QUEEN OF FRANCE

Queen of France

A BIOGRAPHY OF MARIE ANTOINETTE

BY ANDRÉ CASTELOT

TRANSLATED FROM THE FRENCH
BY DENISE FOLLIOT

HARPER & BROTHERS

NEW YORK

This book is published in England and France under the title of
MARIE ANTOINETTE

To Madame S.-R. Carré

Contents

Introduction

"Les pièces originales sont là, telles quelles, elles parlent ou elles se taisent, elles font foi. Les conditions modernes de l'Histoire sont à ce prix."

SAINTE-BEUVE

This book was made possible thanks to unpublished documents principally from the French National Archives and the *Haus-Hof und Staatsarchiv* of Vienna. I did not wish to encumber the pages with footnotes and the reader will find the sources used assembled and commented on at the end of the book. But I would like here to thank M. Bernard Mahieu, of the National Archives, for the valuable help he so kindly gave me during the three years in the course of which I constantly harassed him with endless questions.

Thanks to Mlle la Comtesse Coreth I was able to make use of the unpublished documents concerning Marie Antoinette's childhood and marriage which are preserved in the Vienna Archives. I should like to express my gratitude to her and to M. Nemeth, who carried out very detailed researches for me. I should also like to thank my good friend the doctor and historian Paul Ganière, whose remarkable and valuable explanations can be read; M. Ch. Mauricheau-Beaupré, Keeper of the palaces of Versailles and Trianon, who allowed me to wander through the Château; my friends Pierre Géraudel and Pierre Labracherie, of the National Archives, whose great kindness made my work easier; and finally Mme la Comtesse du Bouchage and her daughter, Mme Maurice Firino-Martell, who were good enough to let me make use of the as yet unpublished *Mémoires* of their ancestor, General Comte de Caraman.

As an unbiased attitude is of first importance I considered it indispensable to give the words of eye-witnesses as often as possible.

A.C.

QUEEN OF FRANCE

1

❧

"A Dainty Morsel"

TOWARDS THE END of the winter of 1770 the servants installed
a second bed in the Empress Maria Theresa's enormous and draughty
bedroom in the Hofburg at Vienna. Every evening it was occupied
by a fair-haired little girl of fourteen, who had no longer been a
child since Thursday, 7 February, at precisely a quarter past five in
the evening—an intimate piece of information which gave the Empress
"extreme pleasure" and which a messenger of the French Embassy
carried at full gallop to Versailles, to Louis XV, whose pleasure, it
appears, was no less keen.

The girl sharing the imperial bedroom was Maria Theresa's youngest
daughter, the Archduchess Antonia—such was Marie Antoinette's
name at that time—who in two months was to marry the Dauphin of
France and who would one day rule with him over the finest kingdom
in the world.

Antonia was to be married!

Only the summer before she had been scampering breathlessly
about with her brothers and the little princesses of Hesse through the
shrubberies of Schoenbrunn's Tyrolean garden. And it was not so very
long since Maria Theresa, passing through the long gallery where the
little Archduchess was "playing at marriage" with Mozart, had heard
the young prodigy ask:

"I shall be your husband, shan't I?"

"Oh yes, no one but you!" cried Antonia earnestly and with shining
eyes.

What a child she had been then!

With an affectionate motherly eye the Empress watched her little Archduchess fall asleep each evening, this girl who was her favourite, perhaps because Maria Theresa felt her to be unarmed against life.

The Empress had certainly settled her children very well. Apart from two daughters given to the Church—the Abbesses Marie-Anne and Marie-Elisabeth—Marie-Christine was Princess of Saxe-Teschen, Marie-Amélie was the reigning Duchess of Parma and Marie-Caroline was Queen of Naples. Of her sons the eldest, Joseph, King of the Romans, Emperor since the death of Francis I, reigned, together with Maria Theresa, under the name of Joseph II, and Leopold was Grand Duke of Tuscany. There were two more sons. It would not be difficult for Maria Theresa to find them a place, or even a throne, in her mosaic of States which was like Europe in miniature.

Within its thick walls the Hofburg was wrapped in silence. How many times during the eight weeks preceding her daughter's departure must "King Maria Theresa," as the Hungarian grandees called her, have leant over the bed of this fair-haired child to whom she had reserved the finest role.

Little Antonia was not pretty—she was something better. In spite of a high, rounded forehead, irregular teeth, a somewhat aquiline nose and a lower lip which was already full of disdain, she was adorable. Her tutor, the Abbé de Vermond, who was of a reserved nature, nevertheless said with enthusiasm:

"You might find faces which are more regularly beautiful, but I doubt if you could find one more attractive."

Another witness praised the silky texture of the girl's fair hair, went into ecstasies over "her eyes, blue but not insipid," and particularly admired her "Greek neck" and the "pure oval of her face." However, a foreigner—admittedly an Englishman—found this oval "too elongated" and thought her eyes unpleasantly "excited." But there was one point on which everyone in Vienna was in agreement—and which was soon to delight Versailles: the pearly whiteness of Madame Antonia's complexion, a "dazzling" complexion, as some said.

One of La Tour's pupils, the pastellist Ducreux, who had come to Vienna the year before to do a portrait of "Madame Antoine," had caught his young model's somewhat proud way of holding her head, "so poised that every movement was full of nobility." The picture gives a hint of that graceful bearing which would one day become Marie

Antoinette's celebrated "queenly carriage." On the occasion of a
festivity at Laxenburg in the previous summer the Abbé de Vermond
had also been amazed by her "noble and majestic posture," which was
really surprising in a child of that age. He had described it to the
Comte de Mercy-Argenteau, Austrian Ambassador to Paris, adding,
"If she grows a little taller the French will need no other indications
for recognizing their sovereign."

For a long time Maria Theresa mused at the bedside of the delicate
child who symbolised the end of the series of wars which had for
centuries set Bourbons against Hapsburgs. During her youth the
Empress had seen her father, Charles VI, struggle against France; in
those days they fought, for Poland, on the Rhine and in Italy. A year
after her accession, in 1741, the Empress had in her turn to fight
France in order to save her inheritance. She had not been able to stop
Frederick II, an ally of Louis XV, from snatching Silesia from her. But
Louis XV, callously abandoned by the King of Prussia, and with his
Spanish and Italian cousins as his sole support, had turned towards
Vienna. As a result, France and Austria, who had fought each other
for so long, after the astonishing reversal of alliances of 1 May 1756
fought side by side. But on each occasion France was the loser. In
seven years she had sacrificed, in helping Frederick II win Silesia from
Maria Theresa, as much in men and money as she had spent over
another seven years in trying, vainly, to reconquer it. Louis XV had
certainly toiled for no reward in the service of the King of Prussia—
that Prussia which, through the fault of France, had ominously risen
from obscurity.

And, after thirty years of slaughter, all the spilt blood, all the forgotten victories, the shameful defeats and the degrading treaties led to
the bed where little Antonia slept, the symbol of the alliance between
France and Austria, or rather, between two peoples—Louis XV and
Maria Theresa, backed by their Ministers, Choiseul and Kaunitz. All
four strove to maintain the union, in spite of the violent opposition
of their peoples and in spite of the French King's unfortunate daughters,
who had been anti-Austrian because their father's mistress, the Pompadour, was not, and would continue to be so because the du Barry was
not either.

For his part the Austrian Emperor was undoubtedly in favour of the
"Alliance," but he was extremely censorious and refused to flirt with

Versailles. According to Kaunitz, Maria Theresa's son "often forgets that one must flirt with Mme la France, just because she is France." To which Choiseul, stung by having his country compared to an elderly coquette, replied, "If the Emperor is not in the mood to make advances, the King is not of the age or temperament to receive them."

But Maria Theresa had not only her son's francophobia to combat. The French diplomats, realising how much the Empress wanted to make her daughter Queen of France, tried to derive as much profit as they could from the situation. M. de Durfort, Louis XV's Ambassador, was given definite instructions: "Leave Maria Theresa in doubt without actually discouraging her."

However, the matter was well settled in Louis XV's mind. The marriage of a son of France with the "daughter of the Caesars" would prevent Austria from drawing too close to Russia and Prussia. The union would consolidate the Alliance and stabilise the balance of Europe. Prussia, Russia and England would be on one side; France, Austria, Spain and Italy on the other. In May 1766 Louis XV had received the Comte de Mercy, and after the interview the Ambassador was able to write to his sovereign, "The King spoke his mind in such a way that Your Majesty may look on the scheme as settled and certain." Louis XV, indeed, appeared pleased at the thought of the arrival at Versailles of a princess whose youth would enliven the court. He too, like Louis XIV, would have his Duchesse de Bourgogne.

Yet for three years, since the Marquis de Durfort's arrival in Vienna at the beginning of 1767, a kind of ballet could have been observed: the Empress offering her daughter and the Ambassador at once refusing and accepting her.

It was one of the Austrian Ministers, Prince Starhemberg, who fired the first shot, in April 1767, by asking Durfort "what he thought of the Archduchess Antonia."

"She is very attractive."

Pleased with this, the Prince went on, "She will be a charming wife for M. le Dauphin."

But Durfort immediately checked this enthusiasm by replying coldly and emphasising the final words, "The morsel is dainty and will be in good hands, *if that is the case.*"

Maria Theresa then decided that she herself would offer the "dainty morsel." After a grand concert given at Schoenbrunn she approached the Ambassador, who in company with the Spanish Minister, Comte de Lahoni, was watching the future Dauphine, and made an undisguised allusion to her daughter's marriage and departure for France.

"I hope she will find success there . . ."

As M. de Durfort remained unresponsive, the Empress turned laughing to Lahoni. "We two can speak more freely, for the French Ambassador has not yet said anything to me about it."

"I pretended not to hear what I could hear very well," sighed Durfort, telling Choiseul of the incident, and he added, "I thought I ought to tell you of a scene which the Empress's air and manner made a rather embarrassing one for me." Choiseul was not concerned with the embarrassment of France's representative at the Hofburg. "You were quite right to be non-committal. The King wishes you to continue to act with the same circumspection until further orders from His Majesty."

The Ambassador's "circumspection" became even more marked when a second scheme was grafted on to the first: the second marriage of Louis XV. As Maria Leczinska had died on 24 June 1767, why should not the King of France also marry a young princess? The Viennese court, which had an ample store of archduchesses, immediately offered one of its daughters, and Antonia's elder sister, Elisabeth, appeared at a masked ball in a domino adorned with *fleurs de lis*. "I fear that this was done on purpose," wrote Durfort, somewhat alarmed by Maria Theresa's eagerness to put into execution the motto of the Austrian monarchy: *Bella gerant alii; tu, felix Austria, nube.*

It was Mercy who had had the curious idea of marrying the two sisters to the grandfather and grandson. At first Louis XV had not said no, "as long as her face was such as not to displease him." But the plan came to nothing and Elisabeth was left to take the *fleurs de lis* off her domino.

Maria Theresa, who always pretended to consider the first scheme settled, busied herself actively with her daughter's education. And heaven knew she needed it! Her governess, Mme de Brandeiss, wrote all her pupil's exercises in pencil and Antonia had only to go over them in ink. The child herself admitted this to her mother. Maria Theresa then instructed the Countess of Lerchenfeld to take the Archduchess's education in hand. But the result was no more successful. Admittedly, as a pupil of Metastasio, Antonio spoke Italian fluently; admittedly she danced with grace under the instruction of the dancer Noverre from Paris; admittedly, thanks to her teacher Gluck, she played the clavichord well; but her French—a Parisian actor had given her some lessons in diction—was studded with germanisms, her German was full of grammatical errors and she wrote with appalling slowness. Through the good offices of Mercy the Empress had finally summoned a French tutor from Paris.

The choice fell on the Abbé de Vermond, "Doctor in the Sorbonne" and librarian in the college of Quatre Nations. He was a typical "blunt courtier," who considered knowledge as good as birth and "treated more highly born people as his equals, sometimes as his inferiors." It was too much for M. de Durfort! He had heard nothing about the "expedition" until the Abbé's arrival and consequently took offence. Vermond paid no attention and set to work—not without difficulty. He explained matters to Choiseul: "A little laziness and much frivolity make it very difficult for me to teach the Archduchess. She understands perfectly well when I put clear ideas before her. Her judgment is nearly always good, but I cannot get her into the way of exploring a question, although I know she is capable of it." Antonia, indeed, was full of good will; she displayed some obstinacy; her character was eager and engaging; but her mind, although intelligent, was not able to concentrate. Furthermore, her mocking nature and constant distractions "counteracted her talent for learning." She neatly evaded her tutor's reproaches and he got results only by "amusing" his pupil.

The Abbé did not succeed in amusing her with writing, and he sighed: "I must confess this is the subject in which I have made least progress." He was more fortunate with French history: "The Archduchess has in this given proof of reasoning ability and good judgement." This is not just a flattering compliment. We possess proof of it in one of Antonia's exercises, an unpublished text which has been preserved by the Vienna *Staatsarchiv* and which one cannot read today without emotion, for in it the future Queen of France judges herself. The little girl, who was then only 12 or 13 years old, draws a comparison between two princesses of the house of Savoy, both daughters of Duke Amédée, the future King of Sardinia. The elder, Marie-Adelaide, Duchesse de Bourgogne and mother of Louis XV, remained something of a Savoyarde even at Versailles, although she had become French by her marriage with Louis XIV's grandson. The younger,

Marie-Louise, Queen of Spain and wife of Philip V, had unhesitatingly adopted her husband's nationality. And Antonia writes:

"The Duchesse de Bourgogne was very scheming. She tried first of all to insinuate herself into the mind of Madame de Maintenon, with whom she tried to do all she could for her father, but not for France, by providing ill counsels and bad generals, who could not lead an army.

"As for the Queen of Spain, she behaved much better, for she interfered in nothing, although she had much to suffer from her father, who caused her much grief and wished to unthrone her, proclaiming Archduke Charles King of Spain. For myself I think that the first was very wrong, for if she wished to have an establishment she should also have been loyal to it and not betrayed the State, and for the other I think she acted well in not interfering in anything and in so loving her husband and her father.

"To continue speaking of the Queen of Spain, I must say that she was not only virtuous, but she had much resolution in affliction . . ."

And referring to various acts and answers showing the "greatness of soul" of the little fifteen-year-old Queen, Marie Antoinette concluded:

"I fear that I should not have done the same!"

She was wrong. After having acted like the Duchesse de Bourgogne, whom she judged so severely, she who would then be called the "Widow Capet" would show even more grandeur "in affliction" than that Queen of Spain, little Louison of the "fiery heart," whose contemporaries described her as "super-natural."

Antonia's reaction to the Duchesse de Bourgogne's "treachery" was the result of Maria Theresa's good advice. In thinking of her daughter's "establishment" Maria Theresa foresaw with apprehension the young Archduchess's bewilderment on encountering the corruption at Versailles after spending all her youth at a homely court—even bourgeois, if Goethe is to be believed—where talent ranked above birth, where etiquette appeared only on ceremonial days and where, in the Prater, the court carriages were passed by the first cab. Maria Theresa constantly repeated to the child: "You must not mention what is customary, nor expect it to be followed. On the contrary, you must adapt yourself entirely to what the French court is accustomed to do."

For, in conformity with her strategy, the Empress continued to act as though the marriage were official. She instructed M. de Mercy to deal with the trousseau in Paris and asked him to send the hairdresser Larseneur. Moreover, in June 1769, on the eve of the feast of St. Antony, she gave a great entertainment in her daughter's honour and placed her next to the Marquis de Durfort. So that there should be no doubt at all in the minds of the guests, the evening ended with a set piece of fireworks showing a dolphin spouting columns of flame through its nostrils.

This audacity had its reward for in the same month Maria Theresa received a letter from her "good brother and cousin Louis XV," who wrote to her without irony that he could "no longer delay" giving expression to his satisfaction at "the forthcoming marriage of his grandson to the Archduchess." And their betrothal was at last officially announced.

The diplomats of both countries were at once assailed by terrible problems. In June 1769, at the request of M. de Choiseul, the Marquis de Durfort went to see Kaunitz to ask him a number of questions about "the marriage contract, the public entry, the solemn demand, the escorting of the bride, the place and formalities for the Remise (or transfer), and the ceremonial to be observed towards the King's Ambassador Extraordinary in all the functions he would have to carry out."

"I promise to fulfil all requests as quickly as possible," Kaunitz had assured him, but six months later, in spite of dozens and dozens of trips by messengers between Vienna and Versailles, hardly any progress had been made. However, Kaunitz constantly claimed to be "making haste." He quite forgot to indulge in his peculiar habits; he no longer smeared his face with egg-yolks, nor was he to be seen cleaning his teeth after dinner with a sponge and a scraper. So that his wig might be evenly powdered he used to walk slowly between two rows of valets armed with bellows which surrounded their master with a cloud of powder. Now Kaunitz paid no attention to his hair-dressing; he had too much to do. How was he in ten months to settle the all-important questions of precedence, etiquette, protocol, ceremonial and gifts so as to avoid any incident? Kaunitz might well be "strong in body, genius and principles," but problems like these can be disconcerting. At Versailles, Choiseul, who was quite as overweening as his Austrian colleague, lost his reputedly unquenchable gaiety; this business forced him to abandon a frivolity which had become a matter of principle, and he bombarded Durfort with proposals and counter-proposals. Who would sign the contract first? The presence of Joseph II, who reigned with his mother, would be another tiresome complication. Would two copies be drawn up, one for France and the other for Austria? In what language would they be written? Louis XV hoped it would be French, "since the law and customs of France will be more exactly and clearly expressed in that language than in any other." And in what order would the Ambassadors, Ministers and commissioners sign? One must read the voluminous correspondence between the diplomats which is preserved at both the Quai d'Orsay in Paris and the Minoritenplatz in Vienna, to grasp all the problems arising out of the marriage of two children. Above all M. de Durfort was to be careful not to invite the future Dauphine to the entertainment he was to give in her honour on the occasion of the marriage by proxy. Why? Had not the Archduchess already visited the Embassy? M. de Choiseul gave him bluntly the reason for this order: "The respect that M. de Durfort, as a subject of the King, will from that moment owe the princess will no longer permit him to seek or invite this honour." "As a result of this same respect" the Ambassador should no longer take an "equal seat" when in the presence of the fiancée. What should he do if he were offered one at the Hofburg? He must manage as best he could! And without a smile Choiseul ordered him "to use all suitable tact in this matter."

These gentlemen blackened reams of paper but hardly mentioned the future married pair. We only know that at the end of February Antonia had a cold, but that blowing her nose "has not effected the slightest change in her countenance or her gaiety." The correspondence is even less expansive regarding the fiancé. Mercy had summed matters up once and for all: "Nature seems to have denied everything to M. le Dauphin" and he appeared, moreover, to possess "only a limited amount of sense." The Ambassador had not dared to put these last words in the plural. Two months before the marriage the Empress realised that her daughter had received no other picture of her fiancé than that of a brilliant, sparkling dolphin belching fire into the sky at Laxenburg. The unfortunate girl risked being somewhat disappointed on her arrival at Versailles. The Empress therefore asked Durfort if she might be sent a portrait of her future son-in-law.

Louis XV hastened to send to Vienna three engravings representing "the Dauphin ploughing." This was hardly gallant ... At the beginning of April, therefore, two portraits of Louis-Auguste in ceremonial dress were at last given to Antonia, who put them "in the room where she sits." "I cannot tell you how much satisfaction these portraits have given," wrote the Ambassador. She who in a few days would be the Dauphine of France mused for long before the image of her future husband. But Maria Theresa warned her that princesses have no right to expect love.

"Domestic happiness consists in mutual trust and kindness," she insisted. "Passionate love soon disappears!"

In the vast bedroom with its heavy white and gold sculpture the Empress continued to pour forth advice.

"Don't show curiosity; this is a point on which you give me great anxiety."

Another question worried her: place-hunters.

"You must know how to refuse ... Don't undertake any recommendations. To avoid trouble don't listen to anyone."

When she thought of her daughter's age—she was fourteen—Maria Theresa trembled. Admittedly, at that time babies who were scarcely weaned became colonels in the musketeers, but for all that the Empress was anxious.

"Don't be ashamed to ask advice from everyone and don't do anything of your own accord."

Until then the Queens of France had always tried to forget their original nationality. Maria Theresa was of another opinion and gave advice which was later to prove serious: "Remain a good German!"

Antonia's temperament gave her the most anxiety. "I realised that her character comprised much frivolity, lack of application and obstinacy in following her own will, together with adroitness in evading intended reproaches." She strove tirelessly to put some ballast into that light head and to tame the stubborn will she could already perceive behind that little round forehead.

On the morning of 15 April 1770, Easter Sunday, M. de Durfort, *Ordinary Ambassador* of His Most Christian Majesty, left Vienna—to return an hour later as *Ambassador Extraordinary*, as though he were coming from France. Little Antonia, together with her sister Maria-Christina, the future Governor of the Low Countries, watched the spectacle from Countess Trauttmansdorff's house.

And what a spectacle it was!

It cost more than 100 million francs of present-day money and M. de Durfort had received only half this from Versailles to pay for all the celebrations. The Ambassador Extraordinary might have ruined himself, but he could at least boast that he had not disappointed the Viennese, who were dazzled by the passage of 48 carriages, each drawn by six horses. Incidentally, the whole stable—including six led saddle horses—was sold the next day by M. de Durfort to help replenish his exchequer.

In fact the Ambassador had had to pay for only 46 carriages, as two travelling coaches had been presented by King Louis XV to his future granddaughter. The Archduchess gazed admiringly at the two enormous carriages with which she was to travel to Versailles, and which had cost 40 million francs of our money. They were the work of the saddler Francien, but had been designed by Choiseul himself. The first was upholstered in crimson velvet on which Trumeau had embroidered the four seasons; the second was upholstered in blue velvet and on its doors were displayed the four elements. On top were bouquets of flowers in gold of different colours and so supple that they nodded gracefully in the slightest breeze.

The two gala coaches were empty, but in the others were the officers of the Ambassador Extraordinary and round the carriages were pages, grooms and servants. In all there were 117 persons dressed in "rich stuffs" of blue, yellow and silver.

On the following day M. de Durfort, after passing through a double rank of noble German and Hungarian guards, was publicly received in audience by the Queen-Empress and the Emperor Joseph II. This was for the official proposal. The Ambassador performed three accomplished bows and made ready to begin his speech, but then—as had been carefully arranged by Choiseul—the Empress invited him to put on his hat, which gave Durfort the opportunity to give another deep bow, cover himself and—in a further improvisation provided by etiquette—immediately remove his hat once more. On ending his speech the Ambassador turned towards the door and made a sign to a rider who seemed at that moment to have arrived from France. He brought Marie Antoinette a letter from her fiancé and a portrait. This was the sixth in six weeks—they were making up for lost time! Maria Theresa summoned the Archduchess, who was waiting in an adjoining room. She came in, made her curtseys and with her mother's approval fastened the "portrait," brought by the rider, on her bosom. One must conclude that the portrait was a miniature. "All this," Durfort related, "took place amid profound salutations." We can well believe it.

On the next day—17 April—in the presence of her mother, her brother, the Marquis de Durfort and all the Ministers, Antonia performed her first political act: her renunciation of the hereditary Austrian succession. In the great hall looking on to the Burgplatz the future Queen Marie Antoinette, having first signed the act drawn up in Latin and later to be ratified by Louis XV and the Dauphin, took the oath before the Coadjutor of the Prince-Bishop of Laylach. It was, in fact, Cardinal Migazzi, Archbishop of Vienna, who should have handed the Testament to the Archduchess and asked her to swear, but the Marquis de Durfort had cried out in protest. In that case he would have had to take second place to the prince of the Church! The Ambassador had accordingly succeeded in arranging that the Cardinal should not take part in *any* ceremony. In the evening Antonia was received by her brother at a great supper in the Belvedere for 1,500 guests. The meal was followed by a ball to which there thronged 6,000 masks and white dominos. A vast ballroom, lit by 3,500 candles, was erected for the purpose, adjoining the palace. The façade, walls and balconies were covered with "appropriate" decorations: it was all torches of love, dolphins, glowing vases borne by seraphim, garlands, hearts and flowers. The Empress had thought of everything: 800 firemen with damp sponges spent the whole evening extinguishing the sparks which fell from the chandeliers. "H.I.M.'s motherly care," the official account tells us, went so far as to order dentists to stand by during the feast in case any sudden toothache required an immediate extraction.

On the evening of the next day, Wednesday, it was M. de Durfort's turn to extend princely hospitality to the Austrian court in the Liechtenstein Palace, in the suburb of Rossau, which he had hired for the occasion. All along the route three rows of illuminated pines gave a light as bright as day, and between each tree and the next was placed a dolphin carrying a lantern.

The feast was given on the eve of the nuptial ceremony, so that Marie Antoinette, not yet the Dauphine, could attend without derogation to her rank. Here, too, flaming dolphins sparkled in the night, but the Ambassador had not considered this symbol to be enough, and pictures lit by 8,000 lamps were disposed on pyramids. One saw Hymen ordering Louis-Auguste to wed the goddess of beauty, then the Danube and the Seine lovingly mingling their waters, and finally "H.R.H. the Dauphine" walking to France "on a carpet of flowers sown by Love."

The classic fireworks, accompanied by the fashionable strains of Turkish music, preceded the supper, which was served by 800 servants to 850 guests.

On Thursday, 19 April, at six o'clock in the evening, the whole court went in great pomp, and to the sound of trumpets and kettle-drums, through the gallery of the Palace to the Church of the Augustines, where the marriage by proxy was to be celebrated. Little Antonia, all smiles, advanced with her mother and brother. She looked enchanting in her dress of cloth of silver.

Archduke Ferdinand, 17 months older than the bride, took the Dauphin's place and knelt at his sister's side before the altar. The *prie-Dieu* for the "married pair" were covered in red velvet embroidered with gold. In order to please Durfort the Cardinal had been asked to stay at home and the Papal Nuncio, Mgr. Visconti, officiated, assisted by the court curé, who bore the warlike name of Briselance.

It was in the vestry of this same church, on 3 November 1755, that little Maria Antonia Josepha, born on the preceding day—all Souls' Day and the day of the Lisbon earthquake—had been baptised in the presence of the Emperor Francis.

The married pair knelt and replied "*Volo et ita promitto,*" to the question put to them by the Nuncio. The rings, one of which Marie Antoinette would give the Dauphin, were blessed and then Briselance drew up the act of celebration, Kaunitz certified it and Durfort legalised it. After the *Te Deum* a salvo was fired in the Spitalplatz and it only remained for them to go to supper—without Durfort, as the Ambassador did not want to yield precedence to Prince Albert of Saxe-Teschen, Marie Antoinette's brother-in-law. Versailles had asked the latter not "to cause any difficulty" and "to arrange matters as best he could." The Prince gave way as far as church was concerned, but being very greedy he wanted to go to the supper; so, in order to avoid dishonour, the Marquis stayed at home. The feast was no less of a success on that account, and the Comte de Saint-Julien, grand master of the imperial kitchens, worked wonders. A hundred and fifty guests were summoned, not to dinner, but to admire the nine princely guests eating off gold plate, while the artillery set off a peal at "the first draught drunk by Their Majesties."

The next day, the eve of the departure for France, was devoted to a final public repast, to leave-taking and to correspondence. Maria Theresa wrote no fewer than three letters to Louis XV, asking the King "to be indulgent towards any thoughtless act" that might be committed by "her very dear child." "I commend her to him yet once more as the tenderest pledge that exists so sincerely between our States and Houses . . ." For her part, Antoine—it was thus that she signed her letter—wrote in a very childish hand to Louis XV, begging "his indulgence" and asking him also "to obtain in advance that of the Dauphin." No document in the archives gives us any details of that last night in the Empress's bedroom, but we can imagine the tears of the little girl who doubtless knew that she would never again embrace her mother, the mother she feared yet adored, and those of the woman who not without anguish saw the departure of the child "who was her delight," but of whose frivolity and thoughtlessness she was also aware. "I am bathed in tears," she wrote the next day when the cavalcade of 366 horses had borne her child away into the distance.

She did not weep alone. The Dauphine's foster-brother wrote: "We did not return home until we had lost sight of the last courier following her, and when we did it was but to mourn among the family for a common loss . . ."

On Saturday 21 April the long procession of 57 carriages preceded by three postillions blowing their horns left the suburb of Mariahilf and passed before Schoenbrunn.

Schoenbrunn!

Never again was Marie Antoinette to see the long yellow façade with its green shutters, nor her apartments on the ground floor where, after hours of play, she and her brothers and sisters would eat pyramids of Viennese cakes dripping with whipped cream.

A few more revolutions of the wheels and the coach crowned with its bouquets of flowers passed the exact spot where, on a summer morning five years earlier, Antonia had embraced her father for the last time. The Emperor Francis, who was on his way to Innsbruck for the celebration of the marriage between Archduke Leopold—the future Leopold II—and the Infanta Maria Luisa, had gone to Schoenbrunn to embrace his children. But when he was a little way from the castle, on the same road now followed by the Dauphine, he had, perhaps, some presentiment of his coming death and stopped his coach.

"Go back for the Archduchess Antonia; I must see her again."

He had gazed at her with indescribable tenderness, and for the rest of her life Marie Antoinette was never to forget that look.

Did she remember too the advice the Emperor left for his children?

"Never be indifferent before what appears to you to be evil, nor attempt to find it innocent . . . We are not put into this world merely to amuse ourselves . . . What kind of people we should frequent is also a delicate matter, for they may often lead us into many things against our will . . . Friendship is one of the pleasures of life, but one should be careful to whom one entrusts this friendship and not be too prodigal of it . . . This is why I advise you, my dear children, never to be in a hurry to place your friendship and trust in someone of whom you are not quite sure."

The future friend of Mme de Polignac and Baron de Besenval was only fourteen years old; one could not hope that she would remember all this advice. Would she even read the recommendations her mother had just given her, which contained a summary of their evening talks? At fourteen one could not expect from her anything more than that her heart should beat faster every time someone in her suite pronounced in her hearing the magic word *Versailles*. Under the orders of Prince Starhemberg, Commissioner Plenipotentiary "in charge of the remise," there were 132 persons: ladies-in-waiting, serving women, hairdressers, secretaries, dressmakers, surgeons, pages, furriers, chaplains, apothecaries, lackeys, cooks and menservants of all kinds, not to mention an escort of noble guards and above all a grand postmaster, the Prince of Paar, assisted by nine masters and 25 employees. They were not too many to watch at each stage over the 376 horses needed for the procession. As the horses were changed at least four or five times a day, a stable of more than 20,000 horses had had to be distributed on the route from Vienna to Strasbourg. All along the road the bells pealed and the artillery fired salutes.

On the first day, after eight hours' travelling, the cavalcade slept at

Mölck, where the Dauphine was welcomed by her brother, Joseph II. At the Benedictine convent, where she spent the night, the pupils performed an opera for her, the monks providing the orchestra. The performance was extremely bad—so bad that Marie Antoinette was "very bored" and became gloomy, at least if we can believe Durfort, who had accompanied the Archduchess so far. Perhaps, however, it was grief at leaving everything she loved.

The following morning she embraced her brother and, alone in her carriage with the Princess of Paar, took the road to Enns, where the Prince of Auersperg received her in his castle. On the 23rd she left the Danube valley and slept at Lambach; on the 24th, after six hours' travelling, she reached Altheim; on the 25th she crossed the Inn and spent the night at Alt-Oettingen; she spent the 26th and 27th not far from Munich at the castle of Nymphenburg, where she was greeted by Maximilian-Joseph, the Elector of Bavaria. There was no etiquette, and, as we are told, "confusion" was the rule. On the 28th she was at Augsburg, and on the 29th nine hours' journey brought the coach to Günsburg, where Marie Antoinette was to spend two days with her aunt, Princess Charlotte of Lorraine, Abbess of Remiremont. The great entertainment offered her was a distribution of food to the people and a visit to the Lorraine chapel of Königinbild, on the Burgau road. As she left twelve young girls presented the Dauphine with wild flowers simply and attractively bound with ribbon, and one of them recited a poem hoping that "the most serene couple" would live more than a hundred years. Then they sat down to table, and 132 people consumed, among other dishes, a trifle of 150 chickens, 270 lb. of beef, 220 lb. of veal, 55 lb. of bacon, 50 pigeons and 300 eggs.

On the next day, 1 May, the long procession of carriages took the road to Ulm and reached Riedlingen. On 2 May they rejoined the Danube, and on the evening of this ninth *Nacht Station* Marie Antoinette stopped at Stockach. On 3 May the suite arrived at Donau-Eschingen, and on the following day, having been nine and a half hours on the road, spent the night at Fribourg. They rested there on the 5th and on the 6th. Having crossed the Black Forest, Marie Antoinette finally arrived at the Abbey of Schüttern, the last stage before the "remise." She had hardly arrived when she received a visit from the Comte de Noailles, Ambassador Extraordinary charged by the King with her reception, who had come from Strasbourg with the Comte de Mercy. This post, which he owed to his friend Choiseul, filled Noailles with pride. He had insisted for himself on "the honours of cannon and troops," and above all on plenty of money. The Treasury being, as usual, in difficulties, the Count had been offered some flattering decorations, but he had replied arrogantly: "I already have enough!"

Choiseul therefore decided to give him a sum corresponding to a good 12 million francs of present-day money, advising him "to be satisfied" with that. The Count consoled himself by thinking that his mission took on the aspect of a family affair, since his wife and his son, the Prince de Poix, were among the imposing suite sent by the King to meet his granddaughter.

M. de Noailles did not stay long with his future sovereign; serious problems were oppressing him and he had to consult with Prince Starhemberg. Three words in the deed of remise—the *Consegna,* as it was called in Austria—stuck in his throat: "Their Imperial Majesties *having been willing* to accede to the King's wish . . ." In this way Maria Theresa and Joseph II seemed to be granting a favour to Louis XV. Could it not rather be said that in common accord Their Imperial and Royal Majesties were "agreed"? Starhemberg gave way, for he too had something to request: in accordance with Austrian etiquette he wanted a dais to be placed in the *salon de remise.* Noailles agreed, and becoming bolder suggested that Louis XV should be named first in the official document. Starhemberg nearly fainted. It was impossible! They went on arguing, night fell, and—to make an end—a compromise was reached: as in Vienna, two documents would be drawn up. In the one for France the King would have precedence, whereas in the one intended for Austria he would come after Maria Theresa and Joseph II.

Everyone then went to bed, except for the secretaries who had to work all night to change the documents. Marie Antoinette, who from now on would bear these names only, was sad. Tears flowed from her eyes and during this last night on German soil her thoughts turned towards her mother. Her ladies heard her sigh through her tears: "I shall never see her again!"

For the official remise it had first been planned to use a house situated on an island in the Rhine and belonging to a Master Gelb. However, it would have been necessary to pull down the partitions, build a reception room on to the brick façade and fill in a pond in front of the house. The scheme was abandoned, much to Master Gelb's relief, and a house was built nearby with two entrances—one French and one Austrian—two antechambers, four offices and a large hall where the ceremony would take place. The room was adorned with carpets lent by the Prince of Lorraine and tapestries borrowed from the old Cardinal de Rohan, Archbishop of Strasbourg. According to Louis XV's envoys everything was done "in order to safeguard the feelings of both courts," but for all that the tapestries caused Goethe much indignation. He was then twenty and often left the courses of the University of Law at Strasbourg in order to visit the hall and look at the tapestries, whose "choice of subjects" revolted him. "They were a copy of pictures painted by very good French masters, but these pictures represented the story of Jason and Medea. On the right of the throne could be seen the unhappy betrothed in the throes of all the anguish of a cruel death; on the left, Jason, seized with horror at the sight of his murdered children, while the Fury rose into the air in a flaming chariot. Such subjects appeared to me to be so little in harmony with the circumstances that I could not help exclaiming out loud: What! At the moment when the young princess is about to step on to the soil of her future husband's country, there is placed before her eyes a picture of the most horrible marriage that can be imagined! . . . Might one not say that the most awful spectre has been summoned to meet the most beautiful and happy betrothed?"

One can guess, in spite of young Goethe's anger, that the tapestries did not find their way back to the archbishopric.

In spite of what Mme Campan said—and after her all the other historians—the little Dauphine was not stripped naked on the Rhine island on the morning of the 7th, so that she might not retain so much as a piece of ribbon from her former homeland. That old custom had been abandoned. As the archives relate Marie Antoinette simply put on, in one of the Austrian rooms, a ceremonial dress brought from Vienna. Her grand mistress of the robes, her tiring woman and her Kammerfraülein, who accompanied her, did the same in the other room and the ladies of her suite dressed in the Gelb house. The little bride was even able to keep on her maiden jewellery: chain necklace, aigrettes, *prétension, boutons de compère, boucles de chien* and a *bec de diamants* for her hair.

Followed by her Austrian escort, the little Dauphine, giving her hand to Starhemberg, entered the *salle de remise* and stood before the large table symbolising the frontier and covered with crimson velvet. On the other side there were only three people: Noailles and his two assistants, the commissioners Bouret and Gérard. Behind her the door giving on to Germany remained open, whereas the French door was still shut. An unpublished document preserved in the National Archives actually informs us that behind the latter door the Prince of Poix and the gentleman usher were looking "through the keyhole." The scene was a short one: Marie Antoinette took her place on the dais dear to Starhemberg—the Lutheran University had had it constructed that very morning. She listened to M. de Noailles making a speech of exceptional banality and submitted to a recital of the official act by Bouret.

That was all: the Archduchess was now French. The Austrian ladies kissed her hand, the French door opened to admit the Comtesse de Noailles and the Comte de Saulx-Tavannes, gentleman-in-waiting. What trouble that entrance had given the Ambassador Extraordinary! The detailed report preserved in the Archives relates: "The Comte de Noailles having informed the usher that he wished the Comtesse de Noailles to come in side by side with the gentleman-in-waiting, who was supposed to give her his hand to enter, the usher, to please the Comte de Noailles, arranged that the second half of the door should be pushed open by the lady-in-waiting's skirts, which might have happened accidentally." The usher, doubtless preoccupied by this manoeuvre, opened the door somewhat too early and from the French antechamber "all could see the leave-taking of the Austrian ladies."

When the former suite had left the German door was closed and the young Dauphine went to meet Mme de Noailles. Surrounded as she was by strangers—only Starhemberg remained present—the poor girl must have felt at a loss, and she threw herself into the arms of her lady-in-waiting, as though for safety. But the severe Comtesse de Noailles considered that this effusion did not come within the protocol and she hastened to introduce M. de Noailles to the Dauphine, to whom he had already been presented the day before. But this time it was in his quality of grandee of Spain and, according to the custom, Marie Antoinette embraced him. Mme de Noailles, who was in her natural element with etiquette, then presented the girl's household to her. Her mistress of the robes, the Duchesse de Villars, and her other ladies of honour, the Duchesse de Picquigny, the Marquise de Duras, the Comtesses de Mailly and de Saulx-Tavannes, had formerly, together with Mme de Noailles, been in the household of Maria Leczinska. In order to avoid intrigue and rivalry, Louis XV had preferred to maintain the former household of the Queen. For years these six ladies had shared the slow-moving existence of their deserted mistress, and neither in their faces nor in their behavior was there any breath of youth or gaiety. Marie Antoinette must certainly have shuddered a little when she thought that she must henceforth spend the greater part of her time with these mature ladies.

However, she smiled politely as she walked gracefully towards the antechamber—and towards France.

The dull rumbling of a storm died away towards the Black Forest, a triple peal of artillery sounded from the ramparts, the bells rang in all the churches and the coach crowned with its bouquets of gold flowers stopped at the first houses of Strasbourg. M. d'Autigny, "head of the magistrature," stepped forward and began a speech in German. The Princess graciously interrupted him. "Do not speak German, gentlemen; from today I understand no language but French."

It is not known whether as a reward for her amiability she was spared the rest of the speech. In any case it is quite possible that this was a "saying" handed down from one foreign princess arriving in France to the next, but certainly no one can have uttered it as charmingly as Marie Antoinette.

In the unanimous opinion of witnesses, and from the first moment of her entry into France, Marie Antoinette's smile charmed and attracted, her "light step," her "archduchess's bearing" and "the somewhat proud carriage of her head and shoulders" made their effect. "As one watches the princess it is difficult to refrain from feeling a respect mingled with tenderness." And in all the accounts one finds the same astonishment of her contemporaries at Marie Antoinette's complexion, a complexion "literally a blend of lilies and roses . . . which can spare her the use of rouge," noted one woman, not without envy. Marie Antoinette's arrival among this decaying monarchy, this cankered age, this unhealthy society had the effect of a fresh bouquet of wild flowers.

"She is like the perfume of spring!" Burke exclaimed.

The spectacle given at Strasbourg was as fresh as the little Dauphine's smile. Children dressed as shepherds and shepherdesses offered her bouquets, girls threw flowers under the horses' hooves and little boys dressed as Swiss Guards lined the route. Marie Antoinette was charmed by this idea and asked that the guard at the Bishop's palace, where she was to stay, should be mounted by this miniature regiment. The request was made so graciously that it was granted with pleasure.

She continued to smile. She smiled at the presentation of the gouty Cardinal de Rohan, the dyspeptic counts forming the cathedral council, and the deputations from the guilds, who were followed by thirty-six ladies of the Alsatian nobility with serious and severe countenances. After an endless dinner, "not being at all tired," she consented, as though it were merely a dessert, to receive the deputies from the grand chapter.

She was not allowed to rest after this heavy day. A feast of Bacchus had been arranged, performed by coopers dancing with their hoops. She smiled, and the elderly Maréchal de Contades, commander of the province, escorted her to the theatre, where she watched performances of *Dupuis et Desronais* and *La servante-maîtresse*. She continued to smile when the Marshal led her back to the bishop's palace, showed her the illuminated town, gave her supper and displayed the garlanded barges on the River Ill which drew alongside the terrace so that, after swallowing her last mouthful, the Dauphine was able to cross the river and see the decorations from the park. The shrubs decorating the barges burst into flame, the fireworks were reflected in the Ill, from which sprang jets of water, while a choir sang "Long Live the King." Hardly had the entwined initials of the Dauphin and Dauphine faded in the sky than the indefatigable Marshal (it was now after midnight) led the little girl to the theatre which was now transformed into a ballroom. It was not until she had watched several dances that Marie Antoinette was allowed to go to bed. She was still smiling and her complexion was as brilliant as ever.

"If one can judge of the Dauphine's constitution from her outward appearance," Noailles wrote that evening to Choiseul, "I do not think one need be uneasy about her health."

The next morning, in the absence of the old Cardinal de Rohan, a strange prelate in a gold mitre received the girl in the porch of the

cathedral. He was young, slender, elegant, and bowed gracefully. This
was the Bishop Coadjutor of the diocese, Prince Louis de Rohan,
later Cardinal de Rohan and one day to be "Cardinal Necklace." "As
pleasant as it is possible to be"—and in those days they were good
judges—he lived in a coterie of pretty women, gave a banquet every
day or hunted the stag and the fox. He sometimes interrupted this
princely and oriental existence to assist his uncle, while waiting to
succeed him. But this prelate-cum-satrap did not forget that he was
an Academician and addressed Marie Antoinette in terms befitting the
illustrious company.

"For us, Madame, you will be the living image of that dear Empress,
for so long the admiration of Europe, as she will be in ages to come.
The soul of Maria Theresa will be united to the soul of the Bourbons."

Into "Madame's" eyes there sprang "two tears" which fell on to her
cheeks "heightened in colour" and under the high, Gothic arches the
soft, caressing voice came to the peroration: "The golden age will be
born from such a union and under the happy rule of Antoinette and
Louis-Auguste our nephews will see the continuation of the happiness
we enjoy under the reign of Louis the Beloved!"

A questionable happiness, no doubt, but the speech was so well
written and nobly spoken that the audience asked for nothing more.
Before the Mass began the man who through ignorance and stupidity
was to bear a heavy share of responsibility in the coming tragedy
blessed "the child's bowed head" with an elegant gesture.

For a whole week, whether at Saverne, Lunéville, Nancy,
Commercy, Bar-le-Duc, Saint-Dizier, Rheims, Châlons or Soissons,
Marie Antoinette had to endure a terrible avalanche of speeches, poems
and compliments. She stoically bore successive comparisons with
Venus, Hebe, Psyche, Antiope, Flora and Minerva. She bravely submitted to triumphal arches, military honours, gala balls, peals of
artillery, deputations, dinners, speeches, shows, entertainments, interminable presentations, bell-ringing. *Te Deum,* illuminations, endless
whirling suns, "sheets of Chinese fire," Pyrrhic columns, cavalcades of
horses "all alight," temples of conjugal love and betrothal, temporary
buildings topped by spirits with trumpets announcing to France the
arrival of her future sovereign. Sometimes, indeed, the programme
seemed not to be full enough. At one stage "as it was very early the
Comtesse de Noailles suggested that the Dauphine might dance," and

she consented. A regimental band was sent for "and she danced in the antechamber with the ladies and gentlemen of her suite." Everywhere she went she seemed happy, and yet, apart from Mercy, Starhemberg and the Abbé de Vermond, she was surrounded by strangers.

The vast procession, preceded by fifty guards, wound its way slowly along the dusty road, which had been remade especially for this journey. Each stage required 386 horses. Reinforcements had to be sent by the posts of Périgueux, Pont-Saint-Esprit and Angoulême. Even the foot servants had been chosen for their physique. The reasons for which some of them were turned down are preserved in the Archives: "not good-looking," "too small," or both "ill-looking and coarse."

Two great wagons, each containing all the furnishings for a bedroom, went in front of the procession. They proceeded in relays so that at each stopping place the Dauphine would find one of the two bedrooms with its armchairs, screens and folding stools in crimson damask "enriched with fringes, gold braid and gold embroidered cushions." Her two beds were both covered with scarlet satin together with a white satin coverlet. In these beds she must have dreamed about the man whose wife she had been for three weeks and whom she knew only by miniatures and an engraving. Could the Dauphin, who was not yet sixteen, do anything besides guiding a plough? Had not Mlle Cosson de la Cressonière exaggerated slightly in the verses published in the Mercure:

> Bearing the wishes of her court,
> She comes, by noble marriage led:
> 'Tis Psyche in the bloom of youth
> Conducted here to Cupid's bed.

"Are you very anxious to see the Dauphin?" one of her ladies asked her.

With her charming smile, she replied mischievously: "Madame, in five days I shall be at Versailles, and on the sixth I shall more easily be able to answer you."

It was not at Versailles that "Psyche in the bloom of youth" was to meet "Cupid," but in the Forest of Compiègne.

2

❧

"Priceless" Festivities

ON THE EVENING of 14 May, not far from the Pont de Berne, on the outskirts of the Forest of Compiègne, lifeguards, light horse musketeers, and gendarmes were drawn up in battle formation keeping back the crowd.

The King was waiting for "my granddaughter," as he called her.

In spite of his sixty years he was still the handsomest man in his kingdom. His reign of half-a-century had not bowed him down. Surfeited with pleasure, he found a distraction in the arrival of the little girl with whom the dispatches of Ministers and Ambassadors had been occupied for the last three years. A few days earlier he had received Bouret, who after reading the official Act in the *salle de remise* had set off hot foot to carry the documents to the King.

"What did you think of the Dauphine?" the elderly libertine asked. "Has she any bosom?"

Marie Antoinette was to make up for it later, but at the moment— as can be seen in Ducreux's portrait—the little Princess's bust was only just developing. M. Bouret confined himself to replying that "the Dauphine had a charming face and very·beautiful eyes."

"That is not what I was talking about," Louis XV interrupted. "I asked you if she had any bosom."

Bouret extricated himself gallantly. "Sire, I did not take the liberty of carrying my eyes so far."

The King burst out laughing. "You are a fool! It's the first thing one looks at in a woman."

The King was waiting. . . . He had forgotten to be bored and to think of death. However, he was, if not anxious, somewhat preoccupied. How would the Dauphine greet Mme du Barry? A fortnight earlier "the King's passion triumphed over his sense of shame," as Mercy wrote to Maria Theresa, and Jeanne Bécu, the illegitimate daughter of a little seamstress of Vaucouleurs, Jeanne Bécu, "the prostitute," as Choiseul said, Jeanne Bécu, called *la Bourbonnaise* by the pamphleteers, had been presented at court, presented to Mesdames, the King's daughters, presented to the Dauphin!

"She is very pretty, she attracts me, that should be enough," the King had written to Choiseul, and to Richelieu, with whom he was more intimate, "the old love-making machine" confided: "She has given me delights I did not know existed."

These were arguments which it would not seem easy to put to the young Archduchess, particularly as Maria Theresa had not thought fit to mention "the creature" to her daughter.

Mesdames, the daughters of Louis XV—a group of crabbed old maids—stood near the King. For some days now they had been feeling very disturbed; their number was now reduced to three. Madame Louise had just entered the poorest Carmelite convent in France, at Saint-Denis. And this decision, which had been hidden from Mesdames Adelaide, Victoire and Sophie, had astounded them. Now merely Sister Thérèse Augustine, and writing to the King only "by permission of our good Mother Superior," she had formerly been an intrepid horsewoman, loving fine clothes and, according to Mme de Boigne, "having a marked inclination for flirting." Indeed, when the King went to his eldest daughter's room to tell her that her sister Louise had left during the night, Madame Adelaide's first exclamation was, "With whom?"

Madame Adelaide, once enchantingly pretty, had withered up and become "as cross as two sticks." Her father called her "rag" or "dishcloth," according to his mood. She played the horn and the Jew's harp and made napkin rings, but in spite of these homely nicknames and simple tastes a haughtier being, more imbued with a sense of ancestry, could not be imagined. She was so proud of her title of "Daughter of France" that any union, even with the son of a reigning prince, seemed to her to be a misalliance and she had preferred to shrivel up at Versailles. Her sister Madame Victoire, plump and pious, retained some faint traces of beauty. Her kindness made one forget her stupidity. It was she, according to Mme de Boigne, who said "with tears in her eyes, during a period of scarcity, when someone was talking of the sufferings of the unfortunate people who lacked bread: 'But if only they could resign themselves to eating piecrust!'" It is only fair to explain that piecrust lay very heavy on her own stomach.

As for Madame Sophie, her "exceptional ugliness" astounded everyone, except the enormous Duc de Luynes, who considered she had "an air of beauty." "I never saw anyone so shy," said Mme Campan. "She walked extremely quickly, and so as to recognise the people she passed without looking at them she had formed the habit of glancing sideways, as hares do." Like Madame Victoire she was "passive"; it was Madame Adelaide who gave orders with the voice of an old sergeant-major. On that day her watchword was: try to get Choiseul and the du Barry dismissed and get the Dauphine on our side. For all that they had done everything possible to avert the marriage. Not only did Madame Adelaide not like Austria, but she would have liked herself to choose her nephew's wife so as to be able to control her. One of the officers of the future Dauphine, who came to ask for Madame Adelaide's orders before leaving for Strasbourg, drew on himself this reply: "If I had any order to give it would not be to fetch an Austrian!"

And this Austrian was now to take from her the first place at court which she had occupied since the death of her sister-in-law, the Dauphin's mother. This child of fourteen would shortly sit at the back of the coach with the King.

Suddenly a great murmur arose. The Dauphine's procession was approaching. The people applauded. The musketeers' drums, trumpets and hautboys sounded. The gold flowered carriage had hardly stopped when the little Dauphine jumped out. She made a few rapid, almost running, steps ahead of the radiant Choiseul, who by the King's special favour had gone to meet her a few leagues off. The girl threw herself at the King's feet; he raised her up and embraced her. He was smiling, for the young Dauphine was charming and beautifully formed. Of her own accord she kissed a great booby of fifteen who was stuck there beside the King, shifting from one foot to the other. This was the Dauphin.

Once seated in the King's carriage Marie Antoinette had plenty of opportunity for looking at her husband, who sat opposite her and did not even turn his vague, short-sighted eyes on his "wife." And yet she was very fresh and charming. It was obvious that this shy, awkward boy wished himself elsewhere. Naturally the fourteen-year-old girl could not guess that the sullen temperament and heavy, uncouth body concealed qualities of mind, heart and judgement which made him, if not a brilliant prince, at least a "good young man" and later a "worthy man." Besides, there was some excuse for his "lubberliness." His father had died when he was eleven and his mother just as he reached his thirteenth year, and he had been very badly brought up by that conceited windbag, the Duc de la Vauguyon. As for his grandfather, he had more frivolous or more serious preoccupations than concerning himself with the mind of an apathetic boy who was a mystery to him. Later he was to say to Mercy: "He is not an ordinary man!"

Fancy stuffing oneself regularly with cakes until one was ill! Fancy having a taste for manual labour, enjoying locksmith's work, or being so fond of mixing plaster that a workman could not enter the castle without the Dauphin hurrying up, lending a hand in the work and going back to his apartments dirty and exhausted!

However, Marie Antoinette knew nothing of all this. Yet although she said nothing and continued to smile, we can imagine her disappointment. She was a long way from the Dauphin of her dreams spouting flame through his nostrils!

And what did the bridegroom think of this blonde girl with the pink complexion who in two days would be brought to his bed? Did he already fear the irony in those somewhat prominent eyes? Did he know that she was given to mockery? Did he guess that the full, pretty lip, now ready to pout, would become very disdainful? But this would attribute to the lout of fifteen years and nine months a perspicacity he did not possess!

Louis XV was progressively more "enchanted." He was shortly to say so to Mercy, who hastened to send a messenger to Vienna, adding that "the whole royal family is infatuated with the Archduchess." Already, in the clearing on the outskirts of the forest, by winningly presenting her cheek she had almost softened the withered hearts of Mesdames and on her arrival at Compiègne she was to make the conquest of her cousins Orléans, Condé and Conti.

In Louis XV's apartments, "in spite of the King's presence," Marie Antoinette greeted the Princes of the Blood, who bowed to her in turn. Although the Duc d'Orléans, grandson of the Regent, the Duc de Penthièvre, grandson of Louis XIV and la Montespan, and the Princes of Condé and Conti seemed old in the Dauphine's eyes, her cousins Chartres and Bourbon, on the other hand, were almost her own age. One of them, the son of the Prince de Condé, was even a few months younger and was already married to Louise Bathilde d'Orléans, sister of the Duc de Chartres, who was nineteen. The son of the Duc d'Orléans, the future Philippe Egalité, was 23 and his wife, the Duchesse de Chartres, daughter of the Duc de Penthièvre, four years younger. The last princess to "salute on the cheek"—a young woman with a sad smile—was Marie-Thérèse de Carignan-Savoie, Princesse de Lamballe. Already two years a widow, she was only twenty-one. Her husband, only son of the Duc de Penthièvre, had died, after a wild life, from the results of a love affair. Since then she had lived a sad existence with her father-in-law, the inconsolable Duc de Penthièvre, who trailed his neurasthenia and his collection of watches from castle to castle.

The Dauphine was conducted to her apartments, where the ladies and gentlemen who had accompanied Louis XV to Compiègne were presented to her. Then, after supper with the King and the royal family, the Master of Ceremonies was ushered into the Princess's room, bearing twelve wedding rings provided by M. Papillon de la Ferté, the *Intendant des Menus Plaisirs*. One of the rings fitted her finger perfectly. It was then taken off, for she was not to wear it until the wedding ceremony.

The Dauphine then went to bed while the Dauphin, in accordance with etiquette, spent the night under a different roof. He was taken to the house of the Comte de Saint-Florentin, Minister and Secretary of State of the King's Household.

Marie Antoinette had nothing to fear. Louis-Auguste was not the kind of person to force his way into his wife's bedroom, as 36 years later, also at Compiègne, Napoleon was to do, after his marriage by proxy to a blonde archduchess.

At M. de Saint-Florentin's house the future Louis XVI, yawning, for he had eaten voraciously, opened his diary—a little notebook bound in grey cloth—and in his fine, small writing entered these five words under the date of 14 May 1770: "Interview with Madame la Dauphine."

For the last month M. de Mercy's life had been a burden to him. It was said that Mme du Barry was to be one of the 39 "ladies of quality" to be invited to supper with the royal family on the next day at the Château de la Muette, the last stage before Versailles. "It seems inconceivable," he wrote to Maria Theresa, "that the King should choose this moment to grant his favourite an honour which has hitherto been refused her."

And all day, as the carriages rolled towards Paris, the Ambassador quaked with apprehension. A ray of hope came to him when they halted at the Carmelite convent of Saint-Denis to present the Dauphine to "Sister Thérèse-Augustine." It would be impossible for the King to let his granddaughter become acquainted on one and the same day with his mistress and with the woman who, it was said, had entered into religion in order, by her sacrifice, to redeem her father's misconduct!

M. de Mercy was barely able to appreciate the applause of the Parisians, who cheered the Dauphine as her procession wound its way round Paris. The King, who had not been cheered for a long time, had preferred to go on ahead, and met his granddaughter at La Muette. On descending from her carriage she met the Dauphin's two brothers, Provence and Artois, the future Louis XVIII and Charles X. The Comte de Mercy began to breathe again. Surely the King would not make these two children of 13 and 14 dine with "the creature"! But suddenly the Ambassador turned pale. Among the ladies of quality Mme du Barry, sparkling with jewels, was bowing to the Dauphine. A little later, at supper, the King asked his granddaughter what she thought of the lady who was smiling at her from the end of the table.

"Charming," Marie Antoinette replied.

Interested, the Dauphine leant over towards the Comtesse de Noailles and asked her what place at court was held by that blonde, black-eyed lady whose complexion was like a rose-petal dipped in milk. The Lady of Honour hesitated, then said: "Her office? . . . To amuse the King!" The little bride at once exclaimed: "In that case I proclaim myself her rival!"

From the other end of the table the Comtesse considered the little girl who on the next day would become the first lady in France. Perhaps it was on that evening that she declared, with the lisp which enchanted her royal lover, "She is a *tsarming* little thing!"

In a month's time the two ladies would be finding each other infinitely less charming.

Twenty-three years before, another German princess—Maria-Josepha of Saxony—had also come to France to marry a Dauphin. She had been handed over on the same island in the Rhine, had been acclaimed at Strasbourg, awaited by the King and her "husband" in the Forest of Compiègne, and had then arrived at a castle where she had met the royal favourite—it was then Mme de Pompadour. Finally, on the following day, her carriage, greeted by the trumpets of the bodyguards, had drawn up before the marble staircase at Versailles. There Louis XV and the Dauphin had conducted her to her room on the ground floor of the palace looking out on to the south lawn.

On Wednesday 16 May 1770 Marie Antoinette in her turn, having made the acquaintance of two little girls—Mesdames Clotilde and Elisabeth, her husband's sisters—was led to the bedroom which had belonged to the Princess of Saxony and where the future Louis XVI, Louis XVIII and Charles X had been born.

The memory of "poor Pepa," as Louis XV had called his daughter-in-law, still clung to this room, which was next to the Dauphin's apartments and had been painted by Martin "in green with a covering varnish." At the beginning of his marriage Louis XVI's father, the widower of a Spanish princess whom he adored, could not enter his new wife's bedroom without bursting into tears. The very furniture reminded him of the one he had lost. The little Saxon had behaved admirably. "Give free course to your tears, Monsieur, and do not be afraid that they will offend me. On the contrary, they show what I have a right to hope for for myself, if I am happy enough to win your esteem."

She did win it, beyond anything she could have hoped for, and an astonished Versailles witnessed a touching idyll of royal marriage.

Would this exceptional phenomenon be renewed?

Marie Antoinette had finally noticed the Dauphin's bad grace. Louis-Auguste was as gloomy as his father had been on his wedding morning, although not for the same reason.

While in their adjoining rooms the bride and groom were being dressed in gold cloth and silver brocade a more serious problem disturbed the great building; a mounting drama had finally assumed considerable proportions. The Dukes and Peers gathered; a bishop— Mgr de Broglie—dared to present to the King a memorandum written in almost insulting tones; and Louis XV, although usually quite indifferent, was "so annoyed" that he threw his hat on the ground and "the tears sprang to his eyes."

And this was all because of a minuet.

The whole affair had begun exactly 274 years before—in 1496. When Charles VIII was reigning in France the younger branch of the house of Lorraine had broken away from the reigning dukes. Since then the elder branch had ended, in the person of Marie Antoinette's father, by sitting on the throne of Austria, while the younger branch—which included the Guises—had continued to serve France.

A few months before the date fixed for the marriage, Mme de Brionne-Lorraine, mother of the Prince de Lambesq and of Mlle de Lorraine, had visited M. de Mercy, to ask him if he could obtain "a distinction" for Mlle de Lorraine on the occasion of the wedding of the Archduchess, who was her cousin in the ninth degree.

The Ambassador considered the request a normal one and referred it to his sovereign, who was of the same opinion, so that one fine day Mercy went to Versailles to speak to the King about this "distinction." Louis XV agreed, and decided that on the day of the ball Mlle de Lorraine should dance the first minuet *after* the Princesses of the Blood and *before* the French Duchesses.

The news had run like wildfire through the palace. The Duchesses nearly fainted. Would not the Lorrainers, "those foreign princes," as they were contemptuously called, take advantage of this precedent to obtain a separate rank, half-way between the Princes of the Blood and the Dukes? The Dukes and Peers promptly got together under the presidency of the Bishop of Noyon and sent the King a petition signed by members of even the high nobility. Louis XV, extremely annoyed and unable to make up his mind, had been evasive. The Duchesses, who were furious, had then decided not to go to the ball. This was how matters stood on this bright spring morning in 1770.

The bride was now ready to make her entrance, for Versailles was like an enormous theatre presenting the spectacle of royalty at home. Everyone could enter to gape admiringly in the Hall of Mirrors at the King on his way to Mass, or to watch the principal characters eating. Louis XV, for example, had a way of slicing the top off his boiled egg which was worth going to see. Only "dogs, mendicant friars and people newly marked with smallpox" could not cross the threshold of the Salon of Hercules. Sightseers with no hat or sword were also turned back, but to get round this one had only to hire a hat and a rapier from the concierge, who did a trade in these accessories. Versailles was an anonymous mob, a public square. "Loose women" were admitted, on condition that they did not ply their "shameful trade" in the apartments. Even managers of performing animals were allowed. Cows went up to the first floor and were milked at the foot of the princesses' beds. If you had been "presented" you might watch the royal family rise, go to bed and have their hair dressed, and if your birth gave you a right to the *grandes entrées* you would have the honour of seeing the master of the house on his closestool. The unfortunate people enjoyed a little privacy only back-stage, that is in their private apartments.

Since early morning the equipages of princes and dukes had been entering the royal courtyard. The harnesses were of tooled leather ornamented with ormolu plaques. Plumes and crimson or blue cockades adorned the tall horses, whose manes were plaited with coloured ribbon. The coachmen wore gold or silver hats with feathers and lace. Four lackeys in full livery hung on as best they could behind the coach and two pages sat next to the coachman.

The selected public—for gala first nights—crowded together in the Hall of Mirrors and the Chapel. For their better convenience and so that they might lose nothing of the spectacle balustrades and tiered seats had been installed by servants of the wardrobe. In principle only ladies in full dress, wearers of the blue ribbon and the many holders of invitation cards were allowed in—making over five thousand. But the order was not rigid and the commandant of the guard was told to allow ladies of quality into the castle "if they are followed by two lackeys or if they are escorted." The "best dressed" ladies were placed in the second gallery.

The curtain rose at one o'clock.

The Grand Master of the Ceremonies, full of his own importance, preceded the bride and groom, who were hand in hand. Marie Antoinette—a symphony in rose, gold and silver sparkling with diamonds—was like a ray of sunshine. As she passed through the Hall of Mirrors and the Grand Apartments she still kept her enchanting smile. She advanced with her "caressing walk," and some erudite courtiers quoted Virgil: *Incessu patuit dea.* At her side, with the rolling gait which was typical of so many of the Bourbons, walked Louis-Auguste, scowling in his gold clothes, which had cost 12,322 livres.

The Swiss Guards lined up in the Chapel beat their enormous drums and blew their fifes to proclaim the King's arrival. The nave and the galleries with their tiered seats were packed and many of the ladies sighed on seeing their panniered dresses squashed as flat as pancakes. It was an extraordinary sight. One seemed to be in a drawing-room rather than in the house of God. The white and gold décor was so pagan! The half-naked angels bearing the instruments of the Passion resembled the disturbed dreams of adolescents, the cherubim of the "heavenly glory" were like cupids and Judah was symbolised, naturally, by a seraph. As for the Eternal Father, who hovered over the nave, he was reminiscent of a bearded and indulgent Saturn.

The bride and groom knelt on squares of red velvet fringed with gold. The King and the Princes stepped forward. The Grand Almoner, Mgr de la Roche-Aymon, Archbishop of Rheims, blessed the thirteen pieces of gold—a reminder of the purchase of the wife—and the wedding rings. Before placing the ring on Marie Antoinette's fourth finger Louis-Auguste glanced at his grandfather, who nodded his head. The Archbishop gave his blessing to the two children kneeling before him and Louis XV returned to his chair. The Mass began, while the King's orchestra, placed behind the altar, played a motet composed by Abbé Ganzargues. The court crowded the transepts. "Members of the bodyguards, stationed at intervals, saw to it that silence was observed and even that people who were inattentive knelt down."

After the *Pater Noster* the Bishop of Senlis, the King's First Almoner, and the Bishop of Chartres, the Dauphine's First Almoner, placed a canopy of silver brocade above the pair. This canopy had been provided by the King's privy purse, but after the ceremony it was claimed by the eight almoners of the district to be sold for their benefit, and this proceeding gave rise to a great deal of argument.

Ordinarily the Dauphin liked to accompany the divine service by singing in a voice both loud and off key. Also, when the blessed bread was distributed, he used to bring out a pocket-knife and cut himself a slice or even bite off a piece. It would appear that on this occasion he did not engage in any eccentricity, for the chroniclers—dazzled, perhaps, by the spectacle—have recorded no picturesque details.

The parish priest of Versailles brought the marriage register. The King signed, followed by Marie Antoinette, whose hand trembled a little, making a blot.

On returning to her apartments Madame la Dauphine received the officers of her household. They took the oath of fidelity to her in the presence of the Comte de Saint-Florentin. After the Lady of Honour and the twelve ladies who accompanied her—the new ones were fortunately younger than those sent to Strasbourg—came the *Chevalier d'Honneur,* the First Maître d'Hôtel, the First Almoner, the Intendants, the serving gentlemen, the First Equerry, the Controllers-General, who had themselves received the oath from an army of employees: fourteen waiting women, two preachers, four almoners, five chaplains, a *Chevalier d'Honneur,* one maître d'hôtel in ordinary, four maîtres d'hôtel, two equerries in ordinary, four equerries, nineteen valets de chambre, five ushers of the bedchamber, two of the antechamber and two of the *cabinet,* two doctors, two apothecaries, four surgeons, a clock-maker, a tapestry-maker, eighteen lackeys, a stable equerry, a fencing-master, two muleteers of the *litière du corps,* a wig-maker, who was also attendant for the bath and Turkish bath, and a bearer of the close-stool, a post also held by a man. A further 168 servants were occupied with her food. For since the morning Marie Antoinette had become the mistress of her own kitchen gardens, cellarmen, *coureurs de vin, hâteurs,* scullery-boys, master cooks, butlers, pantlers, cooks, wine-bearers and fruiterers.

Had she any idea, as she saw these officers bow before her, that any encroachment on their prerogatives would provoke a drama? To use their own expression, it would destroy "all the splendour of their office."

It was a pity—for it would have opened the girl's eyes a little—that her Gentleman of Honour did not tell her about the dreadful struggle in which he was engaged with her maître d'hôtel. The former considered that he had a right to certain functions fulfilled by his colleague which concerned "parts of the Mouth of Madame la Dauphine." He wanted the honour not of drawing some of Marie Antoinette's irregular teeth, but of being able, on the days of the *Grand Couvert,* to give orders to the butlers for serving the wine. And these gentlemen disputed hotly, recalling precedents in force in the time of Queen Marie, wife of Charles VII.

These conflicts had not arisen on the creation of a new household. The King's servants, those of Mesdames, as well as those of His Majesty's grandsons and granddaughters, argued, complained and fought, while continuing to salute each other with elegance and courtesy. For example, the life of His Majesty's wardrobe master was a martyrdom. On Palm Sunday of 1728 a wardrobe boy had taken away "without orders" the folding stool on which that officer was allowed to sit behind the King in chapel. Since that ill-fated day the successive wardrobe masters had remained standing. In vain they sent in petitions, proposals and voluminous memoranda—the stool never returned. And for 42 years they searched their consciences. No! they were innocent! They "had done nothing to draw on themselves such a painful humiliation." Such is the conclusion of their report, which can still be read in the National Archives.

The state furniture—from the Salon de Paix to the Salon of Hercules —was ready. This evening the King was holding a reception. In the Hall of Mirrors the gilded wood furniture—which had replaced the massive silver furniture sent by Louis XIV to the Mint in 1689—had for the first time been taken away and replaced by candelabra of carved and gilded wood each bearing 32 chandeliers. It was as bright as day. Sitting at a table covered by a new cloth of green velvet with gold braid and fringes, the King and the newly married couple played the boring game of *cavagnole*. The ushers, the Swiss Guards and the King's *valets de chambre* received the 6,000 guests at the doors and saw them seated on the benches of the Grand Apartments. If one wanted to see the King play one had to walk along behind the railings in the Hall of Mirrors and go out by the Salon de Paix and the Queen's apartments. Many interested people joined this procession without being invited: they were the "common people." They had been chased from the park by the storm which broke during the afternoon. The barriers were forced and the dripping sightseers mingled with the guests and watched the spectacle.

A second storm broke. Madame Louise trembled with fright. "She was so scared," Madame Campan wrote, "that she approached quite insignificant people. She asked them all sorts of kind questions. If she saw a flash of lightning she pressed their hands. At a peal of thunder she would have thrown her arms round them."

The storm died down. Madame Louise "resumed her rigidity, her silence and her air of reserve" and the royal family moved to the new opera house, where the feast was to take place. Strange sounds of music were heard: they came from the French and Swiss Guards massed in the gallery of the north wing. They had left off their red, white and blue uniforms and were disguised as Turks, making "a great uproar with some music from that country." Along the way the salute was given by the bodyguards in blue coats with silver braid, red breeches and stockings and the Hundred-Swiss in slashed trunks, starched ruffs and plumed caps.

On entering the Opera House, which was being opened for the first time that evening, the guests did not feel that they were in a theatre. The stage was so deep that it had been possible to reproduce on it the balconies of the auditorium, thus forming a perfect oval of green-veined grey marble. On the false floor, which covered the seats and was on a level with the stage, was set up a table 26 feet long and 13 feet wide. The guests took their places in the order prescribed by etiquette:

Louis XV

The Dauphin	The Dauphine
Comte de Provence	Comte d'Artois
Madame Clotilde	Madame Adelaide
Madame Victoire	Madame Sophie
Duc d'Orléans	Duc de Chartres
Duchesse de Chartres	Prince de Condé
Duc de Bourbon	Duchesse de Bourbon
Comte de Clermont	Princesse de Conti
Prince de Conti	Comte de la Marche
Comtesse de la Marche	Duc de Penthièvre
Princesse de Lamballe	

The rest of the Court looked on admiringly with empty stomachs.

Escorted by the bodyguards and by a crowd of waiting gentlemen accompanied by maîtres d'hôtel with their silver-gilt batons, hailed by the rolling of drums, the "King's Meat"—that is, the hundreds of dishes making up the feast—arrived from the Great Offices 600 metres away.

Marie Antoinette ate hardly anything, but the Dauphin, who seemed pleased for the first time since the morning, devoured his food. The

King leant anxiously towards him and murmured: "Don't overload your stomach tonight."

The astonished bridegroom laughed and exclaimed: "Why not? I always sleep better after a good supper!"

The King did not insist and looked at Marie Antoinette rather sadly.

The programme included a gigantic show of fireworks, but the storm had drenched the preparations made by Ruggieri, the pyrotechnist, and the spectacle was postponed until the Saturday evening, to the great disappointment of the people, "who were very wet and said nothing."

All that remained was to put the couple to bed and here too the doors of the "Theatre Royal" were open. Everyone in the court was crushed together on the ground floor to see the Archbishop of Rheims bless the bed, the King hand the shirt to the Dauphin, who seemed progressively more bored and sleepy, and the Duchesse de Chartres help the blushing Marie Antoinette put on her nightgown.

The bride and groom lay down behind the hangings and then suddenly—as was the etiquette—the bed-curtains were drawn aside. All present bowed deeply and followed the King out.

Twenty-four years ago, in the same bed and after an evening of similar festivities, Maria Josepha of Saxony had spent her wedding night consoling her husband who was weeping bitterly as he thought of his first wife. On this evening Marie Antoinette had no one to console. In the bed where he was born the Dauphin, his stomach full, fell into a noisy sleep.

On the next day Louis-Auguste wrote his famous "Nothing," in his private notebook—a "nothing" which was to become distressingly symbolic. However, Marie Antoinette displayed no anxiety so far. Thursday 17 May was too full for the little bride to have time to dream of love. She had to receive the whole court and "present the cheek" to those entitled. In the evening she was taken to see "Perseus," the old opera by Quinault and Lulli, brought up to date for the occasion by a certain Joliveau, who, so as to insert a ballet of his own invention, had had the odd idea of "reinforcing Lulli's music" and of compressing the opera into four acts.

Once the curtain had risen Marie Antoinette had difficulty in stifling her yawns. The chronicler Bachaumon admitted frankly: "The Dauphine was bored to death by an unbearable recitative." She might have been diverted by the machinery, but it worked badly. Arnould, who was responsible, had unfortunately broken his leg just before the rehearsals. He dragged himself to the theatre, but fell a second time. He was there this evening, confined to a stretcher and quite unable to go everywhere in the enormous theatre. He could only watch helplessly the collapse of his work. Even the Eagle—symbol of the House of Austria and the highlight of the spectacle—flopped heavily on to the altar of Hymen, instead of perching nobly, and Arnould contemplated suicide.

At one moment Marie Antoinette seemed to get some pleasure from the spectacle. Perseus, having caught his foot in a floorboard, fell heavily at the feet of Andromeda at the very moment when he should have been freeing his future wife. But when Perseus got up the poor Dauphine relapsed into apathy.

After this soporific play Marie Antoinette had no difficulty in getting to sleep and imitating her husband, who once in bed had fallen into a heavy slumber. At dawn on Friday the 18th he left the conjugal bed to go hunting.

"He is leaving very early," the courtiers murmured.

He came back exhausted and remembered that he had a wife. He found Marie Antoinette playing with a little dog.

"Have you slept well?"

"Yes."

Their badinage went no further. Louis-Auguste went out and, according to the Abbé Vermond, who was present, "the Dauphine played with her little dog. He served as a diversion for a moment, then she fell to musing. My heart was wrung."

On the evening of the third day of marriage again "nothing" happened and the musings became more frequent. Mercy, who was at once informed, told Maria Theresa. He prided himself on possessing some medical knowledge and tried to explain to her that "the Dauphin's development is late probably because his constitution has been weakened by his sudden and rapid growth."

This absence of marital prowess did not alarm Louis XV. He was much more preoccupied by the tiresome business of the minuet, which was becoming serious. Duchesses with the right to a *tabouret* and bearing some of the finest names in France were threatening to leave the court if Mlle de Lorraine danced on the Saturday before they did.

Louis XV humbled himself so far as to write to the Dukes explaining that "the dance at the ball was the one thing which could not form a precedent, since the choice of dancers depended only on his will, without distinction of place, rank or dignity." The King ended his letter by declaring: "I trust that the princes and nobility of my realm, in virtue of the fidelity, submission, attachment and even friendship which they have always shown me and my predecessors, will never occasion anything which might displease me, particularly in the present circumstances."

These lines, judged "hardly worthy of a great monarch," did not settle the dispute, and Louis XV decided to send each lady a personal note enjoining her to appear at the ball.

At five o'clock on Saturday the 19th only the ladies of Lorraine were in the ballroom—once more a perfect oval. Finally a few dancers appeared, though very late. It was not the King's letter, or his personal note, which had made them change their minds, but regret, if they stayed at home, at not being able to show off their new gala dresses. However, the absence of many indomitable duchesses was noticed. In spite of these defections the ball took place as arranged.

After bowing to their grandfather the Dauphin and Dauphine opened the ball by dancing a minuet alone. The Dauphin was as clumsy as his wife was charming and accomplished. Then, still very prettily, she danced a quadrille with the Duc de Chartres, who was the best dancer at court. Then came the minuets in which Mlle de Lorraine and the Prince de Lambesq took part in the place the King had granted them. Did Marie Antoinette observe in the seventh minuet a delightful dancer with large, clear eyes, slender, pretty and shy, who was none other than the Comtesse Jules de Polignac?

When night fell everyone moved to the great gallery and the terrace to see the famous fireworks which had been prepared for the 16th. The bride and groom, the King and Mercy stood at the central window of the Hall of Mirrors, at which a grille had been put up in case of accidents. Then began the most beautiful firework display ever shown in France. Thousands of rockets painted on the sky the arms of the Dauphin and the Dauphine and the inevitable temple of Hymen. While the catherine wheels, the windmills, the spheres and the suns turned, while the pyramids of fire sparkled and the shining cascades flowed, while mortars and "rolling fires" exploded, imitating "the sounds of war," hundreds of musicians could be heard on the Grand Canal.

Only the bouquet "in gold and brilliants" misfired. While they were waiting for it it was already over. The two storms had soaked the fireworks, which gave off a thick smoke. Thousands of people from Paris and Versailles danced until six o'clock in the morning in the illuminated park. The soldiers on duty—700 Swiss Guards and French Guards with a white plume in their hats—did not have to intervene. Everything went quite well.

By the time the festivities ended Marie Antoinette had long since begun her fourth night as a married woman. Louis-Auguste snored at her side. Had she resigned herself to this strange situation? Since according to Mercy's diagnosis her husband's rapid growth had stopped everything, there was, perhaps, nothing to do but wait. This was what her mother was to advise. "You are both so young! As far as your health is concerned it is all for the best. You will both gain strength."

The festivities during May prevented the bride from falling too often into musing. One of the entertainments offered her was a performance of Racine's *Athalie* with additional music and choruses "especially written or taken from operas." Athalie was played by the famous Mlle Clairon, who had left her retirement for the occasion, much to the annoyance of Mme du Barry, who was a supporter of Mlle de Mesnil. Unfortunately the latter could act only after drinking a bottle of red wine, and another bottle placed in the wings went the same way during the performance. Perhaps it was feared that the emotion caused by the Dauphine's presence would cause the actress to exceed the usual amount. For whatever reason Mlle Clairon was chosen. Lekain, as ugly as he was talented, played the part of Abner in a costume of maroon velvet with gold frogging and a braided three-cornered hat. This was the tradition. Mlle Clairon wore a farthingale and chopines—very high pointed shoes. It was in similar shoes that she once fell down when playing Camilla fleeing from Horace's dagger, and Horace was seen to sheath his knife, put on his gloves, help his partner up politely and kill her in the wings.

A few days later the Dauphine saw the famous ballet *The Enchanted Tower*. This was a "mechanical drama" from an original idea by the Duchesse de Villeroy. It was about a princess held prisoner by a wicked spirit. She was, of course, freed by a handsome knight who killed the monster. The "very mediocre" words were by Joliveau and the music was a hotch-potch from various operas "arranged" by a certain Dauvergene. The finale was to be the crumbling of the tower which, full of chariots and knights, was to sink beneath the stage. But the racehorses from the King's stables were upset by the unexpected business and "disturbed the order of the spectacle." Marie Antoinette yawned gracefully behind her fan.

The festivities were over, but who was to pay the bill: the 30,385 rockets for the fireworks, the 90,000 lamps and the 603,611 vases for illuminating the park, the 4,492 roman candles, the 14,444 cartridges fired, the 6,820 pots of fire; the 1,841 costumes made for the theatrical performances—in short the nine millions (nearly 2,000 million francs of our money) spent on the marriage festivities?

"What do you think of my festivities at Versailles?" the King had asked his Controller of Finances.

"Sire, I think they are . . . *priceless!*"

So, as regards many of the expenses, the example was followed of M. de Marigny, who had decided not to settle the bills of the carpet manufacturers who had built the new theatre. Poor Arnould was ruined, having got nothing from the affair but a broken leg. A whole file of the National Archives is filled with the pathetic pleas of tradesmen in want who at the beginning of the Revolution were still asking to be paid at least something on account of what they had spent twenty years before for Marie Antoinette's wedding.

The Dauphine had come triumphantly through the test. She had conquered Versailles. "Her politeness embellished her countenance," we are told by a witness. "She had such a graceful word for everyone and curtsied so prettily that in a few days she delighted everyone . . . There is a charm in her manner which will turn all our heads." "She is all smiles," the stern Mercy admitted.

While waiting to wear the crown of France she wore that of charm and grace. Everyone crowded round her and flattered her. When she did not think of Louis-Auguste's sulkiness she was completely happy.

On Wednesday 30 May, at eight o'clock in the evening, the Dauphine entered her carriage with Madame Adelaide. The Dauphin was heaven knows where, but for all that Marie Antoinette was smiling. For the first time she was going—incognito—to Paris, where there was to be a great evening festivity.

On 28 April Louis XV had commanded the city of Paris to offer gifts to Marie Antoinette. "Do not fail in this," he had advised, "for such is our pleasure."

The Mayor, M. Bignon, and the magistrates had not failed, and gifts had been transported to Versailles on carts. On the wedding day the inhabitants had been enjoined "to shut their shops and illuminate their houses." On the old rampart—the present Boulevard des Capucines —a fair had been permitted where it was "forbidden for anyone to draw his sword, to blaspheme and to swear on God's name."

Furthermore the town had decided that on 30 May a great festival should be held at night in the Place Louis XV—now the Place de la Concorde. On the uneven ground in front of the new houses built by Gabriel and near the King's statue a Corinthian temple had been erected flanked by dolphins and crowned with the ciphers of Marie Antoinette and Louis-Auguste together with "a medallion in their likeness." It was on this that the fireworks were to be let off. Since the early morning essence of bergamot had been poured on the banks of the Seine. At five o'clock fountains of wine began to flow. When evening fell the façades of the two palaces were illuminated and the yews in the square and the trees of the Champs-Elysées were adorned with lamps and vases.

As Marie Antoinette drove towards Paris she was eager to arrive. The carriage had scarcely crossed the Pont de Sèvres when the sky was filled with light and the exploding fireworks could be heard in the distance. The Dauphine had not reached the Porte de la Conférence —the present Place de l'Alma—when the set piece, which was the perennial temple of Hymen, could be seen in the clear May sky. But suddenly the six carriages horses and the escort of bodyguards halted in the Cours-la-Reine. A great clamour arose from the square. People were running in terror. And little by little the Princess learned the details of the disaster. The set piece had hardly gone out when a crowd of 300,000 people, coming simultaneously from the square, the quays and the Champs-Elysées, rushed towards the Rue Royale to see the fair. The pressure was so great that a firemen's cart, which was moving towards the Corinthian temple to put out the beginnings of a fire, was overturned. The flood of people, which was divided into several streams by the carriages leaving the square, clashed with another crowd coming from the Boulevard to see the illuminations in the

Champs-Elysées. In a few moments 400,000 people—according to the report of the Hôtel de Ville—were jammed in the Rue Royale, the Rue Saint-Florentine and the Rue de la Bonne-Morue, now the Rue Boissy-d'Anglas. Men, women and children stumbled over the gutters and were trodden underfoot. Other unfortunates tripped over them and fell. A wafer-seller collapsed with his stall; carriages were overturned. People tried to climb on the carriages, but they gave way under the weight and the horses were suffocated. Soon people were walking on piles of corpses. It was like a scene from Dante: the dead, emptied of blood through the nose and mouth, stayed upright, and were carried along by the crowd. They toppled over only when they were no longer supported.

By the time Marie Antoinette was returning in tears to Versailles in her carriage drawn by six white horses, the panic had died down. The wounded were cared for and the dead taken away.

In the morning the Dauphin, overcome, wrote to the Hôtel de Ville: "I have learned of the disaster which came upon Paris on my account. I am deeply distressed. I have been brought the sum which the King sends me every month for my private expenses. It is all I have to give. I send it to you. Give aid to the most unfortunate." Marie Antoinette, shedding her first tears, followed his example.

On the same morning 132 labelled corpses were laid out in the Cemetery of the Madeleine, in the same grass enclosure where 23 years later the body of Marie Antoinette, the head placed between the legs, would be thrown on the bare ground.

3

❧

One Word

THE FESTIVITIES WERE over. Versailles had relapsed into calm, pending the annual exodus of the court to Marly, Choisy, Fontainebleau and Compiègne. Etiquette held sway, but in between the performances —the *levers*, the *couchers*, midday mass, meals and games—ordinary life was able to go on. At 10 o'clock in the morning and 3 o'clock in the afternoon the King went down to see his daughters in Madame Victoire's great sitting-room on the ground floor under the Salon de la Guerre. Marie Antoinette would be there "in a light dress of gauze or taffeta." She had stopped wearing her sparkling diamonds and looked even more exquisite. But Louis XV did not stay long. He soon left his daughters to their intrigues against Choiseul and their quarrels over etiquette, and went to find his dear, blonde Comtesse, whom he had installed temporarily above his own apartments until the court's absence in the summer, when Gabriel (the architect) would be able to prepare the charming rooms which still exist. Louis XV would often come down again to his daughters' room a little before eleven, after supping in private. Marie Antoinette would be there too, having fallen asleep on a large sofa while waiting for him. She had spent her day embroidering a waistcoat for the King.

"I hope that with God's help it will be finished in a few years," she confessed, smiling.

The Dauphine had as much leisure as ever. Louis-Auguste exhausted himself hunting and in the evenings thought only of repose so as to be able to continue his sporting exploits on the morrow. "I am preaching patience to my daughter," Maria Theresa wrote to Mercy, "and assure her that she will not lose by it." It would seem that one night, after seven weeks of marriage, Marie Antoinette forgot her mother's advice and complained to her husband, for on Sunday 8 July the Dauphin, for the first time, discussed the problem with his wife.

"Rest assured that I am not ignorant of what is involved in the state of marriage. From the earliest days I imposed on myself a rule of conduct which I wished to observe, but the time limit I set myself has been reached. You will find that at Compiègne I shall live with you in the fullest intimacy you could wish."

The Dauphin would be 16 on 13 August. Was this the time limit he had set himself? At Compiègne, on 23 August, however, "nothing" happened.

The whole court was soon informed. Oddly enough, those most alarmed were the King's daughters, who, according to Mercy, "upset Madame le Dauphine and cause her anxiety." The King in his turn was surprised. Marie Antoinette once more gave her husband to understand that she too was "not ignorant of what was involved in the state of marriage" and the Dauphin promised to come to her room on 20 September. Marie Antoinette was so happy that she imparted this piece of news to her aunts who, like all old maids, announced the event to everyone. Madame Adelaide, who could not in fact have known much about it, felt it necessary to "exhort" the Dauphin to give him courage, as Mercy informed his sovereign. The 20 September arrived, and the Dauphin, "scared," remained in his own room. Marie Antoinette sighed and from 400 leagues' distance Maria Theresa advised her daughter "to be prodigal of her caresses." The Dauphine obeyed and her husband weakened, promising to come to his wife on 10 October. The court would then be at Fontainebleau and the Dauphin was convinced that the bracing air of the forest would have a good influence on his behaviour. But the same scene repeated itself: Marie Antoinette confiding in her aunts, Madame Adelaide gossiping and exhorting, and the husband taking fright. The King then decided to intervene and questioned his grandson on his "frigid condition."

"I find my wife charming," the young man replied. "I love her, but I still need a little time to overcome my timidity."

It was decided to wait.

But his "insensibility," as Mercy called it, continued and worried Maria Theresa, who was anxious to have a grandson whose mere existence would consolidate the alliance. "If a girl as pretty as the Dauphine cannot stir the Dauphin," she wrote in despair, "every remedy will be useless."

There was one, however.

Louis-Auguste's "strange behaviour" was to have such repercussions that it is worth dwelling on and listening to the opinion of a doctor. Dr. Paul Ganière, the excellent biographer of Corvisart, wrote to me on the subject: "What was the matter? Did the Dauphin feel physically repelled by the young Archduchess? Not at all. She was charming and expressed her satisfaction in being his wife. Although not very expansive he did not mind revealing his happiness on many occasions. Then was the heir to the throne abnormal? Everyone was soon convinced of it, particularly since rumours and indiscretions whose origin it is very difficult to trace have left the impression that nature had unfortunately endowed him with an anatomical abnormality which, although slight, required surgical treatment at an early age so as not to interfere with his future development. This malformation, which was either ignored or deliberately neglected when action should have been taken, through fear of responsibility, played a serious part in the difficulties surrounding the consummation of the marriage. But this was not all. The descriptions of the Dauphin which have come down to us present him as a boy heavy of mind and body, showing definite backwardness in various features, particularly in the glands to which doctors nowadays attach so much importance. Therefore, together with the physical peculiarity I have just mentioned, or more probably as a result of it, a kind of indifference due to this sluggishness of the genital functions had turned this 15-year-old adolescent into someone completely calm, just when he should have been thanking heaven for giving him a charming wife, quite ready to yield to his desires. Strong principles, natural timidity and an awkwardness increased by bad eyesight do not in themselves explain the marital conduct of Louis XV's grandson. Nature had made him what he was and if the scalpel had been used earlier he might have been different. Tormented by an inferiority complex and vaguely aware of being ridiculous, he yielded to the advice of the doctors who assured him that with the help of a healthy diet and violent physical exercise all would be well. This advice, which in its optimism and simplicity suited his temperament, seemed very sensible and he let weeks go by without thinking that Marie Antoinette, for all her innocence, might experience an indefinable uneasiness, or even a wound to her self-esteem, in having unwillingly to play the part of a wife in name only."

In order to follow his diet the Dauphin ate enormously. Nothing spoiled his appetite, neither the presence of 20 Officers of the Mouth busying themselves round his table, nor the armed guards protecting his "Meat," nor the hundred or so people who, in profound silence, watched him eat.

Marie Antoinette merely nibbled. The Dauphine already had a sense of the ridiculous and could not bring herself to follow the example of Maria Leczinska, who never hesitated to call on one of those standing by.

"Madame?" the spectator would say, coming forward and bowing.

"I think this stew is a fricassee of chicken," the Queen would declare solemnly.

"I am of the same opinion, Madame," the person addressed would reply proudly, walking backwards to his place.

Marie Antoinette preferred to observe the people standing in front of her table. She could not keep her thoughts to herself and would burst into laughter with her young Ladies of Honour. Mercy was soon warning Maria Theresa. "Madame la Dauphine is careless of outward appearances. . . . She makes fun of people who appear to her ridiculous." This was all the more serious because Marie Antoinette "knows how to infuse into her remarks just the amount of wit to make them more telling." The Ambassador often noticed her "whispering in the ears of the young ladies" and then "laughing with them." Maria Theresa scolded her: "It is said that you have begun to make fun of everyone and to burst out laughing in people's faces. . . . By amusing five or six young ladies or gentlemen you will lose the rest." On several occasions the Empress insisted: "Do not give way to an inclination to make fun of others." But the Dauphine shrugged her shoulders.

When Louis XV was informed of his granddaughter's mockery he did not hide his displeasure and sent for the Comtesse de Noailles.

"It is quite right that in private Madame la Dauphine should give way to her natural gaiety, but in public, when she is holding her court, her behaviour must be more reserved."

Marie Antoinette listened inattentively to the lecture brought to

her by her Lady of Honour. She considered that she was no longer a
child and that her education was complete.

So the smiling Archduchess became the mocking, lively Dauphine,
who had only one idea: to amuse herself. She decided she would like
to ride. Mercy, whom this idea frightened "in view of the Dauphine's
extreme youth," warned Choiseul, who went to tell Louis XV. The
King, who was bored by the whole affair, found a compromise and
permitted the use of a donkey, which after several happy expeditions
to Compiègne became a pony and then a real horse. Mercy proposed
a middle course: "that the Archduchess should go only at a walking
pace and rarely trot." Maria Theresa protested: "Riding spoils the
complexion." Marie Antoinette looked in her mirror, and, reassured,
galloped the harder. The Empress sighed: "The donkeys and horses
will have occupied the time needed for reading." But at least let her
daughter not go hunting! The girl promised, but at the beginning of
May 1771, when she was fifteen-and-a-half, she disobeyed on the
pretext of having "accidentally met the hunt." Then she repeated the
offence, following the hunt on horseback or in a cabriolet, which
frightened Maria Theresa still more but has given us a charming scene.
One day the postillion fell and was trampled by the horses. The
Princess refused to go on, had the wounded man tended in her presence
and wrote to her mother: "I told everyone they were my friends,
pages, grooms, postillions. I said: 'My friend, go and fetch the surgeons.
My friend, run quickly for a stretcher, see if he can speak, if he is
conscious!'"

The spoiled child, less felicitously, played the part of a caterer. "Her
Royal Highness," Mercy reported, "has the habit of bringing in her
carriages all kind of cold meats and refreshments which she likes to
distribute to the courtiers following the hunt." Soon "all the young
people in the King's suite" neglected the stag, not for the cold meats
and the refreshments, but to cluster round the carriage in which the
pretty young Princess laughed at the replies of those whom Mercy
called "scatterbrains."

The Empress had to console herself with her one victory. Not
without difficulty she had managed to get her daughter once more to
wear the corset which she had decided to do without at Compiègne.
After serious discussions between Mme de Noailles, the Abbé de
Vermond and the Comte de Mercy, after the exchange of numerous

letters on the subject between Vienna and Paris the Ambassador could at last utter a cry of victory: "Madame la Dauphine is again wearing her whalebone corset."

In spite of this brilliant result Maria Theresa lamented: "Her carelessness, her lack of pleasure in any serious concentration and her indiscretion provide me with many occasions of anxiety."

One evil came from her intimacy with her aunts. At the beginning, when she was neglected by her husband, whose marital failures had plunged him further into awkwardness and misanthropy, the little girl had no other resources than to go four or five times a day to see Mesdames. The Empress herself had advised this. "The Princesses are full of virtue and talent; this is very fortunate for you; I hope you will deserve their friendship." Mercy was of a different opinion. According to him—and he was right—these old maids "had never had the gift of behaving in a way befitting the circumstances." The ground-floor apartments of Mesdames were a hotbed of intrigue and gossip. Even among themselves there was jealousy and almost hatred, and Mercy noted that "Madame Adelaide and Madame Sophie are engaged in inspiring in the Archduchess a coldness for Madame Victoire."

The influence of Mesdames soon became disastrous. Marie Antoinette allowed herself "to be led into sharp remarks in which she indulges only when she is provoked by bad example. I have unfortunately learned," Mercy added, "that of all the ideas which Madame Adelaide contrives to teach Madame la Dauphine there is not one which is not either false or prejudicial to Her Imperial Highness."

It does not appear to have been Madame Adelaide, however, who first revealed to her niece what precisely were the "amusements" of Mme du Barry and the King. It was the Dauphin, and the Dauphine was sickened by the thought that her grandfather had a mistress—and such a mistress! She at once wrote to her mother: "It is pitiful to see the King's partiality for Mme du Barry, who is the most stupid and impertinent creature you can imagine." Fearing her mother's reactions to this outburst, she added: "You can be well assured that I shall commit no fault either for her or against her."

In fact she treated her grandfather's mistress "correctly," but Mesdames were gradually to force her from the line of conduct she had wisely set herself. A trivial incident came to help them.

It began by a women's quarrel. In the little drawing room of the

Château at Choisy the ladies attending court occupied the front benches. Madame du Barry arrived very late with two members of her following, the Maréchale de Mirepoix and the Comtesse de Valentinois. The favourite looked at the occupiers of the benches who showed clearly that they had no intention of giving up their places. No one moved and on both sides the fans fluttered. It was not known who spoke first, but in a few seconds remarks were exchanged, sharp, lively and full of innuendo. One of the Dauphine's ladies, Mme de Grammont, a sister-in-law of the Duchesse de Choiseul and "a leader in this dispute," strongly attacked Mme du Barry, who was forced to retreat and take her place at the back of the room.

On the following day Mme de Grammont received a *lettre de cachet* exiling her 15 leagues from the court, and she begged Marie Antoinette to intervene. The Choiseul family protested, Mesdames became agitated and the Dauphine prepared to act. Fortunately Mercy arrived, calmed the Dauphine and advised her to attack the King in his one weak spot. Marie Antoinette should show that she was "somewhat hurt that a person in her service should have been exiled without anyone mentioning it to her." The Dauphine followed this advice and the King could only murmur a kind of embarrassed apology. But Mme du Barry was on the watch—Mme de Grammont belonging to the clan of her greatest enemy Choiseul—and Louis XV did not rescind the order of exile. At Fontainebleau, a little later on, the young girl, all smiles, returned to the attack. Mme de Grammont was seriously ill and wanted to return to Paris "to receive treatment." The Dauphine became coaxing, and tried out the influence of her fifteen years.

"What a grief it would be to me, papa, if a woman in my service should die while under your displeasure!"

Mme du Barry was the stronger and the King did not yield until a medical examination had been held, but the culprit was still forbidden the court.

The Dauphine's pride had been seriously wounded by this affront. She was soon to suffer another victory by the favourite—the Choiseul affair.

The Minister had approved his sister-in-law's attitude at Choisy, all the more because he himself had undergone something similar at the grand theatre in Rome. He was then French Ambassador and as such regularly occupied a box of honour on the right of that occupied by the Governor. One day it was decided to award this box by lot, as well as the other seats. Choiseul nearly fainted, and on recovering himself threatened to ask for his passport. Apologies were made and the box was given back to him. But the Ambassador demanded reparation. Henceforth he insisted on having the Governor's own box surmounted by the papal arms. It was now Benedict XIV who nearly fainted, but Choiseul would not yield. He declared that he would leave Rome, and finally the Pope, less powerful in his own domain than Mme du Barry at Versailles, had to give way.

One may imagine how Choiseul's pride was offended by Mme de Grammont's exile. His attitude to Mme du Barry became more hostile and the Comtesse persuaded her royal lover to dismiss the Minister.

A pretext was soon found. The King and his Minister were in disagreement because Choiseul was urging war against England in order to support Spain in a complicated affair about an island off St. Malo occupied by English sailors. Louis XV averted the imminent conflict, but his Minister's warlike instincts were a good excuse for exiling him on 24 December and thus offering his pretty mistress the Christmas present she had been angling for for months.

What was Marie Antoinette to do when the man to whom she owed everything was exiled to the provinces? Mercy was on the watch and sent the Abbé de Vermond to this *enfant terrible*. The Dauphine should simply express "a little displeasure," no more. On 6 January Maria Theresa sent her an urgent letter enjoining her "never to forget the gratitude she owed to Choiseul," but also advising her not to "let herself be drawn into any faction" and to "remain completely neutral."

Marie Antoinette thought to obey her mother's wishes by ignoring the favourite's presence and according her not a word or a look. Mme du Barry might have been invisible. Her aunts and the Dauphin encouraged her in this course of action. The whole of Versailles watched the struggle with delight. They almost applauded. Under Mme du Barry's prompting the King spoke to Mme de Noailles about this attitude, but without daring to tackle the problem frankly.

"The Dauphine allows herself to speak too freely about what she sees or thinks she sees," he said. "Thoughtless remarks might produce bad effects within the family."

Louis XV thus placed his Comtesse "within the family." On the

evening of this rebuke Marie Antoinette spoke to her "dear papa,"
who felt very ill at ease, said nothing and confined himself to coaxing
and kissing his granddaughter. Everything was settled, or rather
nothing was settled. The Dauphine continued to refuse even to look
at Mme du Barry, who, however, reigned more securely than ever.
It was not Maria Leczinska's room on the first floor, where Marie
Antoinette now lived, which was "the Queen's apartment," but the
little low-ceilinged but exquisite rooms in which the Comtesse was
installed in December 1770. The seat of the Government was there,
and d'Aiguillon, who through the favour of Mme du Barry had
succeeded Choiseul, worked with the King in the favourite's new
home. It became difficult, not to say impossible, for Ministers from
abroad to avoid the uncrowned queen. Poor Mercy knew something
about this. He found himself in the presence of the Comtesse for the
first time at a dinner attended by the Duc d'Aiguillon, the Nuncio
and the Sardinian Ambassador. The last-named was speaking to the
favourite "as to a person with whom one is acquainted." The representative of His Holiness likewise made a leg. Mme du Barry was
more charming to the Austrian Ambassador than to his Roman and
Sardinian colleagues. Instead of sitting down to table they chatted
like old friends.

Two days later Marie Antoinette, who had learned all about it—
nothing being secret at Versailles—could not help saying to the
Ambassador in a low voice: "I congratulate you on the fine company
with whom you took supper on Sunday."

Mercy bowed. "Today, Madame, an even more remarkable event
is to take place on which I shall have the honour to report to Your
Royal Highness tomorrow."

That evening, indeed, Mercy consented to go and see the King in
Mme du Barry's room. Needless to say, Louis XV was late and the
Ambassador was alone with the beautiful woman, to whose charm
he quickly succumbed. "She bears herself well," he wrote to Vienna.
"She does not appear to have any tendency to malice." Fearing,
however, that his report might offend his sovereign he added: "But
her speech smacks strongly of her former condition." What she
wanted was to persuade Mercy that she had a profound respect for
the Dauphine and that she was in despair at the "kind of contempt"
shown her by Her Royal Highness. The King arrived at last by the

little staircase which linked his room to that of his mistress. The Comtesse rose. "Shall I leave, Monsieur?"

The word *monsieur* astonished Mercy, but left Louis XV unmoved. That was nothing! Yes, he wished to be alone, and at once moved into the attack.

"Until now you have been the Empress's Ambassador. I beg you to be mine, at least for a short time. I love Madame la Dauphine dearly. I think she is charming, but as she is lively and has a husband who is not in a position to guide her she cannot possibly avoid the traps set for her by intrigue."

As was his wont Louis XV did not go straight to his goal. For some time he beat about the question before asking Mercy to use his influence to get the Dauphine "to grant to every person presented the treatment which the latter has the right to expect."

The person presented told the Ambassador what she wanted. "All she wishes is that Madame la Dauphine should speak to her just once." Mercy added an observation on Mme du Barry which caused the Empress to ponder. "If one knows how to go about it it is very easy to make her talk and one might very often gain advantage from this."

Without daring to admit it Mercy was subjugated. He now had to persuade Marie Antoinette. As he had promised, he went to report on the interview and summed it up in the following alternatives: "If the Archduchess wishes to show by her behaviour in public that she understands the part played at court by the Comtesse du Barry, her dignity requires that she should ask the King to forbid the woman to appear henceforth in her circle. If, on the other hand, she prefers to appear to ignore the favourite's real position she must then, without any affectation, treat her as she would any woman presented and, when the occasion offers, speak to her, if only once, so as to put an end to any trumped-up pretext for recriminations."

Her mother's Minister might if he chose imitate the Nuncio and flutter round Mme du Barry in the second-floor attics of the palace— did not M. de Mercy himself live in concubinage with an opera girl?—but she would refuse to speak a single word to this "creature" whose body, before giving pleasure to the Well-Beloved, had been "leased out to anyone who was in a position to pay."

Madame Adelaide supported her niece's good resolutions. Mercy played his last card: policy. He explained to the girl that her attitude was so displeasing to Louis XV that the Franco-Austrian alliance was endangered by it. The Abbé, too, insisted and on 10 July 1771, not without reluctance, the spoilt child gave way. She agreed to say a few words "to la Barry," but in Mercy's presence. The Ambassador would simply have to come with her to the gathering. The Dauphine would stop, speak to Mercy and say a word "as though by chance" to the Comtesse. The Ambassador, delighted, sent word of his success to the woman who was now his "protégée": if she would come on Sunday to the Dauphine's she would be satisfied. On the 11th Marie Antoinette sent a note to Mercy, telling him of her anxiety, but assuring him that "the arrangement still stood." On Sunday, at the beginning of the evening, Marie Antoinette summoned the diplomat and murmured: "I am very nervous, but do not fear, I shall speak."

The play was over. Marie Antoinette began her usual tour of the room, uttering a banality to each person and listening to the banality returned to her with a deep bow. She was only a step away from the favourite and had already opened her mouth when Madame Adelaide broke in, in her sergeant's voice: "It is time to leave! Come, we are going to wait for the King with my sister Victoire."

The Dauphine turned round. She had made the mistake of telling her aunts about her promise. Cut to the quick, Mme du Barry returned to her apartments.

The story spread through Versailles and through Europe. The couriers whipped up their horses to carry the news to Madrid, St. Petersburg and Vienna. But, surprisingly enough, Maria Theresa, who in her own dominions had prostitutes whipped, immediately took the "stupid creature's" part. Austria's interests demanded it. The Empire had now more than ever need of French friendship. If the Alliance should fall apart France would not let Austria draw nearer to Prussia with a view to dividing Poland. In fact, if the "little girl," as Kaunitz called her, refused to speak one word to Mme du Barry the Austrian Empire might say goodbye to its share of the Polish cake which Catherine II and Frederick were getting ready to devour. East Galicia, Russia and two-and-a-half million inhabitants were in the balance. Marie Antoinette would have to sacrifice herself.

"Does one word about a dress or any trifle cost you so much fuss?" the Empress asked. "I can no longer be silent. After Mercy's conversation and all he told you about what the King wanted and what your duty required you dared fail him! What good reason can you put forward? None! You should not know or see the Barry in any other light than that of a lady admitted to the court and to the King's society. You are his first subject, you owe an example to the court and to the courtiers of executing the wishes of your master. If low actions or familiarities were required of you, neither I nor anyone else would advise you to them—but a non-committal word, a few glances, and not for the lady but for your grandfather, your master, your benefactor!"

Maria Theresa had gone rather far and the "little girl" rebelled. "You can be assured that I have no need to be guided by anyone in everything that is honest. If you were able to see as I do everything that happens here you would understand that this woman and her clique will not be content with a word and the whole thing will begin again."

"You made me laugh," Maria Theresa replied, "by imagining that I or my Minister would ever advise you anything against honour or even against the simplest propriety." In the Empress's view the aunts were alone responsible and the cause of all her daughter's *faux pas*. "I can see that you are in great subjection and you need to be quickly and firmly freed from it."

On 2 November 1771 Marie Antoinette was 16. Would she still oppose her mother and Mercy? She was proud and obstinate, as Maria Theresa was constantly repeating, and to yield caused her real suffering. But Austria's interests had spoken.

For the sake of the country which had never ceased to be a little her own—"I shall always glory in belonging to it," she wrote—she gave way. She promised Mercy to speak to Mme du Barry "but not at a fixed day and hour, so that she can let it be known in advance and make a triumph of it."

On the first day of January 1772 Mme du Barry, with the Duchesse d'Aiguillon and the Maréchale de Mirepoix, bowed before the Dauphine. Marie Antoinette said something to the Duchesse then paused for a second in front of the "creature" and remarked: "There are a great many people at Versailles today."

The whole palace heard of it. The aunts, who were furious, sulked, but the King wept with joy. He greeted the Dauphine "with demonstrations of tenderness." Maria Theresa and in particular Joseph II were delighted. Poland could be divided without any obstacle. Mercy arrived all smiles, having triumphed. But the future Queen raised her head and declared: "I have spoken to her once, but I am quite determined to stop there and that woman will never hear the sound of my voice again." She was to keep her word.

4

✤

Madame la Dauphine

THE TRAGI-COMIC STRUGGLE between the two most important women at court—a child and a courtesan—had one advantage. It separated the Dauphine from her aunts. She herself confessed frankly: "I was too young and thoughtless. Now I know where I stand."

In consequence Marie Antoinette became more intimate with her husband. "As for my dear husband," she wrote to her mother, "he is greatly changed, and all for the better. He shows much friendship towards me and has even begun to repose confidence in me." Mercy was soon able to inform his sovereign that "the Dauphin is entirely captivated by his wife." He became almost gallant.

"She is so full of grace," he said, "that she does everything well. It must be admitted that she is charming."

The Dauphine could, of course, do nothing to remedy the "fatal object," as Mercy called it, but she was too much of a coquette not to try her power and at least "smarten up" her husband. At Compiègne, one day after the Dauphin had suffered from indigestion, she stopped him eating so many cakes, and even forbade them to be served to him until further orders. The greedy young man gave way smiling, and seemed very touched.

Emboldened by this Marie Antoinette tried to "wean the young prince from his extraordinary taste for all work connected with building." He would return from his labours covered with plaster. Here, however, the Dauphine, who was "extremely displeased by this conduct," obtained less success. In spite of her forceful complaints she did not succeed in preventing her husband from lending a hand to any workmen he happened to meet.

When he came back from hunting—always very late and often long after the King—the Dauphin sometimes staggered with exhaustion. So on 1 July 1771 Marie Antoinette gave her husband "a lecture on this excessive liking for the hunt which spoiled his health, and on the unkempt and rough appearance resulting from this exercise." Shamed by this explosion, Louis-Auguste retreated to his apartments, but the Dauphine pursued him and "continued to point out, somewhat strongly, all the drawbacks of his way of life. This language," Mercy continued, "so upset M. le Dauphin that he began to weep." Faced with his tears, the girl was affected and wept too.

An incident helped to weaken the influence which the Duc de la Vauguyon still had over his former pupil. "Something very odd has just happened," Marie Antoinette told her mother. "I was alone with my husband when M. de la Vauguyon hurried up to the door to listen. One of the *valets de chambre,* who is either a fool or a very honest man, opened the door and M. le Duc was left standing there like a post without being able to escape. So I mentioned to my husband the disadvantage there was in letting people listen at doors and he took it very well."

Like all Marie Antoinette's letters to her mother, this is written in French and the style is charming.

The Dauphin now consented to join his wife's circle. During these years preceding her reign it consisted principally of the young couples of Provence, Chartres and Bourbon. It was on 14 May 1771 that the future Louis XVIII had married Marie-Josèphe of Savoy, who was very ugly. It was even pretended that she had hair on her chest.

"What do you think of your sister-in-law?" the Comte de Provence asked the Dauphin on the day after his wedding.

"I don't like her very much. I should not care to have her as my wife."

"I am very glad that you have found someone more to your taste," the bridegroom replied, annoyed. "We are both satisfied, for my wife pleases me immensely."

The Comte de Provence began to flaunt bourgeois tastes and declared that he would like to remain by the fire in the winter with his better half. It was soon reported at court that the Comtesse de Provence was expecting a child.

"Is there any foundation for it?" Marie Antoinette asked her brother-in-law.

"A great deal, Madame. There is not a day when it might not be true!"

"Ah! since you reply so well I shall not ask you any more questions!"

The two families were never separated. "We two and my sister and brother get on very well together," wrote Marie Antoinette to her mother on 21 June 1771.

The two families were soon joined by the Comte d'Artois. The future Charles X was certainly to become a cheerful friend to the Dauphine and a gallant companion—even too gallant. But for the present he displayed nothing but "honourable sentiments." In November 1773 he married the Comtesse de Provence's sister, Marie-Thérèse of Savoy, whose appearance was not spared by Mercy. "She has a thin face, a very long nose with an ugly tip, crossed eyes and a large mouth, which all go to make up an irregular face with no charm and very common." She refused to utter a word and had only one wish, to be unnoticed. Her husband was quick to satisfy her on this point and hastened to Paris to his mistress, the beautiful Rosalie Duthé, who had a fancy for his family, having initiated the Duc de Chartres in 1766. Once the Comte d'Artois's escapade was known a jest ran round Versailles: "Having been given indigestion by a sponge cake (*gâteau de Savoie*), the Prince has gone to take tea (*du thé*) at Paris."

No one pitied the neglected wife, who seemed "to take no interest in anything" and was "very repellent." The Dauphine charitably "showed her every kindness" and tried to "rouse her from her apathy." She drew her into the quartet she had formed with the Provences and the Dauphin. The Comte d'Artois was obliged to follow. When there was no public dinner the three families took their meals together and then, unknown to the King, acted plays with Louis-Auguste as the only spectator. In an entresol room in the Dauphin's apartments the young people had fixed up a kind of small folding stage which could be hidden in a cupboard. The Comte de Provence was the most brilliant actor; the Comte d'Artois was graceful; Marie Antoinette was passable; and the two Savoyards extremely bad.

Campan, the father-in-law of Marie Antoinette's future *femme de chambre,* was the producer, prompter and principal actor. But one day, when he was dressed as Crispino, he was surprised behind a door by a servant of the wardrobe, who was so frightened that he fell down backwards with a loud cry. This was M. Campan's most successful part. But they were afraid that this incident might reveal the secret of the performances and the theatre closed its doors, much to the disappointment of the Dauphin, who laughed until he cried.

"It was from the period of these diversions," Mme Campan tells us, "that he was seen to lose his timid childhood air and take pleasure in the Dauphine's society." After a year's intimacy with her two brothers-in-law Marie Antoinette cared less for them. She admitted that she had been mistaken about them and, as Mercy noted with visible satisfaction, these new feelings provided "motives for comparison very favourable to M. le Dauphin."

"I am more and more convinced," she admitted, "that if I had to choose a husband from the three I should prefer the one heaven has given me. Although he is awkward he shows me every possible attention and kindness."

This letter is dated 1775, but these were already the Dauphine's feelings for her husband. Being obviously liked by the girl who was to become the most attractive woman in the court, the Dauphin seemed less clumsy. He began to acquire self-confidence and gave proof of it on the day of his joyful entry into Paris: if he did not succeed in pleasing the Parisians at least he did not go unnoticed.

It seems hardly credible that after living for more than three years in the Ile de France Marie Antoinette knew no more of Paris than the Porte de la Conférence, of which she had just had a glimpse on the evening of the accident of 30 May 1770. This was the fault of Louis XV, who did not at all care to see his grandchildren win the applause he had not received for a long time.

Finally, not without frequent requests from the city, the Entry was fixed for Tuesday, 8 June 1773. At half-past eight in the morning a procession left the Hôtel de Ville to fetch Maréchal de Brissac, the Governor of Paris, who lived in the Rue Cassette. From there it proceeded to welcome the Dauphin and the Dauphine at the Porte de la Conférence.

The horsemen of the watch, the guards and the town orchestra preceded the carriages of the city—that is, of the Prévôt, M. de la Michodière, and of the first and second councillors. But these important personages, who were at that time called the "Gentlemen" of the city, were not in their carriages: they were represented by the *huissiers*. It was the same with the Governor: it was his officers who occupied his four carriages attended by servants in livery holding the doors. The Maréchal, the Prévôt and his two magistrates were seated in the same carriage—called the *carrosse du corps*—preceded by officers on horseback and followed by "the livery of the Governor." Only the third and fourth councillors occupied their own coaches and brought up the rear of the procession with another squadron of horsemen and guards.

The trumpets sounded and at half-past eleven the cannon at the Invalides began to thunder. Everyone gathered at the entrance to the Cours la Reine, and soon the procession of the Dauphin and Dauphine appeared on the hill of Chaillot escorted by His Majesty's bodyguards. After three coaches filled with ladies came the carriage of the old Maréchal de Richelieu. In his capacity of First Gentleman of the Chamber for the year, he had the duty of accompanying the guests of Paris. The Dauphin, who did not care for him, called him a "desiccated mummy." Marie Antoinette blamed him equally for his amorous exploits, which began under Louis XIV and continued until the eve of the Revolution, and for the bad taste he showed in choosing the spectacles for the court, which was part of his office.

"At last, M. le Maréchal, your spectacles are ended," she said to him when his reign finished at the end of the year. "Now we shall be able to amuse ourselves!"

On this particular day the old libertine had nothing to do with the organisation and Marie Antoinette prepared to enjoy herself. She wore the same smile as at Strasbourg and came to conquer Paris. After the presentations the two processions continued along the quays until Notre Dame, while in the Place Louis-XV the *"boêtes d'artillerie"* fired a salute.

After the service in Notre Dame, and after being harangued at the entrance to the college of Louis le Grand and received in front of Sainte Geneviève by the Abbot and his chapter, Marie Antoinette and her husband took a round-about route to the Tuileries for dinner. All along the way the pretty Dauphine and Louis-Auguste himself were wildly cheered. The crowd in the Tuileries gardens were in transports. The young couple had to show themselves to the people ten times, amid cries, shouts and excitement.

"Madame," said Brissac, "there you have two hundred thousand adorers!"

"Tears of emotion mingled with the cries of joy," wrote the clerk of the Hôtel de Ville in his report.

A few days later the Dauphine wrote to her mother, "Last Tuesday I was fêted in a way I shall never forget as long as I live. We received every imaginable honour. But that, although it was very well, was not what touched me the most, but the tenderness and the eagerness of the poor people who, in spite of the taxes which oppress them, were transported with joy on seeing us. When we went to walk in the Tuileries there was such a great crowd that we remained for three-quarters of an hour without being able to go forward or back. The Dauphin and I several times ordered the guards not to strike any-one, which made a very good impression. There was such good order during the whole day that in spite of the enormous number of people who followed us around everywhere no one was hurt. On returning from our walk we went on to an open terrace and remained there for half an hour. I cannot tell you, my dear mother, what transports of joy and affection were shown us in that time. Before retiring we waved to the people, which pleased them very much. How happy we are, in our position, to win the friendship of a people so easily. And yet there is nothing so precious. I was well aware of that and I shall never forget it."

The people of Paris wanted to make it clear that they put their hope in their future sovereigns. They did not confuse them with "the old gallant" and his Bourbonnaise. In order to lessen the slight to her grandfather Marie Antoinette said to him as they returned to Versailles: "Sire, Your Majesty must be greatly loved by the Parisians, for they have fêted us well!"

From now on the Dauphine had but one wish: to return to Paris. On 16 June she went with her husband to the Opera. Louis was applauded, in spite of "two rather awkward little bows" which he made on entering his box. Disconcerted, he stepped back to give way to Marie Antoinette, who was cheered. She was cheered again on 23 June at the Comédie Française, where they were performing *Le Legs* and *Le Siège de Calais,* and she gave permission for the public to applaud the actors in her presence, which was contrary to etiquette. On 30 June it was the turn of the audience in the Théâtre des Italiens to fête the young woman. Clairval played the part of Montauciel in *Le Déserteur* by Sedaine, and at one point in the text had to cry "Long live the King!" and throw his hat in the air. With great presence of mind—well-thought-out beforehand—he added: "And long live his dear children!"

"All this is addressed to Madame la Dauphine," Mercy wrote. "One could fill volumes with the moving remarks which were made, the comments on the appearance, charm and gracious, kindly air of the Archduchess."

The Ambassador was moved and was ready to shout with the Parisians. Marie Antoinette often managed to disarm him. He was touched when the little coquette said to him with an angelic air: "I shall make as few mistakes as I can. When I do make any I shall always admit it."

But Maria Theresa was not blinded. She replied that she knew how much her daughter liked to get her own way and how well she could "turn round and about in order to reach her goal. She is compliant only when it is a question of something which does not particularly affect her. She did not hide it from you when latterly she said to you, on two separate occasions, that 'when one has adopted a line of conduct it is very difficult and painful to change it.' Her behaviour towards the favourite, her excursions on horseback and what is even more dangerous, her rides in the cabriolet, furnish enough proofs of a character which is impetuous and too closely wedded to its own ideas. In spite of her good qualities and her intelligence I always fear the consequences of her frivolity and obstinacy."

Mercy tried to defend his pupil by guaranteeing that the Dauphine was "in good faith when she confessed her little faults of the past and the one or two opinions which H.R.H. finds it difficult to renounce. But in so doing she does but give proof of the candour and truth of her mind."

The Ambassador was all the more moved by this candour, which in his opinion compensated for many faults, since it had "softened" the Dauphin. From the end of 1773 the latter hardly ever left his wife.

One morning he gaily entered his wife's room and eagerly announced that he had just inherited 2,000 crowns through the death of someone to whom he paid a pension from his privy purse. Marie Antoinette calmly asked him: "But have you found out if the dead man has not left a widow, children or relatives in need?"

Louis was startled for a moment and then replied cheerfully: "As to that, I must admit that you are quite right to remind me." He at once went "to make inquiries and did not fail openly to give Mme la Dauphine the credit for his charitable intentions." His wife's charm and charitable disposition and her extraordinary popularity, which all reflected on him, had combined to transform Louis-Auguste. "H.R.H. shows in the best possible light," wrote Mercy, "and M. le Dauphin fills this position much better than his physical and moral constitution would have led one to hope."

The booby of Compiègne was no more than a memory. Marie Antoinette said so herself. "M. le Dauphin has been wonderful every time he has been to Paris and if I may say so he has won the good opinion of the people on account of the air of perfect understanding between us. This is perhaps what has given rise to the rumour that he has kissed me in public, although it is not true." And she concluded: "For a long time everyone has noticed his attentions to me." "There is, however, no sign of pregnancy," Mercy observed, "but one may hope every day for this longed-for event."

They might indeed "hope every day," but we must hear again what Dr. Ganière has to say.

"The phase of waiting could not last indefinitely. As he grew older, his fortifying diet and particularly the presence of this fresh, tender girl ended by awakening the Dauphin's sluggish senses, but on account of the pain caused at certain moments by his malformation he had to give up his attempts. The doctors had to admit that only surgery could put an end to the real torture, both physical and mental, resulting from these fruitless and exhausting experiences. But he had not the courage to submit to it. Nature had already allowed him to make some progress, since now he did not immediately fall asleep on reaching the marriage bed; surely it would allow him to make more, and to be able to avoid the scalpel he relied on a spontaneous cure."

This drama often brought tears to Marie Antoinette's eyes. Shy and touched, the Dauphin embraced her. "Do you really love me?"

"Yes, you cannot doubt it. I love you sincerely and I respect you even more."

"The young Prince seemed very moved by this remark," Mercy reported. "He tenderly caressed the Archduchess and told her that when they returned to Versailles he would continue with his régime and hoped that all would go well."

But on 18 December, when the court had returned to Versailles, Mercy again sighed: "By the most incredible misfortune our hopes in that direction, instead of increasing, seem to have become more remote."

As a consolation Marie Antoinette went in for amusement. As often as she could she went to Paris. Nothing was more delightful than the masked balls during carnival time in 1774. There were so many people to mystify. On Sunday 30 January she arrived shortly after midnight, wearing a domino and a black mask, and recognised in the crowd a young foreigner who had been presented to her on Friday 19 November and whom she had again seen in the following month at two of her Monday balls. In true carnival spirit she went up to him and spoke to him for a long time without his recognising her. He was tall, handsome, well made and pleasant, but not at all foppish. They laughed together until the Dauphine, who was beginning to be recognised by the crowd, was obliged to move away. She soon left the ball, enchanted by her evening.

He was the son of a field-marshal and a member of the Royal Council of Sweden. He was making the tour of Europe for his education; would be 20 years old in a few months and was called Axel Fersen. "A masked ball, a domino, a mask, two hearts," wrote the last biographer of Marie Antoinette and the handsome Swede. This is all very pretty, but the two hearts were not yet beating in unison. Whereas his meeting with the Dauphine takes 10 words in Fersen's private diary, two other carnival adventures occupy two pages.

At Versailles the balls, held on Mondays at Marie Antoinette's and on Wednesdays at Madame de Noailles', went on until six o'clock in the morning. To please the Dauphine more festivities and more balls were organised and everywhere the Dauphine laughed, danced, made fun, enjoyed herself and, in the words of the Goncourts, bounding and fluttering "passed by like a song."

"At the end of Louis XV's reign," writes Pierre de Nolhac, "the most serious fault with which Marie Antoinette could be reproached was excused by her age: an excessive love of pleasure. With her health and youthful eagerness she found there a natural compensation for the strict and tedious court duties to which she had to submit." This is true, but there was something else which the most recent adorer of the Queen did not dare to touch upon.

The marital drama was becoming more serious: the "indolent husband" went to visit his wife with increasing frequency. A staircase had been built just behind his room on the ground floor which came out on the first floor quite near the Dauphine's bedchamber, at the spot where later Marie Antoinette's *Méridienne* was to be established. Before climbing these stairs this semi-invalid would have been wise to wait until he had the courage to undergo an operation. But Louis-Auguste, as conscientious as he was awkwardly embarrassed, persisted in his unfortunate attempts. In the words of Dr. Ganière: "Night after night, in the silence of the nuptial chamber, this clumsy and well-meaning young husband inflicted moments of real nightmare on his companion without ever attaining the desired result, except no doubt for some defilements on her flesh which these two innocents might believe would result in a pregnancy that would put an end to all the court's gibes."

This young girl, thus awakened but not satisfied, had no other palliative than to amuse herself, throw off all constraint and seek after every possible pleasure except—and this is to her credit—that of deceiving her husband. Melancholy, frivolous whims, mad gaiety and bad temper followed each other, to the terror of Maria Theresa, who did not guess the cause of the trouble. In those days there was no science of neurology.

Yet for the moment this thirst for pleasure did not go beyond the bounds permitted to an eighteen-year-old Dauphine. Her popularity was as great as ever. The Parisians, indeed, were glad to see that their future Queen could laugh as well as a Bécu or a Poisson. To please her the public was ready to abuse the King and his Bourbonnaise and even to adopt her tastes. "Paris is completely charmed by the Archduchess in a way that cannot be described," wrote Mercy.

This was to enable Marie Antoinette to get Gluck accepted.

Marie Antoinette was happy to welcome Gluck when he arrived from Vienna at the end of the autumn of 1773. Her former clavichord teacher seemed to bring a breath of her youth with him into the little rooms behind her bedroom where she received him. She remembered the *Parnasso Confuso,* a poem by Metastasio which Gluck had set to music and to which she and her brothers and sisters had danced at Schoenbrunn for the marriage of Joseph II, when she was eleven. Leopold had played the clavichord. She had indeed been brought up on music. And since her arrival at Versailles, in spite of the donkeys and the cabriolet, she had not neglected the clavichord and particularly her "dear harp." She sang Mozart and Gluck in a voice which, although only just true, was pleasant. She was therefore very disappointed when she had to listen to French operas. Rameau was no longer alive and to arouse the apathetic audiences whole operas were composed of potpourris of popular works. And there were the never-ending overtures. Lulli had once and for all set the pattern: "A slow passage, called serious, which was generally played twice, and a quick return of the subject, called gay, which was usually in the form of a fugue."

When Gluck had sent the Paris Academy the first act of his *Iphigenia*, inspired by Racine's tragedy, the director had frankly declared "that such a work would only kill all the old French operas" and with the same frankness had done everything he could to prevent "M. le Chevalier Gluck" from coming to Paris. But Mercy, who was on extremely good terms with Rosalie Levasseur of the Opera, had connections with the theatre and *Iphigenia* was accepted.

On his arrival Gluck was to play his opera on Marie Antoinette's clavichord. He explained what he had tried to do: "Reduce music to its real function, that of aiding the poetry so as to reinforce the expressions of feeling and the interest of the situations without interrupting the action of holding it up by superfluous ornamentation."

This music "with no other adornment than its own beauty" delighted Marie Antoinette and the rehearsals began, not without difficulty, however, for the cast were somewhat out of their depth. They were used to "seeking the model for the singing voice in the voice of declamation" and were astonished by Gluck's profession of faith: "I have taken great care not to interrupt an actor in the heat of a dialogue in order to make him listen to a tedious *ritornello* nor to stop him in the middle of his speech at a favourable vowel."

Not to be interrupted or stopped upset the French singers. The rehearsals went all the more badly since everything on the stage was at sixes and sevens. Faced with this anarchy, Gluck went into terrible rages.

"I am here, ladies, to put on *Iphigenia*. If you want to sing, so much the better; if not, it is as you please! I shall go to Mme la Dauphine and say to her: 'I find it impossible to get my opera performed.' Then I shall get in my carriage and take the road to Vienna."

On leaving the Opera House he was sometimes so excited—singing every part in the opera to himself—that one day a crowd followed him in the Tuileries, taking him for a madman, and warned the Swiss Guards, who arrested the composer.

He went into similar rages in Vienna and the Emperor Francis soothed the orchestra, who wanted to leave everything and go, by saying kindly to them: "You know what he is like, my children! But at heart he is a good man."

Like her father, Marie Antoinette calmed the cast, through the agency of Mercy, and herself took charge of the composer. She wanted "her" musician to have a triumph. She wanted this all the more since Mme du Barry appears to have declared that she detested Gluck and preferred Piccini. Versailles promptly divided into two parties: the Gluckists, partisans of clarity and truth of expression, and the Piccinists, who extolled the charm and sweetness of melody. The opinion of Gluckists such as Jean-Jacques Rousseau or Grimm, or of Piccinists such as Marmontel or d'Alembert, no doubt had its value, but the majority of the Versailles weathercocks either defended Gluck through hatred of the favourite or attacked him to please her. M. de Breteuil, French Minister at Naples, was even ordered to "buy" Piccini and bring him to Paris. Incidentally, the two rivals became the best possible friends and took their meals together, while their partisans devoured each other, until the day when Piccini began to write like Gluck.

But that had not yet happened and all Paris was getting ready to go to the first performance of *Iphigenia* on 13 April 1774, when Legros, who was to sing the part of Achilles, fell ill. Gluck announced calmly that the tenor would not be replaced and that the first performance would be put off for a few days. Everyone was scandalised. The royal family had reserved their evening and this would show a grave lack of respect. But Gluck declared that he would rather tear up the score and take his carriage back to Vienna. Marie Antoinette supported him and the performance was postponed until 19 April— an unprecedented event.

The Dauphine went with her husband, the Comte and Comtesse de Provence, the Duchesse de Bourbon, the Duchesse de Chartres and the Princesse de Lamballe. The French audience were somewhat taken aback by the long recitatives and the absence of trills. Certain passages seemed flat and even mediocre but the majority of the spectators were "very much struck by the many new beauties, grand, strong and simple, which burst forth in passionate, moving and dramatic music."

"Since one can have such great pleasure for two hours," Rousseau exclaimed, "I feel that life has some advantages."

The Dauphine never ceased applauding. "The Princess seems to have joined a plot," remarked a contemporary chronicler, and the sulky spectators clapped too, "in order to please Madame la Dauphine."

On the following day the throng was enormous and there were no more criticisms. Guards had to be called out to restrain the crowds. The call for the composer went on for ten minutes. The Dauphine had triumphed. "In Paris no one thinks or dreams of anything but music," wrote Grimm. "It is the subject of all our disputes and all our conversations, and the preoccupation of our suppers, and it would even seem ridiculous if one were to be interested in anything else."

German music—"music, simply"—took its place thanks to Marie Antoinette. Her success and the clever way she had managed it proved to Mercy what a great part his "pupil" would later be able to play. "I see approaching the time when the great destiny of the Archduchess will be fulfilled. The King is growing old . . ."

It would surely be she who would govern. "M. le Dauphin will never have the strength or the will to reign by himself," Mercy declared. "If the Archduchess does not govern him he will be governed by others." Now the Archduchess cared nothing for affairs of state. "She is very much afraid of them . . . The result is that her character tends towards passivity and dependence." Mercy concluded: "It is most important that the Archduchess should learn better to know and appreciate her own strength."

The Empress replied with wisdom: "I confess frankly that I do not wish my daughter to have a decided influence in affairs. I have learned only too well from my own experience how crushing a burden is the government of a vast kingdom. Moreover, I know my daughter's youth and frivolity and her dislike of concentration—and she knows nothing!—all of which makes me fear for her success in governing a kingdom as dilapidated as France is at present."

Marie Antoinette may have felt that her mother was right. On the evening of 27 April 1774, eight days after the first performance of *Iphigenia*, her heart beat fast as she approached the bed of the sick King, who had been brought back from the Trianon wrapped in his dressing-gown. Had the moment come for those two children to take up the dishonoured crown? That evening the King's condition did not appear serious. He had a fever and a bad headache and asked his children to leave him alone: he only wanted Mme du Barry.

When the Dauphine saw the invalid again towards five o'clock on the following day he had become worse. He had already been bled twice. Around his bed were six doctors, five surgeons and three apothecaries. But the King thought there were too few. "He would have liked to have the number increased," a witness relates. "He had his pulse taken by all fourteen six times an hour and when this large faculty were not all in his bedroom he called the one who was missing so as to be constantly surrounded."

"Sire," said Le Monnier, the first doctor, "Your Majesty must show your tongue."

The King put it right out, left it there for more than five minutes and drew it in again only to say: "Your turn, Lassone!"

The second doctor stepped forward, looked, felt, bowed. The King put his tongue in. "Your turn, Bourdeau!" Again the King put out his tongue. The business was repeated. "Your turn, Lorry!"

The fourteen filed past one after the other "each showing in his own way his pleasure at seeing the beauty and colour of this precious royal organ." Next it was the turn of the stomach. "He made each doctor, each surgeon and each apothecary come past, calling each by turn and in their proper order." But to Marie Antoinette, the Dauphin and his daughters the King said nothing.

Around the bed were a crowd of useless people who were thinking only of the "third bleeding."

"A third bleeding," the King had exclaimed. "I am really ill, then!"

There was a tradition at court: "A third bleeding entails the reception of the last sacraments," and consequently, in the present case, it would decide the King to dismiss Mme du Barry.

"A third bleeding would reduce my strength," Louis XV had sighed. "I should very much prefer not to be bled a third time!"

The whole court were on tenterhooks. They cared nothing for the invalid; the only thing that mattered was the Comtesse's position.

The doctors were torn in two directions. If they ordered a third bleeding they would make a mortal enemy of Mme du Barry and M. d'Aiguillon, for no one doubted that the King would be on his feet again in a week. But if the favourite was dismissed would she return? "It is worth taking the chance!" declared the clique of Mesdames.

At 10 o'clock in the evening the Dauphine returned to the bedroom. The King had been placed on a small camp bed. He had sunk a good deal. In default of a third bleeding the Master Apothecary, M. Fargeau, and his assistant had given the King an enema. The fourteen doctors were still busy about him. The room was almost in darkness for the patient's eyes were hurt by the slightest light. Suddenly a servant of the bedchamber accidentally raised a torch. The King's face appeared in full light: his forehead and cheeks were covered with little red spots. The doctors looked at each other. The King had smallpox.

Marie Antoinette, who had been inoculated at Vienna, hastily led away the Dauphin, who had never had the terrible illness. But she was not to enter the King's room again.

However, she saw her "dear papa" again at dawn on 7 May. That night she had been awakened at five o'clock. The King wished to receive Communion. The dying man had just summoned the Abbé Maudoux and for the first time in 38 years was making his confession to the priest. This decision put an end to all the intrigues which had been disturbing Versailles for a week. When the doctors appeared hopeful the shadow of confession faded and everyone hurried up Mme du Barry's staircase. When the King's condition grew worse she was abandoned and M. de Beaumont, the Archbishop of Paris, went to see the dying man. But, having been lectured by Richelieu and Aumont, he did not dare mention confession.

"Archbishop," the Duc de Richelieu had said, "if you are so anxious to hear confessions come into a corner; I shall make my confession and I swear that it will interest you as much as the King's!"

But this time all was over. The night before the King had asked his mistress, who came down every evening, not to come again, and at four o'clock in the afternoon she had left for Rueil in a hired carriage, having wept for a long time in the arms of M. d'Aiguillon, whom she was to drag down in her fall.

On the eve of her reign Marie Antoinette was trembling. Had not

Mercy repeated that "to assure her own happiness" she should "take over the authority which in the Dauphin's hands would never be anything but precarious"? Was she capable of reigning?

It was six o'clock. In the *cour royale* the drums beat a ruffle. Mgr de la Roche-Aymon, Grand Almoner of France, left the chapel bearing the ciborium between a double row of bodyguards and Hundred Swiss. The Dauphin walked behind the canopy. He was very pale. For three days he had been repeating: "I feel as though the universe were falling on me!"

He stopped at the foot of the marble staircase, which owing to the infection he could not mount. On the top landing Marie Antoinette had come with the Princes to meet the Holy Sacrament. In her turn she walked through the state rooms following the canopy, which was borne by four gentlemen of the bedchamber. As they approached the King's room a dreadful odour became more pronounced. In the anteroom, whose door led into the apartments, the infection took one by the throat and was suffocating, in spite of the windows open on to the Marble Court. Here the Queen of tomorrow knelt down. Through the open door she could see the dying man holding the crucifix which Madame Louise had sent him from the Carmelites. His face, blackened, swollen enormously and covered with suppurating sores, was unrecognisable. The countenance of the Well-Beloved to which so many women had bent their lips was now only a carnival mask with bituminous reflections.

La Roche-Aymon had finished. He was about to leave, but the Abbé Maudoux plucked him by the rochet and whispered in his ear: the King wished to make a public confession. This was the price exacted by the Abbé for absolution. The Cardinal, who had promised Richelieu and d'Aiguillon that everything would go off without incident, was obliged to obey the confessor. He advanced towards the Cabinet Room, where the court was massed behind Marie Antoinette, and cried in a loud voice: "Gentlemen, the King has charged me to tell you that he asks pardon of God for having offended him and for the scandal he has caused his people."

There was a silence. Then from the thick, blackened and deformed lips in the Negro-like countenance ten words escaped: "I wish I had the strength to say it myself."

On 10 May, at a quarter past three in the afternoon, the flame of a lighted candle in one of the windows of the royal bedroom was extinguished. The appalling agony was ended.

Marie Antoinette was in her own apartments. The Dauphin was there, striding about the room. Suddenly, in the words of a witness, "a terrible noise, exactly like that of thunder, was heard": it was the crowd of courtiers running through the Hall of Mirrors to salute the new King. At this strange sound Marie Antoinette and Louis XVI started. They had understood, and the first comers to the room saw the young Queen of eighteen and the King of nineteen on their knees, weeping bitterly.

"Oh God," they repeated, embracing each other. "Oh God, protect us, we are too young to reign!"

5

❧

A Fashionable Little Queen

OWING TO THE infection the new King could communicate with his grandfather's Ministers only by letter. The all-important question was: "Will dispatches and commands be signed Louis or Louis-Auguste?" For the first time, in the margin of the same letter, Louis XVI wrote the five letters of the name he had chosen. He wrote them again, on the same day, at the foot of the documents concerning his grandfather's burial.

When a King of France died his body was opened and the heart taken out and sent to one of the churches of Paris. But on 11 May the Archbishop of Paris received word from Versailles that the putrefaction of the late King's body was so far advanced that there was no question of opening it and that consequently it was impossible to send him "in trust the entrails of that prince."

Louis XV was therefore the only King of France to be buried at Saint Denis with his heart. This special treatment, incidentally, resulted in the viscera of the Well-Beloved not being used, twenty years later, by Martin Drolling in painting his famous "Interior of a Kitchen." During the Revolution Drolling bought the royal hearts—which owing to the spices used had become mummified—to put into tubes and thence on to the canvas, to which they imparted "a wonderful shine."

No prayers were said at the deathbed. The monks, who could no longer stand the air of the bedroom, moved into the council room. Furthermore—as a last privilege—the body was transferred to Saint Denis in the middle of the night at full gallop in a "coloured coach,"

surrounded by forty bodyguards and thirty pages of the Great and
Little Stables carrying torches. Along the route the inns were full of
drinkers, crying out in a head voice: "Tally-ho! tally-ho!" in imitation
of the rather ridiculous tones used by the King to urge on his hounds
after the game.

Fun was made of the Abbé of the Church of St. Geneviève, who
had brought the famous relic in order to obtain the King's cure. His
patron saint must have very little credit in heaven! "Well, what are
you complaining about?" answered the Abbé, laughing. "He's dead,
isn't he?"

Only one person wept—Mme du Barry, who was "entrusted to
the police." She was made a prisoner of the State and taken the same
evening to the Abbey of Pont-aux-Dames.

In spite of the hard times the great mourning machine was set in
motion. Whereas the equipages of princes and those having "the
honours of the Louvre" were draped in black, the King and Queen
rode only in carriages covered with violet cloth. It cost 322,650 livres—
64 million francs—for this one item alone. For the same sum were
furnished the headstalls for the horses and the helm, coat of mail,
gauntlets and spurs to be thrown into the tomb with the coffin. But
the furniture and beds had to be covered with dark drapery, and all
the officers and livery servants dressed in black, which cost nearly
300,000 livres. The mourning required 1,365 new suits for the Great
Stable alone. No more gaudy liveries. Only large shoulder-knots of
blue, fringed with gold or silver, according to the wearer's position,
lightened the vast sepulchre that Versailles had become.

Although the décor was funereal, hearts were joyful. Everything was
hoped for from the new reign and *resurrexit* was written on the
pedestal of Henri IV's statue. Abundance would come again. The
women wore in their hair nothing but ears of corn, and the dandies
bought mourning snuff boxes adorned with portraits of the King and
Queen and lined with shagreen. This signified "consolation in the midst
of grief" (*chagrin*). Everyone wept. Eyes "wet with tears" were
fashionable and indicated not grief but tenderness—tenderness towards
the nineteen-year-old King who admittedly possessed no grace, no
gallantry, but who seemed so simple and natural and such a "good
fellow" in spite of his youth. Had he not commanded M. d'Estissac,
the Grand Master of the Wardrobe, who had come to take his orders

for the first time, to make him eight suits of frieze cloth? Had he not been seen at Choisy walking around the château like any bourgeois? And on returning from his walk had he not sat down on a park bench with his wife and sisters-in-law, who were eating strawberries and drinking milk? Was this not just like a picture by Greuze, "divine" and of an "indescribable grace"? And at this point in the story it was fashionable to shed "a torrent of tears."

There was tenderness, too, for the pretty eighteen-year-old Queen who so charmingly took her husband's arm when walking in the alleys at Choisy, the little Queen of whom Walpole wrote: "Hebes and Floras, Helens and Graces are streetwalkers to her." She had refused to touch the *"droit de ceinture,"* which went back to the distant times when queens carried their purse at the waist and was an additional tax raised after "joyful events" and levied in Paris on wine and coal.

At this refusal the tears flowed faster. "How I love the French at this moment!" exclaimed Maria Theresa. "What depths there are in a nation with such good feelings!"

Marie Antoinette was moved, and having recovered from her first anxiety she was intoxicated by the three words: Queen of France. "Although God caused me to be born into the rank I occupy today," she wrote to her mother, "I cannot refrain from admiring the disposition of Providence which has chosen me, the youngest of your children, for the finest kingdom in Europe."

But although Maria Theresa was full of emotion she faced the reality, and sighed: "My daughter's destiny can only be either completely great or very unhappy. . . . Her palmy days are over." On 18 May she wrote to the new sovereigns: "You are both very young and your burden is a heavy one. I am distressed, truly distressed by it." Although 400 leagues distant from the Ile de France, she seemed already to have guessed that now that her "Antonia" was her own mistress she would ride over Versailles and its customs like an escaped colt.

In fact she did not even wait to return to Versailles. After a short stay at Choisy the new court went to La Muette, a royal house originally intended for the erection of mews for the stags. Here Marie Antoinette received the "mourning respects." The women, in plain dresses of black *raz de Saint Maur*, coifs, black stockings and gloves, and carrying crêpe fans came to bow to the new Queen. The ceremony was endless and there was nothing cheerful in the dark scene. One of the young ladies of the palace, the Marquise de Clermont-Tonnerre, declared that she was tired and sat down on the floor, hiding behind the screen formed by the dresses of the Queen and her Ladies of Honour. This should have been enough to have her sent away from court, but Marie Antoinette said nothing. Indeed, when the Marquise began to play "all sorts of pranks" Marie Antoinette could not keep her countenance and "put her fan to her face to conceal an involuntary smile," Mme Campan reports. Other witnesses declare that "the Queen most improperly burst out laughing in the faces of the sexagenarian Duchesses and Princesses who had thought it their duty to appear at the ceremony."

This last description appears to be the more truthful since on the following day some ladies announced that they would never again set foot in the court of "this mocking little thing." Marie Antoinette shrugged her shoulders and called them "strait-laced" (*collets montés*). This nickname was her own invention. Similarly she described as "centenarians" ladies who were not necessarily very old. "When one has passed thirty," she remarked, "I cannot understand how one dares appear at court."

There were, too, the "bundles"—also so-called by Marie Antoinette, heavy, ill-dressed women at whom the Dauphine had formerly laughed behind her fan but at whom the Queen now laughed without any restraint. Belleval realised this: "She unfortunately makes fun of everybody without putting the least restraint on herself."

She was not able to restrain herself either during these "mourning respects" when the Duchesse d'Aiguillon made her bow. Not only did Marie Antoinette not speak to her, but "she looked down her nose contemptuously," a witness reports. On the next day the "Aiguillon clique" —formerly the coterie of Mme du Barry—was singing:

> Little Queen, have a care;
> If you behave with such an air
> You'll be sent back over there.

And she had only been reigning for a month!

The Abbé Baudeau, a contemporary, asserted that the first pamphlets against Marie Antoinette came from "the Chancellor's Jesuitical cabal." There is no serious proof in support of the serious accusation that d'Aiguillon was the organiser of this "shower of red bullets," to quote the Abbé's expression. But there is one disturbing hint. A dossier in the Archives of the Bastille proves that the Chevalier d'Abrieu, the Chancellor's private secretary and friend, had made an agreement with the pamphleteer Dubec for the elaboration of the well-known *Nouvelles à la main.* Shortly afterwards, on 28 July, Dubec was arrested for being one of the presumed authors of *Lever de l'Aurore,* an abominable pamphlet which described as an orgy an innocent vigil spent by Marie Antoinette at Marly to watch the sun rise. It is unfortunate, to say the least, that the name of M. d'Aiguillon's secretary should be coupled with that of the scribbler.

Marie Antoinette had not even noticed the discordant note in the symphony of praise surrounding her. She was intoxicated by the clouds of incense about her.

On the day after his predecessor's death Louis XVI asked his aunts' advice on how he should govern. They had no hesitation: the Dauphin their brother would have called on M. de Machault. The King consented. Then he asked them a further question: what should be decided about the funeral celebrations held a month after the death; who should be approached? Madame Adelaide's reply was: "No one is more fitted, by his recollections and traditions, to take care of these details than M. de Maurepas."

The same courier took the two summonses. In spite of his 73 years M. de Maurepas made haste and arrived first at Versailles. He had been forbidden to come to court ever since the reign of the Pompadour, when, so it was said, he had sung at supper a song stigmatising "the low-born whore who turned the court into a hovel."

Clever and insinuating, he paid his respects to the King and when the usher came to tell Louis XVI that the Council was assembled the old courtier bowed as though the news concerned him also. The King was confused and left his companion without daring to take his leave. M. de Maurepas followed and sat down at the Council table.

"Does Your Majesty wish to nominate me Prime Minister?" he asked.

The King gathered up his courage. "No, that is not my intention."

"I quite understand," Maurepas replied, smiling. "Your Majesty wishes me to teach him how to proceed without one."

M. de Machault was forced to return home and Maurepas, who in fact was virtually the Prime Minister, governed together with his nephew d'Aiguillon, who, to everyone's astonishment, retained his portfolios and his title of Chancellor.

> Maurepas was impotent;
> The King restored his power anew.
> The grateful Minister then went
> To see the King and told him: "Sire,
> The only thing that I desire,
> Would be to do the same for you."

The rhymester did not realise how accurate he was. The new Minister feared that the "separation" between husband and wife would give Maria Theresa more influence over her daughter. But Maurepas had no need to worry. Marie Antoinette could stand on her own feet. "I was very struck by her behaviour in the d'Aiguillon affair," the Empress was able to say.

In less than a month, indeed, the Queen was able to obtain her chief wish: the dismissal of the "creature's" friend. She importuned her husband every day. The Queen of France could not forget the injuries done to the Dauphine, and Maurepas, who was secretly delighted at being able to keep the power to himself, advised his nephew to give up the unequal struggle. At the beginning of June the Chancellor sent the King his double designation. "Being unable to restrain her animosity," wrote Mercy, "the Queen brought about by herself the dismissal of the Duc d'Aiguillon, who but for her would have retained his position."

But Louis XVI, who had taken one step forward, now took two back and granted the ex-Chancellor a gift of 500,000 livres, or 100 million francs, which caused Marie Antoinette to sigh, as she was not concerned: "I am afraid the King is too kind and easy-going."

The "horrid man's" disgrace should automatically have entailed the return of M. de Choiseul to be Minister of Foreign Affairs, for during the first few months of the new reign this enemy of Mme du Barry was still cooling his heels at Chanteloup with Mme de Choiseul. And he cared "neither for his wife nor for the country." But Louis XVI did not wish for his return; he did not want to play the part of Louis XII either. Choiseul had unfortunately once said to him: "I may one day have the misfortune, Monseigneur, to be your subject, but I shall never be your servant."

The young King had not forgotten this. Choiseul would not be his servant; he would not return to Versailles for two months. Marie Antoinette then played her last card. According to Mercy she "demanded this concession from the King, and without delay." And Louis yielded, but when he saw Choiseul again on 15 June he confined himself to saying: "You have lost a lot of hair since I last saw you, M. le Duc."

What would Vienna say on seeing the "champion of the Alliance" so badly received? However, the Empress seemed satisfied by this partial success. She did not wish Choiseul to return to power. "In the present state of affairs a Minister of Choiseul's character would not suit us," she informed Mercy. This being her mother's opinion, Marie Antoinette asked for nothing more. She was content with the dismissal of M. d'Aiguillon.

Something much more important weighed on her and forced her to constant restraint: etiquette. In extenuation of the Queen's desire to throw off this perpetual yoke one should remember how tyrannical were these outworn customs, some of which dated from the time of Francis I. When she woke Marie Antoinette could not take her breakfast in peace: those with the right of the *petites entrées* were present. Perhaps it was all very well for the First Physician, the First Surgeon, a physician in ordinary and the Reader, the Abbé de Vermond, but why should the King's four first valets de chambre, their reversioners, and his First Physicians and Surgeons also come to see the young woman drink her morning chocolate? Admittedly she had a short respite afterwards in order to take her bath—a tub which was wheeled into her room. Only women were present. But towards mid-day the Queen, who had gone to bed again, had to rise. She sat at her toilet table in the middle of a circle of folding stools reserved for women of high office while the men with a right to the *grandes entrées* remained standing and watched Marie Antoinette do her hair and put on her rouge. Gentlemen were constantly entering the room and bowing. Marie Antoinette interrupted her toilette to incline her head and smile. In the case of Princes and Princesses of the Blood etiquette required her to put her hands on the arms of her chair as though she were about to rise, but to remain seated.

Then the men retired, jostling each other, for the most polite went out first so as to give others the happiness of contemplating their sovereign for as long as possible. She began to dress. One would do well to re-read the celebrated passage by Mme Campan: "The dressing of the Queen was a masterpiece of etiquette; everything went by rule. The Lady of Honour and the Mistress of the Robes, both taking part if they were there together, aided by the first waiting woman and two ordinary waiting women, performed the main functions, but there were distinctions between them. The Mistress of the Robes handed the petticoat and presented the dress. The Lady of Honour poured water for washing the hands and handed the chemise. When a Princess of the Royal family was present the Lady of Honour yielded her this latter office, but did not yield it directly to Princesses of the Blood. In their case the Lady of Honour handed the chemise to the first waiting woman, who presented it to the Princess of the Blood. Each of these ladies observed these customs scrupulously, as they were privileges. One winter day the Queen, who was quite undressed, was about to put on her chemise. I was holding it unfolded; the Lady of Honour entered, hastily took off her gloves and took the chemise. There was a knock at the door, which was opened; it was the Duchesse de Chartres. She took off her gloves and came forward to take the chemise, but the Lady of Honour could not present it to her. She gave it back to me and I gave it to the Princess. Another knock: it was the Comtesse de Provence; the Duchesse de Chartres handed her the chemise. The Queen held her arms across her chest and seemed to be cold. Madame noticed her discomfort and merely throwing aside her handkerchief kept on her gloves and in putting on the chemise disarranged the hair of the Queen, who began to laugh to conceal her impatience, but not without having muttered several times: 'How odious! what importunity!' "

When the King had spent the night with the Queen a mixed service began its ballet. Towards eight o'clock the menservants, to whom the Queen's women had opened the door, extinguished the torch which had been burning all night in a silver basin, drew open the bed curtains on the side on which Louis XVI was, and presented him with his slippers and dressing gown. The King left his wife to continue her night's sleep. He retired to his apartments followed by a manservant bearing the short sword which on the previous evening had been placed on a chair "within reach of His Majesty's hand."

Therefore when the ceremony of the royal *lever* began at half-past eleven, Louis XVI had already been up and dressed for over three hours. He had paid a visit to his little forge, asked his chief locksmith Gamin all sorts of questions, shot at the cats on the terraces of the château or, seated in an armchair on the roof, had watched through a telescope the people arriving at the château to be present at his *lever*. And he now had to take off his suit of plain cloth and put on his night clothes. During the long ceremony Louis XVI did not sigh like Marie Antoinette. He played games and dodged, and they had to run after him to put on his shirt or breeches. In summer he liked to edge his visitors on to the balcony, which was covered by canvas continuously watered by hoses. Laroche, the guardian of the Menagerie and the dirtiest of his pensioners, was often the butt of the royal jokes. The King guffawed when his pages succeeded in snatching off Laroche's wig. If the Duc de Villequier was present Laroche was left in peace, for he was distantly related to the First Gentleman of the Bedchamber. Louis XVI then made up for it by tickling an elderly valet de chambre, who was so sensitive that he fled in fear, pursued by the King's loud laugh.

Often, too, he would lift at arm's length a page sitting on a fire shovel. His strength was famous; he was the only man in the court who did not fall down when he used an arquebus belonging to one of the Swiss Guards which kicked like a little cannon.

But the strong man side of him did not make him forget what was due to etiquette. He knew well that if the Queen came to see him in the morning it was the Grand Chamberlain or the First Gentleman of the Bedchamber who must "take the dressing gown at the first door," whereas, no one knew why, the first valet de chambre had the privilege of carrying it as far as the bed railing.

At the least step Marie Antoinette was accompanied by an armed battalion.

"For whom is the detachment of warriors I found in the courtyard intended?" the Abbé de Vermond asked her ironically one day. "Is some general going out to inspect his army?"

Her Reader extolled the simplicity of the court of the House of Lorraine. When one of Marie Antoinette's ancestors had to levy a tax he went alone to the church, stood up after the sermon and, waving his hat in the air, stated the sum he needed. Marie Antoinette, who could not take two steps by herself, loved to tell this story. The smallest of her actions set in motion a cohort of officers, employees and servants, of whom she now had more than five hundred.

One might well think that Marie Antoinette could console herself by thinking that thanks to this antique pageant she was the best served woman in France. But the Queen was not surrounded by professionals and the holders of the great posts were only clumsy amateurs, fixtures imbued with a strong sense of their prerogatives. If Marie Antoinette saw dust on the counterpane and, with the help of several intermediaries, summoned the servants of the bedchamber, the latter replied that the dust did not fall within their jurisdiction, "the Queen's bed being considered furniture when Her Majesty was not lying in it." It was therefore the first upholsterer of the bedchamber who should be approached. When the Lady of Honour and the first waitingwoman were absent Marie Antoinette could not drink if she was thirsty, as these ladies alone had the right to present their mistress with a glass of water—a glass of tepid water, incidentally, on account of the number of hands through which it had passed.

When Marie Antoinette opened the windows of her little apartments a terrible stench rose from the courtyard of the *Œil-de-Bœuf*, for the château was a veritable sink. "The passages, the courtyards, the wings and the corridors," reports a contemporary witness, "were full of urine and faecal matter. The park, the gardens and the château made one retch with their bad smell." Viollet-le-Duc tells how in 1830 he visited the château with an old Marquise who had lived at the court of Marie Antoinette. She seemed bewildered and could not find her way in the unfurnished rooms. Suddenly the two visitors found themselves at a place where "a waste plug, which had burst owing to the frost, had covered the floor with filth." The smell drove them back. The old Marquise cried out with joy: "Ah! I know where I am now! That was Versailles in my day. . . . It was like that everywhere!"

To these smells was joined a harsh odour of the soot with which the walls were impregnated; it lasted until August, for the chimneys drew very badly. An inventor did indeed try to create a "capnebalic" and "capnephaltic" apparatus which, according to him, would absorb all the smoke. A trial was made at the Château de Saint-Hubert, but the machine—a turret with valves—creaked so much that no one could sleep a wink and it was considered preferable to keep the smoke which had filled Versailles since the days of the Great King and which was borne with as an old acquaintance.

It was impossible to alter the château. Marie Antoinette had to be content with modernising the most out-dated customs. "The most ancient custom," Mme Campan tells us, "required that in the eyes of the public the Queens of France should appear surrounded only by women; the absence of servants of the other sex obtained even at meal times for the service of the table. Although the King ate publicly with the Queen he too was served by women with all the objects directly presented to him at table. The Lady of Honour, kneeling with a napkin on her arm, and four women in full dress presented the dishes to the King and the Queen. The Lady of Honour poured their drink. This service was formerly performed by girls of honour. On her accession the Queen abolished this custom. She also freed herself from the necessity of being followed everywhere in the Palace of Versailles by two of her women in court dress at those times when her ladies were not with her. From then on she was followed only by a single valet de chambre and two foot servants. All Marie Antoinette's faults were of the kind I have just mentioned. Her wish gradually to substitute the simplicity of the Viennese customs for those of Versailles did her more harm than she could possibly have imagined."

It was no good submitting problems of etiquette to her or reminding her of what Maria Leczinska used or used not to do, unless one wanted to draw on oneself such replies as: "Madame, manage these matters as you wish, but do not imagine that a Queen, born an Archduchess of Austria, can give so much interest and enthusiasm to them as a Polish Princess who became Queen of France."

"Her Majesty dislikes constraint," wrote a chronicler of the time, "and will not submit herself to an etiquette she had already thrown off when she was Dauphine."

Her first care, indeed, was to simplify the famous *lever*. Once her hair was dressed she left her ladies in their full court dress—their annoyance can be imagined—and followed only by her women returned to her private rooms, where, with no spectators, she could quietly get dressed and undertake the serious business of looking over her wardrobe. In any case she could not possibly do all this in the bedchamber, for the "artists" who took care of her—Mlle Bertin and the three Léonards—had no right of *entrée*.

Custom forbade any "underling" with a post at court to exercise his "art" outside. But Marie Antoinette feared lest the imaginations of Rose Bertin and the "Physiogonomist," as Léonard was called, should become provincialised among the "centenarians" of Versailles. The Queen therefore insisted that her favourite artists should continue to look after the dresses and the hair of the ladies of Paris. The devotees of etiquette shuddered.

It was scarcely two months after the death of Louis XV that the Duchesse de Chartres had presented Rose Bertin to the young Queen, and as soon as the blue and black of the "little mourning" ended in November Mlle Bertin threw herself into what she called "her work with Her Majesty." Several times a week, at the peep of day, the pretty Rose would arrive at Versailles followed by a graceful troupe of blushing girls bearing enormous boxes from which the dressmaker brought out dresses called "Indiscreet pleasures," "Stifled sighs" or "Masked desire." With each visit the boxes became larger, for panniers were soon to be two or three yards in circumference.

One morning the Queen hesitated in what shade to order the dress which Rose called "Honest compromise." Perhaps in this brown taffeta? At this point the King entered. "That's the colour of fleas!" he declared contemptuously. And so puce became fashionable. Distinctions were soon drawn between *ventre de puce* and *cuisse de puce*. But a few days later Marie Antoinette chose an ash-blonde silk. "It is the colour of the Queen's hair," said the Comte de Provence, who was more gallant than his brother.

That too became the rage. A fashionable woman was obliged to wear this "divine" colour. Couriers were sent to the Gobelins and to Lyons with a lock of Marie Antoinette's hair, so that the weavers could reproduce the colour exactly.

From the boxes there also came shoes whose heels were adorned with a row of emeralds—the *venez-y voir*. But Mlle Bertin's triumph was her *poufs aux sentiments,* coiffures designed in collaboration with the "Physiognomist." The day after Louis XV's death elegant women wore a cypress and a horn of plenty in their hair—mourning for the King and hope for the new reign, or a rising sun symbolising Louis XVI (they did not know him very well) and an olive tree, emblem of peace and plenty. "More simply" one saw fields of corn being harvested by Hope. One morning the Queen bore lightly on her head a whole English garden, with its lawns, hills and silver streams.

The Duchesse de Lauzun, who was not afraid of headaches, arrived one day at Mme du Deffand's house with a built-up *pouf* representing a whole countryside in relief. One could see a hunter aiming at the ducks flapping at the edge of a lake ruffled by the wind. On the heights was a mill with the miller's wife being courted by a sprightly curate, while the miller, who knew how to behave, went off with his donkey in the direction of the Duchesse's ear.

Mlle Bertin was once nearly dethroned by a certain Beaulard, who invented mechanical coiffures. One pressed a spring and a rose flowered. There was also a real piece of machinery, called "The good miller's wife," which with the aid of a winch hidden in the chignon could be lowered or raised when an old lady with retrograde ideas entered or left the room. Mlle Bertin went pale with jealousy. But Marie Antoinette remained faithful to Rose, who in collaboration with Léonard invented for the Queen coiffures *au Lever de la Reine, à la puce*—naturally! *à l'Iphigénie, à l'Eurydice*—to please Gluck, *à la Modestie* and *à la Frivolité*. But above all Marie Antoinette liked feathers. The coiffure *à la Minerve* had as many as ten, which were so tall that one day she found it impossible to enter her coach to go to a ball given by the Duchesse de Chartres. At the beginning of February 1775 Maria Theresa sharply criticised her daughter's "plumage" and when the Queen sent her a portrait of herself with her head covered in feathers the Empress sent it back, feigning to imagine that there had been a mistake in the destination of the present. "I did not see the portrait of a Queen of France but that of an actress."

Mercy, while admitting that "the feather head-dresses were somewhat exaggerated," pointed out that "in this matter the Queen is merely following a fashion that has become general." But the Empress would have none of it. "A young and pretty Queen, full of charm, has no need of all this nonsense."

Marie Theresa was not aware of the other disadvantages of Marie Antoinette's craze for Mlle Bertin. Mme Campan, an impartial witness, tells us: "The Queen was naturally imitated by all the other women. Everyone immediately wanted to have the same head-dresses as the Queen, to wear the plumes and garlands which were made infinitely charming by her beauty, which was then at its height. The young ladies' expenses were enormously increased; mothers and husbands grumbled; a few scatterbrains contracted debts; there were unpleasant family scenes and coldness or quarrels in several homes. And it was widely said that the Queen would ruin all the French ladies."

Rivarol observed justly: "Always more of a woman than a Queen, she forgot that she was born to live and die on a real throne." For Marie Antoinette, in the words of another witness, "the title she most desired was that of the most fashionable pretty woman."

To be fashionable one had to please—please oneself and please others. To be fashionable was to be constantly surrounded by a court of adorers. The Queen could not imitate the elegant woman of the day, the Parisienne of 1775, who in the mornings, dressed in her "night mantle" held together by a pink *désespoir*, smiled at the folly of her friends, while a sprightly abbé fanned himself in his armchair and hummed a popular tune. But just like a "belle" she could always be surrounded by crowds of young or not quite so young people.

At this time her favourite companion was her brother-in-law. In the eyes of the Comte d'Artois, who according to Mercy was interested in nothing but frivolity and whose behaviour was very much that of a libertine, "there was only one King of France: the Queen." When he met his brother he crowded him, "almost treading on his toes," never called him "Your Majesty" and considered that he lowered himself by paying his daily court. As for his sister-in-law, paying court to her consisted in amusing her. He asked her to distribute the prizes to the winners of the tilting at the ring, took her driving in a *diable*— an open two-wheeled carriage—or with his cousin, the Duc de Chartres, organised horse races. This was a novelty. Until then racing was carried on only at Newmarket. Now, on 9 March 1775, the two Princes invited the Queen to preside over the first races, at the gates of Paris on the outskirts of the Bois de Boulogne. In spite of the rain and the wind which tugged at her skirts, Marie Antoinette remained stoically on the uncovered platform to which she had mounted by a shaky ladder. The horse of one of her friends, the Duc de Lauzun, won the race, but died of its victory.

A large crowd was present at this "meagre spectacle" but, significantly, Marie Antoinette was very much less applauded than usual. She hardly noticed, thinking only of her next outing. During this first winter of her reign she was chiefly preoccupied by her balls, and the papers of Papillon de La Ferté, Keeper of the Privy Purse, reflect the Queen's frequent requests "which never cease to entail rather heavy expenses, in view of the large number of plumes and fine gilding ordered by H.M." Marie Antoinette paid no attention to Papillon's sighs; her main desire was to amuse herself with her friends. The carnival of 1775 "gave the young people too easy an access to the Queen," Mercy complained, but Easter did not restore calm. The Queen was constantly surrounded by a whole troupe of thoughtless, gilded youth. For all these "feather brains," to use a contemporary expression, who had very little in their powdered heads, Marie Antoinette was truly "their Queen." For them the faults which distressed Maria Theresa and Mercy—"hostile impulses," "remarks on her superior rank," "grudges," "feelings of revenge"—did not exist. She was just a pretty, fashionable woman who laughed delightfully and wanted to please her dear friends. With them she was exquisitely charming and kind. "It is always the same when she is given the opportunity of amusing herself," Mercy noticed bitterly. And her set was adept at doing this.

There was the Comte d'Adhémar, whose real name was Montfalcon. His dubious nobility was forgiven, for he was "very fashionable" and could sing while accompanying himself on the harp. Vaudreuil had presented him. Some people thought that the latter had a "charming" face; others found him "frankly ugly." The former were probably women and the latter men, for the Princesse d'Hénin said: "I know only two men who know how to speak to women: Lekain and M. de Vaudreuil."

"The Comte de Vaudreuil, who governs the Queen," said Tilly, "does not always know how to govern himself." This man, so exquisitely polite, went into dreadful rages. He was not a man but a weathercock: he changed his opinions as he changed his wig.

There was Esterhazy, a Hungarian who had just arrived at court. This officer was possessed of "brutal good looks" and was surrounded by legend: his line could be traced to Attila and his family owned 60 townships and 414 villages. But this did not satisfy him. He wanted to have his debts paid and asked for a regiment. The Queen hastened to satisfy him on both points and even occupied herself with garrisoning his hussars. "Is it enough for him to be one of my friends," she said to the Minister of War, "for you to persecute him? Why have you sent Esterhazy's regiment to Montmédy, which is a bad garrison? See that it is sent somewhere else! Let M. d'Esterhazy be satisfied! You will report to me on the matter."

The Hungarian obtained Rocroy—a much-sought-after garrison—where he occupied his leisure moments in receiving and writing a great many letters to the Queen.

Another foreigner was a member of the coterie: the Prince de Ligne, "an Austrian in France and a Frenchman in Austria," who adored Versailles. "The love of pleasure first brought me here; gratitude brings me back." At the slightest pretext he covered the distance between Beloeil and Versailles in 24 hours. He was the most disinterested of Marie Antoinette's friends and his love for the Queen was respectful and noble. For him "her soul was as beautiful and white as her face."

Another friend was the Duc de Coigny. In 1774, he was 38 years old. At the moment he was "simple and temperate," but he was soon to change. The friend with the most influence was Besenval, pronounced *Baiseval*. Polish on his mother's side—she was the Comtesse Bielinska —the Baron de Besenval was Swiss on his father's side and for this reason bore the rank in France of lieutenant-colonel of the Swiss Guards. His 53 years enabled this "old Celadon" to proclaim himself the young Queen's counsellor and to pay respectful court to her. He amused her. According to him, Marie Antoinette "with no fund of personal gaiety" was interested only in "the gossip of the day, little carefully veiled familiarities" and "in particular the kind of scandal heard at court." Besenval was king in that line, having, it is said, an excellent style of bad manners and "being able to risk impertinences which suited him perfectly." One has only to see his portraits, of which his descendant, the present Prince Amédée de Broglie, has a whole series, to realise that one is in the presence of a witty man. When he was away Marie Antoinette was bored—that perpetual disease of the great.

The most dangerous of them all was undoubtedly Lauzun, towards whom the Queen was much too friendly. It was a pity that she did not listen to Mercy when he declared that this irresponsible man was "very dangerous on account of his restless mind and his collection of all kinds of bad qualities." But for two years Marie Antoinette refused to take notice of the evidence. Like Besenval, Lauzun amused her. He too knew how to talk the "nonsense" which was popular in Marie Antoinette's circle.

"Tell me, Monsieur," she said one day to an old marshal who could talk of nothing but his two war horses, "which of your two horses do you prefer?"

"Madame," replied the Marshal with "comic gravity," "if on a day of battle I were mounted on my piebald I should not dismount to mount my bay; and if I were mounted on my bay, I should not dismount to mount my piebald."

A moment later the conversation turned on two pretty women at court.

"Monsieur," said the Queen, turning to one of her "associates"—Lauzun or Vaudreuil—"which do you prefer?"

"Madame," he replied, as gravely as the Marshal, "if on a day of battle I were mounted on—"

"That will do!" the Queen exclaimed, laughing.

Such was the prevailing tone.

Sometimes a spoilsport would come to spend the evening with the Princesse de Guéménée, with whom the coterie gathered: it was the King. Luckily he liked to go to bed early and retired at eleven. Then the conversation became much freer. So one evening, in order to hasten his departure, someone risked putting the clock forward, and the King disappeared, leaving the field clear. All Versailles got to know about it. The "centenarians" and "strait-laced" ladies were very severe on this joke, but the Queen shrugged her pretty shoulders. The important thing was to be among friends and chatter.

What did they talk about? According to Mme Campan, who cannot be accused of severity, these pretty scatterbrains in furbelows thought of nothing but trivialities. "To be childish" was the mode and it showed itself in a profound ignorance. Marshals of France or infantry lieutenants, cardinals or curates just leaving the seminary—all were ignorant! The Prince de Ligne confirmed this. And in this sphere Marie Antoinette was the most fashionable. She never opened a book, unless it were a licentious work, which caused Joseph II once to reproach her with "the trashy reading she filled her mind with."

It was all the more difficult for the Queen to fix "her attention on interesting objects," as Maria Theresa said, since her conversation was "inconsequent and sprightly, flitting from one thing to another." We learn this from Besenval, who knew what he was talking about. Now the Swiss colonel and the Queen's "associates" were ambitious. The rôle of clown must be made to pay off. In April 1775 the coterie urged the Queen to demand a marshalship for the Duc de Fitz-James. Marie Antoinette, who liked the Duchesse, undertook this and the King agreed. The Minister for War was horrified. "No one knows anything of M. de Fitz-James' actions in war!"

Louis XVI tried to go back on his promise, but the Queen had already informed the new Marshal, who was waiting in the ante-chamber to present his thanks. Nothing could be done. All Paris laughed at the nomination. So in order to mitigate this incredible promotion the King nominated seven other Marshals, who were hardly better qualified than M. de Fitz-James, and Paris sang:

> Rejoice, ye happy French, break forth and sing!
> The Marshals who have been made by the King
> Will bless us with eternal peace, for sure,
> Since not a single one is made for war!

But the Queen had had her way and Besenval now considered that they could go further. He had formed a scheme: to persuade Marie Antoinette that her pride would no longer tolerate the presence of M. d'Aiguillon a few leagues from Versailles. He must be exiled, not to his château of Veretz in Touraine, but to Aiguillon itself, on the Garonne. After all, was not the former Chancellor the instigator of the libels and pamphlets which were poured out on Marie Antoinette daily? Besenval and Mercy were convinced of it. The Ambassador declared: "As a result of extensive research and observations I daily receive more indications that it is the Duc d'Aiguillon who is the principal actor in all the little intrigues formed against the Queen."

The Ambassador reported his discoveries to Marie Antoinette. The Queen seemed indifferent to the steps taken by her mother's councillor; nevertheless she asked the King to exile d'Aiguillon to his lands in the country. "Somewhat embarrassed," the King first consented and then, after consulting Maurepas, withdrew under some vague pretext. The Queen made no comment and, said Mercy, "the matter stayed there."

Now it was Besenval's turn. The Swiss had one gift which the diplomat would never possess: he could get what he wanted out of Marie Antoinette by pulling a long face, and so he sulked. For the sake of peace and to make her entertainer resume his rôle the Queen yielded to his importunities, as she was later to yield to Mme de Polignac, who used the same technique.

M. de Besenval belonged to the "Choiseul party." "The Queen's concern in the matter would have sufficed to make me attack M. d'Aiguil-

lon," the Baron confessed unashamedly in his memoirs, "but I was led
to it by other considerations. He was responsible for the fall of M. de
Choiseul. It suited my personal feelings to punish him. I could not
flatter myself that there was any hope of M. de Choiseul's return as long
as M. d'Aiguillon was in a position to wield any power." Soon, thanks
to M. de Besenval, the Queen "felt how important it was to be rid of
M. d'Aiguillon." "There was not much reason for exiling him," wrote
Besenval. "I advised the Queen to stress his audacity in attacking the
Comte de Guines."

Guines, a "fashionable man" of whom Marie Antoinette was really
fond, was French Ambassador in England, but he stayed at Versailles as
often as he could. The little time he spent in London did not prevent
his enjoying the pleasures of smuggling by means of the diplomatic
bag. Unmasked, Guines had protested loudly and thrown all the blame
on his secretary, Tort de la Sonde. The two men were confronted in a
trial. The Ambassador's guilt quickly became obvious and in order to
defend himself Guines declared that it was all sheer calumny and
accused M. d'Aiguillon of trying to ruin him.

When the Minister fell Guines attacked him with redoubled violence.
Maurepas supported his nephew and Marie Antoinette the Ambassador.
It was a cut-and-thrust fight, said Besenval, who was delighted by the
turn things had taken. "One cannot hold out against a queen," sighed
Maurepas, and left the field clear for Marie Antoinette. She persuaded
the King to intervene and Guines was acquitted. He remained Ambassador. However, the Duc d'Aiguillon had to be punished for daring to
attack Marie Antoinette's friend. "I have spoken to the King," she
announced to Besenval, who was managing the intrigue alone. "He is at
last beginning to suspect that M. d'Aiguillon is flouting him, and I think
that he will settle matters."

Whatever the Queen might say, Louis XVI, like Mercy, had the idea
that Besenval had "with treacherous cunning made the Queen discover
in the protection she accorded the Comte de Guines a means of vengeance against the Duc d'Aiguillon." The King therefore tried again to
temporise. Marie Antoinette was furious, and when the Duc d'Aiguillon
came to receive her orders for the annual review of the King's Household, in which he was to ride at the head of his company, she exclaimed
harshly: "My orders? Why do you not go and seek those of Mme du
Barry?"

On 30 May, at Marly, when the light horse commanded by the Duc d'Aiguillon rode past, Marie Antoinette drew down sharply the blinds of her carriage. The ex-Minister asserted even that she put out her tongue at him. That evening she insisted that the King exile "the creature's" friend.

"My hair stands on end every time I see that man!"

Louis XVI sighed and allowed his wife to settle the matter. The Queen promptly summoned Maurepas. "What new offences has my nephew committed?" he asked. Naturally, there was nothing new. "No matter!" retorted the Queen. "The measure is full to the brim; the vase must overflow."

"But Madame, it seems to be that if the King must harm someone it should not be through you."

"You may be right, and I shall not do it again, but I wish to do it this time."

The "Prime Minister" could only give way. "My nephew is too obedient a subject to do anything which might displease the Queen. He will leave in a few days."

Marie Antoinette confessed: "This departure is entirely my doing. The measure was full to overflowing. This wretched man was carrying on all kinds of espionage and evil designs. He tried to defy me more than once in the affair of M. de Guines. I asked the King to exile him. It is true that I did not want a *lettre de cachet*, but nothing was lost by this, for instead of remaining in Touraine, as he wished, he was asked to continue as far as Aiguillon, which is in Gascony."

Now that the ex-Minister had been relegated to a half-ruined château in the heart of the Agenois, Marie Antoinette would have liked to continue with no more worries in what Maria Theresa called "her dissipations." But Louis XVI's coronation at Rheims had been fixed for Sunday, 11 June 1775, and it would interrupt the fashionable little Queen's happy existence.

She yawned as she listened to the Abbé de Vermond reminding her, on Mercy's behalf, that formerly "it was a fairly frequent custom that when kings were consecrated at Rheims their queens were consecrated at the same time." According to the Ambassador and his messenger, Marie Antoinette would have to take part in the great ceremony being prepared. But once again the Abbé returned empty-handed to the Petit Luxembourg, where Mercy lived. "He found the Queen completely indifferent in this connection." Maria Theresa's two confidants were hardly surprised. They well knew that these presentation days brought no amusement to their royal pupil. She much preferred to be queen of her coterie than Queen of France. The public were already beginning to be aware of this. And yet, once again—perhaps for the last time—her charm and the impulses of her heart would provoke enthusiasm and recall the first hours of her reign.

6

※

"The Feather-head"

IN RHEIMS CATHEDRAL, decorated in "the antique style" and brilliant with lights, the King was stretched before the altar on a fleur-de-lis covered carpet. At his side, in the same posture, was the Archbishop of Rheims. This was the only moment of the very wearing day when the two principal actors could draw breath, particularly needed by the Archbishop, who was 78 years old and already exhausted by the first two hours of the ceremony.

The anointings began. There were nine of them, accompanied by prayers which the Archbishop chanted in a trembling voice. Those who were following the ceremony could hear a sentence which was almost a thousand years old: "May he not abandon his rights over the kingdoms of the Saxons, the Mercians, the people of the north and the Cimbrians." The Cimbrians were the English.

Before the final anointing the King was clothed with the tunic, dalmatic and mantle covered with fleurs-de-lis. The Keeper of the Seals, M. de Miromesnil, raised his voice: "Monsieur, you who represent the Duc de Bourgogne, present yourself at this act!"

The Comte de Provence stepped forward. Miromesnil turned towards the future Charles X, who in 50 years' time was to come there on his own account.

"Monseigneur, you who represent the Duc de Normandie, present yourself at this act!"

Then one by one, wearing the great ducal mantles of violet cloth edged and lined with ermine, their coronets on their heads, the collar of the Order of the Holy Ghost round their necks, the Ducs d'Orléans,

Chartres, Condé and Bourbon represented the other lay peers—Aquitaine, Toulouse, Flanders, and Champagne, and surrounded the King together with the six ecclesiastical peers. The Archbishop intoned further prayers, one of which has a curiously Oriental flavour: "May the King possess the strength of the rhinoceros, and may he drive the enemy nations before him, like a raging wind, to the uttermost ends of the earth."

The King had need of such strength to support the heavy crown of Charlemagne, studded with rubies and emeralds, which the Archbishop placed on his forehead with the help of the twelve peers, who laid their hands on it symbolically—a remnant of the elevation on the shield of the Frankish kings.

A hinge in the crown was unobtrusively opened and it was fastened on the forehead of the King, who bent under its weight. Those around him heard him sigh: "It hurts me!"

But Marie Antoinette did not hear. When from her seat she saw her husband holding the sceptre bearing the lily of enamelled gold and the hand of justice made from the horn of a unicorn, when she saw him looking just like the crowned kings adorning the manual from which the Abbé de Vermond used to teach her French history tears of emotion rolled down her fair cheeks.

The Constable, M. de Clermont-Tonnerre, who was 84, had difficulty in holding "Joyeuse," Charlemagne's heavy sword, in his wrinkled hands. He preceded the King, who walked slowly towards the rood-loft. This was the Enthronement.

The Archbishop and the peers kissed the King and cried three times: *"Vivat rex in aeternum!"* The doors of the cathedral were opened. The crowd filled the nave, crying: "Long live the King! Noel! Noel!" The fowlers freed hundreds of birds which, dazzled by the light, fluttered among the crystal chandeliers. Outside, salvos of musketry were fired and all the bells in the town answered the great bell of the cathedral.

"Noel! Noel!"

The applause, the clapping and the shouts increased. The Queen could not bear it and burst into tears. When she was seen to take her place again a few moments later the whole church, Mercy reported, in spite of the sacred character of the building "rang with shouts, claps and demonstrations difficult to convey." During the long ceremony which was only just beginning, the King, who was deeply moved, frequently turned his eyes towards the Queen "with a look of adoration impossible to describe." As though in a dream Marie Antoinette saw Louis receive a loaf of gold and one of silver, give the kiss of peace to the twelve peers and communicate in both kinds.

Husband and wife were both so moved that perhaps they did not notice that the sword of Charlemagne fell from Clermont-Tonnerre's trembling hands and that the Comte d'Artois, whose "careless attitude" shocked everyone, had thrown down his coronet, exclaiming: "Oh, to the devil with it!"

A little later, still as a spectator, the Queen was present at the interminable royal banquet. To the sound of hautboys, flutes and trumpets a whole crowd watched hundreds of dishes borne along, to be eaten under their eyes by about thirty privileged persons.

In the evening, the King, who had put off his stifling robes and heavy accessories, took the Queen's arm and without guards, like honest bourgeois, they went to walk among the crowd in the garden of the Archbishop's palace. Their reception was almost hysterical. People pointed out the envoy from Tripoli, "that barbarian," who was also weeping with emotion.

With admirable stoicism Louis then underwent the exhausting ceremony of the Order of Saint Sulpice—about a hundred bows to be received and returned. On the following day, riding his horse *Vainqueur* with silver trappings which had cost 27,543 livres, followed by all the nobility on horseback and preceded by trumpets, Louis XVI went to the Abbey of Saint-Rémy. Behind him were led two other horses, *Fier* and *Monarque*, in case the King should take a wish to change his mount. After Mass, surrounded by doctors and surgeons, he touched 2,400 persons afflicted with scrofula. "May God heal you, the King touches you," the Prince de Beauvau repeated 2,400 times, while the King "rested his hand on the head of each sick person."

In the evening Louis XVI went for a walk, on the arm of the Queen, in the Bois d'Amour outside the town. The applause was unceasing. The crowd pressed in from all sides. There was even a boy of fifteen there, who was not very good-looking. He had come from Troyes and his name was Danton.

On 16 June the Queen drove towards Compiègne, with the cries of admiration and affection still ringing in her ears. She repeated that if she lived until a hundred she would never forget the day of the coronation. Why were Mercy and the Abbé constantly scolding her? Was she not loved, adulated? Was she not acclaimed in spite of her "dissipations" and "mistakes"? As the Ambassador wrote to her mother on 23 June, she did not realise that all this was merely "a momentary success which should not dazzle" since "there is not sufficient foundation for it."

The diplomat may have been farsighted, but the Queen was not. "I did my best to respond to the eagerness of the people," she wrote to her mother. "It is at once amazing and gratifying to be so well received, in spite of the dearness of bread. . . . It is a remarkable trait in the French character to be carried away by evil suggestions and then to return at once to the right road. What is certain is, that seeing the people who in the midst of their unhappiness treat us so well, we have an even stronger obligation to work for their happiness. The King seemed to me to be struck by this truth."

The King was struck by it and would do what he could, but would she? Bread was not merely dear; there was a shortage. Did she know that as the carriages went along the road to Rheims the labourers making up the road "knelt down, raising their hands to heaven and brought them back to their mouths to ask for bread"? In the same year, 1775, at the time of the "flour wars," the rioters talked of going to "shake up" the Queen—and this was only one year after her accession, and fourteen years before the Revolution. That was indeed a warning. But once the Queen was back in Versailles she resumed her life of pleasure. For her "the happiness of the people" had nothing to do with her amusements. Maria Theresa, speaking of the inevitable consequences of this "endless dissipation," exclaimed: "I cannot put it too strongly to you so as to save you from the abyss towards which you are rushing."

Mercy was about to discover the reason, and the excuse, for this "thirst for pleasure" which had such "a mysterious power" over the Queen and wrought "such havoc" in her character. One day, when the Ambassador was repeating his reproaches, Marie Antoinette became "sad and thoughtful" and with a heavy sigh "went into a few details of the distress caused to her by her situation" as a "married" woman. "I must have some distraction and I can find it only in increased amusements."

Louis XVI was now undoubtedly in love with his wife "in every sense of the word," but the "fatal object" was still in the same condition. At the end of 1774 he discussed this subject with his doctor, Lassonne, who earnestly recommended an "incision." As Marie Antoinette told her mother on 17 December, the King was very favourably disposed, but a little later, when the surgeon showed the King all his tools, which were real instruments of torture, "His Majesty wished to put it off once again," as a chronicler relates. This did not stop him from visiting his wife. In the spring of 1775 a small, secret corridor was built between the bedrooms of the King and the Queen, passing under the Hall of Mirrors and emerging behind Marie Antoinette's bedroom. "The King's passage," of which only fragments remain today, enabled Louis to avoid the *Œil-de-Bœuf*, which was like a public square, and thus continue his too conscientious and vain attempts.

"The old Roman proverb, *Tota mulier in utero*, throws a striking light on this conjugal drama," writes Dr. Ganière. "If it is true, and daily instances prove it to doctors, that the uncertain female equilibrium is often based on the satisfaction of the senses, how can one be surprised if the young Queen, undoubtedly endowed with the impetuous temperament which has characterised so many members of the Hapsburg family, appeared to the eyes of her intimates and through them to her whole people as frivolous and capricious? Nearly every night she had to submit to her husband's demands, which, although they might not yet have any real result, aroused without appeasing her senses. 'There is certainly no indifference on my side,' she wrote to the Empress, 'but my dear mother must understand that mine is a difficult situation.' She did not fully understand the unfortunate effects of these unavailing onslaughts, but had ended by instinctively shunning them after having for months lamented her husband's indifference. She stayed up as long as possible in the hope of finding her husband asleep, when formerly that peaceful sleep had seemed an insult to her youth. By day she tried to lose herself in a whirl of sometimes questionable pleasures. She sought, certainly in no unhealthy spirit, friendships which would appease her ardent need of affection."

The reign of the favourites was about to begin.

It was the fashion of the times. In 1775 it was the accepted custom to have a woman friend—a completely respectable relationship, one must emphasise—of whom one said with a sigh: "She has such an attraction for me! There is such conformity in our way of life!"

Such a friend was "inseparable" until "a caprice or a trifling dispute brought about a rupture." This was called "friendship's flirting." It was so much in vogue that the Sèvres factory had to make groups "of a passionate sensibility" representing "The tender friends" or "Confidences between two young persons."

The first "young person" to whom the Queen "confided" was the Princess de Lamballe.

Marie-Thérèse of Savoy, Princesse de Lamballe, was not pretty "but seemed so at a little distance." The young woman had suffered so much and was so "naïve" that Marie Antoinette had a kind of protective feeling for her. She was emotional to the point of fainting when she saw a lobster in a painting. Were these faintings, which were then very fashionable, sincere? The Empress considered these swoonings to be "affectations" and for his part Mercy had every reservation about "the appearance of this Principal Lady in Waiting." During 1775, in which Madame de Lamballe rose to the height of her favour, Marie Antoinette had the Princess from Savoy appointed Principal Lady in Waiting in her Household.

"Picture my happiness," the Queen wrote on 13 July. "I shall make my dearest friend happy and I shall benefit even more than she will."

The nomination was not brought about without trouble. It had been necessary to plead with Louis XVI. On Marie Antoinette's assuring him that it "would be the greatest pleasure of her life," he yielded—as he always did. Faced with the extra expense entailed by the creation of this post, the Controller General protested loudly. But in spite of her father-in-law's huge fortune the Princess protested even more loudly, and she was able to enter on her duties "with the wages, pensions, lodging allowance, liveries and other rights" formerly granted to Maria Leczinska's Principal Lady in Waiting, Mlle de Clermont, who had had no personal fortune. Moreover, Mme de Lamballe received an extra 50,000 livres "to provide her with the means to maintain herself in this important post"—so important, indeed, that the two first Ladies of Honour resigned, considering their prerogatives attacked.

Marie Antoinette consoled herself by spending hours alone with the Princess and, as a chronicler tells us ingenuously, "appreciates her even more and enjoys herself immensely."

This friendship and these long *tête-à-têtes* did not suit M. de Besenval, who wanted the Queen to "create Ministers on whom she could rely." The Chevalier de Vergennes had been nominated "without the

Queen's being informed and without her paying the slightest attention." She took no interest either in the nomination of the upright, honest Turgot. Besenval thought this situation should change. Seeing her entertainer become gloomy, Marie Antoinette set about the dismissal of La Vrillière, Minister of the King's Household, whom Besenval did not like, and she succeeded without too much difficulty.

This victory was followed by a defeat. To succeed La Vrillière Marie Antoinette and her friends put forward Sartines, who was Minister of the Marine, although he had never seen a ship in his life, and intended to put in his place M. d'Ennery, another friend of the coterie. But the question was, how to bring about this general post, for Maurepas, whom the Aiguillon affair had placed firmly among the Queen's enemies, had other plans.

"What is to be done?" Marie Antoinette asked Besenval.

"Use the occasion to be on good terms with M. de Maurepas, so as to obtain the Ministry you want. You must therefore send for him and tell him you will make no recriminations about the past and have decided to forget it and in future to have a good understanding with him, and that you imagine he will be sufficiently aware of the advantages for public affairs, for the King, himself and you resulting from such an understanding, to strive to deserve your friendship and trust; that you ask nothing better than to grant him both, but that you must have proof of his good intentions so as to destroy even your slightest distrust; and that this proof would be the placing of M. d'Ennery in the Ministry of the Marine."

Marie Antoinette strongly approved but, complained Besenval, "I had no sooner left her room than everything was forgotten. A hunt succeeding a walk, a spectacle, caused it to be four days before the Queen held the conversation she had promised."

The conversation was a failure. Maurepas was sorry, but it was too late. M. de Malesherbes had been chosen for M. de la Vrillière's post. Consequently, M. de Sartines would remain at the Ministry of the Marine and there would be no portfolio free for M. d'Ennery. But unexpectedly Malesherbes refused. Maurepas insisted, but Malesherbes stood firm, in spite of two urgent notes sent to him in one night. The third letter was a real cry of alarm: "If the Queen prevails on this occasion, all is lost!" wrote Maurepas and Malesherbes finally accepted. "The Queen," wrote Besenval, "received what in the language of intrigue is called a rebuff." Marie Antoinette took it very badly. The King bore the blow courageously, but for all that advised Maurepas, who wanted to make his apologies, not to go and see the Queen. "Don't go, it is not very fine there today."

Besenval had made an error in tactics. It was not towards Maurepas he should have directed his scheming but towards the King "in love with his wife in the fullest sense of the word." When she applied to her husband Marie Antoinette was rarely refused. Indeed, at Rheims the Queen had obtained the King's permission to meet M. de Choiseul, although Louis XVI had an increasing aversion for him. It was true that on that occasion the Queen had been really artful. By recounting this to her childhood friend, the Comte de Rosemberg, Marie Antoinette caused a sensation. "You can be sure," she wrote, "that I did not see M. de Choiseul without mentioning it to the King, but you could never guess the skill I exercised so as not to appear to be asking permission. I told him that I wished to see M. de Choiseul and that I was only in difficulty about the day. I managed so well that *the poor man* fixed the most convenient time for me to see him. I think I made good use of a wife's privileges at that time."

"The poor man!"

Also to the Comte de Rosemberg she wrote: "My tastes are not the same as those of the King, who cares only for hunting and machinery. You must admit that I would be somewhat out of place in a forge!"

"The poor man!"

Here again Marie Antoinette was very fashionable. It was extremely bad taste to love one's husband. An affectionate husband who begged his wife to call him *tu* was thought ridiculous, but everyone was charmed by her reply: *"Eh bien! va-t'en."*

Unconcern and indifference were the two rules of the day. Men gave as good as they got to their wives. Métra tells us of this dialogue between two of the Queen's friends, the Duc de Coigny and the Marquis de Conflans.

"You know, I am very embarrassed."

"Why is that?"

"I have never once had supper at your wife's."

"Well, neither have I. Let us go together and back each other up."

Marie Antoinette had adopted the prevailing tone and in Paris they sang:

> The Queen imprudently let out
> To Besenval, her friend, one day:
> "My husband is a sorry lout."
> The other answered, winking,
> " 'Tis what all think, but do not say,
> You say it without thinking."

These three words, "the poor man," horrified the Empress when Rosemberg showed her the letter. Marie Theresa, who was unaware of what constituted a fashionable Frenchwoman, was shocked and wrote to Mercy: "My daughter is simply hurrying to her destruction. . . . What a style, what a way to think! This does but confirm my forebodings: she is hastening to her ruin and will be fortunate if, when she is lost, she retains the virtues owing to her rank!"

Rosemberg also showed the letter to the Emperor. Joseph II did not spare his sister: "You meddle in a great many matters which first of all do not concern you, which you know nothing about and in regard to which the cabals and associates who flatter you and know how to arouse your *amour propre* or desire to shine, or even foster a certain hatred or rancour, cause you to take one step after another calculated to spoil the happiness of your life and certain to bring *extreme unpleasantness* upon you sooner or later, and, by diminishing the King's friendship and esteem, to lose you the good opinion of the public and all the consideration which, with the aid of that opinion, you might acquire, and have acquired, astonishingly enough, until now. Why do you think it your business, my dear sister, to transfer Ministers, to send one to his estates, to have a particular office given to this man or that, to help another to win his lawsuit, to create a new and expensive post at your court, and finally, to talk about public affairs and even to use expressions by no means suited to your position? Have you ever asked yourself by what right you interfere in the affairs of the government and the French kingdom? What studies have you ever made? What knowledge have you acquired that you dare to imagine that your advice or opinion can be of any use, particularly in affairs which require wide knowledge? You are a pleasant young woman who all day thinks of nothing but frivolity, your appearance and your amusements. You never spend more than a quarter of an hour a month in reading or hearing anything intelligent. I am sure you never ponder or think out anything or reflect on the consequences of what you do or say. You act only from the impulse of

the moment, and the words and arguments of the people you are protecting and in whom you trust are your only guides. Could anything
more rash, unreasonable and improper be written than what you observed
to the Comte de Rosemberg concerning the way in which you arranged
a conversation at Rheims with the Duc de Choiseul? If such a letter
ever went astray, if, as I have no doubt, you let slip similar words and
observations to your intimate friends, I can only *foretell great unhappiness for you,* and I confess that on account of my attachment for you
this distresses me very much."

Maria Theresa begged Joseph II to soften his letter. However, the
expurgated text which Marie Antoinette received sent her into a passion.
She made a scene to Mercy. After "an agitation lasting half-an-hour,"
the Queen, astonished by the Austrian Ambassador's silence, stopped.
"In all conscience, what do you think of it?"

With great frankness Mercy replied that "his respectful observations"
having so far been without result, he no longer knew what to say. "I
therefore give myself up in silence to painful ideas which depress me
by showing an unhappy future for the Queen . . . It must be admitted
in good faith that everything is going badly, that Your Majesty does not
trouble to examine any question, acting solely from the prompting and
the passions of her associates. By engaging only in futile or dangerous
dissipations Your Majesty risks losing all the trust, respect and love of
the public."

Marie Antoinette looked at her mother's friend with astonishment.
For the first time she seemed uneasy. The Comte de Mercy believed
that she had understood the cry of alarm uttered by the Empress and
Joseph II.

As usual the court went to Fontainebleau in the autumn. It was an
incredible removal. Actors, singers, dancers and wigmakers all took
the road to Fontainebleau. All these had to be lodged, as well as "people
who have neither post nor service, but who constantly come to pay
their court and who have to be lodged." The château had only 172
apartments, and only the four walls were provided. When the château
was full lodgings were taken in the town and the guests found their
names written in chalk on the doors as at a halting-place. Only Princes
had the right to yellow chalk.

In 1775 it rained at Fontainebleau nearly every day and Marie

Antoinette, who had caught cold, hardly ever went out. She was present at several spectacles, which were not very good, but which, for all that, cost no less than 100 million francs. For reasons of economy the dresses of some of the actors had been made from the coronation robes and in spite of his short sight the King noticed it.

This more peaceful life allowed Mercy and the Abbé to continue with their exhortations. Their task was the harder and more delicate in that Marie Antoinette was at that time a victim to one of those "changes of affection" from which, according to Mercy, "there result only trouble and inconvenience." If one can believe what Lauzun says in his Memoirs, or if, to be more exact, one can believe Lauzun's Memoirs, which were possibly embellished by their first publisher, it was at Fontainebleau in 1775 that the favour of the future Biron rose to its highest peak—to such a peak indeed that people made transparent allusions in the presence of the favourite. According to himself Lauzun one day hastened to Marie Antoinette.

"I feel I must inform Your Majesty that some people are so bold as to blame her for the kindness with which she honours me. I take the liberty of begging her to demonstrate it less frequently and to allow me not to present myself before her so often."

Marie Antoinette refused. "I must beg Your Majesty," Lauzun insisted, "I must even demand, as the only reward of my complete devotion, that you do not compromise yourself by supporting me."

"What! You would wish me to be so cowardly! No, M. de Lauzun, our cause is inseparable; they will not ruin you without ruining me."

"I threw myself at her feet. She held out her hand, which I kissed ardently several times without altering my position. She leant towards me with great tenderness; she was in my arms when I rose. I was tempted to grasp the happiness which seemed to be offered to me."

Was this scene entirely invented? Did the Gascon's habitual complacency cause him to interpret as a yielding what was perhaps only a feeling of affection? One fact is certain: a few days later the Queen admired a white heron's plume adorning her favourite's military headdress. Lauzun gave it to her and she wore it one evening.

According to Mme Campan "his conceit exaggerated the worth of the favour which had been granted him. Shortly after the gift of the heron's plume he asked for an audience. The Queen accorded it, as she would have done for any other courtier of his high rank. I was in the next room to the one in which he was received. A few moments after his arrival the Queen reopened the door and said in a loud, angry voice: 'Begone, Monsieur.' M. de Lauzun bowed deeply and disappeared. The Queen was very upset. She said to me: 'That man will never enter my doors again.' "

The "handsome Lauzun" makes no mention of this incident. But it is possible that the stories of the courtier and the waiting-woman are both true. Having misunderstood the Queen's affectionate gesture a few days earlier, Lauzun might on this occasion have tried "to grasp the happiness which seemed to be offered." Later on, when he had certainly lost favour, he followed Marie Antoinette all one day, disguised as a foot servant, in order to attract her attention. The Queen did not even notice him. "He seemed to have given his services for nothing," wrote Mme d'Oberkirch, "when, just as the Queen was to return in her carriage from a walk in the Trianon, he had the idea of kneeling on one knee so that she might place her foot on the other, instead of using the velvet step. Astonished, Her Majesty looked at him for the first time, but, like the witty and sensible woman she was, she pretended not to recognise him and called to a page: 'Please see that this servant is dismissed. He is very clumsy and does not even know how to open a carriage door.' "

"It is said," adds Mme d'Oberkirch, "that M. de Lauzun was deeply wounded by this rebuke and that afterwards he hardly ever presented himself to Her Majesty."

For this conceited fool the Queen's behaviour and her perpetual "changes of affection" may have been somewhat of an excuse. Marie Antoinette was already reaping what she had sown.

The Princesse de Lamballe had only just been nominated to her new post when, at Fontainebleau, Mme de Polignac came into favour. Mercy told his sovereign that "the Queen has an even stronger affection for her than for any who have gone before."

Mme de Polignac's reign was to last, with a few breaks, for fourteen years. For some people her face bore the marks of "her shameful villainy"; for others "no face ever expressed more charm and sweetness. . . . One of those countenances to which Raphael knew how to impart an expression of intelligence and infinite kindness."

"Her character," said Besenval, "was even more perfect than her face." She possessed "a calm which no situation, circumstance or object could shake." One might conclude that she had not a very open disposition. Mercy certainly asserted it.

In 1775 Mme de Polignac was 26 years old. She was married to a colonel, the Comte Jules, who had very little money. According to the best traditions the Comtesse's lover was her husband's best friend, the Comte de Vaudreuil, a tyrannical lover, who made very violent scenes. The family was completed by her sister-in-law Diane, née Polastron, who was ugly and hunchbacked, but a real live-wire and far and away the most intelligent, and the most full of intrigue, of the four.

It was at a concert at which "Comtesse Jules" was singing that Marie Antoinette had been touched by the young woman's charm and by her sweet, tender voice. Then she was attracted by her candour, her "careless grace" and the sensibility which constantly melted into tears. Soon she was to explain: "When I am alone with her I am no longer a queen, I am myself!"

According to Diane de Polignac the Comtesse first responded to the Queen's advances without enthusiasm, but cleverly: she had no fortune and informed her sovereign that it would be best if she retired from court. Marie Antoinette, much affected, strongly opposed this. Was she not there to help her friend? At Fontainebleau, feeling that the "Lamballe clan," especially the Chevalier de Luxembourg, was preparing to give her a hard time, the Comtesse burst prettily into tears and declared to Marie Antoinette: "We do not yet love each other so much that we will be unhappy if we are separated. I can feel it coming, and I shall soon be unable to leave the Queen. Let us anticipate this and let Your Majesty permit me to leave Fontainebleau."

This scene, which was reported by the Prince de Ligne, ended in a general outburst of emotion. The Queen mingled her tears with those of her pretty friend and then took her away to the park.

But a Queen of France had no more the right to laugh at the follies of a Lauzun than to put her arm round the waist of a Lamballe or a Polignac. The pamphlets and songs increased. It was "an epidemic," the Queen exclaimed, adding lightly: "I was not spared. Both tastes were freely attributed to me: for women and for lovers."

The people were easily "carried away by evil insinuations," particularly as these came from Versailles. As a pamphleteer said at the time: "A despicable courtier hatches them in the dark; another courtier puts them into verse or couplets and with the help of the flunkeys distributes them to the Halles and the herb markets."

Marie Antoinette's exaggerated and demonstrative affection for Mme de Polignac set all Paris talking and at court unleashed a positive drama. The astonished Mercy related that "the two favourites, mutually very jealous, are constantly complaining about each other and quarrelling." Fontainebleau was a battlefield for these ladies, who had each her partisans, enemies, jealousies and intrigues. The Queen suffered from these perpetual disputes. She would have liked her two friends to get on together and love each other, and she would then have been quite happy. "I should enjoy the pleasures of private life which do not exist for us if we have not the intelligence to secure them."

The evening was "the most critical moment of the day," the Austrian Ambassador assures us. After supper Marie Antoinette went to see the Princesse de Guéménée, where she found Mme de Polignac, Coigny, Vaudreuil, Besenval and a number of young people who were the terror of poor Mercy. Mme de Guéménée, Governess of the Children of France, now governed only Madame Elisabeth (Madame Clotilde had just married the heir to the Prince of Piedmont) and her office gave her a great deal of leisure. She busied herself with her many dogs, with whom she claimed "to be in communication, thanks to mediating spirits." Sometimes the Princess stopped dead in the middle of a conversation and fell into a trance: a "mediating spirit" was informing her of the wishes of her pack. When the Governess was receiving her spirits and her dogs the Queen preferred to visit Mme de Lamballe, to whom came the Duc de Chartres and "everyone connected with the Palais Royal," that is, with the younger branch of the family. "Guéménists" and "Lamballists" insulted, slandered and dragged each other elegantly in the mud. They agreed only on two points: backbiting and begging. "Every day," continued Mercy, "there come from both these sources so many insinuations and requests that it would be impossible to explain even part of them to Your Majesty without entering into endless details."

During the greater part of the stay at Fontainebleau Besenval and his friends were seething with excitement about the nomination of a new Minister for War. Besenval's candidate was the Comte du Châtelet, son of "the divine Emilie." Mme de Polignac and Vaudreuil preferred the Marquis de Castries. But prompted by Maurepas and Malesherbes, the King chose a Minister unconnected with any court intrigue. He was sent for from Alsace, where he was cultivating his pear trees. It was

M. de Saint-Germain who was appointed "to the applause of the whole army." The clan was greatly disappointed. M. de Saint-Germain—"a Jean-Jacques Rousseau in boots and a helmet"—cut down the parade establishment. Henceforth the gendarmes and the light horse would number only 88.

"I suppose they are to escort the King to the *lits de justice?*" the Queen asked ironically.

"No, Madame, they are to accompany him when the *Te Deum* is to be sung."

A more serious grievance was that he was not a courtier. One evening Marie Antoinette was bombarding her husband across the table with bread pellets.

"What would you do, brave soldier, if you were fired on like this?" Louis XVI asked the new Minister.

"Sire, I should spike the gun!"

There was a chilly silence.

Another drama, that of expenses, was unfolding. The end of 1775 saw the purchase of a pair of diamond earrings for 100 million francs of present-day money, to buy which Marie Antoinette got into debt. A little later she bought for 250,000 livres bracelets which "loaded her with debts." When Maria Theresa wrote that this "filled her with anguish for the future," she replied lightheartedly: "I would not have believed that anyone would have tried to occupy my dear mother's kind attention with such trifles." The trifles were bracelets worth 50,000,000 francs.

Marie Antoinette had soon forgotten her brother's lecture and during the winter her "taste for dissipation" revived strongly. On 11 February she went to a ball at the Opera, stayed there until five o'clock in the morning, came back to Versailles at half-past six and left again at ten to attend the races in the Bois de Boulogne. Conforming to the prevailing fashion of anglomania, the Queen had developed a passion for horse-racing. The Comte d'Artois and the Duc de Chartres organised a race every Tuesday in the Bois de Boulogne. On that day the Queen should have received the Ambassadors. The diplomats waited in vain, and one may imagine their acid remarks on leaving Versailles after their fruitless journey.

It was terribly cold in January 1776. Wrapped up in furs, the Queen went by sledge along the boulevards. Louis XVI put on an old overcoat and walked in the country, where he paid poor people to break the ice or pardoned wood-stealers arrested by the guards in the forest of Ville-d'Avray. One morning, on his return, he met the Queen, who was coming back from a ball at the Opera.

"Did the public applaud you? How did you find them?"

"Cold."

"Apparently, Madame, you were not wearing enough plumes."

"I should like to see you there, with your Turgot. I think you would be well and truly hissed."

Like "the lords and the grocers" Marie Antoinette did not care for Turgot. It was not because the Controller-General could not "come to terms with human weaknesses," nor because he treated Parliament, industry, finance and the nobility roughly, nor because, like Sully, he was kind only to the farmers, nor because he behaved more like a brutal vivisectionist than a careful surgeon. It was because M. Turgot had dared to recall M. le Comte de Guines from his Embassy in London.

This recall was to cost Turgot his portfolio. The Controller's sudden departure, willed and planned by Marie Antoinette, put an end to the famous economic reforms, which might perhaps have saved the monarchy and avoided the clash in 1789.

The pretty "feather-head," as Joseph II called her, might protest to her mother that she had had nothing to do with her enemy's dismissal (for she sometimes told a lie), but in fact her responsibility was equalled only by the King's weakness. Marie Antoinette made her husband rewrite three times a letter according de Guines, in exchange for the loss of his Embassy, "permission to bear the title of Duc." "The Queen's scheme," wrote Mercy, "was to demand that the King should dismiss Turgot, and even send him to the Bastille, on the same day that the Comte de Guines was declared a Duc." Not without difficulty the Austrian Ambassador managed to avert "the results of the Queen's anger" against a man "who enjoyed a great reputation for honesty and was loved by the people." But Turgot had to leave without even having been able to complete and submit to the King his plan for reorganising the finances.

Further, Vergennes, whose policy was successful, nearly lost his Ministry of Foreign Affairs, also "on account of the Comte de Guines." Mercy realised how astonished Maria Theresa would be and he explained: "The key to this enigma can be found in the Queen's associates, who are banded together in favour of the Comte de Guines. Her Majesty is *obsessed* and wants to be clear of it all. They manage to arouse her *amour-propre*, to irritate her, to blacken those who, for the sake of the general good, might resist her wishes. All this goes on during the races or other pleasure parties and in evening conversations with the Princesse de Guéménée. In fact, they are so successful in putting the Queen beside herself and in intoxicating her with dissipation that, given also the King's extreme compliance, there are times when it is quite impossible for reason to break through."

The Abbé de Vermond, entrusted by Mercy with the task of helping reason to break through, was so discouraged that he wanted to leave court. The Ambassador made him stay, but he too was in despair. During the summer of 1776 Mercy admitted that there existed "no active authority capable of opposing the Queen's wishes."

The Ambassador considered as particularly harmful the Queen's recent decision to appoint Madame de Polignac's husband "reversioner" of the Comte de Tessé, her First Equerry. "H.M. imagines that she has paid tribute to friendship, but the public sees in it only blind infatuation for the Comtesse de Polignac, who at the moment is completely in the ascendant." Again, he complained: "The late Queen had only 150 horses. When M. de Polignac has bought those he has to have as reversioner, the Queen's stable will have 300 horses and the expenses will be 200,000 livres more than in the time of the late Queen."

The poor man thought that was all, but he did not know everything. He knew nothing of the positive looting the Comte de Polignac was to engage in and which is revealed by a file in the National Archives whose contents have been overlooked until now.

It must first of all be noted that as the reversioner—that is, successor —to the Queen's First Equerry the Comte de Polignac had the right to horses and carriages which, according to a document, "are destined solely for the personal use of M. le Comte Jules and not for his service with the Queen, since every time he has the honour to follow H.M., whether in town, on an excursion or at the hunt, he is in a carriage of the Queen's suite and not in his own."

A staff had to be formed. The Comte was given fourteen "liveried servants"—footmen, coachmen, ostlers and postillions. He not only doubled this number but decided, using the King's money, to give his grooms a salary of 1,143 livres instead of the usual 756. His footmen's wages were raised from 503 livres to 759 and those of his chairmen from 596 livres to 893.

M. de Polignac thought that his servants, animals and carriages would be rather cramped in the King's stables. He therefore hired a house at Versailles, one at Compiègne and another at Fontainebleau. And "M. le Comte Jules, so as to have no difficulty in getting what he wants, has taken all the workmen from the Queen's stables," sighs an anonymous controller.

This was not all, however. The Queen granted the new reversioner two teams of seven horses and four saddle-horses—in all eighteen horses, which the Comte soon increased to 25. In the Little, as in the Great, Stable it was customary to spend 1 livre 12 sols per day per animal for the horses' upkeep and food. Comte Jules demanded 9 livres 6 sols a day for each horse. This useless post of reversioner consequently cost the State, in present-day francs, 13 millions in 1777, 15 in 1778, 19 in 1779 and nearly 23 in 1780. This was not surprising, since the reversioner's horses ate nine times more oats than those of the First Equerry.

An amusing and unpublished text, emanating from some discouraged controller, can be seen among these fabulous accounts. "If M. le Comte de Tessé refuses to pay, M. le Comte Jules will complain to the Queen, who will get the increases from the King, and M. le Comte de Tessé will simply appear to be acting with a bad grace."

A year after M. de Polignac's appointment the bitterness between the Grand Equerry and his successor became so violent that a duel was feared. M. de Tessé, who like his father and predecessor was completely absorbed by his profession (he said of a woman: "She is gentle—as gentle as a well-made carriage"), could not understand the careless frivolity with which his reversioner undertook the duties of his post. He decided to make a journey to Italy and asked for 15 months' leave to get over his irritation. Comte Jules replaced him and ran the stables in accordance with his own calculations. One set of figures will be a sufficient indication. Until now shoeing had cost 6,000 livres a year; henceforth it would cost 20,000.

Although he was unaware of these details, Mirabeau was in the right when he exclaimed: "One thousand crowns to the Assas family for having saved the State, one million to the Polignac family for having lost it!"

In the summer of 1776 Mme de Lamballe was in semi-disgrace, which did not prevent her "from causing annoyance and expense in connection with lodgings at Versailles, Compiègne and Fontainebleau." But worst of all, continued Mercy, "are the favours which the Principal Lady in Waiting manages to extract." Her brother, Prince Eugène de Carignan, who had entered the French service, received 40,000 livres as pension, together with 14,000 livres for his colonelcy, although the allowance for colonels was only 4,000 livres. These expenses, Mercy pointed out, were entirely the Queen's doing.

Marie Antoinette was incapable of refusing. She was too afraid that her coterie would imitate Besenval's procedure by sulking and giving her a hard time, for these bandits imagined that they could do what they liked and they played on their mistress's emotions. "The Queen is impulsive," wrote Mercy, "and nearly always accepts what her petitioners report. Before making requests she ought to find out their importance and extent, together with the services and rights of the petitioner. The Queen's credit is considered so high that most of the Ministers can only obey her without venturing to remonstrate. The Queen takes it upon herself to make requests as much from a dislike of refusing as from a real desire."

When Maria Theresa received this letter, which was sent to Vienna on 17 September 1776, she wished that her "dear daughter" might have a few setbacks to put her on the right road again. For some months she had taken the line of not scolding "Antonia," for she had lost her influence, but she now changed her mind. "I can no longer be silent, as I love you for your own good, not to flatter you. Do not lose by frivolity the credit you gained to begin with. The King is known to be very easy-going, and you would get all the blame. I hope I do not live to see such a change."

Marie Antoinette's credit with the public was already much diminished. In the preceding spring she had not managed to get Gluck's *Alcestis* accepted by the Parisians. The opera was a failure and Marie Antoinette's lavish "signs of approval" did not, as before, carry the public with them. At the beginning of the autumn of 1776 the cheers were much less enthusiastic and they became even fainter after the stay at Fontainebleau in October and November 1776 when the notorious races organised by the Comte d'Artois and the Duc de Chartres took place.

The lack of constraint shown at these race meetings horrified Mercy.

Marie Antoinette installed herself with her suite in a salon prepared at the top of a wooden grandstand. She was surrounded by "a swarm of young people in boots and *chenilles*" who shouted and yelled. "There was such a mob and so much noise one could not hear oneself speak." Between races they plundered the buffet. The most excited was the Comte d'Artois, who ran down the stand, hurried through the spectators to go and encourage his jockeys, returned to the "mob," presented the winner to the Queen, insulted the loser, whom he wanted to thrash if he had betted on him. He whined if he lost, indulged in "pitiful exhibitions of joy" if he won. Amid all this "pell-mell"—Mercy's word—the Queen managed to keep "her air of graciousness and grandeur," but the crowd of spectators were "unable to notice this difference" and were dumbfounded. They were even more so on 13 November.

The Comte d'Artois had bought in England the famous racehorse King Pepin, belonging to the Marquess of Rockingham, and the Duc de Chartres had acquired Glow-worm, a son of the celebrated Eclipse. The King had promised to watch this "futile" spectacle and risked three livres either on his brother's horse or on that of the future Philippe-Egalité—the reports do not agree. The Comte d'Artois wagered a fortune. Many English had crossed the Channel and one of them bet 10,000 louis against King Pepin. In fact 5,000 of these belonged to the Marquess of Rockingham, who knew that his former horse's legs were too long and would trip him up at the turnings. Glow-worm, indeed, was the winner. The Comte d'Artois flew into a rage, wanted to kill his jockey and, to the surprise of the King, who did not suffer from hippomania, was very harsh on the Duc de Chartres. "I am tired," he exclaimed, "of being continually cheated, either at the races or at play."

On the occasion of the performance of *Don Japhet d'Arménie* by Scarron, after the return to Versailles from Fontainebleau, the King asked the leaders of the troupe "to imitate the behaviour, poses and grimaces of the Queen and the Comte d'Artois at the famous Fontainebleau race meeting." The parody was so successful that Marie Antoinette recognised herself and her anger was appeased only by the King's loud laughter. These details seem to indicate that perhaps Marie Antoinette had not always kept an "air of graciousness and grandeur" during the race between King Pepin and Glow-worm.

Although Louis XVI disapproved of his wife's passion for horse-racing, he tolerated gambling, although it was forbidden elsewhere.

In the evening, after their visit to the Turf, the Queen and her friends sat round another, clandestine, green carpet, but the King did not play.

"I can understand your playing heavily," he said to one of the gamblers, "you are playing with your own money, but I should be playing with other people's."

Marie Antoinette did not grasp this distinction and plunged recklessly. She even persuaded her weak husband to get someone from Paris to hold the bank at faro.

"It will not matter as long as you play for only one evening," the King conceded.

The banker, M. de Chalabre, arrived on 30 October. Somewhat intimidated by the crowd of gamblers, he asked for an assistant. A M. Poinçot, a Knight of the Order of Saint Louis, volunteered, but he had not the right to sit down to the game as he was only a captain. The rank of colonel was the "lowest grade giving this right." Moreover, he was there *"en polisson"*—a recognised expression signifying that the captain's nobility did not go back beyond 1400 and that consequently he had not been presented at court.

This made no difference. "A chair for M. Poinçot!" the Queen ordered. This chair was to cost the *polisson* several months' pay.

They played all night and into the morning. The Queen left at four o'clock, having lost only 90 louis, about 430,000 francs, whereas the Comte d'Artois had won six times as much. The game was continued on the evening of 31 November at Mme de Lamballe's house. Marie Antoinette went to bed at three o'clock, but the game went on well into the morning of All Saints' Day. Louis XVI was displeased.

"You allowed one gambling session, without fixing its length," Marie Antoinette explained, "so we had a perfect right to prolong it for 36 hours!"

"Really!" exclaimed the King, laughing, "you are all a worthless lot!"

But his weak nature was not very admirable either, for on 11 December he proposed of his own accord to bring back the bankers. Once more the session lasted all night at Mme de Lamballe's house.

Inevitably, Mercy one day found the Queen anxious and "worried about the state of her debts, of whose total she was not herself aware." The diplomat turned into an accountant and, although the Queen's allowance had recently been doubled, found a tidy deficit of 487,272 livres—100 million francs. The Queen was "somewhat surprised" but showed no signs of panic.

Marie Antoinette's insensibility in this matter was more excusable. The expenditure all around her appeared to have been instituted and regulated by a madman. On opening some of the files in the National Archives one feels obliged to read every item twice, for fear of having misunderstood. The Queen's personal apothecary received the sum of 2,000 livres a year for his drugs, whether Marie Antoinette was ill or not. The army of domestic servants was given a yearly travelling allowance even if no moves were made. One also notes that when the gentlemen of the watch were on guard they were reimbursed their outlay for "straw and mattresses," although this rule was two centuries old and the watch had for a long time been provided with mattresses from the furniture store. To illuminate the suppers the ushers received every three days a torch of yellow wax which was never used. Leakage was a recognised thing. For example, the Queen's victualler received no salary, "the profit he makes on his supplies standing in its stead." The story is well known of the scullery boy whose task was to keep up a roaring fire in the furnace every night "to make ashes," which ashes were sold the next day for the benefit of the chief cook.

One of the files in the Archives proves how insincere were the complaints made by Papillon de La Ferté in his *Journal*. His outlays were very profitable. Ferté, "who had a good understanding with his contractors," simultaneously authorised and checked the expenses. This is why, to take one example out of many, one sees invoiced, for *Athalie*, shepherds' crooks and straw hats, but further on we learn "that there was no occasion to make use of them," which in the case of *Athalie* is not surprising. And the clerk to the Privy Purse sighed as he bent over his accounts: "I should never finish if I went into all the details of the waste and useless expenditure I see every day, for the underlings, taking their example from the master, think they can do as they please and are not supervised."

There were very strange customs, too. Why did the Queen's dentist receive six dozen handkerchiefs? Why did the chief footmen yearly draw a mysterious "parasol allowance"?

"Tipping" was universal. The Queen's servants of the bedchamber collected a toll for the oaths of senior officers and for the stools of duchesses and grandees of Spain, apart from their salary, New Year's gift and the "charge on the replacement of candles."

Oh, those candles! The moment the Queen left her bedroom for her private apartments the candles were extinguished. Even if they had burned for only a few moments they were not used again and fell to various privileged people who resold them for their own account. The candles in the antechamber, the *grand cabinet* and the corridors were given to the servants of the bedchamber; those in the private rooms, the gambling room and the Queen's bedroom were presented to Marie Antoinette's women. One evening when the chandeliers and standard lamps were not lit the servants collected an indemnity of 80 livres. This "right to the candles" brought in yearly to each of the Queen's four waiting-women 50,000 livres, or 10 million present-day francs. There were burned, or to be more exact, there were *lit,* 109 livres' worth of candles on summer evenings and 145 on winter days. If, for reasons of economy, it was decided to cut down the festivities the women demanded an extra payment.

"Charities, gifts and pensions" for Marie Antoinette's Household alone amounted to 867,383 livres, 18 sols, 11 deniers—or 175 million francs. The Queen's unpublished accounts reveal some curious obligations. Marie Antoinette had to give 252 livres a year to the Recollect Friars "instead of a carp on abstinence days." By a reverse process she had to give 120 livres to the nuns of "Pique-puce" "on account of the herb salads which they customarily present to the Queen," and which they never presented.

These accounts are amusing, but they did not help settle the Queen's affairs. Somewhat embarrassed, Marie Antoinette decided, on Mercy's advice, to speak to her husband about her 487,272 livres of debts. Just as he had allowed faro, tolerated the "swarm of young people," permitted the dissipations and granted the Ministerial portfolios, Louis XVI now declared to the Queen "without hesitation and with the best possible grace," that he would pay her debts out of his own pocket. There was not a complaint or a word of reproach. "This indulgence of the King's, which covers everything, is extremely unfortunate," Mercy declared, "since it makes it impossible to divert the Queen from things which cannot be for her real good."

But Louis XVI had an excuse, and it was Maria Theresa who guessed it from afar. The King preferred to shut his eyes so that his wife—who was still not yet his wife—"may not become attached to other, less suitable, pleasures." Louis XVI may have realised that his wife's dissipations were a necessary palliative and prevented the worst.

The courtiers might make jests and the rhymers verses about this paradoxical situation, but the "fatal object" obsessed some people's minds. On New Year's Eve 1777, when Marie Antoinette and Louis XVI were returning from the chapel, an Abbé rushed forward, knelt down on one knee and presented the King with a "Memoir giving the secret of perpetuating his august race." This was the root of mandragora "to be eaten or applied." The Abbé and his "memoir" were politely shown the door. The King laughed loudly, but Marie Antoinette had to force herself to smile.

Having so much to be forgiven, Louis XVI became more and more indulgent. He ordered the number of balls, entertainments, games and spectacles to be doubled. During carnival time in 1777, as Marie Antoinette realised and Mercy confirmed, he urged his wife to go as often as possible to the Opera, although she behaved there "with an air of familiarity to which the public would never be accustomed." Neither did it become accustomed to see its sovereign indulge, under the walls of Paris this time, in the "pell mell" and rowdiness of the Fontainebleau races. Parisian society, too, did not become accustomed to travelling fruitlessly to Versailles to pay court. The reception days were unchanged, but Marie Antoinette, whose moods were very uncertain, would change her mind at the last minute, and Paris began to hold aloof from its sovereign's invitations. "The small number of people who make up what the Queen calls her 'coterie' keep away the majority of courtiers of both sexes," wrote Mercy, "and deprive the latter of any occasion and possibility of paying their court."

But Joseph II was about to break in on their enjoyment and try to restore order. It was to be seen if he would succeed.

It was not the first time that Marie Antoinette had once more seen one of her brothers. At the beginning of 1775 the Archduke Maximilian had come to Versailles accompanied by the Comte de Rosemberg and this visit had caused a great deal of trouble. Since the fourteen-year-old Archduke was there incognito, under the name of the Comte de Burgau, the Princes of the houses of Orléans, Condé, Conti and Penthièvre considered that the Queen's brother should visit them first. They awaited his arrival, but in vain. Marie Antoinette showed "excessive warmth" and remarked haughtily: "My brother will be sorry not to see the Princes, but he is spending only a short time in Paris and has many things to see. He will do without it."

The affair grew considerably and Paris applauded the Duc de Chartres, who refused to appear at Versailles during the "Comte de Burgau's" stay.

This time, with the arrival of Joseph II, it was an Emperor who wanted to shelter behind an incognito. He wished to be known only as the "Comte de Falkenstein." The Princes were in great anxiety. They wished to behave correctly, but there were so many problems. Should they provide an armchair for the Emperor if he came to see them? Should they themselves sit on a folding stool or allow themselves a chair with a back? Should they reconduct the Comte de Falkenstein to the door of the salon or as far as the antechamber?

Joseph II, indeed, was very eccentric. When he was dictating his orders he took pleasure in snipping off the ends of his secretaries' pigtails. An unpublished text in the Archives recounts that he would amuse himself by firing from his window at the dogs passing along the ramparts and that he would drive away "with blows from his whip the girls bringing petitions." This anonymous report declares that the Emperor's greatest enjoyment was to go and watch the women in labour in the great hospital in Vienna or to spend hours at the top of a tower overlooking a courtyard full of shrieking madmen.

Marie Antoinette was very nervous about her brother's visit. She expected criticisms and, according to Mercy, was prepared "to sidetrack him on a good many subjects."

On 18 April, at 7:30 in the evening, the Emperor's sedan chair entered the courtyard of the Petit Luxembourg, where Mercy, who was kept in bed by a painful attack of rheumatism, was waiting for him. For nearly two hours the Ambassador discussed with his master the different aspects his first interview with Marie Antoinette might take. Mercy need not have been anxious. On the following morning the first meeting between the brother and sister in the Queen's private room went off extremely well. The Emperor remarked jestingly: "If you were not my sister I should not hesitate to marry again in order to have such a charming companion."

Marie Antoinette was softened and confided her deep distress to the Emperor. Of course she felt nothing for the King, as Joseph II wrote to his brother, but the "fatal object" was the cause of real tragedies. When the Comtesse d'Artois's son was born, the fishwives who had come to congratulate the King's brother had followed the Queen "right to the door of her private room, shouting in the coarsest terms that it was for her to provide heirs." She still wept at the thought. The Emperor promised to speak to the King and meanwhile took advantage of his incognito to see, and criticise, everything.

He mingled with the public. "Yesterday," he wrote to his brother on 29 April, "I saw Sunday celebrated *in publico* at Versailles: the *lever*, the mass, the formal dinner. I mixed with the crowd so as to watch everything. I must admit that I enjoyed it, and having to act a part so often myself I now take the opportunity of seeing other people do so." The public was in ecstasies over his simplicity. He had refused to sit at the back of the King's carriage and had taken his seat "on the front." He was lodging with a simple bath-attendant of Versailles, who had rented him two rooms. He slept only on a bearskin. He drove around in the rain in a "mean little open carriage."

> Majesty without pomp our eyes have seen,
> Amazed at Falkenstein's simplicity.
> But here how shameful has the contrast been,
> He has found only pomp, no majesty.

What first astonished him was the "strange spectacle" of Louis XVI and his two brothers. "Their behaviour was so free and easy that on rising from table they amused themselves with childish jokes, ran about the room and threw themselves on the sofas."

Through these "incongruities" Joseph II made rapid judgements: Artois was only a fop, his wife "a complete idiot," Provence "nondescript and very frigid" and Madame, "ugly, coarse and full of intrigue, is not a Piedmontese for nothing."

The King made a better impression. "He is rather weak, but no fool. He has ideas and good judgement, but his body and mind are apathetic . . . The *fiat lux* has not yet been spoken, the matter is still in a lump." The Emperor was particularly anxious for the *fiat lux* regarding the "fatal object" and Louis XVI, who had explained the position to his brother-in-law, promised that he would no longer put off the operation advised by his surgeon.

The Emperor thought his sister more and more enchanting and was the first to applaud at the Opera when, in Gluck's *Iphigenia,* the chorus sang on seeing Clytemnestra: "Let us extol our Queen." "She is good natured and charming," he wrote. "I have spent hour after hour with her and not noticed their passing . . . Her virtue is unassailed and indeed she is austere by nature rather than by reasoning . . . With all this she has wit and a penetrating judgement that has often amazed me. Her first impulse is always correct." He was dazzled, like everyone who approached the Queen, but this did not prevent him from criticising her. "The Queen is a very pretty and good-natured woman, but she thinks of nothing but enjoying herself!" To the actor Clairval he said: "Your Queen is very giddy, but fortunately you French do not dislike that!"

On the fourth day of his arrival at Trianon, after a dinner in private, the Emperor took his sister into the garden and began to lecture her on her "everlasting dissipation." "He developed his ideas," wrote Mercy, "and drew a striking picture of the Queen's position, of the pitfalls surrounding her, of the ease with which she let herself be seduced by the deceptive allure of dissipation. He showed the *infallible and terrifying* consequences of this for the future. Under this heading were included neglect of the King, the Queen's companions, the absence of all serious occupation and the passion for gambling."

Joseph II was particularly shocked by "the bad tone of society" and by the air of license prevailing at Mme de Guéménée's house as a result of the games of faro. "That house is simply a gambling den!" he declared.

The Queen was full of good intentions. She promised to reform, but only after the Emperor's departure. "I do not wish to appear to be managed."

Joseph II was full of emotion on leaving Versailles. "It was all I could do to drag myself away." France, too, had affected him. "A government could lead it anywhere at the touch of a finger. I beat my Germans and they never move an inch!"

Marie Antoinette was very grieved by this separation. In the evening of 31 May she had a violent nervous attack. "It is true," she wrote to her mother, "that the Emperor's departure has left a gap I cannot fill. I was so happy during that short time that now everything seems like a dream. But what will never be a dream for me is all the good counsel and advice he gave me, which is engraved on my heart for ever. I will confess to my dear mamma that one thing he left me, which I begged for, gives me particular pleasure. This is the written advice he left me. At present this is my principal reading, and if ever I should forget what he told me (which I doubt), I should always have before me this paper which would soon recall me to my duty."

This "recall to duty" did not mince its words. "You are getting older and no longer have youth as an excuse. What will you become, if you delay any longer? An unhappy woman and a still more unhappy Princess!" He then entered on a lengthy criticism of the Queen's behaviour towards the King. "When he caresses you, when he speaks to you do you not show irritation, even repugnance?" He then attacked her "associates." "Have you ever thought what effect your intimacies and friendships, if not bestowed on people in every way irreproachable and reliable, may and must have on the public, since you will seem to share in them and to authorise vice? Have you weighed the terrible consequences of games of chance, the company they bring together and the tone they set?"

He then spoke of the masked balls at the Opera of which the Queen was fond and of the adventures, or rather misadventures, in which she was involved there. "In itself the place has a bad reputation. What do you go there for—respectable conversation? You cannot have this with your friends, for the masks prevent it. Nor can you dance. Why, then, all these adventures and dubious behaviour? Why mingle with a crowd of libertines, prostitutes and strangers, listening to their remarks and perhaps making similar ones? How indecent! . . . I must confess that I could see that this was what most shocked those who love you and who have a proper way of thinking. The King is left alone all night at Versailles and you mix in society and mingle with the riff-raff of Paris! . . . I really tremble for your happiness, for it cannot turn out well in the long run and there will be a cruel upheaval (*révolution*) unless you take steps against it."

"You will have a fall unless you are careful," was what the Emperor meant, but one's mind cannot help pondering on that *révolution cruelle* mentioned here 11 years before the fall of the Bastille.

The effect of these reproaches did not remain long with the Queen and Mercy confessed his amazement. "I cannot get over my astonishment over the short duration of the impression made by H.M. the Emperor on the Queen's mind. When one has for *two months* seen this august Princess imbued with the useful truths which were presented to her it seems unbelievable that everything should return to a state which is really worse than it was before the Emperor's stay in this country. I have reason to believe that the rule of conduct written by H.M. has been torn up and thrown on the fire."

The favourites reigned as never before. Mme de Polignac and M. de Coigny were at the height of their power. "These two persons," Mercy complained, "extort from the Queen favours which give rise to continual complaints by the public. The protégés of the Duc de Coigny snap up the financial posts and the Comtesse de Polignac's satellites constantly receive pecuniary favours to the detriment of those whose right it should be to have them. No Minister dares resist the Queen's wishes."

In the summer of 1777 there began the famous walks on the terraces of Versailles which, as Mme Campan wrote, "absorbed the attention of Paris, France and even Europe in a way very detrimental to Marie Antoinette's character." Mme Campan and Mercy both say that in order to profit by the cool of the evening Marie Antoinette would walk on the terrace of the château arm-in-arm with one of her sisters-in-law or one of her ladies. Soon, at the suggestion of the Comte d'Artois, the musicians from the chapel were summoned and installed on a rostrum, where they played far into the night. The inhabitants of Versailles "wanted to enjoy these serenades" and there was soon a crowd, with which the Queen imprudently mingled. There is a well-known story of Marie Antoinette, thinking herself unrecognised and sitting on a bench with a clerk from a Ministry and then with one of Monsieur's bodyguards and striking up a conversation with them. These two innocent little scenes were embellished and ended up as a veritable saturnalia.

"How many times," wrote the author of the pamphlet, *A Reprimand to the Queen,* "have you left the nuptial bed and the caresses of your husband to abandon yourself to bacchantes or satyrs and to become one with them through their brutal pleasures?"

This torrent of filth would fill more than a hundred volumes. Shortly after the famous promenade concerts a whole collection of songs against the Queen was thrown into the *Œil-de-Bœuf.* Joseph II scolded from Vienna, but the Queen "brushed it all aside and replied merely by evasions which seemed almost like jesting."

Joseph II had more success with his brother-in-law. In July Louis XVI finally made up his mind. "No doubt his self-esteem conquered," writes

Dr. Ganière, "and enabled the King to overcome his repugnance for the knife." It was a mild enough operation in itself, but very cruel when one thinks that it was carried out with no help from anaesthetics. A few incisions—a kind of anatomical retouching, in fact—and the job would be done, as long as the operation did not leave a painful impression for a few days. Louis XVI, proud of his endurance, bravely overcame these discomforts, and looked forward to achievements of which he had merely dreamed for the last seven years. The revelation took place. In spite of the long delay neither of the two partners seemed disappointed. Louis XVI confessed to his aunts: "I very much enjoy this pleasure and I am sorry to have been deprived of it for so long." And Marie Antoinette confided to Mme Campan: "I am now experiencing the most important happiness of my life." And yet, when one thinks of it, although during an August night in 1777 Marie Antoinette at last became true Queen of France, one is free to imagine that the reality must have been very different from what her thoughts had idealised during that hopeless period of chastity.

One has no need to imagine, for Marie Antoinette soon admitted it to one of her "associates": "I should be neither grieved nor very annoyed if the King were to develop a passing and temporary attachment, as he might thereby acquire more vitality and energy."

As a result of the King's lack of skill and experience the operation, which should also have appeased the Queen's thirst for pleasure, brought about no change in her behaviour. Three months after the beginning of this "most important happiness" she was already shunning the conjugal bed, and explained to her mother "that the King does not like sleeping two in a bed." Mercy explained matters more correctly. The King had never felt this dislike, but during their stay at Fontainebleau Marie Antoinette's passion for gambling caused her to return home at an ever later hour. Consequently, the King, who retired early so as to rise early, preferred to remain in his own room rather than have his night's rest interrupted by his wife's noisy return.

Once again faro was all the rage in the evening at the Princesse de Guéménée's house. The passion for gambling had become sheer madness: "The Duc de Chartres has lost 30,000 louis"—that is, 44 million present-day francs. In vain Mercy told the Queen that "as the government recognised the danger of games of chance and was attempting to check their spread, it was unheard of and scandalous that these very games should be admitted by the Queen, particularly when they occupied those moments which should be given to etiquette." The only reply he obtained was: "I am afraid of being bored."

And play continued. "It is the one subject," wrote Mercy, "on which she will admit no protest. On 25 October 1777 H.M. had lost her last crown. On the next day she ordered her treasurer to bring her her November allowance, which was also consumed in a few days, without counting a debt of 500 louis which is still not paid." Marie Antoinette was enjoying herself more than ever and would not listen to any cries of alarm. She made a wager of 100,000 francs, which would be 20 millions today, that the Comte d'Artois would not manage to have a château built in the Bois de Boulogne in six weeks, during the stay at Fontainebleau. The future Charles X accepted the challenge and declared that he would give a feast in the Queen's honour at Bagatelle —as the little château was called—before the return to Versailles. He won his wager thanks to 900 labourers who worked day and night. "The most extraordinary thing was," Mercy sighed, "that as there was a lack of building materials, particularly freestone, lime and plaster, and no time could be lost in looking for them, M. le Comte d'Artois gave orders that patrols of the Swiss Guards should search the high roads and seize all the carts they found loaded with the above-mentioned materials. The price of the materials was paid right away, but as the goods had already been sold to other individuals, there was a kind of compulsion in this method which revolted public opinion. No one can understand how the King can allow such flightiness and unfortunately it is also supposed that it would not be tolerated without the protection accorded by the Queen. H.M. often deigns to assure me that she is very far from approving the rashness of the Prince her brother-in-law, but that she has no means of stopping his misconduct. The Queen speaks truly on the first point, of which I have had many proofs, but as regards the second point, the one way of preventing the Comte d'Artois's disorderly conduct would be to refuse to attend the pleasure parties which cause it."

But Marie Antoinette did not refuse. She visited the little château. We do not know if her brother-in-law showed her the entresol adorned with frescoes and high-reliefs among which the Marquis de Sade would have been quite at home, but the public was convinced of it.

After one incident the Queen became involved in the Comte d'Artois's unpopularity. On Shrove Tuesday of 1778 Marie Antoinette spent the whole night at the Opera in the company of her brother-in-law and Monsieur. During the masked ball Artois, as usual, mixed with "the worst company," and a little later on was seen walking arm-in-arm with Mme de Canillac, the companion to the Duchesse de Bourbon, who had just dismissed her as she was also companion to that Princess's husband. The Duchesse was not a model of virtue, far from it, but she was as jealous as a tigress. Recognising her rival, she uttered a few acid remarks in an audible tone. The Comte d'Artois, who was also masked, came forward and replied sharply.

"Only M. d'Artois or a rascal could speak to me like that!" exclaimed Mme de Bourbon. On this gracious remark she tore off the mask of the King's brother. One can guess the scandal. The excitement increased the next day, when it was learnt that the Comte d'Artois had boasted to Mme de Polignac of having hit the Duchesse right in the face with his fist. Mme de Bourbon promptly styled her aggressor an insolent personage. Although her husband thought very little of his wife, he considered it his duty to intervene and challenge his cousin to a duel.

"Do your duty and fear nothing," his father ordered. The Prince de Condé then ordered relays of horses to be set up along the road to Belgium in case his son killed the King's brother. Vaudreuil and Besenval organised a meeting and on 16 March, in spite of Louis XVI's orders and Marie Antoinette's attempts to prevent the duel, the two opponents took up their position in the Bois de Boulogne. After a few minutes' fencing the Comte d'Artois's sword slid under his adversary's arm, scratching him slightly.

"That is more than is needed to settle the question," exclaimed Crussol, the Captain of the Prince's guards.

Artois raised his sword. "It is not for me to have an opinion, but for M. le Duc to say what he wishes. I am at his orders."

"Monsieur," replied the Duke, lowering the point of his sword, "I am deeply conscious of your goodness. I shall never forget the honour you have done me." Whereupon the two adversaries embraced.

Nevertheless, the affair had two victims, who were not the combatants: the Duc de Chartres, brother of the Duchesse de Bourbon, who was reproached with not having taken the quarrel seriously, and Marie Antoinette, who, it was asserted, had taken sides with her "insolent" brother-in-law. This was certainly false, but the Queen was now reaping what she had sown.

Whereas the future Philippe-Egalité prudently refrained from appearing at the Comédie Française on the evening of the duel, the Queen rashly went there with her brother-in-law. The Prince de Condé and the Duc and Duchesse de Bourbon were applauded at length, but Marie Antoinette and the Comte d'Artois were accorded only a few handclaps, so sparse that they appeared ironical.

This dispute in the Carnival season gave the Queen her first opportunity of measuring the road she had travelled in five years, since the time when the Parisians in tears showed her their "tenderness and attention."

At dawn on Thursday before Ash Wednesday 1778, at a time when there was once more a shortage of bread, the Queen travelled along the boulevards in her sleigh which had cost 10,000 crowns, followed by 21 coaches. Marie Antoinette had just left the Opera ball and was still laughing uncontrollably. The evening had been full of surprises. For a few minutes the Queen had mingled with the prostitutes and then a masked man, disguised as a fishwife, had approached her box, called her "Antoinette" and scolded her for not being with her husband, who "must at that moment be snoring in the conjugal bed." In a cascade of laughter Marie Antoinette leant over to speak to the stranger "until he could nearly touch her breast."

And while the sleigh crunched over the icy road in the direction of Versailles, she exclaimed with disarming unconsciousness: "Ah! I have never enjoyed myself so much!"

7

✣

Less Conspicuous Amusements

AT THE BEGINNING of 1778 France, which had for a long time fought for the King of Prussia, very nearly had to fight for the Emperor of Austria. The Elector of Bavaria, Maximilian Joseph, had died on 30 December 1777 and Joseph II, who saw in this the long-awaited opportunity to seize Bavaria, made great play with rights going back to the fifteenth century. These rights over certain districts had been confirmed by a secret convention between Austria and Charles Theodore, the Elector Palatine and successor to the deceased.

The Queen's first fear on hearing of the death of the Elector was, as she wrote to Comtesse Jules, that her brother would be "up to his tricks." He soon was, and 12,000 men were sent to occupy Lower Bavaria, a "district" claimed by Austria.

"This rounding off of territory is of inestimable value," declared Joseph II, much to the dismay of Maria Theresa. "We may be able to bring it off without a war!" He meant without a war against Prussia, which would acquiesce in the "rounding off" *if* France showed itself "firm in the Alliance" and *if* Marie Antoinette were willing to support the Austrian view. Now a letter written by the Queen to Mme de Polignac shows that Marie Antoinette shared French opinion concerning Joseph II's ambition. Besides France had taken sides with the English colonies in America and was preparing for war with England. Would it have to fight simultaneously against the English in America and against Prussia in Europe?

Seeing that Marie Antoinette had no concern for the interests of Austria, Mercy acted, and spoke decisively: the Queen of France must remember the Archduchess. Maria Theresa went further: "I have need of all your feeling for me, for your house and for your country."

"Your country!" "My two countries," Marie Antoinette said. By yielding to her mother's wishes she became the first Queen of France to act in such a way. The Empress did not care, and brought a kind of blackmail to bear on her daughter's feelings: the King of Prussia would certainly do everything he could to upset the Alliance to his own advantage. "And this would be my death," sighed Maria Theresa.

Mercy, who was present, saw Marie Antoinette pale as she read these words. The Ambassador pressed the Queen. She must act and speak to the King. The Abbé de Vermond seconded him. The Queen's Reader was a Frenchman, and paid by the Treasury, but as always he acted as an Austrian agent. Marie Antoinette decided to see the King and spoke sharply to him. Louis XVI replied unexpectedly: "Your relations' ambition will upset everything. They began with Poland and now Bavaria will be the second chapter. I am sorry on your account."

"But, Sir, you cannot deny that you were informed about the Bavarian affair and were in agreement."

Apparently Louis XVI had no recollection of the allusions which Joseph II was supposed to have made, for he replied: "I was so little in agreement that the French Ministers have just been ordered to inform the courts to which they are accredited that this dismemberment of Bavaria takes place against our wishes and that we disapprove of it."

This was a failure. Marie Theresa, who at the bottom of her heart did not approve of her son's action, acknowledged her daughter's "critical position." The Queen, she repeated, must act "with all prudence and skill" so as not to be accused of betraying French interests. "If the Ministers ever became aware of it many of them would not hesitate to take advantage of it to weaken her credit and counteract her influence in public affairs."

But events moved fast. In March the King of Prussia made an official protest against the Hapsburg claims and demanded the withdrawal of the Austrian troops from the Bavarian districts. Maria Theresa, frightened by the gravity of the situation, no longer recommended prudence to her daughter and begged her openly to support Mercy, who was to ask France to fulfill the treaty of 1765: in the event of aggression the King was to supply the Emperor with 24,000 men or with money.

To begin with, Marie Antoinette, "much occupied with the dissipations and long evenings of the Carnival of 1778," gave little help to her mother's Ambassador, who complained: "If the Queen would only put some method into her proceedings and into the use of her power everything would go off here without a hitch, but I am very far from obtaining such a desirable state of affairs and Your Majesty need not fear that her noble daughter will interfere in affairs of state in such a way as to compromise herself. I am disturbed only by her lack of action in this respect."

However, between 20 and 25 March, as a result of the urgent and almost daily prompting of Mercy, Marie Antoinette decided to take action and summoned Maurepas and Vergennes. "They responded very well on the subject of the Alliance," she wrote to Maria Theresa, "and seem strongly attached to it, but they are so afraid of a land war that when I pressed on them the hypothesis of the King of Prussia commencing hostilities I could not get a clear answer from them."

The Empress considered her daughter's action insufficiently vigorous. She received this letter on 31 March, the courier having taken only six days, and two days later she wrote to Mercy: "In fact my daughter does not change. She is so taken up by her dissipations that she is hardly capable of reflecting coherently on major matters. We will have to be satisfied by what can be wrung from her by remonstrances."

Following another letter from her mother and another conversation with Mercy, Marie Antoinette interfered a second time in the middle of April. She again summoned Maurepas and Vergennes. "I spoke to them with some force and I think I made an impression on them, particularly the latter. I was not very pleased with the arguments of these gentlemen, who are only trying to compromise and to accustom the King to do the same."

The "arguments of these gentlemen" in reply to her pro-Austrian language had been clear: France could consider intervention only in the event of the King of Prussia threatening the Low Countries. This was also the King's opinion. The treaty did not guarantee new "acquisitions" by Austria in Poland and Bavaria which were nothing but thefts accomplished by the House of Hapsburg since the agreement of 1756.

But a "long-awaited, long hoped-for" event was to enable Marie Antoinette to act with new authority and to oblige the royal Government to take up its attitude in accordance with the wishes of Vienna.

Marie Antoinette was at last expecting a child. Mercy wrote: "The Queen's pregnancy has so greatly increased her credit from what it was in the past that there would be very advantageous changes here in every direction if this noble Princess could properly estimate her position and realise the profit to be gained from it, in view of the King's turn of mind and character and the disposition of his present Ministers. I am doing all I can to enlighten the Queen in this respect."

On 20 April 1778 Maurepas and Vergennes sent a rather "sharp" dispatch to Vienna, informing Austria that it could not count on France. Strong in her "increased credit" Marie Antoinette spoke out strongly. "I indicated my displeasure as soon as I heard of it. It is extraordinary what a gift the Ministers here have for drowning affairs in a flood of words. Nevertheless, after everything Mercy had told me, and as a result of the reflections which I cannot help constantly making on the most important event of my life, I pressed them so hard that they were obliged to alter their tone somewhat. They have sufficiently admitted their mistake as regards this wretched dispatch."

"As a result of the fear instilled in them by the Queen" the Ministers reversed their position on 26 April and formally guaranteed the safety of the Low Countries. If Frederick should attack Austria in the Belgian Provinces he would find the French troops at the side of Joseph II's army.

Maria Theresa was delighted with this success and henceforth considered her daughter as a real agent of Austrian policy. "As you have entered with so much affection and zeal into our interests and situation," she wrote from Schoenbrunn on 17 May, "I feel I must continue to keep you informed." Marie Antoinette approved her mother's decisions all the more since, without telling her, the King and his Ministers were explaining everything to the King of Prussia and revealing their real sentiments. In other words they gave him to understand that his hands were free in the south, towards Bohemia, but not in the west, towards France. It was through Mercy and not through the King's Ministers that the Queen learned of this secret warning. "I objected very forcibly to such a neglect of the Queen," he wrote, "and I made her see how disrespectful it was to her and added that if she overlooked such liberties she would no longer be able to maintain her influence and her credit. The Queen was struck by my remarks and decided to speak to the King."

This time there was a violent scene between husband and wife. Louis XVI, who was much annoyed, remained silent during the lecture and then sighed: "You see that I am so much to blame that I have not a word in reply." And Marie Antoinette concluded: "I would ask you to speak to your Ministers about the incivility of their silence towards me. It seems to me extremely important that they should not get into the habit of it."

Frederick II was not a man to postpone his schemes indefinitely. In the certainty that France would not move he turned his back on the Rhine, crossed the Bohemian frontier and at the beginning of July entered Nachod. The Queen's distress was so great that the King declared "he could not bear to see her so anxious, that he would do anything in the world to appease her grief, that he had always wished to do so but that his Ministers had prevented him." "The welfare of my kingdom does not allow me to do more than I have done."

As her husband claimed to have been prevented by his Ministers, Marie Antoinette attacked Maurepas, who evaded the storm by having recourse "to his usual subterfuges." Marie Antoinette raised her voice: "This is the fourth or fifth time, sir, that I have spoken to you on affairs and you have always given me the same reply. Until now I have been patient, but matters are becoming too serious and I will no longer put up with such defeats." She described how, in her opinion, "France had yielded to the coaxing of the King of Prussia and instead of holding him back had, if possible, made him more obstinate."

This was perfectly true, but it was in France's interest. The Austrian Alliance ought not to have been diverted from its principal aim, which was to maintain the balance between Prussia and Austria intended by the Treaty of Westphalia.

Marie Antoinette was launched, and continued to worry her husband and the Ministers. Even Maria Theresa exclaimed on 2 November: "I am grateful for the interest my daughter is taking in our affairs. I only hope she is not being too impetuous, with the sole effect of making herself importunate to the King, suspect to the Ministers and odious to the nation."

"Odious to the nation!" One would think one was suddenly in the year 1792.

But French policy was to meet the wishes of Austria. The weakness of the Hapsburgs and the new strength of the Hohenzollerns threatened to upset the balance of Europe. Consequently when in August the Queen, urged by Mercy, suggested "as though of her own account and without any appearance of prompting," that France should mediate, this was all the more welcomed since the Hanoverians might well take a hand and create a second front. Negotiations were begun and thanks to France and Russia, both powerful mediators, culminated in the following spring in the Peace of Teschen.

This war, in which three of her brothers risked their lives and which in the summer of 1778 threatened the road to Vienna, had a very good effect on the Queen. Mercy related that he had never seen the Queen so oppressed. "In a burst of confidence and kindness she deigned to tell me that she wished to make a general confession and went on to speak of her amusements and her friends and all the details of her private life generally, commanding me to give my humble opinion on each point and on each individual. I acquitted myself with zeal and did not omit a single point bearing on the Queen's interest. She deigned to listen to me with every mark of kindness and added that her present sadness made it a favourable time for her to reflect seriously on her future conduct and that she really felt the necessity of coming to a decision."

Once more Mercy trembled with hope.

Shortly after midnight on 19 December 1778 the Queen awoke with a start: her first pains were beginning. Once more Marie Antoinette was to be a victim to the tyranny of etiquette. At the end of the morning, when the accoucheur Vermond cried: "The Queen is about to give birth!" the crowd of curious people who poured into the room was so unruly, as is related by Mme Campan and confirmed by Mercy, "that it nearly caused the death of the Queen." Marie Antoinette's waiting-woman draws a picture of this public delivery which is not without its picturesque side. "During the night the King had taken the precaution of having the enormous tapestry screens around Her Majesty's bed fastened with cords; without this precaution they would certainly have fallen down on her. It was impossible to move in the bedroom, which was full of such a mixed crowd that one might have been in a public square. Two Savoyards climbed on the furniture to get a better view of the Queen, who was lying facing the fireplace on a bed erected at the time of her confinement. Either all this noise, or the sex of the child, which the Queen was able to learn by a sign agreed

on, it was said, with the Princesse de Lamballe, or an error of the accoucheur, temporarily obstructed the natural consequences of the confinement. The blood went to her head, her mouth twisted and the
accoucheur cried: 'Air, warm water, she must be bled in the foot!' The
windows had been stopped up. The King opened them with a force
that can have been derived only from his affection for the Queen, as
they were extremely high and stuck down their entire length with
bands of paper. As the basin of warm water did not arrive quickly
enough the accoucheur told the Queen's First Surgeon to make a dry
incision. He did so, the blood gushed forth and the Queen opened her
eyes. It was difficult to restrain the joy which so quickly followed the
liveliest alarm. The Princesse de Lamballe had been carried unconscious through the crowd. The valets and ushers seized the indiscreet
sightseers, who were not in a hurry to leave, in order to clear the room."

The couriers immediately hurried off in all directions. The Paris
municipality, which had been assembled since five o'clock in the
morning, received the news of the birth of Madame Royale at half-past
twelve from one of M. le Gouverneur's pages and at five past one from
the Comte de Bevi, representing the King. As a reward the Comte
received a snuff-box of gold and enamel worth 1,440 livres.

In the evening Paris was given up to rejoicing "for the opening of
H.M.'s womb." The "Gentlemen" of the city, in their red and black
robes and with bouquets in their hands—they wore garlands and bracelets of flowers only for a prince—came down into the square in front
of the Hôtel de Ville. To the sound of drums and trumpets the Gentlemen, the ushers in livery, the foot-servants bearing torches, the Swiss
guards shouldering their partisans, all walked three times round the
square, in the middle of which was a bonfire of 500 faggots which the
Mayor lit. An hour later the fireworks were set off and all the *"boetes"*
and guns of the city pealed forth.

Admittedly a Dauphin had been hoped for, but the rejoicing was
not diminished. The event proved that Marie Antoinette and Louis
could have children, and this was all that mattered. A Parisian dairy-
woman—they were poets in those days—hung these verses under her
sign:

> The Nation had from heaven a Cupid sought:
> A Grace comes to announce him to the court.

On the following morning a bulletin, of which 800 copies were printed, announced that "the Grace" was in good health. "The lochia were abundant" and "the Queen's condition is as satisfactory as can be expected." It was a Sunday and the rejoicings continued in Paris. The Gentlemen did not strain their imagination. They organised another procession around another fire, which was lit as on the day before.

On Monday a second printed bulletin informed that "the belly is supple and not at all painful," that "last night the Queen had a very peaceful sleep" and that "the perspiration is maintained," a point on which Lassonne and Vermond were particularly satisfied.

Two further bulletins were published, giving details in the crude terminology of the age which I will spare the reader. Everything was going well, "the lacteal matter is arriving normally." The Queen was taking nourishment, eating "cream of rice with biscuit" and on the 26th she ate some chicken and was "extremely gay during dinner."

On Monday, 8 February, Paris was in a ferment from early morning. The city was to receive the King and Queen. Previously 100 poor girls were married to whom Marie Antoinette gave a dowry corresponding to 100,000 present-day francs. The betrothed, with their hair "curled and arranged," went to their parish priest. The wedding parties then piled into the city coaches and drove to Notre Dame.

While the wedding ceremonies were taking place the city corporation, accompanied by the guards, waited for their sovereigns at the Porte de la Conférence. When the long procession of coaches appeared, surrounded by bodyguards, light horse and pages, the Gentlemen advanced towards the Queen's carriage, which was occupied merely by her Grand Equerry, M. de Tessé. Marie Antoinette had taken her seat with the King in the *"voiture du corps,"* which was preceded by "trumpeters in ordinary" and accompanied by twenty-four footmen and six pages on horseback. The Prévôt came to the door of the carriage and declared: "May this first fruit of your mutual tenderness and those destined by heaven for the future unite to the graces of their illustrious mother the virtues which Your Majesty will transmit to them by example and inheritance."

The King grasped only the intention of this verbose speech and replied "in the most gracious manner." The procession continued by the Quai des Tuileries to Notre Dame, where the hundred couples "lined up in order formed a very touching and moving sight."

But in spite of this sight, in spite of the monthly bonus of 15 livres to be given to the brides if they themselves suckled their future off-spring, in spite of the liberation of 132 prisoners sentenced for not having paid their child's monthly nurse, in spite of the buffets of cold meat, in spite of the curtseys of Mlle Bertin and her 30 assistants from a balcony in the Rue Saint Honoré, in spite of the fireworks let off on the Ile de la Cité and the illuminated fountain in the middle of the Pont Neuf, Paris's welcome was icy. From Notre Dame to Sainte Geneviève, from Sainte-Geneviève to the Place Louis XV, by way of the Rue des Francs-Bourgeois and the Pont Neuf, there were only a few shouts. In certain quarters the gilded procession passed through a double rank of completely silent idlers.

Marie Antoinette was furious. Mercy tried to explain to her that "the idea of her dissipation and the expense she caused, and finally the appearance of an excessive love of amusement in a time of calamity and war might combine to estrange people's minds and required a little tact."

The Queen agreed. She promised once more to change her way of life and "to renounce too conspicuous amusements."

But the evil had been done. Henceforth Marie Antoinette would be the victim of her slightest actions. Whatever she did would be turned against her.

On Shrove Tuesday 1779 she decided to go to the masked ball at the Opera in the strictest incognito. She left Versailles accompanied by the Princesse d'Hénin and drove in a coach to the house of the Duc de Coigny, the King's Grand Equerry. There, in order not to be recognised on her arrival at the ball, she changed into a plainer carriage without any coat of arms and so old that it broke down during the journey. The ladies got out. They could not remain in the street and, laughing over the adventure, the Queen and her companion, both masked, entered the first house they came to, which was that of a cloth merchant. The carriage could not be mended and the Duc de Coigny's footman went to look for a cab, and it was in this unexpected vehicle that the Queen arrived at the Opera.

"It is I in a cab! Isn't it amusing?" she said, laughing to her friends.

The story is well known. "All Paris soon knew of this adventure with the cab," wrote Mme Campan. "It was said that there was something mysterious about this evening adventure, and that the Queen had had a rendezvous in a private house with a gentleman honoured with her

favours. The Duc de Coigny was openly named. . . . Once these
ideas of light conduct had been awakened there were no limits to the
calumnies about the Queen which were rife in Paris." Mme Campan
adds that as a result of the "affair of the cab" every time the Queen
spoke to any young men either at play or at the hunt they were "so
many favoured lovers."

How could it have been otherwise when, in the following month,
the public learned that Marie Antoinette, who had measles, was remaining at Trianon for three weeks, with Coigny, Guines, Esterhazy
and Besenval? These gentlemen announced their intention of not leaving the Queen all night.

"I strongly opposed this ridiculous idea," said Mercy. "I called in the
doctor, Lassonne, who was always weak and undecided and did not
dare oppose things which his position gave him the right to forbid.
Finally the Abbé de Vermond and I made so much fuss that it was
decided that the gentlemen would leave the Queen's bedchamber at 11
in the evening and would not come back until the morning."

The court roared with laughter and amused itself by choosing the
four ladies who would watch over the King if he fell ill. Neither Louis
XVI nor the usual servants had the right to enter the bedchamber. An
exception was made for the Abbé de Vermond, who on Mercy's orders
begged the Queen "to write a few friendly lines to the King." Marie
Antoinette rejected the suggestion "with great warmth." Not without
difficulty the Abbé finally extracted a short note which "the poor man"
received with emotion.

One may imagine the gossip of the town about this little Queen
going disguised to the Opera in a cab or shutting herself up in her
bedroom for three weeks with four men. Two of these nurses, Coigny
and Guines, were named as the Queen's lovers. Had the former, while
"extorting" numberless favours from Marie Antoinette, gone so far as to
obtain the ultimate favour? Letters exist, it is said, but their present
owner refuses to part with them out of respect for the Queen's memory.
We are therefore reduced to conjecture.

According to public rumour, when the Duc de Coigny fell in love
with Mme de Châlons, Marie Antoinette accorded her favour to the
Duc de Guines. This is a calumny. The former Ambassador was far
from being an Adonis. He had become enormously fat and for each
of his suits had two pairs of breeches, one normal pair for the days

when he would have to sit down and the other tightened as much as possible to make him look slimmer. In the morning, before helping him to dress, his valet would ask: "Will M. le Duc be sitting down today?" "When he was to remain standing," the Duc de Levis recounts, "he climbed on to two chairs and descended into his breeches, which were held by two of his servants."

He was not the Queen's lover, but he amused her better than anyone and his favour was so high that Mercy revealed his anxiety in a letter written during the summer of 1779. In order to get rid of this fat man, "as intriguing as he is ambitious," Mercy suggested that Maria Theresa should write to her daughter "that it is generally rumoured that the Queen is so much under the influence of the Duc de Guines that she makes no decisions without consulting him." The Empress followed this advice and the Queen, annoyed, claimed that these were slanders, "which are the usual thing in this country"; but the ruse was successful and gradually the Queen treated her favourite more coldly. Soon, in the autumn of 1779, Mercy, enchanted with his stratagem, was able to write that "the falling off of the Duc de Guines's favour" was complete.

In 1779 the danger, if there were a danger, did not come from that direction.

In August of the preceding year Axel Fersen had arrived at Versailles. Marie Antoinette had recognised him at once: "Ah! Here is an old acquaintance!"

In spite of this flattering welcome the Swedish officer had visited the château only at very irregular intervals. Surprised, perhaps even intrigued, by a reserve to which she was hardly accustomed, Marie Antoinette had displayed some astonishment and had questioned Creutz, the Swedish Ambassador in Paris. "The Queen, who is the prettiest and most amiable Princess I know," Axel wrote to his father, "was so kind as to ask after me often. She asked Creutz why I did not come to her card games on Sundays, and learning that I had come one day when there was no play she took that as a kind of excuse."

Although naturally modest, Axel was obliged to realise that he pleased the Queen, and every Sunday he went to Marie Antoinette's card games, where she treated him "with kindness" and "always spoke" to him. One day she expressed a great wish to see him in his uniform of a Swedish Light Dragoon. The young man complied and for the first time was received in the Queen's private apartments. Very carefully, according to a witness, Marie Antoinette studied the blue doublet, over which was a white tunic, the tight-fitting chamois breeches, the black shako topped with a blue and yellow plume—and admired.

During the spring and summer of 1779 Fersen, "without intrigue and without seeking notoriety," as the Comte de Tilly recounted, became an intimate of Versailles and Trianon. And the inevitable happened: he fell in love with the Queen. For her part Marie Antoinette felt drawn to this rather melancholy young man of 23, who perhaps possessed none of the French levity or brilliance, but whose grave masculinity charmed all the women. She was not yet in love with him, but expressed a lively affection for him. Axel's favour increased. "If there were anything which might cause it to be thought excessive," wrote the Queen's page, "it was a more restrained and respectful attitude which perhaps partook somewhat of the affectation of a courtier. . . . But M. de Fersen is not at all affected and all his art is in simplicity."

The feeling which he thus carefully concealed within his heart became so violent that Fersen decided to flee and signed an engagement with one of the expeditions which were then being prepared for America.

Versailles was thunderstruck. "What! sir, are you deserting your conquest?" Axel replied simply: "If I had made one, I should not desert it, but I am going without leaving any regrets behind me."

The announcement of this forthcoming departure made Marie Antoinette realise that, according to the expression of the time, she had an "inclination" towards the Swedish officer. When he came to take his leave "she could not take her eyes off him," a witness recounts, and "as she watched him they filled with tears."

But it was a false alarm. After a long wait at Le Havre the expedition was postponed and Fersen was obliged to return to Versailles. Although he did not ask for any post, thanks to the Queen he was appointed supernumerary officer to the regiment of the Royal Deux Ponts. Some of Marie Antoinette's associates began to find the Swede's attitude much less "restrained" and the officer wrote to his father: "The kindness she has shown me and this post of colonel have won me the jealousy of all the young men at court."

At Trianon Axel was invited to the intimate receptions. One evening the Queen, with obvious meaning, sang verses from the opera *Dido*, which was not performed in France until 1783:

> Ah! I was well inspired
> When I received you at my court.

Twenty-six years later, on hearing *Dido* performed at the Opera in Stockholm, Axel exclaimed: "How many memories and painful regrets does this opera recall to my heart!"

According to the Comte de Saint-Priest, "Mme de Polignac did not oppose her friend's preference. No doubt Vaudreuil and Besenval schemed for her because an isolated foreigner who was not very enterprising suited them much better than would a Frenchman, surrounded by relatives, who might win all the favours instead of themselves and perhaps end as head of a clique which would eclipse them all. The Queen was thus encouraged to follow her inclination, and she indulged in it without much prudence."

So as not to compromise the Queen any further Axel once more did all he could to go and fight in America. Finally, in March 1780, thanks to Breteuil and Vergennes, he was appointed aide-de-camp to General Rochambeau and left for Brest, where he embarked on 13 April in the *Jason*, a ship of 16 guns.

The Swedish Ambassador, boasting to Gustavus III of this "wisdom and prudence beyond his years," added: "Incidentally, the Queen is behaving with much more circumspection and wisdom than formerly."

Marie Antoinette had given Mercy her promise and this time she kept it. Two things helped her: the birth of Madame Royale and her inclination for Axel Fersen. The years 1779 and 1780 were certainly a decisive turning-point in Marie Antoinette's life. The whirlwind ceased and the classic countenance of the Queen of Trianon so dear to her later admirers appeared. It was at this time that Marie Antoinette left off feathers and wore instead "shepherdess hats" of simple straw. During this year she ordered 93 dresses, 41 formal dresses and 56 coats, but for all that everything was in "the simple style" for which Trianon was the ideal setting.

The year 1780 "marks the most interesting period in the history of Trianon," according to Pierre de Nolhac. Life went on in the "simplest" possible way. When the Queen entered the drawing-room the piano did not stop playing, the ladies' tapestry frames continued to work and the men did not break off their game of billiards or backgammon. The women wore dresses of white muslin with gauze fichus and straw hats. The men wore dress coats or long coats of cloth, the colour of "London soot," and lightened only by a collar of scarlet velvet.

Unfortunately Marie Antoinette was reproached for playing at the lady of the manor. Too many people were excluded. In June the only person staying at the château was Mme de Polignac, who shortly before had been made a Duchesse after giving birth on 14 May to Charles X's future Minister. Marie Antoinette had been so upset by her friend's confinement that the whole court had had to move to La Muette, so that the Queen could go every day to see Mme de Polignac, who lived at Passy. In this same month of May the new Duchesse had married her daughter, who was still an adolescent, to the Duc de Guiche. The girl, who henceforth was always called "Guichette," received a dowry of 800,000 livres (160 million francs) from Louis XVI, although dowries given by the King were usually not more than 6,000 livres. As a reward for having established her daughter so well the Duchesse received 400,000 livres (80 million francs), a duchy for the new-born son and the promise of lands with an income of 35,000 livres. Her lover, M. de Vaudreuil, was given an allowance of 30,000 livres (6 million francs) under the pretext that as his possessions were "in the islands" he was drawing no revenue, on account of the war.

One may imagine the disgraceful tone of the books and pamphlets. There was a jest current in Versailles: "Is Mme de Polignac's child the Queen's or M. de Vaudreuil's, since M. de Polignac has been in the country for a year?"

Marie Antoinette merely shrugged her shoulders. She was so glad to have the Duchesse in her little château of Trianon, that nothing else counted. On the second floor was "Guichette," whose husband, in view of his wife's youth, had been asked to stay at home. For the same reason a third guest, the young "Bichette," who had been married on 5 June to the Vicomte de Polastron, the brother of the Duchesse Jules, was also without her husband, who had been dispatched to his regiment the day after the wedding. Two cousins of the Polignacs made up the party: the beautiful Comtesse de Châlons, née d'Andlau, more than ever loved by the Duc de Coigny, and the brilliant Comtesse d'Andlau, daughter of Helvétius.

Even the ladies of honour remained at Versailles. As for the King, he occasionally came to dinner, when four entrées and two roasts were added to the menu. Louis XVI would not have had enough to eat with the meal served to the Queen and her guests—three soups, two main dishes, twelve entrées, four roasts, two medium entremets, fourteen little entremets and two dishes of pastries.

After the meal the coterie maintained a certain reserve for fear of a harsh remark from the King. "With the best intention of being polite to someone," writes Mme de Boigne, "he advanced towards them until they were against a wall. If he could think of nothing to say, which often happened, he gave a loud laugh, turned on his heel and went away." Five years of reign had not polished him, and he still possessed "no more gallantry in his manner," which was a great grievance to this dying society. Sometimes he would sit on the lap of young Narbonne and imitate a baby wanting to be nursed. Admittedly he was good, simple and natural, but these qualities were not greatly prized by Marie Antoinette's friends, for whom the possession of wit was the most important thing.

Sometimes, after dinner, the Queen gave a party in her own rooms and received a few privileged persons. But people slipped in uninvited and the porter asked the architect for double locks to all the doors.

The guests wandered in the famous garden of which all Europe was talking. The Hamlet was not built until later, but in the summer of 1780 the gardens were nearly finished. Marie Antoinette's own part had been important. It was she who had influenced the development of the final stage of the art of gardening in the 18th century. Neat rows, trim scalloped flower-beds, embroidered hedges, yews shaped like dragons, and "well-turned" bowers all seemed the height of boredom, melancholy and ugliness.

"Nature plants nothing in a line!" exclaimed M. de Wolmar in the *Nouvelle Héloïse,* and he added that it was amusing to see men "as though they were already tired of their walk on beginning it, construct it in a straight line so as to arrive at the end more quickly."

Marie Antoinette considered that Le Nôtre had massacred nature "by subjecting everything to the standard of architecture." But, as the Marquis de Girardin said, it is not enough, under the pretext of realism, "to substitute a winding garden for a square garden," one must "compose landscapes to interest the eye and the mind at the same time."

Marie Antoinette, fortunately, was concerned only with the eye and not with the mind. Away with those gardens Laborde speaks of, "containing a moral lesson," where "each tree has its sentimental motto," where "every rock utters something tender." Having "a thirst for rusticity," she wanted to "create reality." She intelligently rejected both the "turco-chinoiserie" of Antoine Richard and the artificial ruins advocated by Gabriel. She would have none of the fallen temples which so enthralled the Prince de Ligne. The Queen settled on the plan conceived by the Comte de Caraman. The former Lieutenant-General of Louis XV's armies proposed an uncultivated hillock covered with yews and box, a grotto and waterfall—this was the "Montagne de l'Escargot" —a "Swiss" rock, and a belvedere surmounted by a pavilion mirrored in a lake. The lake fed a river which meandered through the garden and after winding round a Temple of Love died away in two branches in front of the château.

Everything had to be constructed in record time, "for you know your mistress," we read in a report in the Archives, "she wishes to enjoy her garden very soon." In spite of the cost—352,275 livres in a single year—the garden rapidly took shape. A whole forest was transported from the royal nurseries of La Rochette, near Melun, to Versailles.

In 1780, too, Mique was working on the Queen's dwelling. In Marie Antoinette's boudoir there was a mechanism permitting mirrors to be moved to cover the windows in the evening: this was "the room of the moving mirrors." In the same year the library was painted in off-white and adorned with apple-green taffeta curtains. A lot of space on the shelves was given up to collections of plays—*French Drama* in fourteen volumes, *Bourgeois Drama, Dramatic Proverbs, Italian Plays, Society Plays, Country Plays*. These last two volumes were the favourites in 1780, for this year saw Marie Antoinette's début on the stage of the papier-mâché theatre at Trianon, which was completed that summer. Marie Antoinette was the leader of a "troupe" composed of Madame Elisabeth, her young sister-in-law, who was now one of her friends, the Comte d'Artois and the coterie—the new Duchesse de Polignac, her daughter "Guichette," her sister-in-law Comtesse Diane de Polignac, the Comte Esterhazy, Adhémar, Crussol and Vaudreuil, who was reputed to be "the best actor in Paris society." In the balcony there were only the King and the royal family. The Comtesse de Provence had been asked to join the troupe, but she was shocked and had refused. "It is beneath me!"

Astonished, the Queen remarked: "But if I, the Queen of France, act, you should not have any scruples."

"I may not be a Queen, but I am the stuff of which they are made."

This was the only memorable saying of her life and Madame remained a spectator, together with the King and the other members of the royal family. Even the Princes of the Blood were not admitted. In the boxes and the pit were those in service at Trianon. Campan had resumed his role of prompter, much to the fury of the First Gentleman of the Chamber, the Duc de Fronsac, son of the Maréchal de Richelieu, who, as one of the prerogatives of his position, should have had the ordering of "Her Majesty's amusements."

"You cannot be the First Gentleman when we are actors," explained the Queen. "Besides, I have already told you my wishes concerning Trianon. I hold no court here. I live here as a private person."

The troupe performed comic operas, or comedies with music: *L'Anglais à Bordeaux* by Favart, *Le Sorcier* by Poinsinet, *Rose et Colas* and *La Gageure Imprévue* by Sedaine. In the latter Marie Antoinette played the maid Gotte, who exclaimed: "We servants. . . ."

In Berthe's *Les Fausses Infidélités* Marie Antoinette chose the part of the charming Angélique, betrothed to the choleric Dormilly, played by Vaudreuil, whose temperament was far from placid.

"It's lifelike" declared the King, not without malice.

Louis XVI was delighted and applauded wildly, "particularly when the Queen performed her part of the play." During the interval he went on the stage, watched Marie Antoinette's "toilette" and congratulated her with tears in his eyes. And yet, it is said, it was "royally ill-played."

Marie Antoinette was an accomplished actress compared with the Comte d'Adhémar. In *Le Devin du Village* by J. J. Rousseau, in which he played Colin, his voice was so trembling that Marie Antoinette as Colette had difficulty in keeping a straight face when she saw him, disguised as a shepherd, on his knees declaring his love.

"Malice would be hard put to it to criticise the choice of such a lover," she said when the curtain fell.

But malice had something to go on with *Le Sabot Perdu*, a play with songs by Piis and Barré, which was staged a little later. It was the

Queen who, in the part of Babet, lost the famous sabot after having long resisted her suitor. The latter ended by kissing her and Babet sang:

> Dans l'plaisir où ton coeur s'épanche
> C'n'est pas agir d'une magnière franche
> Comment te pardonnerai
> De m'prendre ainsi c'que jallions donnai?

It was true that the scene was supposed to be taking place in the snow—hardly an exhilarating spot—and that the lover Colin was played by the Comte d'Artois. As Pierre de Nolhac has said "it was a kiss given in the family," but the pamphleteers did not see it that way.

When there was no performance, they played at *tire en jambe*—you mounted astride a stick and fought in that position. The King took part, but without amusement. There was also the famous *Descampativos*. This was the blindman's buff in reverse. The players were all covered with a large white sheet, except for the one who was "it," whom each in turn touched with a napkin and who had to guess the name of his assailant. There were forfeits, which had "to be redeemed by some odd penance, and the bustle occasioned by this often continued far into the night," according to Mercy. Needless to say, under the acid pen of the pamphleteers *Descampativos* became a veritable orgy.

In September the diversions at Trianon were somewhat overshadowed by the economies of Necker, Turgot's successor. The coterie was furious. Four hundred "principal idlers" and twelve hundred "subordinate idlers" of the King's household were dismissed.

"I want to bring order and economy into every part of my household," Louis XVI had declared. "If anyone has any objections I shall break them!"

Marie Antoinette was one of those who had objections. She is said to have warned Necker "that she did not care to manage her house in the style of the Rue Saint-Denis and to carry the keys of the cellar in her pocket."

Necker realised that his task would not be easy—in the following spring he abandoned it—but meanwhile, in default of large savings, he launched his famous loans, the interest on which encumbered the Treasury with a heavy burden which finally crushed it once and for all.

The coterie plucked up courage—it was not much affected by the plans of the Director-General of Finances—but the spectacles at the

Trianon were interrupted in October by the death of the Duchesse de Polignac's uncle, who was also a relative of M. de Vaudreuil, and the troupe rested. As the favourite and her lover were prevented by their mourning from treading the boards they consoled themselves, at the beginning of the winter of 1780, by taking on the role Besenval had asked them to play with the Queen. It was simply a question of "creating a Minister for War."

On 18 October 1780, after rather confused intrigues on the part of Marie Antoinette, Sartines had been replaced at the Ministry of the Marine by the Marquis de Castries.

"Is the Queen going to stop there?" Besenval asked Mme de Polignac. "Now she has the prestige of having created a Minister of the Marine, would she not also like to make a Minister for War?"

"Indeed, we should now turn our attention quickly and seriously to M. de Ségur."

It was a scheme dear to Besenval—to have the Prince de Montbarrey dismissed and his portfolio given to the Maréchal de Ségur. But, knowing the female mind, he had managed it so that Mme de Polignac should take an interest in this appointment and now the pretty scatter-brain thought that the idea had come from her. "I never stopped urging Mme de Polignac," relates Besenval, "so that she would stir up the Queen, who always replied that she was persisting with her plan, but that matters could not be hurried."

Maurepas certainly considered that Montbarrey should no longer remain in his post, but he, too, had his candidate: M. de Puységur. He therefore cleverly succeeded in persuading Marie Antoinette that "Mme de Polignac had taken advantage of the influence she had over her." Mercy had on several occasions tried out the worth of this argument with the Queen. Marie Antoinette was really angry and addressed bitter reproaches to her friend: "You wanted to sacrifice me to your personal wishes."

The Duchesse burst into tears and declared that she would leave the court. Marie Antoinette was in despair, "tears streamed down her face and she finally threw herself at Mme de Polignac's feet, imploring her to forgive her." The Duchesse's tears flowed faster, but they were tears of affection. The two friends fell into each other's arms, embraced—and Marie Antoinette promised to protect the Maréchal. Then the scene was forgotten and the appointment was delayed. Besenval returned to the attack, and "strongly urged" Mme de Polignac, reproaching her with not employing "the necessary energy."

With dramatic suddenness the Queen announced to her friend on 30 December that Puységur had been appointed. The coterie was amazed. On instructions from Besenval Mme de Polignac sent a note to Marie Antoinette, asking to see her urgently. The Queen obeyed and arrived at her friend's house at 11 o'clock in the evening. Well coached by the Baron, the favourite "represented forcibly to her how humiliating it was for her that M. de Maurepas should triumph on this occasion."

"Everyone is on the watch to see who will win—you or M. de Maurepas. It will be a shocking rebuff for the one who loses."

Marie Antoinette saw the distress in her friend's face and promised to see the King the next day. At seven in the morning she went to the King and did not mince her words. Maurepas, who lived above the King, in the apartments of Louis XV's mistresses, was called and put forward rather weak arguments against the appointment of Marie Antoinette's candidate. Louis XVI, who had just put up with a violent scene, yielded to his wife's wishes and agreed with all she said. Maurepas, unconvinced, looked at the King.

"Monsieur," pronounced the Queen, "you have heard the King's wishes. Go at once and send to M. de Ségur."

Maurepas bowed. "It was the severest blow of my life," he said later.

However, the choice was not a bad one, and the Maréchal would have been a worthy successor to Saint-Germain, were it not for his ruling of 22 May 1781, forbidding promotion to officers not possessing four quarterings.

Maria Theresa was not to know of her daughter's victory over Maurepas. Since mid-November the great Empress had been seriously ill with "a hardening of the lungs." She retained consciousness until the end. On 29 November she sighed: "This is my last day!"

At eight o'clock in the evening she was seized with choking, rose and supported by her son went to the window. Joseph II, seeing her terribly oppressed, asked: "Are you ill?"

"Ill enough to die."

Turning to her doctor she ordered: "Light the mortuary candle and close my eyes."

A minute later she expired in the arms of her son before the still-open window.

At Versailles the Abbé Vermond was entrusted by Louis XVI with breaking the news to Marie Antoinette. The Queen was overwhelmed. On 8 December the court went into mourning, the liveries became black and the court coaches were draped in violet and black. On the 10th Marie Antoinette tried to write to her brother, but could only trace a few lines while she shed tears. "I can no longer see what I am writing."

Her tears flowed faster when she learned that 48 hours before her death her mother had given her blessing to her absent children. Raising her hands to heaven, she had named each in turn: Leopold, Grand Duke of Tuscany, Maria-Cristina, Duchess of Saxe-Teschen, Amelia, Duchess of Parma, Maria-Carolina, Queen of Sicily and Naples. Then, after a moment's silence, she had almost shouted the last name: "Marie Antoinette, Queen of France!" And she had burst into sobs.

Since 31 July 1775, when the Empress had written to Mercy from Schoenbrunn: "My daughter is hastening to her ruin," she knew there was no hope. Marie Antoinette, in the Empress's own expression, was "hurrying to destruction." Maria Theresa had not complained about the amusements at Trianon—"I regard them as transient," she said to Mercy—but with her astonishing clear-sightedness she had not concealed her anxiety at the dangerous void Marie Antoinette had brought about at court so as to remain with her dear friends. In her last letter to Mercy, on 3 November, she had approved and judged "very sound" the observations the Ambassador had thought it his duty to make to Marie Antoinette on her return from Trianon: "A great court must be accessible to many people, otherwise hatred and jealousy turn everyone's heads and give rise to complaints, dislike and a kind of estrangement."

In the calm of her private apartments, where she had shut herself up with the Duchesse de Polignac, Marie Antoinette could re-read the last letter sent to her by her mother: "I am very glad that you intend to resume your state at Versailles. I know how tedious and empty it is, but believe me, if there is none the disadvantages that result are much greater than the little inconveniences of holding state, particularly in your country, with such an impetuous nation."

Marie Antoinette had in fact promised her mother to stop being merely "Queen of Trianon." But, unfortunately, it was too late and the "kind of estrangement" Mercy had spoken of had taken place. At the end of the previous year she had made an effort to be in her apartments three days a week, but no greater number of people came to Versailles.

Her coterie had finally kept at a distance all who might surround the throne in case of danger. Marie Antoinette did not yet realise this isolation. The great machine was still in motion and its wheels hardly creaked. But during ten years at Versailles and six years of reign the Queen had succeeded in estranging for ever all those she had ignored, those she had despised, those she had mocked, those who were not among her beloved "associates," those who seemed to her too old, those who had come so many times to Versailles without getting a glimpse of their sovereign, those to whom she refused to speak and above all those who had been her friends, her companions of pleasure and whom she now ignored, such as the Duc de Chartres, who was already the centre of a group. The sister-in-law of the future regicide, the Princesse de Lamballe, who was barely tolerated at court in 1779, was also excluded from the gatherings of 1780, and in the autumn she left court to take refuge with the Duc de Penthièvre. She had yielded, but the Duc de Chartres was far from being resigned to his disgrace. Marie Antoinette had not even defended him after the Battle of Ouessant, where his conduct as commodore had been despicable. It was even said that she had sided with the jesters who did not spare the Duke with jokes about his "cowardice." Moreover, in July 1779, in order to spare him "the severity of an order from the King," the Queen had written to him advising him to leave the army, which was threatening England from Saint Malo, and return to the Palais Royal. Louis XVI did not like his cousin and had no intention of running the risk of seeing the man who was to become head of the younger branch be more successful on land than on sea. The Duc de Chartres obeyed and returned to the Palais Royal, where, at a distance from the court, he retired into private life while waiting to throw himself into the opposition. But in 1780 the Palais Royal clan was already attracting the malcontents and opposing itself to that of Trianon.

While waiting to send each other to the scaffold they continued to wage war with pinpricks. Marie Antoinette did not seem to attach much importance to it. In this she resembled the Duc de Chartres, who when faced with the attacks of his enemies—for he also had a great many— merely repeated his famous: "Je m'en f. . ."

With her eyes shut to all this, Marie Antoinette asked M. de Boufflers to compose a song "in which he would successively enumerate all the faults with which she was reproached in libellous publications." The Chevalier did so, and drew a picture of the Queen under the name of Thémire.

> Air: "Phyllis asks for her portrait"
> Are you concerned to hear
> What's said about Thémire?
> At moments, it is said,
> You'd think she'd lost her head.
> Is that really so?
> Yes, but you must know
> She can so fashion it
> That her strange lack of wit
> Would even captivate
> A mind of Cato's weight.
>
> Too much good sense, 'tis said,
> Has never plagued her head,
> But incense, so they say,
> Enchants her all the day.
> Is that really so?
> Yes, but you must know
> So full of skill is she
> That every deity
> Would come down to adore her
> And burn incense before her.
>
> If she has promised you
> A private rendezvous
> Or business talk, they say,
> She soon forgets the day.
> Is that really so?
> Yes, but you must know
> That when you meet once more
> Her faults fly through the door,
> And time itself will fly
> Only too quickly by.
>
> Self-centredness supreme—
> That is her guiding theme.
> She loves herself, they say,

> As dearly as she may.
> Is that really so?
> Yes, but you must know
> She must be left her creed.
> Can she be blamed, indeed,
> For loving as she does
> What everybody loves?

The Queen was not angry. On the contrary, the author of the *Mémoires secrets* goes so far as to assert that "Her Majesty deigned to sing it herself to her court." It must be admitted that Marie Antoinette's lively intelligence, mentioned by certain historians, is no more than a pious legend!

When she finally opened her eyes and understood, she was in a cell in the Conciergerie and the executioner was binding her hands.

8

✤

The Pure Soul

IN 1781 MARIE ANTOINETTE was pregnant for the second time. She would be 26 on 2 November. What had become of the little Arch-duchess with the slender bosom and childish eyes? She now possessed what, on a throne, is better than flawless beauty—the bearing of a Queen.

"If I were not a Queen," she said to Mme Vigée-Lebrun, "one would almost say I looked insolent, don't you think?"

They said so, in spite of her position. How many of her contemporaries, from the Comte de Séneffe to the young Camille Desmoulins, seeing her behind the windows of her coach, were struck by her "haughty air" and her "arrogant look."

Her page, the Baron de Tilly, who did not like her, drew this portrait of her: "She had eyes which were not beautiful, but could assume every expression. Kindness or dislike were mirrored in this look more strikingly than I have ever seen elsewhere. I am not sure that her nose matched the rest of her face. Her mouth was decidedly unattractive; that thick, prominent and sometimes drooping lip has been quoted as giving her countenance a mark of nobility and distinction, but it could only be used to indicate anger and indignation, and that is not the habitual expression of beauty. Her skin was admirable and so were her shoulders and neck. Her bosom seemed rather too full and her waist might have been more elegant. I have never seen such beautiful arms and hands. She had two ways of walking: one decided, rather hurried and always noble; the other more relaxed and swaying, I would almost say caressing, but without provoking any loss of respect. No one ever curtsied with so much grace, saluting ten people in one single bend and giving each his due in look and inclination of the head. In a word, unless I am mistaken, just as one offers a chair to other women, one would almost always have been inclined to draw up her throne."

Looking at her portraits we can realise the defects in this face, which was yet so attractive: a forehead too broad, a rather thick nose, short-sighted eyes and a heavy chin. With age the famous Austrian lip had become more pronounced. Burgundian lip would be more accurate, for Charles the Bold was the first to have it. But what would mar another face is hardly noticeable here. One sees only that dazzling colouring of a blonde, the incomparable texture of the skin, that Greek neck, that long waist, the somewhat heavy but beautiful breasts and the body that seemed made for love.

"She was then at the height of her youth and beauty," wrote Mme Vigée-Lebrun, who had watched her for many hours as she painted her. "Marie Antoinette was tall, beautifully made, rather plump, but not too much so. Her arms were superb, her hands small and perfectly shaped and her feet charming. She walked better than any woman in France, holding her head high with a majesty which made one recognise the sovereign among all her court. . . . Her features were not regular. She had inherited from her family the long, narrow oval, peculiar to the Austrians. But what was most remarkable in her face was the radiance of her complexion.

"I have never seen any so brilliant, and brilliant is the word, for her skin was so transparent that it held no shadows. For this reason I could never reproduce it as I wished. I had no colours to paint that freshness, those fine shades which could be seen only in that charming face and which I have never found in any other woman."

Mme Vigée-Lebrun has painted another picture of Marie Antoinette which, though not on canvas, is still charmingly coloured. Suffering from an advanced pregnancy, Mme Vigée-Lebrun missed an appointment the Queen had given her, and on the following day, distressed and confused, she arrived at the château at the very moment when Marie Antoinette was about to enter her carriage.

"My heart was beating, for I was all the more afraid since I was in the wrong. The Queen turned towards me and said gently: 'I waited for you yesterday all the morning. What happened to you?'

" 'Alas! Madame,' I replied, 'I was so unwell that I was not able to obey Your Majesty's orders. I have come today to receive them and I am leaving again at once.'

"'No, no! Do not go,' replied the Queen. 'I would not like you to have made the journey for nothing.' She dismissed her carriage and gave me a sitting.

"I remember that in my eagerness to respond to her kindness I seized my paint-box so quickly that it was upset. My brushes and pencils fell on the floor and I stooped to repair my clumsiness.

"'Leave them,' said the Queen. 'In your condition you should not bend down.' And in spite of my protests she picked everything up herself."

Another thing that emerges from the portraits of Marie Antoinette is a great purity. Joseph II, who made a short stay at Versailles in 1781, several times expressed his astonishment, in view of the Queen's "associates" and "the prevailing licentious tone," at seeing his sister's virtue untouched. According to the Prince de Ligne, "her discretion inspired as much respect as her majesty. One could no more forget it than forget oneself. In her presence no one dared venture an indelicate remark, a ribald story or a marked piece of spite." It had certainly not been so before 1780, during the "reign" of the Comte d'Artois, but the Prince de Ligne was gallant and remembered only the Queen's "pure soul." Prudery had come with the birth of Madame Royale.

"I do not meet women separated from their husbands," she declared, when refusing to receive the Princesse de Monaco.

When in 1781 young Tilly wrote a comedy taken from a story by Marmontel and entitled *Laurette, or Virtue Rewarded By Love*—a "delightful play in the best of taste," if the author is to be believed—Marie Antoinette forbade her page to give it to the actors.

"But, Madame, is there any harm in having it staged?"

"No harm, no, but it is not seemly. A gentleman should not advertise himself."

And when the young man persisted and quoted the example of M. de Boufflers and the Cardinal de Bernis, she interrupted him: "You will oblige me by giving no more thought to it."

Tilly, incidentally, behaved badly, spent too much and went in for amusements. Having read Mercy's letters one is surprised to find this lecture from the Queen: "Behave according to your duty and you will get from me all the support you would wish to receive. You should dress more simply. In the last two days you have had two embroidered suits. Although you have a sufficient fortune it will not be enough if your tastes outrun it. Why this hair style and these curls? Are you going on the stage? Simplicity will not make you noticed, but it will bring you esteem."

Reading Tilly's *Memoirs*, edited by Christian Melchior-Bonnet, we can almost hear the sound of Marie Antoinette's voice. The scene begins one morning in the Hall of Mirrors, when the Queen was on her way to chapel. "Having noticed me, she did me the honour to greet me and to speak to me as she walked, so that I followed her. After putting several questions she was silent for a moment, and I seized the opportunity to take the liberty of telling her that I very much wished to throw myself at her feet and that I begged Her Majesty to hear me for a minute. 'Come to see me before five o'clock,' was her answer."

Tilly presented himself at the appointed hour. "An usher informed me that the Queen was not in her room but that she would soon return. In fact before five minutes had elapsed she came back.

" 'Good day. Where did you dine?'

" 'With Mme de Beauvilliers, Madame.'

" 'My Mme de Beauvilliers?'

" 'No, Madame, Madame Adelaide's.'

" 'Does she give dinners?'

" 'Yes, Madame, at least she does for me, whom she knew as a child and with whom she makes no ceremony.'

" 'If M. de Champcenetz had been at Versailles you would have dined with him. There is someone who is good company!'

" 'Madame, he has some wit and much gaiety.'

" 'Oh! he is charming. He will go far! Well, Monsieur, what do you want? Come in.'

" 'I beg the Queen to listen to me with indulgence, because I may take longer than I should.'

" 'But of course I shall listen to you.'

" 'Madame, there is a gentleman arrived here, a sort of magistrate, to whom my parents wish well, as I do also. He would like to obtain a post at Alençon, it is vacant—here it is written on a piece of paper—it all depends on M. de Miromesnil. My friend is a very worthy man and I should be happy if he had this post. One word from the Queen to the Keeper of the Seals and it is clear . . .'

" 'Well, it is clear . . .'

" 'Yes, Madame, that he could not refuse . . .'

" 'Is that all?'

" 'Yes, Madame.'

" 'I shall write. Give me that paper.'

" 'Madame, it is very crumpled.'

" 'Give me that paper. Come back tomorrow at half-past three. The letter will be ready. Goodbye.'

" 'I do not know how to express all my gratitude to the Queen.'

" 'By behaving well.' "

Let us follow the affair and see how posts were "wangled" in those days. The page went to see Miromesnil and explained the "gentleman's" wishes. The Keeper of the Seals leapt: "My God! your head's been turned, bold youth! You ask for a post which is the reward of the highest services and demands a degree of competence of which you have given no proof!"

Smiling and triumphant Tilly showed Marie Antoinette's letter. Miromesnil was taken aback and stammered: "Monsieur, I am sure that Her Majesty did not know what difficulty . . . How it is, I should say *almost* impossible . . . However . . . All my happiness is in obeying the Queen's orders."

When Joseph II made his second journey to Versailles in July 1781 Marie Antoinette gave an evening party for her brother in her beloved Trianon. The Comte de Liedekerque-Beaufort, page to the Comte de Provence, gives an account of it in his *Souvenirs,* of which only a few fragments have appeared in the *Revue de Paris.* "We arrived at the château, where all was confusion and freedom. In our gold livery we had no difficulty in entering. We passed one antechamber and were making our way towards the smell of food in the dining room. We were very surprised and embarrassed, although we were pages, to find ourselves in the salon where coffee was laid out for the royal party. As we were about to leave through one of the doors the two sides opened and we were face to face with the Queen and Joseph II, who was handing her out before the rest of the company into the coffee room. You may imagine our fright. It did not last long. The Queen was amused and said with gaiety and kindness: 'Well, where are you going, my little friends?' Her gentle smile reassured us and we confessed that as we were dying of hunger in the garden, her beautiful feast would be rather depressing for us unless someone gave us a piece of cake, which we had come to ask for in the pantry, but had mistaken the door.

" 'Well,' she said to her brother, 'they are very nice, they are not afraid to speak the truth.'

"She made us come back with her into the coffee room and made us sit down in a corner and help ourselves to cakes, brioches, etc., and there we were taking our coffee together with all the distinguished people, to whose teasing, including that of Joseph II, we replied gaily, without losing a bite. We were delighted to be told afterwards that we could follow the royal party all through the gardens, as for the moment we were part of Monseigneur's suite. We followed, as may be imagined, at a respectful distance. Soon a trellised door was opened leading to a private alley, in which, however, there were already a great many distinguished people who had come in beforehand by means of private tickets, so that there was already a great crowd of strollers. They were needed, too, to give a better idea of a crowd at a fair. To this end stalls had been erected on either side of the alley, as in a real fair. Ladies attached to the court, and elegantly disguised as vendors, invited the purchase of lottery tickets at their stalls, offering them on credit. No one waited to be asked twice. They knew that that meant that the number they received corresponded to one of the little things on show, which were thus intended as gifts, and everyone seized their little prize."

Where can Marie Antoinette be better evoked? Perhaps in that salon at Trianon "where coffee was laid out for the royal party," in which garlands of wild flowers adorned the wood panelling, that salon upholstered in green velvet with gold braid "*à la Bourgogne,*" where one can still see on the marble violet chimneypiece the two vases of petrified wood sent from Vienna in 1780 by Joseph II. Better still, in her bedroom next door. It was indeed *her* bedroom, for the King never slept in this mezzanine room whose walls were covered with muslin and embroidered silk in bright colours. In the adjoining boudoir doves, incense-burners, crowns, quivers and rose trees adorned the delicate woodwork. Is it here that her presence can still be felt by lovers of the past? Either here or at Versailles in her little apartments looking out on the courtyard of the Œil-de-Bœuf. In spite of the lack of light in these delightful little rooms, one can understand that Marie Antoinette preferred to live in these charming jewel boxes which suited her so well, rather than in her sumptuous bedroom shimmering with gold and silver brocade on a background of crimson, or in her marble and stucco salon looking out on the south lawn.

She liked best to stay in her "inner room," the most modern room in the château, whose winged sphinx and smoking antique tripods presaged the Empire style, where she sat on a couch in an alcove of mirrors draped in silk. There were her writing desk, her workbasket and her clavichord, on which she often played Mozart's music.

It was in this room that she received the famous singer P. J. Garat, "the Bordeaux wonder," who was presented by his father, a magistrate in Parliament, and accompanied by the musician Salieri.

"How is this, M. Garat," she reproached him, "you have brought your son to Paris, an excellent musician and an accomplished singer, and you have not presented him!"

The younger Garat defended himself, explaining that he knew only dialect songs of Aquitaine.

"'Well, let us hear your Gascon songs.'"

Salieri sat down at the piano. Marie Antoinette was delighted, particularly as Garat took care to translate each poem into French.

"But, M. Garat, do you know no music from the French operas?"

"I have not learnt any, Madame, as my father has allowed me to waste my time only in studying law."

The Queen laughed, and the magistrate was enough of a courtier to follow her example.

"What, nothing at all?"

"Well, Madame, I went to the Opera yesterday and heard *Armide*. I might be able to remember some of it."

"Ah! good! M. Salieri, would you take the music and accompany M. Garat?"

His memory did not betray him and young Garat sang all the solos from the famous opera. Marie Antoinette was overjoyed and applauded.

"We shall meet again, Monsieur," she said, giving him her hand to kiss.

When she rested after dinner during her second pregnancy, which in September 1781 was entering its eighth month, Marie Antoinette deserted her bedroom dominated by the vast bed with its great arched canopy surmounted by a "coping richly sculptured with flowers and garlands." She opened the door of the alcove and entered the little passage she had asked Mique to arrange for her, "Her Majesty wishing to be alone whenever she thinks necessary, without disturbing her suite or being disturbed by them." Only too rarely did she open the door on the right leading to her library, which had just been completed and where that very year Campan had arranged the Queen's books, which she never opened. Sometimes she would pull open one of the drawers by its handle in the form of a two-headed Austrian eagle and turn the pages of a book of engravings. But after dinner she preferred to retire to her new *Méridienne*, which Mique had finished in September 1781, and lie down in the mirrored alcove in which from a certain angle one could see oneself without a head. How many times must her blue eyes have wandered over the admirable frames—gems chiselled by Forestier—which surrounded the plate glass and repeated the design of the admirable woodwork, by the Rousseau brothers: branches and crowns of roses, royal lilies, cupids, hearts pierced with an arrow, Austrian eagles and dolphins. An allegory of the love and power of the Dauphin she was awaiting with so much impatience, the Dauphin who was stirring within her, for this time she was sure she would give birth to a king.

No one could have been more maternal. How she had trembled at the beginning of October in the previous year, and how distressed she had been at the sight of Madame Royale's "great pain," when "several of her teeth were coming through at once." On 11 October, in her last letter to the Empress, she had described how touched she had been "by the sweetness and patience of the poor little thing in her suffering." Then there was the day, not so long ago, when someone had asked the little Princess where her mother was. "Without anyone telling her, the poor little thing smiled at me and held out her arms. This was the first time she had shown that she recognised me. I confess that it gave me great joy, and I believe that I now love her even more."

Louis XVI, in the whole of his lifetime, wrote two narratives: one page concerning the birth of Madame Royale and two sheets recounting the Queen's confinement on 22 October 1781. Let us have it in his words: "The Queen had a very good night from 21 to 22 October. She had a few small pains when she woke, but they did not prevent her from taking her bath. She left it at half-past ten. The pains continued slight. I gave orders for the shoot I was to have held at Saclé only at midday. Between noon and half-past the pains increased. She lay down on her delivery bed and at exactly a quarter-past one by my watch she was successfully delivered of a boy. During her labour there were in the room only Mme de Lamballe, Monsieur, the Comte d'Artois, my aunts, Mme de Chimay, Mme de Mailly, Mme d'Ossun, Mme de Tavannes and Mme de Guéménée, who took turns to go into the Salon de la Paix, which had been left empty. In the *Grand Cabinet* were my Household and the Queen's, the *grandes entrées*, and the sub-governors, who entered when the final pains began and stood at the back of the room so as not to impede the air."

Infinitely preferable to this official report is the extract from a letter to King Gustavus of Sweden from M. de Stedingk, Fersen's friend: "After a quarter of an hour's suspense one of the Queen's women, all dishevelled and excited, entered and cried: 'A Dauphin! But you must not mention it yet.'

"Our joy was too great to be suppressed. We hurried out of the apartment, which led into the hall of the Queen's Guards. The first person I met there was Madame, who was rushing to the Queen's room. I called out to her: 'A Dauphin, Madame! What happiness!' It was only the effect of chance and my extreme joy, but this seemed amusing and it is retold in so many ways that I am very much afraid that it will not make me liked by Madame. . . .

"The Queen's antechamber presented a charming sight. Everyone's joy was at its height and all heads were turned. People who hardly knew each other laughed and wept by turns. Men and women fell on each other's necks and even those who cared least for the Queen were carried away by the general rejoicing. But it was very different an hour after the birth, when the two doors of the Queen's room were opened and M. le Dauphin was announced. Mme de Guéménée, beaming with joy, held him in her arms and was wheeled across the apartments in her armchair to take him to her rooms. Everyone wanted to touch the child, or even just the chair. A crowd followed him, adoring. When he had arrived in his apartments, an Archbishop wanted to decorate him with a blue ribbon, but the King said he should first of all be a Christian. The baptism took place at three o'clock in the afternoon.

"At first no one had dared tell the Queen it was a Dauphin, for fear of arousing too strong an emotion. Everyone around her held in their feelings so well that the Queen, seeing only constraint about her, thought it was a daughter. She said: 'You see how reasonable I am. I have asked no questions.'

"Seeing her anxiety, the King thought it was time to reassure her. With tears in his eyes he said: 'M. le Dauphin begs to enter.'

"They brought her the child and those who witnessed the scene say they have never seen anything so touching. She said to Mme de Guéménée, who took the child: 'Take him, he belongs to the State, but I now take back my daughter.'"

In Paris the "Gentlemen," the ushers and the Governor took part in the traditional ceremonies and in full procession walked three times round the bonfire. This time they wore garlands and bracelets of flowers, artificial flowers, "in view of the season." The tocsin rang without ceasing for three days and nights, money was distributed to the people, buffets were set out under the wind and for two days all work in Paris was stopped. The women replaced their gold cross by a dolphin; the locksmiths presented the King with a mysterious lock which he could not manage to open; the chimney-sweeps brought to Versailles a chimney "large enough for one of them to hide in it"; the bakers made bread "in the Queen's vestibule" which "Her Majesty found delicious"; and finally the fruiterers presented a charming silver cauldron for the newborn child's food.

The Parisians dispatched verses and songs. Even a certain Collot d'Herbois sent the Queen an ode which ended with the lines:

> O sheltering heaven, protect
> The life of Antoinette!

This was the future regicide Collot d'Herbois!

Another poet preferred to make fun of his colleagues and sent this quatrain to the château:

> O Monseigneur, you are indeed in luck,
> Not for being born to govern France,
> But on account of your total ignorance
> Of all we're grinding out in the way of poetic muck.

The fishwives came from Paris and recited to the King a song whose verses made a point of being, in the words of those ladies, "broad and unkempt," so unkempt, indeed, that we can transcribe only the first three lines:

> *Notre charmante Antoinette*
> *Vient de faire un petit bout*
> *Et j'avais vu la croquette. . . .*

The description of the said "croquette" apparently delighted Louis XVI and he laughingly demanded an encore. The ladies did not wait to be asked twice and began again "with contortions, grimaces and gestures" to help. Side by side with its beribboned graces the 18th century offers us these surprises reminiscent of the Middle Ages.

On Friday 26 October the "Gentlemen" went in ceremonial dress to Notre Dame, where a *Te Deum* was sung in the King's presence. Two days later they again put on their robes and went by carriage to Versailles to inform His Majesty of their wish to admire the Dauphin. Louis XVI granted them this favour, but, according to the report, "ordered the Mayor to use the title of Monseigneur" to the child who was not yet a week old. The "Gentlemen" bowed and "advanced towards Monseigneur, who was in his cradle, and the Mayor offered congratulations on behalf of the city." At his side stood his appropriately-named nurse, Mme Poitrine, superintended by a *"gardienne du Ventre,"* who never left her "so as to report to the Faculty on her state of health."

On Tuesday 31 October the city authorities returned to congratulate Marie Antoinette, who received the city clerk and told him that she was "as well as could be wished."

Paris then considered it had done enough. Times were hard and the capital would have preferred to postpone the festivities, *Te Deum* and entries until the fine weather. The city's finances were in a bad state. During the preceding year seven Princes or Princesses allied to the royal family had died: Louise of Brunswick, the Comte of Modena, the Duke of Wolfenbüttel, the Duchess of Württemberg, the Electress Dowager of Saxony, Prince Charles of Lorraine, Marie Antoinette's uncle and finally Maria Theresa. Admittedly, the King was generous enough each time to present the "Gentlemen" with a "mourning robe" with weepers, but all this mourning had cost the city a great deal, 2,700 to 3,000 livres for each death. On the preceding 30 May Paris had been obliged to have a solemn service celebrated at Notre Dame for Maria Theresa and to dress the heralds in a violet velvet dalmatic, and the king-at-arms and the official crier in a black robe with the Empress's arms on the front—not to mention the church, which had to be draped in black, and the costly allegories which were constructed above the portico and around the catafalque.

M. de Caumartin, the Mayor, in view of the frequent and costly journeys of the city council each time a member of the royal family had a "tertian fever," was of the opinion that on this occasion the rejoicings could be postponed until later. Feasts in the middle of winter were twice as expensive, and besides there was already a shortage of bread. But Marie Antoinette asked laughingly if they were waiting until Monseigneur was old enough to dance at the ball to be given in the Hôtel de Ville and the "Gentlemen" obeyed. The feast would take place on the 21 and 23 January. But the citizens, who were at close quarters with the poverty in the city, grumbled, and the rejoicings started badly.

Some precautions were therefore taken. The simplest consisted in increasing the number of charcoal braziers, buffets and orchestras so as to disperse the ordinary people and prevent them from gathering in a mass before the Hôtel de Ville, where the fireworks were to be set off. So that the King and Queen could see better, a long wooden gallery was built at the site of the display. Although Marie Antoinette was to stay only a few hours at the Hôtel de Ville, a room was fitted up in blue damask with the ceiling "mingled with flowers," as well as a wardrobe room draped with crimson material. In order that the sovereigns would not have to bring their own Officers of the Mouth, the "Gentlemen" created the post of "city maître d'hôtel."

M. de Caumartin might well sigh. A contributory cause was that the Princes of the Blood, who had been invited only to the reception after the banquet, had told the King that "being unable to be of any use to him on this occasion," when they would be "mixed up with everyone else," they preferred to remain at home. A great deal of trouble was caused by this princely bad humour.

The Dukes, too, were discontented. They had actually been invited with the same formula as that used for the nobility. The Mayor did not know what to do, for if there had been two formulas the nobility would have been offended.

By the morning of 21 January everything was ready. The weather was superb. During the night the mud under which Paris was submerged had been cleared away and the inhabitants had carefully swept before their doors and prepared the "fire pots" to illuminate their houses in the evening. For their part the city authorities had 6,201 fire pots and 3,141 lamps placed on the public monuments, and M. de Caumartin sighed again at the thought of the bill.

The Queen arrived from La Muette alone at nine o'clock. As it was her churching she had the right to a special entry. In her carriage were Madame Elisabeth, who now attended all the ceremonies, Madame Adelaide, the Duchesse de Bourbon, the Princesse de Chimay and Mme de Lamballe, who now came to court only to carry out the duties of her post.

At the Porte de la Conférence the Governor, according to custom, knelt on one knee to make his speech to the Queen, and Marie Antoinette "replied with all her own particular grace."

This time Paris's welcome was as it should be. It was, of course, far from the wild applause at the beginning of the reign, but as the Queen had assured the succession people wanted to show their joy.

After the ceremony in Notre Dame, where she knelt on the flagstones to say the prayers for her churching, and after the visit to Sainte Geneviève, Marie Antoinette proceeded to the Pont au Bled, to the sound of the tocsin and the city artillery. In front of the old Hôtel de Ville she descended from her carriage, not without having to hear another speech, and went to wait for the King in her blue damask room.

Louis XVI, who had left La Muette in grand array at a quarter-to-one, arrived in the Place de l'Hôtel de Ville an hour later, accompanied by his two brothers, the Grand Equerry, Prince de Lambesq, the First Equerry, Duc de Coigny and the Captain of the Guards, Duc d'Ayen.

Only Provence and Artois were to sit at the royal table, in company with 76 women. M. de Caumartin presented the King's napkin and tasted each dish by putting a small piece of bread to the food. Mme de la Porte, the Mayor's sister, served the Queen. The other "Gentlemen" bustled round the Princes and Princesses, while the ladies were served by 70 valets in scarlet uniform with gold frogging. The other tables were served by 230 valets dressed in the same way—and M. de Caumartin's sighs were by now innumerable. The dishes were brought by 150 city guards in uniform but without rifle or hat.

Tiers had been built on either side for the "people of the highest consideration," but this consideration did not go so far as to offer them anything to eat. There was an endless file of people behind the railings which had been set up "to give everyone the opportunity of enjoying a noble and magnificent spectacle." The meal, which began at a quarter-to-three, ended at five, but only for the royal table, for there had been a certain amount of disorganisation in the kitchens. The Dukes' table, among others, had only reached the *hors-d'oeuvre*, and according to the clerk's report: "MM. les Ducs had only radishes and butter to eat, as His Majesty rose from the table." One can imagine their ill humour, particularly as "MM. les Ducs" had to be turned out in order to clear the large room. It was from here that after the reception the sovereigns would watch the fireworks being let off from a Temple of Hymen adorned with dolphins. "The fireworks," the clerk reported frankly, "did not come up to expectations, either because of the bad management of the artificer, Master La Varinière, or because of the bad weather."

The city officials then all went back with the King and Queen to La Muette. In the Rue Saint-Honoré the Queen stopped her carriage in front of the Hôtel de Noailles, where stood, bare-headed, the Marquis de Lafayette, who had just returned from America covered with glory and had not yet been able to present himself at Versailles. He came to the door of the coach to bow, and Marie Antoinette gave the hero of the day her hand to kiss.

The coaches then resumed their way towards the Cours la Reine and, the clerk concluded briefly, "the Governor went away and the Gentlemen also."

Two days later the masked ball took place. It was the last great festivity of the old régime. Thirteen thousand people had been invited. More than twice as many came and complete confusion reigned over the evening. Marie Antoinette, who came although she was not expected, was nearly suffocated. The buffets were rifled and every corner of the Hôtel de Ville invaded, although places had been set aside "where people who were tired or who wished to leave could rest and more conveniently wait for their carriages." Marie Antoinette left at two o'clock, but the ball went on until seven in the morning. On the same day the indefatigable Mayor and four magistrates went to Versailles to thank the King and Queen, and much to M. de Caumartin's relief, they received 30,000 livres to cover part of the expenses.

The "Gentlemen" were touched by this gesture and when, a little later, Marie Antoinette was suffering from erysipelas a city officer went every day to inquire after her health. And when, at Pont Notre Dame, a Parisian fisherman caught a sturgeon six-and-a-half feet long (times have changed somewhat), the magistrates hastened to buy the fish and to have a "bath" made to carry the monster to Versailles to be presented alive to the King and Queen. They arranged for a whole cavalcade of mules with barrels "to refresh and change the water from time to time," but the sturgeon died and was taken by coach to Versailles, where it was admired by everyone before being sent to the kitchens.

On 30 January M. de Caumartin was again at Versailles to "stroll about" at the ball given to the Queen in the opera house of the château by the bodyguards, still in honour of the Dauphin's birth.

"Have you come to learn how to give a party?" a masked figure asked him, bursting into laughter.

It had to be admitted that the evening was particularly successful. Marie Antoinette opened the ball at five in the afternoon with M. de Moret, the oldest bodyguard. Artois danced with Mme de Condé and "Guichette" with the Duc de Bourbon.

At six o'clock the guards let in the common people and showed them to the buffet "which contributed not a little to their applause expressed by cries of 'Ah! that's good!' and clinkings of glasses accompanied by 'Long live the King! Long live the Queen! Long live M. le Dauphin and all the family!'" During a silence a voice was even heard to cry: "Long live the wine and pie the Guards have given me!"

At eight o'clock the people were shown out and the bodyguards sat down to eat. The French Guards, "who had been keeping order indoors," succeeded them.

The evening was not yet over, for the masked ball was yet to come. The King came back at about eleven, "but His Majesty was overcome by sleep and went to bed at half-past eleven." Marie Antoinette stayed, and enjoyed herself. She had come in a black domino, but as she was soon recognised she changed her disguise three times during the night.

She was still fond of balls but considered that at her age—she was not yet thirty—she ought not to dance as much as she used. In three or four years she would allow herself no more than a quadrille or a *colonne anglaise* in an evening. When the King was present etiquette required him to dance without ever turning his back on his wife. Hampered by this acrobatic feat, he was sometimes overtaken by the music, "but then," Horace Walpole declared gallantly, "it is wrong to dance in time!"

Ah! those balls given by the Queen! In fifty years' time the last supporters of Charles X, exiled in Prague with the former Comte d'Artois, would speak of them with emotion. In those days they had been pages "charged with doing the honours." At a gracious smile from Marie

Antoinette, who supervised everything, they would accompany the ladies "with the easy manner of their age and the politeness of their rank," to give them refreshments and return them to their places. The ballroom was on the left of the royal courtyard, on the spot where there is now a passage leading to the park by the princes' courtyard.

In a few hours the department of the *Menus Plaisirs* would enlarge the pillared hall by means of wooden pavilions. "One entered first into a leafy grove adorned with statues and rose trees and ending in an open temple, where the billiard room was," related one of the Queen's pages. "On the right little paths led to the ballroom and to the gaming room, and so that those who were playing could see the dancing without losing the warmth of this fine room one of the doors had been made of an enormous piece of plate glass, so transparent that a Swiss Guard had to be placed as a sentinel to prevent careless people from trying to walk through it. The ballroom was a rectangle, to which one descended by a few steps. All around was a gallery, which allowed people to walk about without interrupting the dancing, which could be watched between the pillars. It was from here that people not presented and admitted to the boxes surrounding the ballroom could see the dancing."

In winter heating pipes warmed the apartments and in summer cascades of water falling into vast marble shells brought a pleasing freshness to the ballroom. From the gallery one could watch the dancers, whose black suits embroidered with jet and plumed hats shimmered and sparkled in the light.

Newcomers were watched with particular attention. Woe betide anyone who might commit a gaffe, like the "almost fashionable" M. de Chabannes, who had the misfortune to fall during a quadrille, exclaiming "Jesus Maria!" The nickname stuck. "He went to fight in America," Mme de Boigne tells us, "and gained some distinction, but he came back 'Jesus Maria' as he had left." The Duc de Guines had reason to tell his daughters on the day of their presentation at court: "Remember that here vices are without importance, but ridicule can be fatal."

Certain "elderly young men" danced bare-headed, for, by a characteristic quibble of the age, "they were supposed not to have come to dance and consequently were not dressed for it." Refreshments could be found nearby in a semi-circular hall, where there were enormous baskets of fruit and pastries and large urns full of wine. In some small rooms there were maids to repair the dresses disarranged in dancing.

The Queen supervised everything and, like a hostess of today, prevented the young men from remaining together to talk about horses and politics. At midnight supper was served at tables with twelve places each, waited on by footmen of the King and Queen in red and silver livery. The King would arrive after supper, play a game of billiards, risk a crown at backgammon, send back to their regiment those who were playing too heavily, and then watch the dancing from the gallery before going to bed.

"Once Louis XVI had left one could laugh and enjoy oneself," the Queen's page related much later. Dawn put an end to the ball, which finished with the farandole of the *colonne anglaise* in which Marie Antoinette took part, laughing. Then the most wide-awake pages conducted the ladies to their carriages, having first given them soup and "restoratives," while others slept in corners, overcome with exhaustion.

Those who were staying at the château would meet the Swiss Guards in the corridors or on the stairs, patrolling with their spaniels, which had been trained to search in corners. Without this precaution the château would have been a playground for prostitutes and a haunt of thieves.

Late in the evening, or early in the morning, the patrols would sometimes meet a pale, haggard man "like one whose mind is wandering." But the Swiss Guards said nothing. It was M. de Castelnaux, Marie Antoinette's elderly adorer, whose life consisted in gazing from afar at the woman he loved. "Always alone, he would calculate the moments when he might find himself in the Queen's presence." He would stay for hours in the Hall of Mirrors, and never missed a state dinner. "Did he hear wheels? He was at once at the foot of the stairs." Even the cold did not put him off. "While the Queen was staying at the Little Trianon," relates Mme Campan, "this unhappy man's passion became even more importunate. He would snatch a bite of food with one of the Swiss Guards and would spend the whole day, even when it rained, walking round the garden, always walking at the edge of the ditches. The Queen often met him when she was strolling alone or with her children." One day she asked M. de Sèze to try to make the unhappy man see reason. After agreeing to "retire to his estates," he recanted. To withdraw seemed to him beyond his powers.

"Ah well!" sighed the Queen. "Let him vex me, but let no one take away from him the happiness of being at liberty."

At the beginning of the summer of 1782 Versailles and Trianon were enlivened by fresh festivities. The Comte and Comtesse du Nord, otherwise the future Tsar Paul I and his wife, born a Princess of Württemberg, were in Paris. Marie Antoinette was not aware of the Tsarina Catherine II's dislike for her, but she gave a very courteous reception to "those Norths," as she rather contemptuously called them, and organised a feast for them at Trianon. The Comtesse du Nord proudly wore on her head a little jewelled bird which "at her slightest movement sways on a spring above a rose." Marie Antoinette thought it so pretty that she wanted one like it. Scaffoldings of hair were now out of date and instead flowers were worn with their stems "in little, flat bottles, curved to fit the head." "When one finally managed it," recounts Mme d'Oberkirch, who wore just such a headdress on 6 June at Trianon, "it was charming. The spring flowers on the head in the midst of the snowy powder produced a unique effect." But one hardly dared move one's head, for fear of being drenched.

Dresses and hair styles were in garden or wild flower fashion. One dressed as a lavender seller or country girl, and Marie Antoinette was soon to ask Mique to construct a simple, unpretentious hamlet at the bottom of the park. Like an ordinary, artless shepherdess, she enjoined, her simplicity should be her sole ornament.

But we must hear again from the Baroness d'Oberkirch, who had been invited to the formal ball given by the Queen in honour of "those Norths." "I still cannot get over the difficulty of managing one's dress and one's hair in the carriage from Paris to Versailles. One was extremely uncomfortable, and the women who follow this postillion's calling several times a week must be very tired. The ball was wonderful. The Queen danced with the Grand Duke and no one could display more grace and nobility than our august sovereign. Her figure and bearing are wonderful. At one moment I was standing behind her and the Grand Duchess. 'Madame d'Oberkirch,' said the Queen, 'say something to me in German, so that I can see if I remember it. I now know only the language of my present country.'

"I said a few words in German and she mused for a moment without replying. 'Ah!' she said at last, 'I am charmed by the sound of the old German. You speak like a Saxon, Madame, without any Alsatian accent, which surprises me. German is a beautiful language, but French!

On the lips of my children it seems to me the sweetest tongue in the world.' "

She instilled similar sentiments into her children. When Mme d'Oberkirch went to see little Madame Royale, the child asked her name.

"You are a German then, Madame?" she said.

"No, Madame, I am French—from Alsace."

"Ah! I am glad of that, for I should not wish to love foreigners."

At the end of the summer of 1782 her children's education caused Marie Antoinette a great deal of worry, M. de Guéménée's startling insolvency—33 million livres—forced the Princesse to give in her resignation. Who should replace her? Marie Antoinette thought of the pious Princesse de Chimay or the learned Duchesse de Duras. But Besenval was on the watch—the Queen must nominate Mme de Polignac.

"Any other nomination would give the idea that Your Majesty no longer had enough influence to have the post given to her best friend."

"I should have thought you knew the Duchesse better. She would not want this post."

But the Swiss was clever, and he had touched the Queen on a sensitive spot. She interceded and, naturally, the King yielded. One can imagine the murmurs of the public. The Polignac family's revenues were to become even larger, and even Joseph II, in Vienna, declared himself "shocked" by this choice. Marie Antoinette was to be very much blamed for this appointment, but she consoled herself by saying that she would have "the opportunity to supervise her children's education—in particular that of her daughter—without the risk of wounding the governess's vanity."

The little Marie Thérèse—Madame Royale—never left her mother's rooms, and every "important or serious business," as Mercy wrote to Joseph II on 28 December 1782, "is interrupted by the little incidents of the royal child's games, and this inconvenience so chimes with the Queen's natural disposition to be superficial and inattentive that she hardly listens to what is said to her, and understands even less! . . . Consequently I find myself kept more at arm's length than ever."

With all respect to the Ambassador, that was a good thing. To draw Marie Antoinette into the question of the free navigation of the Scheldt, so dear to Joseph II, or into the eternal Austro-Prussian quarrels, would have harmed the Queen a great deal in public opinion. We shall see this later.

"One can no longer calculate the effects of the Queen's vacillating ideas," wrote Mercy in the same letter. But this vacillation had its good side, for in spite of the new favour granted to the "clan," the great "passion" had lessened somewhat. Mme de Polignac was still Marie Antoinette's "most tender friend," but sometimes her credit waned. She wearied the Queen with her perpetual demands. Recently she had taken it into her head to ask for the post of Minister of the King's household for the Comte d'Adhémar, who with his quavering voice had played Marie Antoinette's lover in the *Devin du village*. The Queen refused. Mme de Polignac, annoyed, had sulked. Marie Antoinette consoled herself more easily, perhaps, than she would have done two years before, for she had found a new friend—Geneviève de Gramont, Comtesse d'Ossun, her Mistress of the Robes since the previous year.

This time one may be thankful for Marie Antoinette's "vagaries of affection," which always upset Mercy. Mme d'Ossun was not an intriguer and never asked for money. She received 600 livres salary, 4,000 living allowance, 3,600 for *plat* (?) and 886 for her "coaches and hackneys," in all less than 10,000 livres. And she asked for nothing more. Marie Antoinette, who often invited herself to dinner with her Mistress of the Robes, together with four or five other people, had difficulty in getting her to accept a few thousand crowns in recompense.

Marie Antoinette's wardrobe was a real Ministry, and Mme d'Ossun had a large staff under her. "Everything was under her authority," wrote Mme Campan, "and nothing was released without her signature, from shoes to suits embroidered at Lyons. . . . The Mistress of the Robes had under her a first tiring-woman, entrusted with the care and upkeep of all the Queen's clothes; two women to fold and press anything that needed it; two valets of the wardrobe and one wardrobe boy. This last had to bring to the apartment every morning baskets covered with taffeta which contained everything the Queen was to wear during the day, and large dress-covers of green taffeta, in which were wrapped the ball and other dresses. Every morning the wardrobe valet on duty gave the first woman of the bedchamber a book containing patterns of the dresses, ball dresses, négligées, etc. A little portion of the trimming indicated what kind it was. The woman of the bedchamber presented the book to the Queen when she awoke, together with a pincushion. Her Majesty marked with pins everything she wanted for the day: one for the ball dress she wanted, one for the formal dress, for gambling or for supper in the small apartments. The book was taken back to the wardrobe and soon everything needed for the day arrived in the taffeta covers."

One of these daily "gazettes," in which one can still see the marks of Marie Antoinette's pins, has been preserved for us in the Archives. One cannot help musing over these patterns of "spotted green" or "white braid on a lilac ground." In the spring of 1782 she wore dresses of "white spots on a lavender ground," or of "striped satin," or a dressing-gown of "gosling-green figured with white spots." The ball dress at the head of the list, perhaps the one she wore for the feast given at Versailles to the "Norths," is of "mottled lilac," and the "paniered dress," perhaps for Trianon, was made of "gold-embroidered muslin, *présence de l'Impératrice.*"

According to Mme Campan, Marie Antoinette "usually had for the winter 12 ball dresses, 12 small, so-called fancy, dresses, 12 rich hooped dresses for when she played or for supper in the small apartments. The same number for summer. The spring dresses served for autumn. All these dresses were scrapped at the end of the year, unless she kept back one or two she preferred." The Queen's devoted waiting-woman tried to hide part of the truth from us, and indeed, she succeeded, for the figure of 100 new dresses a year is that usually given by historians. Now, by consulting the files of the Archives and taking the year 1782, which was a year below the average, we arrive at a total of 170 dresses. "On being cast off, the dresses were given, by order of the Mistress of the Robes, to the waiting-women." Mme Campan skates over this question. In reality, still according to the Archives, the first women of the bedchamber each received in 1782, apart from their candle rights, 12 coats, 22 wrappers and at the beginning of each season "a ball dress or a day dress," not to mention all the little taffeta underskirts, shoes, silk stockings, gloves and mittens. And it was not a question of worn clothes. A note points out that the "outfits were so numerous that they could not all be used and that many are cast off without having been worn." It must also be mentioned that the remainder, principally dresses and ball gowns, came to Mme d'Ossun, who might sell them for her own profit. This was only fair, for the Mistress of the Robes was the only one of the Queen's women who, apart from her titular rôle, did any real work.

The unfortunate Comtesse d'Ossun was scared by her mistress's expenditure. Marie Antoinette received between three and four million livres a year—between 600 and 800 million present-day francs—for all the expenses of her household and privy purse, the latter post totaling 300,000 livres in 1780. For clothes there was a budget of 120,000 livres, which was never enough. In 1776 a supplement of 28,000 livres was required, in 1780 one of 74,118. In 1783 Mme d'Ossun had to ask the treasurer for 73,067.

And Mme Campan dares tell us that Marie Antoinette's love of adornment, after "the first years of her reign, had given way to a love of simplicity, which was carried to unwise lengths." The truth can be more accurately found in the accounts of Mme d'Ossun, who when asking for the payment of these "truly excessive" sums, to use her own expression, added: "In bringing these statements to the King's notice, I would ask you to express to him my regret at having to request such a large supplement."

Incidentally, the treasury was not able to pay at once and it was not until February 1784 that the Mistress of the Robes received the money for the excess expenditure of 1782. "This deficit is the work of Mlle Bertin, among others," wrote Mme d'Ossun, when she sent in her accounts. The Queen's dressmaker was the Comtesse's *bête noire*. Rose Bertin, indeed, delivered directly to the Queen, instead of to the wardrobe. She sent in her bill three or four months later and "no one could remember anything about it . . . which means that one is often forced to agree in her invoices to things which one has neither seen nor used, and to pay for them without even being sure that they were furnished." Mlle Bertin's prices were "exorbitant." She actually asked 6,000 livres for a ball gown for New Year's Day—1,200,000 francs for a dress. "A sum as large as this might well have been given in some detail," sighed the secretary of the wardrobe, and he suggested "the employment of a specialist to review Mlle Bertin's invoices." But, he went on, "it would seem much more desirable to make Mlle Bertin give these details herself in her invoices, under pain of having those articles crossed out which are given without explanation. She has been asked to do this for a long time, and she cannot be brought to do it." And without consulting anyone he cut down one of the bills by 9,000 livres.

Rose Bertin was not the Queen's only dressmaker. Besides the "outside sewing-women" there was at the château a whole staff of "ordinary sewing-women," twelve of them, sewing-women for extraordinary dresses, sewing-women who specialised in dressing-gowns, tailors for riding-habits, not to mention the "manufacturers of hoops and collarettes," bonnet-makers and even a certain Demoiselle Brisemiche, whose job was "to construct the flounces on the Queen's petticoats." This troupe, which was paid on a different budget from the one managed by Mme d'Ossun, could not have been overworked, since the mending was done outside, by among others Mme Eloff, who repaired dresses and shoes. She also provided Marie Antoinette with her basques, brocade dresses and her bodices.

The Queen did not feel in the least guilty about this prodigality which distressed her new friend. Her disbursements were as nothing compared to those of the Comte d'Artois, who had debts of 21 million "as a result of heavy expenditure and much dishonesty on the part of his business men," says Mercy. But Marie Antoinette was no more anxious than her brother-in-law. In 1783 the new Controller of Finances, Calonne, appeared, who refused them nothing, in accordance with his famous principle: spend a great deal in order to appear rich. Meanwhile Marie Antoinette did not observe that her extravagance was as harmful to her as her past follies. A contemporary, the Abbé de Véri, wrote at the beginning of 1783: "The people of Paris are attached to the King merely because they cast on the Queen all the reproaches they might make to Louis XVI. The continual changes in the fashion of adornments, hairdressing and clothes, together with a few small showy expenses, are the real reason for popular feeling against the Queen. The middle-class man says he is ruined by the fancies of his wife and daughters, who want to imitate all the Queen's changes of taste. The merchant and the manufacturer have no fixed standard for predicting what will sell. And as these people know that the King has none of these tastes and that his way of life is simple, he is loved for the contrast between his taste and the Queen's."

How should she feel guilty, since when she wished a simple way of life she was reproached with that too? Witness Mme Vigée-Lebrun's picture of the Queen in a *gaulle,* a kind of blouse made fashionable by the creoles of Santo Domingo, which was exhibited in the Salon of 1783. People gathered before the picture to see Marie Antoinette "dressed as a chamber-maid." She wanted to ruin the silk merchants and weavers of Lyons in favour of the Flemish drapers, her brother's subjects.

The picture was given a title: "France, under the features of Austria, reduced to covering herself with a rag."

The Queen, annoyed, had the portrait withdrawn. Since, on the one hand, Calonne asked it of her and, on the other, the public thought she was ruining the country's textile industry by dressing in batiste and muslin, why should she worry? And the wardrobe expenses mounted sharply from 199,957 livres in 1783 to 217,652 in 1784 and 258,002 in 1785.

Although "less conspicuous," her amusements were none the less ruinous.

9

※

"Limited Lovers"

ONE AFTERNOON TOWARDS the end of June 1783 Marie Antoinette was playing the harp in her gilded drawing-room when an usher scratched at the door. A moment later Axel Fersen stood before her. How changed he was! "As handsome as an angel" when he left for America, he had "aged by ten years." The Queen stopped playing and gave him her hand to kiss.

It was certainly not grief at being separated from Marie Antoinette that had preyed upon the "supernumerary" colonel, but the fatigues of war. During these three years spent in America he had certainly not forgotten his "conquest," but it would be ridiculous to try to make an inconsolable lover out of him. Before embarking for France he had even considered renewing, on his return, his plans for marriage with an Englishwoman, Miss Leijel, whom he had once known, and he wrote to his father: "After taking care for my promotion and satisfying my self-esteem, I must now think of a more solid establishment. I am now at an age when marriage becomes necessary, however little vocation I may have for that sacrament. A marriage with Miss Leijel would have many advantages. I have not lost sight of her and during my stay in America I continued to correspond with her. I wrote her five or six letters, but have had no reply. . . . If she failed me and persisted in her rejection I have my eyes on someone else. This plan will depend entirely on your wishes. I have no other influences except what you would exert: it is the daughter of M. Necker."

But then he met Marie Antoinette again. A month after his return, hearing that Miss Leijel had married during his absence, Axel wrote to his sister Sophie and confessed his love for the Queen. "I am very glad that Miss Leijel is married. She will not be mentioned to me again, and I hope no one else will be found. I have made up my mind. *I cannot belong to the one person to whom I should wish to belong, the one who really loves me,* and so I wish to belong to no one." His scheme for marrying Mlle Necker was also abandoned—Staël had just entered the lists.

Marie Antoinette seemed to have renewed her "inclination" and soon Axel had but one wish: to remain in France and obtain from Louis XVI the command of a foreign regiment. The proprietor of the Royal Swedish, Comte Alexandre de Sparre, was ready to sell it to him for 100,000 livres. Axel spoke to his father, asking him to help pay this sum, which would allow him to remain for part of the year at Versailles, and begging him to consent to "the one thing which can make me happy for ever" and for which, he said, "there were a thousand other reasons I dare not put on paper."

Senator Fersen replied in a stern letter: "I would willingly consent to your scheme, if I did not see in it a physical impossibility. Neither you nor I have the necessary capital."

Fortunately King Gustavus intervened and asked Louis XVI to grant a commission to Count Fersen "who has served in Your Majesty's armies in America to the approbation of all and has thus rendered himself worthy of your benevolence." On 12 September Axel handed the letter to the King and on the same day reported to Gustavus III: "The King consented at once and displayed the strongest desire to do something to please Your Majesty. The Queen also wished to take a hand in it." On 20 September Marie Antoinette also wrote to the King of Sweden to assure him that she would "omit nothing to second the wishes of her brother and cousin." And on the following day, 21 September, Louis XVI appointed "M. le Comte de Fersen commanding officer and proprietor of the Royal Swedish." Axel paid the Comte de Sparre the 100,000 livres, which he had borrowed, but "His Majesty, on this same 21st day of September, granted the Comte de Fersen a *brevet de retenue* for the said 100,000 livres," which would enable him to discharge his debt.

Axel had by that time left Paris and was on his way to join King Gustavus, who was travelling in Germany under the name of Count de Haga and had asked Axel to accompany him. On 9 November he noted in his correspondence book: "(Wrote) to the Queen to thank her for the regiment."

Did he also express his regrets for the accident which had befallen her nine days before at Fontainebleau? Marie Antoinette had then "given birth, without much pain, to what is commonly called a false germ." No complications arose and the Queen was quite well again when on 29 November peace with England was solemnly proclaimed. Twelve trumpets, 12 hautboys and eight drums of the Great Stables marched through the streets of Paris and at each crossroads an officer announced the news.

Fersen was then in Italy. He was not a man to play at the faithful lover—he never would be. In Florence he made the conquest of Lord Cowper's stepsister, "the fair Emily." In Naples he consoled Lady Elizabeth Foster, daughter of the Duke of Bristol and unhappily married to John Thomas Foster. The pretty Englishwoman found Axel the most charming of consolers and considered a separation from her husband, and when Fersen left Naples a correspondence was carried on between the lovers.

On 7 June 1784 Count de Haga and his suite arrived at Versailles. Louis XVI, who had not been forewarned, was hunting at Rambouillet and returned in a hurry. His servants were not there; he dressed as best he could and presented himself before the King of Sweden with two different shoes.

"Have you been dressing for a masked ball?" asked Marie Antoinette laughing.

The visit lasted six weeks. "We are in a whirl of feasts, pleasures and entertainments of every kind," Axel wrote to his father. "We are constantly occupied and always in a hurry. We never have time to do everything arranged for us. This giddy life suits the Count de Haga very well. It does not suit me nearly so well and I am exhausted. We have already had a grand opera at Versailles and a state ball, not to mention numerous dinners and suppers. Tomorrow there is a feast in the Queen's large garden at Trianon. This will be the last, but there are still many suppers and spectacles in Paris. We never miss any of them, and we would rather go without drinking, eating and sleeping than not be present at the spectacle from the beginning right to the end. It is a mania!"

We know what the feast at Trianon was like through Gustavus III, who wrote to his brother: "In the little theatre they performed the

Dormeur réveillé by M. de Marmontel, music by Grétry [it was the *Dormeur réveillé* with music by Piccini] with the whole ballet company from the Opera, together with the Comédie Italienne. The spectacle ended with the diamond transformation scene. Supper was served in the garden pavilions and after supper the English garden was illuminated. It was perfectly enchanting. The Queen had opened the gardens to respectable people who had not come to the supper and who had been warned that they must dress in white, which really provided an elysian sight. The Queen would not sit down at table, but did the honours like any mistress of the house. She spoke to all the Swedes and entertained them with great care and attention." Marie Antoinette seemed transfigured. "She is miraculously beautiful," writes the Baroness d'Oberkirch.

The "inclination" was to become a "passion." But feasts and distractions did not make Marie Antoinette forget that Fersen had no fortune and before he left for Sweden Axel was given 20,000 livres a year income in his capacity as colonel of a French regiment.

At each stage of the long journey Axel wrote to a mysterious "Josephine." "Under this name," wrote the admirable archivist Alma Söderjhelm, "Fersen kept up a secret correspondence with Marie Antoinette." Doubt has recently been cast on this interpretation by M. Henry Valloton. Now, from Luneberg, on 27 July, and from Vernamynde, on 29 July, Axel wrote to "Josephine," as he notes in his correspondence book, to ask her "what name should be given to the dog" she had asked him to buy and "if any secret should be made of it." Josephine presumably replied that the purchase need not be secret, for on 9 November he wrote from Stockholm to M. de Boye and summarised his letter in his correspondence book: "Asked him to send me a dog, not small, the size of those owned by M. Pollett. Said it was for the Queen of France."

Much later, during the Revolution, we read in his private diary: "I went to see Mercy to ask him if he had taken care of Josephine's diamonds. He had the face to tell me that he did not know if there were any, that he had received a box, but that he had given the key to the Archduchess [Christina] on his arrival." Now we know that when the Queen was about to leave for Varennes she had her diamonds taken to Mercy so that he could give them to her sister. Marie Antoinette, then, was definitely "Josephine."

However—and it is this which gives rise to M. Henry Valloton's mistake—there must have been a second Josephine. The correspondence book shows that he wrote "to Josephine" to ask her to make "a straw hive." Obviously this could not be the Queen. Mrs. Sullivan, one of the Swede's mistresses, had a chambermaid called Josephine. Fersen sometimes lived on the same floor as the servant in the house belonging to Craufurd, Mrs. Sullivan's protector. What was this Josephine to Axel? Apparently no more than "the obliging friend" who even undertook to deliver letters from Fersen to her master, witness these words in the private diary: "Wrote to Craufurd by Josephine."

Axel, then, was in continuous correspondence with Marie Antoinette. These letters have disappeared. About sixty letters addressed to Fersen by Marie Antoinette had been preserved at the castle of Stafsund in Sweden. A grand-nephew of Axel, the Baron Klinckowström, published them in 1878, but the letters were incomplete, whole sentences being replaced by dots. According to the Baron, Fersen himself, or else his brother Fabian, had crossed out certain lines to make them illegible.

According to Fersen's grand-nephew, "when the Comte de Fersen had answered these letters they were sent to the King of Sweden so that from the Queen's remarks he could judge of the political situation and its dangers. But so that the King of Sweden might not be tempted to challenge some of the Queen's expressions on delicate points Fersen, through his erasures, rendered all indiscretion impossible. These are perfectly adequate reasons for Fersen to have concealed by erasures certain sentences in the Queen of France's letters. The friends of that noble martyr will find them quite sufficient to dispel all malicious conjecture . . ."

Very few friends of "that noble martyr" found them sufficient. The famous rows of dots indicating erased passages have been closely studied. For example, would Marie Antoinette talk of political questions at the beginning or end of the letters, in between affectionate phrases? When she writes: "How is your health? I am sure you are not looking after yourself and you are wrong . . . (erased passage) . . .; as for myself I am bearing up better than I ought," would she have slipped in remarks likely to offend Gustavus III? And when, later, Marie Antoinette wrote: "Farewell . . . (erased passage) . . . I shall not be able to write to you again . . . (erased passage)" would the King of Sweden, on reading the complete text of the letter, have been annoyed by "some of the Queen's expressions" on political affairs placed among affectionate sentiments?

Baron Klinckowström realised how improbable his explanation was. He was afraid that modern science might succeed in deciphering the erased passages and one evening, feeling death approaching, he called to his bedside an elderly woman friend and a faithful servant—this is historical fact and not a scene out of an old melodrama—and under the Baron's eyes the faithful servant lit a fire and the old friend consigned Marie Antoinette's letters one by one to the flames.

"Now let the world know what it will, it will never know more."

Fortunately, in the house of Countess Nordenfalk, née Sophie Piper and a descendant of Axel's favourite sister, Mme Alma Söderjhelm discovered a mass of documents: the end of the private diary, the correspondence book, letters from Axel to his father, a letter from Sophie to her brother, etc. These enable one to realise that, contrary to the opinion of the historian Heidenstam, the love of Marie Antoinette and Fersen was something other than a feeling of all purity "worthy of the troubadours and the Knights of the Round Table."

Moreover, Lucien Maury had the luck to discover in the castle of Stafsund an important letter which escaped the old Baron's holocaust. It is in cipher, and Baron Klinckowström probably thought it without interest. This letter is from Marie Antoinette. It dates from the return from Varennes and has been deciphered by M. Maury. There is no erasure, and it begins: "I can tell you that I love you and indeed that is all I have time for." It ends: "Let me know to whom I should address the news I may write to you, for I cannot live without that. Farewell, most loved and loving of men. I kiss you with all my heart." These kisses are not an exception. "Farewell, my dear Rignon," she ended on another occasion—this was her name for him—"I kiss you tenderly."

M. Henry Valloton, for whom Fersen is "the pattern of the discreet knight deeply devoted to his lady," writes in this connection that "epistolary embraces were customary at that time. The Baron Stedingk, Swedish Ambassador in Moscow, sends kisses to Fersen, his old friend and comrade of the American war; Fersen kisses von Taube; Louis XV gives the accolade to the future King of Sweden at their first meeting in Paris; the Comte de Provence kisses Gustavus III; Lafayette 'kisses with all his heart' General Bouillé, whom in fact he cordially detested. It is needless to insist," he concludes, "on the poverty of such a 'proof.'"

M. Valloton merely gives examples of embraces between men—men kissed each other easily by letter—but "I kiss you tenderly," when it is a question of a Queen of France writing to a colonel in the Light Dragoons is, if not a proof, at least an indication all the more disturbing as it is coupled with other presumptions.

Alma Söderjhelm wrote: "The way in which Fersen received the rumours which circulated about Marie Antoinette is very significant. Would he in 1791 have noted that 'it is said the Q. sleeps with Barnave' as being something in itself quite possible unless he had reasons which forced him to admit this possibility?" Mme Söderjhelm further relates that "when, after Marie Antoinette's death, he went to one of his estates in Sweden, which, in its time, had been given by Queen Hedvig Eleonora to her lover, Count Gyllenstierna, he made a note of this fact and added that 'the parallel' made him even more attached to this estate."

There is, too, the famous *resté là* (stayed there).

On the evening of Monday, 13 February 1792, the Swede, disguised, managed to gain entrance to the Tuileries, where the Queen was a prisoner of the Revolution. One can read in his diary: *"Allé chez elle, passé par mon chemin ordinaire; peur des gard(es) nat (ionnaux) son logement à merveille, pas vu le Roi."* (Went to her by my usual road; afraid of the National Guards, her room wonderful, did not see the King.) There follow two words crossed out. Mme Alma Söderjhelm considers that "in spite of the erasure one can see that the crossed out words are *resté là*" and that, indeed, it emerges from the context that the Swede did not leave the Tuileries until the following evening. M. Valloton was able to submit the page of the diary to experts. "For the sake of clarity," he writes, "let us summarise the conclusions: the Swedish Institute admits, without prejudice, that the erased text *appears* to be *resté là* and the Director of the Swedish Institute *has the impression* that this reconstruction of the text *might well* correspond to the reality." At all events, I am of the same opinion as my eminent colleague when he writes that this *"resté là"* in no way constitutes a proof of adultery. Fersen may have spent the night in the château through fear of the National Guards, but elsewhere than in Marie Antoinette's bed.

Of course the morning ballet laid down by etiquette had never found Axel Fersen in the Queen's bedroom, but at Trianon, as at Versailles, Marie Antoinette was able to escape from her "cloud of enemies." In Besenval's memoirs we read that one March morning in 1778 Marie Antoinette summoned the Swiss Baron to discuss with him the duel

between the Comte d'Artois and the Duc de Bourbon. "I began by
going to the King's *lever*. I had hardly entered his cabinet when I saw
Campan, the Queen's secretary, who motioned to me with his head. I
went to him and he said, without appearing to speak to me: 'Follow
me, but at a distance, and let no one notice.'

"He made me pass through several doors and by staircases which
were quite unknown to me and when we were out of sight and hearing
he said: 'You must admit, Monsieur, that this looks odd, but it is not
what it seems, for the husband is in the secret.' 'My dear Campan,' I
replied, 'when one has grey hair and wrinkles one does not expect a
young and pretty Queen of twenty to have one brought through the
back ways for anything but business.' 'She is waiting for you,' he
replied very impatiently. 'I have already sent twice to your house and I
looked for you in all the places I thought I might find you.'

"As he finished speaking we were under the roofs, in a dirty corridor
and opposite a mean little door. He inserted a key and having pushed
vainly several times, exclaimed: 'Oh heavens! the bolt is shot on the
other side. Wait for me here. I shall have to go round.'

"He returned shortly and said that the Queen was very annoyed,
that she could not see me at that moment because it was nearly time for
Mass, but that she asked me to come back to the same place at three
o'clock.

"I did so and Campan introduced me by a side entrance into a room
with a billiard table, which I knew from having often played there
with the Queen, then into another room, which I did not know, simply
but comfortably furnished. I was astonished, not that the Queen should
have wanted these facilities, but that she had dared to procure them."

In her Memoirs Mme Campan, while trying to defend the Queen's
virtue, confirms the accuracy of this account and gives details of the
use of this lodging, which was intended for Her Majesty's Lady of
Honour "in case of confinement or sickness." When Marie Antoinette
was not unwell she appropriated "this very small antechamber, this
bedroom and this sitting room, situated above her private apartments."

We must not leave Mme Campan without reproducing the "confession" of Georges Laguerre, which appeared in the *Intermédiaire* in
March 1906: "My family was very friendly with M. Jean-François
Barrière. François Barrière, publicist and man of letters, born in 1786,
had published Mme Campan's Memoirs in 1823. M. Barrière died in

August 1868 in the Rue de Monceau, where he lived opposite my parents. My father, Léon Laguerre, a doctor of law and an enthusiast for *belles-lettres* and history, often used to go and talk with M. Barrière and explore his very fine library.

"One day, about 1867 (my father has often told me of it), François Barrière lent him, on his promising to return it the same evening, a small manuscript, a few pages only, by Mme Campan, which was not included in the Memoirs. My father read it with great interest. Mme Campan said that horrible calumnies had attributed many lovers to Queen Marie Antoinette, that they were pure invention, against which she protested, but that, since she was on this delicate subject, she had to admit that she was aware that the Queen had had a partiality for the young Chevalier de Fersen. She pleaded extenuating circumstances on behalf of her unhappy mistress. . . .

"Faithful to his word, my father returned the precious pages that same evening. Shortly afterwards François Barrière died at the age of 82. My father made the inventory of his papers and set about winding up his estate. He had not forgotten the famous unpublished fragment of Mme Campan's Memoirs and not finding it, he asked Mme Barrière, who was a very distinguished woman and an inspector of schools in the city of Paris, what had become of the manuscript. Pointing to the fireplace of the study, she replied that shortly before her husband's death they had together burned it there 'out of respect for the memory of Queen Marie Antoinette.' "

After reading all that has been written on this delicate question can one really come to a decision? Can one, without any reservation, believe Saint-Priest when he affirms that Marie Antoinette and Axel were lovers? Their amours must certainly have been rather limited, and as a result of this "limitation" we need hardly dwell on the hypothesis that Fersen was the father of the future Louis XVII, who was born on 27 March 1785, nine months after Axel's stay at Versailles. In any case, even had their love affair been more "extensive," "the risk of committing the crime of *lèse-dynastie*," as Pierre Audiat has very justly remarked, "would have been enough to confine Fersen, who was an ardent royalist, to his role of a limited lover."

Limited as was his love affair, Axel none the less considered himself bound to Marie Antoinette. This "burning spirit in a shell of ice" would undoubtedly have many more adventures, but Axel always refused to commit his life. His two conquests in Italy, Emily and Elizabeth, whiled away their time far from the man who had crossed their life. Both Englishwomen would have liked their Italian adventure to end in marriage, but Fersen refused. He dealt first of all with Emily and wrote to her "that it could never be and must no longer be thought of." He charged Lord Cowper to console his sister. During the winter, from the castle of Gripsholm, where the Swedish court was, he replied to Elizabeth Foster, stating the reason for his refusal, in his notebook, in two words, which he himself underlined: "Declared everything."

Axel thought only of returning to France. During the winter of 1784-5 the talk was all of a possible war with the Low Countries, a war in which France, and consequently Axel's regiment, would be involved. Moreover, the fighting would have been against Austria, and from a distance he could imagine Marie Antoinette's distress.

Once more it was the Mouths of the Scheldt which threatened to set Europe aflame. In the previous year Joseph II had drawn nearer to Catherine II, with a view to planning the dismemberment of the Ottoman Empire: this year he wanted to let some air into Antwerp. The Netherlands had been in possession of the Mouths of the Scheldt since 1460—in fact they still are—and they kept the estuary closed, much to the fury of the Emperor, who would have liked France to intervene with the Dutch. Louis XVI and Vergennes, having been at peace with England for a year, knew perfectly well that to make the Scheldt an Austrian river would displease both London and Berlin. So when on 1 September 1784 Marie Antoinette, at Mercy's instigation, brought up the question of the Scheldt with Vergennes, the Minister prudently replied that "the court of Versailles could not lay down the law for the Dutch." Learning of this, Joseph II was extremely annoyed and wrote to his sister: "It is quite certain that M. de Vergennes' conduct is hardly calculated to strengthen, or indeed even to maintain, the bonds of alliance and policy which united us."

Not maintain the Alliance! All Maria Theresa's work would crumble, and consequently Marie Antoinette began a campaign against Vergennes. "I spoke openly to the King about it more than once. Occasionally he replied with anger, and as he is incapable of discussion I was not able to persuade him that his Minister was deceived or was deceiving him."

An event took place which enabled Marie Antoinette to revive the affair. As the Dutch continued to refuse to free the Scheldt estuary, Joseph II ordered one of his ships to leave Antwerp and to force a passage. On 4 October the Austrian ship, a brigantine called *Le Louis,* was fired on not far from the mouth of the river, opposite Saftingen.

The Emperor mobilised an army of 80,000 men to avenge the outrage, and to complete matters the United Provinces asked for Louis XVI's protection. Mercy and Joseph II insisted that the Queen should act "energetically," and the events at the time of the Bavarian affair were to be repeated, with all the more serious results as the King, according to Mercy, no longer had "any credit in the affairs of State, as he brings to them no energy and very little knowledge." Consequently we have the spectacle of Vergennes dictating to Louis XVI a letter for Joseph II in which the King seemed to be trying to make excuses for the Dutch. Marie Antoinette considered the letter "impossible," and did all she could to obtain another letter from her husband which he would write by himself. Louis XVI, who had a horror of scenes, gave way and made his brother-in-law an offer of mediation in a letter which was delivered to the Emperor on 6 November. Without waiting for the reply Vergennes, backed up by the Council of Ministers, decided on 12 November to send a "very stiff note" to Vienna. This time France put all the blame on Joseph II and announced a concentration of troops on the Netherlands frontier. The King signed the note on 15 November. Marie Antoinette made her husband another scene and succeeded in having the "odious dispatch" delayed for five days.

Joseph II was no less furious, but proposed a curious peace offer: the Elector of Bavaria should cede his State to Austria; in exchange he would receive the Netherlands, and the quarrel over the Mouths of the Scheldt would end.

Louis XVI and Vergennes distrusted this scheme. The Minister was faithful to the old principle of Henri II: "Keep Germany's affairs in as much difficulty as possible." They did not care for the idea of seeing Germany installed all the way from Dunkirk to Bâle, and so they found a compromise. They would agree to the scheme on condition that Joseph II obtained the consent of the King of Prussia. This was to condemn the scheme to failure, for Frederick II would never accept.

Discussions began again and the threat of war became more urgent. Two army corps under the command of the Prince de Condé encamped in Flanders and on the Rhine. Marie Antoinette redoubled her activity.

During all this time, it must be sadly admitted, she was much more her brother's Minister than Queen of France. Joseph II sent her two letters by the same courier—one she would show to her husband and one she must keep secret. In the latter, dated 19 November, he urgently advised her "to take no step without the authorisation of the Comte de Mercy," and Marie Antoinette obeyed. She even ran counter to the French point of view, which was in favour of gaining some advantage from the affair. Breteuil talked of the cession to France of Luxembourg and Namur; "the Queen gave him a rough handling," writes Mercy, and the Minister held his peace.

It is somewhat embarrassing to read the congratulations Mercy bestowed on his master's sister for her "true zeal" in the service of His Austrian Majesty. Almost condescendingly he acknowledged that "in the present situation the Queen has been less unsuccessful than in any other, in her attempt to be of use to her august brother." Urged by her monitor, who was quite shameless about it, Marie Antoinette kept Ambassador Mercy informed about what went on in the King's Council and continued to hold up the courier. "All things considered," she wrote to Mercy, "I shall not give the King his letter [from Joseph II] until late this evening or tomorrow morning." She would then see her husband before he had time to confer with Vergennes. She thus obtained promises from Louis XVI which were in contradiction with the Council's decisions.

The following day there was a violent scene between Marie Antoinette and Vergennes in the presence of the King, who was very vexed at the turn taken by the discussion. The Queen, moreover, was only half successful and on the 31st she made her excuses to Joseph II: "M. de Vergennes's delays and difficulties would make you impatient, my dear brother. They would be much worse if I had not spoken to him in a way that had its effect."

Joseph II was impatient, in fact, and demanded a solution. A month later he wrote to his sister: "I insist on it and shall not cease my requests."

The Emperor's courier crossed that of the Queen. He carried a letter in which Marie Antoinette declared: "You certainly have a right to complain about the methods of this country. Remember what you have seen and what you know of it." "This country" is indeed the language of an Archduchess. Marie Antoinette finally obtained what she wanted: in a note France promised not to declare war on Austria in the event of a conflict between Joseph II and the United Provinces and to confine itself to sending "an army to watch the frontier."

The Dutch, feeling themselves abandoned, gave in. They would send an embassy to Vienna and apologise for firing on the brigantine. They would also pay a reasonable indemnity, and France, which had had nothing to do with the firing, promised to pay a share.

This was the beginning of the legend of the cases of gold crossing the frontier and of the famous 200 million sent by Marie Antoinette to her brother to enable him to make war against the Turks.

The Parisians knew that France's disgraceful attitude in the affair of the Netherlands and the tithe paid to the Emperor were both the Queen's doing. Henceforth they always called her the "Austrian," a nickname she was to keep right up to the scaffold.

In the spring of 1785 it was quite usual to hear the public say: "We are going to Saint Cloud to see the waters and the Austrian." For since 20 February Marie Antoinette was the owner of the château of Saint Cloud, which the King had bought from the Duc d'Orléans for the attractive sum of six million. One may guess the cries and murmurs of the opposition—for one can already use that term: "So the mania for English gardens is beginning again!" "M. Mique is preparing plans for enlarging it, estimated at several millions!"

And a councillor exclaimed in Parliament: "It is both impolitic and immoral for palaces to belong to a Queen of France."

When, on 24 May, Marie Antoinette made her entry into Paris after giving birth to her second son, she received no applause whatsoever. Fersen, who had just arrived in Paris, wrote sadly to King Gustavus: "The Queen was received very coldly. There was not a single cry of welcome, but a complete silence."

On returning to Versailles she wept for a long time in Louis XVI's arms. For the first time she realised how deep was the gulf separating her from the French, but the motives for this icy reception escaped her.

"What have I done to them? What have I done to them?" she asked through her sobs.

10

❧

The First Thunderclap

MARIE ANTOINETTE WEPT, but a very important event soon absorbed her attention and dried her tears—she was to rehearse the part of Rosina in *The Barber of Seville*. With complete lack of intelligence she deliberately chose a play by the author of the *Marriage of Figaro*, which had been prohibited by the King, a play by M. Caron de Beaumarchais, of whom Louis XVI said: "That man undermines everything that should be respected in a government."

But the Queen's coterie, who loved to scoff, had had the *Marriage* performed at Vaudreuil's, and thanks to Marie Antoinette the play was given on 27 April 1784 in Paris, where its triumph is well known.

"There is only one thing madder than my play," said Beaumarchais himself, "and that is its success!" There was something madder still— the delight of the great lords at seeing themselves castigated, and the Queen's intervention in the affair.

At Trianon Marie Antoinette was to be Rosina, "the prettiest and most provoking little thing," Vaudreuil was to play Almaviva and Artois Figaro. There were rehearsals every day and the performance was fixed for 19 August.

On 12 July 1785 the Queen was at Versailles when the crown jeweller, Böhmer, arrived, bringing her a diamond epaulette and buckles, a gift of the King on the occasion of the baptism of the Duc d'Angoulême. At the same time the jeweller gave Marie Antoinette a note from his partner Bassenge.

Madame,

We are filled with happiness and venture to think that the last arrangements proposed to us, which we have carried out with zeal and respect, are a further proof of our submission and devotion to Your Majesty's orders, and we have real satisfaction in thinking that the most beautiful set of diamonds in existence will belong to the greatest and best of Queens.

Marie Antoinette looked up from her reading. She seemed not to understand a word of this jumble. What was it all about? But Böhmer had vanished. The arrival of the Controller General had caused the jeweller to disappear. Marie Antoinette ordered him to be sent for so that he might give her the key to the mystery. Perhaps he was still in the Gallery—but he could not be found. The Queen read the note to Mme Campan, who could not understand it either. And yet, said the Queen laughing, she was so good at solving the riddles in the *Mercure*. This Böhmer must certainly be mad. In 1774 and on several other occasions he had begged Marie Antoinette to buy an extraordinary necklace *"en esclavage,"* which incidentally was rather ugly, like a collar for a circus horse, made up of 540 admirable diamonds. The Queen had refused to buy this 1,600,000-livre breastplate, and Böhmer, who had sunk all his fortune in the necklace, had even thrown himself at her feet and made a ridiculous scene, threatening to "go and throw himself into the river." Marie Antoinette had told him sharply to stand up and not to give way to these "despairing contortions."

This affair of the unsold necklace had evidently deranged poor Böhmer's mind. "That man exists to torture me. He has always some mad scheme in mind! I do not think I shall make use of him any more. If I want my diamonds reset I shall use my valet-jeweller, who will have no ambition to sell me a carat."

A lighted candle stood near, and Marie Antoinette put the note to it. "It is not worth keeping!"

This apparently insignificant gesture is dramatic and was to have terrible consequences. For this brief moment, the most poignant of the drama, as Funck-Brentano has remarked, was the only instant when the Queen was in contact with the intrigue of the necklace.

On 1 August Madame Campan left for her country house, where she had a visit from Böhmer, who was "very worried at having no reply to his note." The waiting-woman tried to make him understand that there was no hope of the Queen changing her mind. She did not want to buy any more diamonds.

"If I had any money to spend," Marie Antoinette had told her recently, "I would much rather enlarge my estate at Saint Cloud." And she had even asked Mme Campan to take the first opportunity of telling the jewellers so.

"But," exclaimed Böhmer, who seemed astounded, "to whom should I address myself for a reply to the letter I presented the Queen?"

"To no one! Her Majesty burned your petition without even having understood what you were trying to say."

"Ah! Madame, that is not possible. The Queen knows that she must give me some money."

"Money, M. Böhmer? But we settled your last accounts for the Queen some time ago."

"Are you not in the secret, Madame? It is not a settlement if one ruins a man by not paying him when one owes him more than 1,500,000 francs."

"Have you lost your wits? For what object could the Queen possibly owe you such an exorbitant amount?"

"For my necklace, Madame," replied Böhmer coldly.

"What!" said Madame Campan. "That necklace you vainly worried the Queen about for several years?"

"But the Queen wanted to have it and caused it to be purchased by the Cardinal de Rohan."

"You are quite wrong," exclaimed Madame Campan. "The Queen has not spoken once to the Cardinal since he returned from Vienna. There is no man less in favour at court."

"It is you who are wrong, Madame," retorted Böhmer. "She so well receives him in private that she handed His Eminence 30,000 francs, which were given to me on account and which she took, in his presence, from the little Sèvres porcelain desk near the fireplace in her boudoir."

"Was it the Cardinal who told you that?"

"Yes, Madame, the Cardinal himself."

On Madame Campan's advice Böhmer hastened to Trianon, but Marie Antoinette was rehearsing her rôle as Rosina.

"He is mad. I have nothing to say to him and do not wish to see him."

But two or three days later, when she learned from Madame Campan exactly what Böhmer wanted, she was stupefied. "The whole thing was a mystery to her. She could not see her way through it." She quickly summoned the jeweller, who came at once and began his extravagant and incredible tale.

The jeweller's confused remarks involved only Cardinal Louis de Rohan. After the blessing at Strasbourg Marie Antoinette had often heard about this curious Eminence, who knew women so well—even too well. His tastes had driven the Empress Maria Theresa to despair when he had been sent to her as Ambassador at the time of Mme du Barry's reign. In nearly every one of her letters to her daughter and to Mercy she had mentioned the licentious prelate. "All our young and plain women are bewitched by him," sighed the Empress and she remarked that the court ladies went eagerly to the dinners given at small tables in the Embassy.

Scandalised, Marie Antoinette's mother saw the "young and plain women" dance and flirt with this priest, who frequented masked balls, or went hunting in lay dress and fired 1,328 shots from his gun in one day. "He is stuffed with extremely improper remarks, which ill beseem his position as an ecclesiastic and a Minister, and which he impudently lets out to everyone he meets . . . His turbulent suite is exactly the same, a mixed lot of people without merit or morals." After two years of his Embassy Maria Theresa could no longer put up with this "incorrigible" man.

At Versailles Rohan was supported by d'Aiguillon and at Vienna by Joseph II, whom the prelate amused "by his follies, chatter and buffoonery." Even Kaunitz got on very well with this Ambassador, who "did not disturb him and was submissive to him in every way." Maria Theresa had to wait for her son-in-law's accession to see an end put to this "horrible and shameful embassy." She then dreaded the possible havoc which might be wreaked on her daughter by this man who was so "supple, flattering and eternally amusing." In fact, all through 1776 Rohan had tried to find "opportunities to ingratiate himself with the Queen," but Marie Antoinette had refused to receive the Cardinal, for whom she had a pronounced antipathy.

When he was still at Vienna he had written to d'Aiguillon: "I did indeed see Maria Theresa weep over the misfortunes of oppressed Poland, but this Princess, who is a past mistress of the art of concealing her thoughts, seems to me to be able to cry at will. In one hand she holds a handkerchief to dry her tears and with the other she seizes the sword, so as to be the third sharer." The Minister had given the letter to the du Barry, who had read it aloud at one of her suppers. Marie Antoinette had heard of this and had been all the more wounded since the epigram was true. Would Rohan ever manage to get that unfortunate letter forgotten?

"Although my daughter holds the Coadjutor of Strasbourg at a distance, I think her quite capable of changing her mind, either as a result of her incapacity for reflection or from her habit of yielding to the whims of her favourites of both sexes."

Fortunately Prince Louis had had to go back to Strasbourg, where he had succeeded his uncle. But he might be returning to court, as he was certain to succeed Cardinal de la Roche-Aymon, the Grand Almoner of France, who had one foot in the grave. Louis XVI had let this promise be forced from him by the Comtesse de Marsan, Rohan's cousin. When at the request of Marie Antoinette, who had been well coached by Mercy, the King wanted to take back this stupid promise, Mme de Marsan had protested loudly and reminded the King of his word.

"My cousin," sighed Louis XVI, "I know I promised to make your cousin Grand Almoner, but it is now impossible."

The discussion became bitter. The Comtesse would not give up her point.

"I cannot do it now," Louis XVI almost implored. "I have given the Queen my word."

"I respect the Queen's wishes, Sire, but Your Majesty cannot have two words. The Queen would not wish that the King, in order to please her, should do what the threat of death would not force from the meanest gentleman! I therefore take the respectful liberty of assuring Your Majesty that having published the promise he gave me I should find myself urgently compelled also to make known that the King has broken it merely to please the Queen."

He had to give way. And so, on the death of Mgr de la Roche-Aymon, M. le Prince de Rohan, Bishop of Strasbourg, Cardinal of the Holy Church and member of the Académie Française, became Grand Almoner of France. He was present at the King's *lever*, officiated at all the great feasts at court, and had just baptised the little Duc de Normandie, but Marie Antoinette never addressed one word to him. It was hardly likely, then, that the Queen would have asked this man to be her intermediary in the purchase of a necklace.

Another name kept on coming up in Böhmer's story, that of "Mme la Comtesse de la Motte-Valois," who claimed to be descended from Henry II. Marie Antoinette sat up. There were no more princes of the Valois family and no lady at court with that illustrious name. She had never heard of this woman. But Böhmer explained how he and his partner had been put in touch with Mme de la Motte. He knew a certain Louis-François Achet, attorney in the court of appeal, whose son-in-law, the lawyer Laporte, was friendly with the Comtesse. According to the attorney the lady was in favour with the Queen, and she had even shown the lawyer letters written to her by Marie Antoinette.

"We would willingly give 1,000 louis to anyone who could sell the necklace," the jewellers had said, seeing a ray of hope.

This was at the end of November 1784. Urged on by his father-in-law, M. Laporte, who was riddled with debts, had spoken to Mme de la Motte about the necklace and the difficulty the jewellers were in. If they did not sell this regal piece they would be ruined, as they had borrowed heavily in order to assemble the stones. Since the Comtesse was in favour with the Queen why should she not intercede for them?

"Have you seen this necklace?" Mme de la Motte had asked Laporte.

"It is a marvel, Madame! The crown jewellers have worked on it for years and from the value of the stones alone it is a treasure."

Yet Mme de la Motte did not seem in a hurry to admire the treasure. It was not until 29 December that she went to see "the Böhmers," as they were called, and appeared to think the necklace very fine, in spite of the ungraceful heaviness of its setting. On 21 January the Comtesse arrived with Maître Achet. She had come to inform the jewellers that a "very great nobleman," acting "in the Queen's name," would perhaps acquire the necklace.

The jewellers nearly fell over themselves thanking her, and offered her a trinket, which she refused. On 24 January the Comtesse reappeared at seven o'clock in the morning to announce a visit from the Cardinal de Rohan, the "very great nobleman" mentioned four days earlier.

A few hours later His Eminence arrived at the Böhmers' house, saw the necklace, asked the price, which was 320 million present-day francs, and "did not conceal his intention to negotiate, not for himself, but for a person whose name he might get permission to mention."

On 29 January the Cardinal proposed to buy the necklace from the Böhmers for the agreed price of 1,600,000 livres, to be settled in four payments spread over two years. The necklace was to be delivered on 1 February and the first payment made on 1 August. The Cardinal wrote out these conditions himself and they were signed by Charles Böhmer and Paul Bassenge. On 1 February the two jewellers received a hurried note from the Grand Almoner, asking them to bring him the necklace. Carrying the case, the Böhmers hastened to the Hôtel de Rohan.

"The jewels are for the Queen," the Cardinal told them and showed them a sheet containing details of the transaction signed on 29 January by the jewellers and written by the Cardinal. At the side of each article was the word "approved" and at the bottom was the signature "Marie Antoinette of France."

"Take a copy of it."

The jewellers copied the sheet "without the peculiarity of the signature raising any doubt in their minds" and they left the Cardinal the jewel case to be presented to the Queen.

After that they had again met Mme la Comtesse, had invited her to dinner to show their gratitude and had themselves gone to the Rue Neuve Saintes Filles to a meal given to them by "the Queen's friend" in her house.

On 1 August Böhmer and his partner had received a visit from the Cardinal. His Eminence did not bring the first payment of 400,000 livres, but on behalf of the Queen asked them to grant a delay of three months. Mme de la Motte had on the previous day brought the Cardinal a letter signed Marie Antoinette and telling him of her financial difficulties. The Queen promised to pay 700,000 livres on 1 October and meanwhile paid 35,000 livres as interest on the debt. This sum had been given to the Cardinal by Mme de la Motte, and His Eminence had the money on him. The jewellers had taken the matter rather badly, as they had obligations to pay their creditors, among them M. de Saint-James, who was pressing them. The Cardinal had promised to take the matter up with the Queen and on this 1 August things had gone no further.

Two days later, to the astonishment of the jewellers, Mme de la Motte had summoned Bassenge.

"You have been deceived. The written guarantee the Cardinal possesses bears a forged signature, but the Prince is rich enough and will pay."

Böhmer had then seen Mme Campan, who had opened his eyes, and then, with beating heart, had gone to see the Cardinal and told him of his interview with Marie Antoinette's waiting-woman.

"The Queen said she did not know what we were talking about and that the whole thing confused her." In his distress the jeweller had added: "Are you sure your intermediary has not deceived you both?"

The Cardinal had hesitated and then replied: "If I hesitate to answer, it is not because my answer is not ready. I am merely wondering if I ought to tell you everything." And after a silence he had added: "I ought and I can. If I tell you that I have dealt directly with the Queen will you be satisfied?"

"Yes, Monseigneur."

"Well then, I assure you that I have dealt directly with the Queen and I affirm it by raising my right arm as a sign of affirmation."

The Grand Almoner had then claimed to have seen Marie Antoinette take the money out of a "small desk of Sèvres porcelain." Moreover, the Cardinal had given a similar assurance to M. de Saint-James, asking him to wait before exacting payment from Böhmer of the money due to him.

On hearing this tale Marie Antoinette was thunderstruck by this monstrous audacity. Even if she had wanted to buy the necklace, were not the jewellers made suspicious by the purchase being carried out without the King's knowledge? They were not, for in June 1776, without telling His Majesty, the Queen had had two bracelets made for 300,000 livres in exchange for which the jewellers had bought back some stones cheaply. Moreover, this had not been enough, particularly as there were also earrings to be paid for, and Marie Antoinette had been obliged to confess her purchase to the King. Mercy had told Maria Theresa about it: "The monarch received this proposal with his habitual equanimity, merely permitting himself to say kindly that he was not surprised that the Queen had no money, in view of her taste for diamonds. After this remark the 2,000 louis were given to her the following day." The Empress had declared that this event "filled her with alarm for the future," but the "madcap" was not frightened, and had said lightly to the Abbé de Vermond: "Now my bracelets have got as far as Vienna!"

"Does the Empress sound angry?"

"A bit. See for yourself," Marie Antoinette had contented herself

with replying as she handed the letter to the Abbé, and she had not
given it another thought.

The jeweller remembered very well, too, that in the same year the
Queen had bought chandelier earrings for 600,000 livres, also without
the King's knowledge, and that she had finally had to speak to her
husband, who had once more paid the debt by four annual instalments
from his own purse.

Marie Antoinette felt the ground giving way under her. But only
a few days ago she had said to Mme Campan: "I do not like diamonds
any more. I shall never buy another."

That might be, but she had liked them very much. The jewellers
were still living in the time when the Queen adored them. And so
Böhmer and Bassenge had been no more surprised than the Cardinal
when Mme de la Motte had told them that the Queen wanted secretly
to buy the necklace she had officially refused.

When her first emotion was over Marie Antoinette must have thought
that the affair was no more serious than that of Mme Cahuet de Villers,
wife of a treasurer of the King's Household, who in 1777 had made
use of her name to get money out of various people. She too had claimed
to be frequently received by the Queen. She too had written, or caused
to be written, what claimed to be a request from the Queen for 200,000
livres, and she had found a farmer-general, one Béranger, who was delighted to render a service to Marie Antoinette so as to obtain "the
honours of the court."

But was the Cardinal another Béranger, or had he appropriated the
necklace himself? Was he a fool or a swindler?

According to Marie Antoinette, who wrote of it to her brother, the
Cardinal, "who had an urgent need for money, had thought he would
be able to pay the jewellers at the appointed time without anything
being discovered."

On 9 August 1785 Marie Antoinette still knew nothing of the notorious story of the grove where she was supposed to have given Rohan a
secret interview, and so she wanted this "strange romance," as she
called it, to be cleared up as soon as possible. She asked Böhmer to
draw up an account of it, which the jeweller brought on 12 August.
It was at once made known to the King, and on 15 August, Assumption
Day and the Queen's feast day, Marie Antoinette, Louis XVI, the
Baron de Breteuil, Minister of the King's Household, and M. de Miro-

mesnil, Keeper of the Seals, met in conference in the King's cabinet room. The Queen wanted the Cardinal arrested. "He has used my name like a vile and clumsy forgerer." It was a swindle. The strongest proof was in the flagrant lie made by the Cardinal to the Böhmers and Saint-James, that solemn oath which the Prince of the Church had dared take to them. How had he dared to raise his arm and affirm that he had dealt directly with the Queen?

Miromesnil counselled prudence, but Breteuil supported Marie Antoinette. He detested the Cardinal, whom he had replaced in Vienna and who since then had never stopped making fun of him. According to Breteuil, the Cardinal was riddled with debts and had invented the whole plot in order to lay hands on the necklace. Like Miromesnil Louis XVI considered that "Rohan's rank and family entitled him to be heard before being arrested," but Marie Antoinette displayed such exasperation that he sent immediately for the Cardinal, who was with the *grandes entrées* in the Council Room while waiting to go to the chapel.

It was eleven o'clock. Wearing a scarlet watered silk soutane and lace rochet, the Cardinal entered the room. The King questioned him.

"My cousin, did you buy diamonds from Böhmer?"

"Yes, Sire."

"What did you do with them?"

"I thought that they had been given to the Queen."

"Who gave you this commission?"

"A lady called the Comtesse de la Motte-Valois, who had handed me a letter from the Queen, and I thought that by carrying out this commission I was paying my court to Her Majesty."

Here the Queen interrupted him. "How could you believe, Monsieur, you to whom I have not spoken for eight years, that I had chosen you for these negotiations, and through the intermediary of such a woman?"

"I can see that I have been cruelly deceived," replied the Cardinal. "I shall pay for the necklace. My desire to please Your Majesty blinded my eyes. I saw no trick and I am very sorry."

The Cardinal did not dare look at the Queen, who was red with anger. He took a wallet from his pocket; it contained the contract signed "Marie Antoinette of France."

"This is neither the Queen's writing nor her signature," exclaimed the King. "How could a Prince of the House of Rohan and a Grand

Almoner of France think that the Queen would sign 'Marie Antoinette of France'? Everyone knows that Queens sign only their Christian names. Explain all this mystery to me," continued the King. "I do not want to find you guilty; I should like you to be justified. Tell me the meaning of all these negotiations with Böhmer, these assurances and these notes."

The Cardinal was as pale as death; they thought he would fall. He clung to the table. "Sire, I am too distressed to reply to Your Majesty in a way which . . ."

"Calm yourself, M. le Cardinal, and go into my room. You will find paper, pen and ink there. Write down what you have to tell me."

The report he handed the King a quarter-of-an-hour later was as confused as it could be. One thing was clear: "A woman called De Valois had persuaded him that the necklace was to be acquired for the Queen, and that woman had deceived him."

"Where is this woman?" asked the King.

"Sire, I do not know."

"Have you the necklace?"

"It is in the hands of that woman."

The Baron de Breteuil read the report written by the Böhmers, and then the King asked: "Where are the alleged authorisations written and signed by the Queen and which are mentioned in the report?"

"Sire, I have them; they are forged."

"I know quite well they are forged!"

"I will bring them to Your Majesty."

The King looked at him with contempt. "I must warn you that you are to be arrested."

The Grand Almoner paled. "Ah! Sire, I shall always obey Your Majesty's orders, but let him spare me the pain of being arrested in my pontifical robes in the eyes of the whole court."

"It must be so!"

Rohan persisted, and recalled that his cousin, Mme de Marsan, had brought up the King. At this recollection Louis XVI was about to weaken, but Marie Antoinette's eyes were full of tears, and he made up his mind.

"Monsieur, I shall try to console your relatives as best I may. I should be glad if you could exculpate yourself. I am doing my duty as a King and a husband."

Pushing the Cardinal in front of him, Breteuil went to the door opening on to the Salon de la Pendule. All the *grandes entrées* were there, while the rest of the court were massed in the Council Room, the State Room, the *Œil-de-Bœuf* and the Long Gallery. A voice—that of Breteuil addressing the captain of the Bodyguards—made everyone jump.

"Arrest M. le Cardinal!"

If a bomb had exploded in the Hall of Mirrors it would not have caused more fright and stupefaction. Only the Cardinal retained his calm, and standing at the entrance to the gallery, he wrote a note to his *alter ego,* the Abbé Georgel, asking him to burn all the letters contained in the "red portfolio."

These were the notes which the Grand Almoner had imagined were written to him by the Queen and which had been delivered to him by Mme de la Motte.

There was a considerable scandal. "Only in France," wrote the Archduke Leopold to his brother Joseph II, "could one see a Cardinal-Archbishop, Grand Almoner to the King, without religion or morals arrested as a forger of letters, a swindler and a cheat." "It is incredible!" he also exclaimed. The Emperor was of the same opinion. "I should not have thought him capable of such roguery and such a sinister trick as he is accused of." One can see that Marie Antoinette's two brothers had doubts about the Cardinal's guilt. They did not dare ask if their sister was entirely unconnected with the intrigue, but in Paris they had no such reticence.

All unconscious, Marie Antoinette heaved a sigh of relief. "As far as I am concerned," she wrote to her brother, "I am delighted at the thought of not having to hear this wretched business talked of any more."

For her everything was finished, and on the day after the accusation, while the Cardinal, who had spent the night at home, was on his way to the Bastille, Marie Antoinette took the road to Trianon, where the final rehearsals of the *Barber* were awaiting her.

As she listened to her partner, Don Basilio, repeating his famous speech on calumny, did she realise that the scene might be a dramatic representation of her own case? Yesterday, as the Comtesse de la Marck said, "the Queen was going to the Opera and to the Comédie, piling up debts, canvassing for lawsuits, covering herself with feathers and pompoms and caring nothing for anybody." Yesterday calumny had been no more than a "faint noise, skimming the ground like a swallow before the storm." But today the Queen's name was to be dragged in the mud, coupled with those of a prelate "without religion or morals," a forger, a cheat and a prostitute. Calumny then would be seen to "raise its head, hiss, swell and grow before one's eyes." And this chorus of hate was to attribute the Grand Almoner of France to Marie Antoinette as a lover.

The principal accused, the Comtesse de la Motte-Valois, was at Bar-sur-Aube, where before her arrest she was given plenty of time, with the help of her friend Beugnot, Louis XVIII's future Minister, to burn the passionate letters written by the Cardinal to the Queen of France.

On the next day, 18 August, she was arrested and taken to the Bastille. It was then discovered that the prisoner was not entirely an adventuress. She really was descended from the Valois and her arms were "argent, one fess azure charged with three fleurs-de-lis or." Four generations separated her from Henry de Saint-Rémy, acknowledged son of King Henri II, and Nicole de Savigny, Dame de Saint-Rémy, but from a misalliance to misalliance the family had sunk into poverty. Jeanne's father, Baron Jacques de Saint-Rémy, had died in the poorhouse. She herself had had an unhappy childhood. Her mother, a peasant, had set up with a soldier and both of them beat the child and forced her to beg, imploring passers-by "for the sake of an orphan of the blood of the Valois." It was in this condition that a noble lady, the Marquise de Boulainvilliers, had discovered her by the side of the road leading to Passy. She was moved, and taking the child and her sister brought them up in her house, then apprenticed them and finally sent them to the convent of the Abbey of Longchamp, where only daughters of the nobility were taken. Mme de Boulainvilliers had had her protégées' genealogy established by the famous Hozier. From the end of 1776 the King granted a pension of 800 livres to his distant cousins. The two little "Princesses," as they called themselves, rewarded the Marquise for her kindness by running away from their convent to finish up in an inn at Bar-sur-Aube. A second protector, Mme de Surmont, took charge of the runaways and it was in her house that Jeanne, now a very pretty young woman, met an officer of the gendarmes called Marc-Antoine Nicolas de la Motte. The marriage was celebrated at Bar-sur-Aube on 6 June 1780 and the couple, who on their own authority had become "Comte and Comtesse de la Motte-Valois," set out to seek their fortune. The young Comtesse decided she had found it the day when Mme de Boulainvilliers, who did not bear grudges, presented her to the Cardinal de Rohan on the way from Saverne to Strasbourg.

A few months later, the "Comte," now a "supernumerary captain in Monsieur's dragoons," came with his wife to Paris. The first months were very difficult, in spite of the frequent charity of the Grand Almoner, and in spite of the visits of "military men and men of the gown," whom Mme de la Motte received while, like a well-behaved husband, the "supernumerary captain" disappeared. "The inheritor of the blood of the Valois" decided to use cunning and to faint from inanition in the antechambers of Versailles. Twice she fell in a swoon in the presence of the Queen, who did not even notice. She was no more successful in the apartments of the Comtesse d'Artois. Only Madame Elisabeth was moved when she saw this pretty girl with clear eyes sink to the ground in her "servants' hall." She had the royal pension increased to 1,500 livres, but after another swoon, possibly less well counterfeited, Louis XVI's sister suspected the truth. Mme de la Motte then transformed herself into "a promoter of business in the offices of Ministers and at court," which was almost a recognised profession. This occupation was much more paying than syncopes, as Jeanne succeeded in making people, including even the Cardinal, believe that she frequently saw the Queen, and soon affluence was reigning in the la Motte home.

The two principal accused were now behind bars. The Cardinal's defence was that he had bought the necklace in the Queen's name and that the Comtesse de la Motte had been the link between Marie Antoinette and himself. On the evening of 1 February he had gone to Versailles, where Mme de la Motte had a small property. He took with him the large case containing the necklace. Mme de la Motte was alone. "The Queen is waiting; this necklace will be given to her this evening."

A few minutes later someone announced "coming from the Queen." "From discretion" the Cardinal retired into a "half-opened" alcove and had seen a man dressed in black hand over a note and then leave the room. Mme de la Motte approached the alcove and showed the letter. It was a word from the Queen "giving orders for the box to be handed

to the bearer." The man was brought back, the jewel case handed to
him and he disappeared into the night.

"Who was that?" asked the Cardinal.

"He is attached to the Queen's Bedchamber and Music."

To these details the Comtesse de la Motte replied that the story of
the handing over of the jewel case was pure invention. "By way of
conversation" with the Cardinal she might, one day, have made allusion
to the necklace, but the prelate had replied to her "with the same indifference." "The next day, or two days later, M. de Rohan had asked
her for the address of the Böhmers." She knew nothing more. The
paper signed "Marie Antoinette of France" was in the hands of the
Cardinal, who had written it in the presence of the jewellers. It was
the Cardinal who had dealt with the Böhmers. According to her, "it
was without the Queen's knowledge that the Cardinal negotiated."
Prince Louis was in straitened circumstances as a result of the fire at
his château of Saverne and as a result of his extravagance. Everyone
knew that. Then suddenly the prisoner made an accusation: the chief
culprit was Cagliostro.

What had the brilliant alchemist to do with it? He was not concerned
in the swindle, but Mme de la Motte considered that by dragging the
famous charlatan into an affair which was already pretty much confused she would do herself no harm, but on the contrary distract everyone's attention. In Paris no one talked of anything but this Comte de
Cagliostro, who claimed to be two thousand years old, to have been
present at the Marriage of Cana and to have walked with Christ on the
shores of Lake Tiberias. When a disbeliever pushed him further, he
answered arrogantly: "I am who am!"

In reality his name was Joseph Balsamo and he was no more a
Comte than Jeanne was a Comtesse. He had managed to gain the
Cardinal's confidence, to become intimate with him and to make gold
and diamonds for him. The Cardinal had said to the "Comtesse": "He
is a great man, a god! He should be spoken of with the greatest respect.
He is going to make me a Minister!" He had also promised to reconcile
the Cardinal and the Queen. The Cardinal, as he was fond of proclaiming, was inconsolable "at having incurred his sovereign's hate." "It
brings a bitterness to my heart which poisons my happiest days."

In order to console His Eminence Cagliostro made Marie Antoinette
appear in a carafe. Of course the Cardinal saw nothing by himself,

but through the intermediary of a child who must be "as pure as an angel." The latter was dressed in an apron woven in silver and with "a large sun in the middle," and wore the blue ribbon. He was the child the Queen was to give birth to in March, the future Louis XVII. Cagliostro then drew his sword, placed his hand on the child's head and blew on his hair as he waved his rapier. Then he drew him behind a screen, where there was a carafe of clear water on a table.

"I command you," cried Cagliostro, "to make me see everything I wish. What do you see, child?"

With beating heart the Cardinal held his breath.

"Nothing," replied the "seer."

"Strike with your foot, child. What do you see?"

"Nothing."

"Strike again! What do you see?"

"I see a tall, beautiful pregnant woman dressed in white. I see her in her bed."

"Do you know the Queen? Have you seen her? Do you recognise her?"

"Yes, Monsieur, I see the Queen."

"The Cardinal was in ecstasies," related Mme de la Motte. "He crawled at the magician's feet and kissed his hands."

The "Comtesse" detested the alchemist, who where swindling was concerned was a dangerous rival. So at her first interrogation, on 20 August, she accused Cagliostro. It was he who had helped the Cardinal steal the necklace. This mountebank was the accomplice of the Prince of the Church.

But there was too much evidence involving the "Comtesse" for the lieutenant of police to believe this version. How was it that since 1 February the La Mottes had been living like princes? Forty-two carriages had brought sumptuous furniture to Bar-sur-Aube. They had bought six coaches and twelve horses and engaged a large staff—cooks, lackeys, kitchen maids, a coachman and even "a Negro covered with silver from head to foot." It was nothing but feasts and receptions, and to defray the expenses they were constantly selling diamonds. The "Comte" had even gone to London to negotiate the sale of 240,000 livres' worth of stones, "some of which were damaged as though they had been hastily and carelessly prised from a piece of jewellery with a knife." These must have been the diamonds from the necklace.

"Perhaps," replied Mme de la Motte, when she was interrogated on 26 August, "but it was the Cardinal who had told me to sell them to pay the instalments. On two occasions he gave me a large quantity of diamonds."

On Monday 25 August she began to write her defence. Her arguments were skilful: "If I were guilty, I should not have stayed in France. I should have fled to rejoin my husband, who is at present in England."

In spite of this argument the lieutenant of police was convinced that Breteuil and the Queen were mistaken. The Cardinal was innocent. Mme de la Motte was not his accomplice but the instigator of the swindle. Rohan had been speaking the truth in his account of how the "Comtesse" had hoaxed and plucked him.

For the police officer the affair was now clear. For the Queen's enemies, reinforced by the tribe of Rohan, Marson, Brionne and Soubise, the Cardinal was not the victim of an adventuress but of the Queen. "In the town," relates the *Correspondance secrète,* "they accused Mme de la Motte and the Cardinal; but at court they accused the Queen."

The opposition members of Parliament were delighted. "What a great and fortunate affair!" cried one of them. "A swindling Cardinal, the Queen involved in an affair of forgery! . . . What mud on the crozier and sceptre! What a triumph for the ideas of liberty! How useful for Parliament!" and from hatred of the Queen these gentlemen began immediately to campaign for the "illustrious victim."

But suddenly a story pre-dating the theft emerged from the first interrogations and explained the Cardinal's hitherto incomprehensible credulity.

This was the affair of the grove, more serious perhaps than that of the necklace and already a year old. And, like us today, Marie Antoinette, by studying the memoranda and documents of the case, could reconstruct "this horror," as she henceforth called the affair.

Mme de la Motte had formed a plan to take advantage of the stupidity of the Cardinal, that great fool in purple. She claimed to have spoken to the Queen about the Grand Almoner and his grief with "such enthusiasm that she had gradually dispelled her prejudices." One day the "Comtesse" declared joyfully to the prelate: "I am authorised by the Queen to ask you for a written defence to the faults imputed to you."

The Cardinal, moved to tears by gratitude, wrote. The Queen

answered, and soon a correspondence was carried on through Mme de la Motte. The Queen's letters were written by a friend of the "Comte," a former gendarme called Marc-Antoine Rétaux de Villette. To his talent as a forger he joined that of a singer, and when he sang Rameau's music or recited his own verses his voice was so captivating that the "Comtesse" had allowed herself to be captivated.

Needless to say, consoling the Cardinal was of no interest to the triangle unless there was money in it, and so Mme de la Motte began to dictate to her lover letters in which Marie Antoinette, on various pretexts, asked His Eminence to lend her money. The Grand Almoner found this quite natural. At that time everyone was talking about the Queen's reckless expenditure and debts.

Meanwhile, in exchange for services he was delighted to render, and which permitted the trio to live in luxury, the Cardinal wished to have an audience with Marie Antoinette. This was where matters became complicated. Unlike Cagliostro, Mme de la Motte had no means of summoning the Queen to her house in a carafe. Some other way had to be found, and Jeanne had an idea. Everyone was aware that Marie Antoinette walked in the park in the evenings—there were countless stories about these walks. Why should not the Cardinal be granted an audience at night in the gardens? All that had to be done was to find a woman who in the darkness could play the part of the Queen. This bold project did not daunt the Comte de la Motte, who began to search. Soon he found in the gardens of the Palais-Royal a fair young woman who was astonishingly like the Queen. This was Mlle Oliva, the "street walker." He entered into conversation with her, seduced her and after nine visits brought her to the Comtesse, and then faded away.

Jeanne did not beat about the bush. She called Oliva "dear heart" and declared: "I have the Queen's complete confidence. She and I are hand in glove. She has just given me further proof by ordering me to find a person to do something which will be explained in due course. If you wish to undertake it I shall make you a present of the sum of 15,000 livres."

The girl was dazzled. "I should be very flattered by doing anything that might please the Queen."

"M. le Comte de la Motte will come to fetch you tomorrow evening in a carriage and will take you to Versailles," ended Jeanne, leaving the young woman, in her own words, "intoxicated with joy and hope."

The next day the "Comte" took the girl to Versailles. When the carriage drew near the gates of the château it was stopped by the "Comtesse," who ordered her husband: "Take Madame to my house." La Motte obeyed, left the girl in the Rue Dauphine and disappeared. Two hours later he came back with Mme de la Motte. "Their faces were alive with gaiety."

"I have told the Queen of your arrival," Jeanne announced, "and she was very pleased at it. She is impatient to be there tomorrow to see how things will go."

Mlle Oliva was surprised. "But what is it, then, that you want me to do?"

"Oh! it is nothing at all. You will soon know."

On the next day Mme de la Motte dressed the young woman. "I was dressed in a white robe of spotted linen; as far as I can remember, it was a *robe à l'enfant* or a *gaulle*." This was the dress the Queen was wearing in Mme Vigée-Lebrun's portrait, which was exhibited in the Salon in the same year, 1784.

The "Comtesse" then gave the girl a letter with no name on it. "I shall take you into the park this evening and you will give this letter to a very great nobleman you will meet there."

On 11 August 1784, between 11 o'clock and midnight, M. and Mme de la Motte came to fetch Oliva, who had a white tippet round her shoulders and a *Thérèse* on her head. When they came to the grille of the Orangerie the "Comtesse" handed her companion a rose. "You will give this rose with the letter to the person who presents himself before you and you will say to him only this: 'You know what this means.' The Queen will be there to see how the interview goes off. She will speak to you, she will be behind you."

Oliva, seized "with trembling all over," began to stammer with emotion. She was only a poor girl and did not know what title she should give the Queen.

"You must always say 'Your Majesty,' " declared the former gendarme.

The "Dame de la Motte" stationed the young woman in an arbour. "Stay there. I am going to fetch the great nobleman."

She went away, and the girl's heart beat fast. The "great nobleman"—it was the Cardinal—arrived and bowed, while Jeanne remained at a short distance. "I was trembling so much that I cannot even now imagine how I was able to do even half of what I had been commanded." In fact the young woman merely handed the rose to the Cardinal, uttering the agreed phrase, and forgot the letter. The Grand Almoner had scarcely taken the rose when one of the Queen's valets—it was Rétaux in disguise—ran up, saying: "Here are Madame and Madame la Comtesse d'Artois!"

Madame de la Motte hurried up, took the girl's arm and led her away, saying "urgently": "Quick, come quickly!"

She handed the young woman over to M. de la Motte and returned to the Cardinal, who was intoxicated with joy. He thought he had heard the "Queen" say to him: "You may hope that the past will be forgotten."

His Eminence was dazzled and not in the least surprised. It was currently said that Marie Antoinette received her lovers in the park. The court and the town had mentioned the names of Guines, Coigny, Lauzun and Fersen.

Henceforth Mme de la Motte could make all kinds of demands on him "in the name of the Queen" and they would be received with "a deep sentiment of respect and gratitude." August 1784 was not over when Jeanne asked the Grand Almoner for 60,000 livres "for some poor people in whom she knew the Queen was interested." Until the end of the year demands for money and passionate letters written by the former gendarme Rétaux de Villette succeeded each other. As for the Cardinal, he replied by letters "which no man with any self-respect could read right through," related Beugnot, who was able to read them before the holocaust at Bar-sur-Aube.

The Cardinal was all the less suspicious since Jeanne, in order to deceive him, continued to ask him for a few louis to help her to live. Faced with such an outstanding example of imbecility, Mme de la Motte did not hesitate for a moment when Maître Laporte asked her, on behalf of the jewellers, to intercede with the Queen. Her mind was soon made up: she would have the Cardinal buy the necklace and would keep it for herself.

Everything seems clear to us today, but at the time it was not so.

"It is impossible," cried the Archbishop of Tours, "that the Cardinal should be guilty of being involved in such a gross swindle!"

Fersen, who was with his regiment, noted these rumours. "It is said that the whole thing was only a game between the Queen and the Cardinal, that he was on very good terms with her, that she had in fact commissioned him to buy the necklace, that the Queen pretended not to be able to bear him in order to conceal her aims, that the King had been informed of it, that he had reproached her with it, that she had been made very ill by this and had pretended to be pregnant."

In the opinion of her enemies Marie Antoinette must have been mixed up in the affair one way or the other. The most tolerant assumed that the scene in the grove had been stage-managed to amuse the Queen, who was hidden in an arbour. With the complicity of Breteuil —some even said of Jeanne de la Motte—Marie Antoinette had wanted to fool His Eminence. After that Jeanne had gone on with the intrigue on her own account. Everything then appeared more normal: the Cardinal was no longer an imbecile and Mme de la Motte was no longer the moving spirit in the intrigue. Others were surprised that Rétaux de Villette, who was arrested at the same time as Oliva, should confess everything, the forgeries as well as the scene in the grove, give all the required details and yet deny having played the part of the man in black who came to fetch the necklace from Mme de la Motte in the night of 1 February. Others were surprised that a special messenger had not been sent to Bar-sur-Aube on 15 August to arrest the "Comtesse." Why wait three days? Finally, everyone was astonished at Jeanne's calm, having left for Bar-sur-Aube on 5 August, receiving and paying visits there, living like a Princess and making no attempt to escape. Was someone trying to protect her?

And so Mme de la Motte's consummate cunning, the mistakes made by the investigators and the accused, and the details which did not come to light all turned against Marie Antoinette. The victim of her reputation, was she now to see opening before her feet that "abyss" of which Maria Theresa had once spoken?

As unconcerned as ever, and instead of avoiding the Parisians, who were dragging her in the mud, she showed herself—and in great array. On 5 October, having made up her mind to go to Fontainebleau by the Seine, she decided to embark "at the beginning of the plain of Issy" and to cross Paris on board a *hyac*. On the bank 15 horses drew the little boat, which sailed up the Seine as the cannon of the Invalides thundered. Marie Antoinette came on deck and took care "to be seen by all the assembled people."

Soon all the actors in the drama, even those with only walking-on parts, were in the Bastille, with the exception of La Motte, who having taken refuge in England was selling off the rest of the diamonds. The truth was becoming clear. Everyone confessed, but Jeanne, although overwhelmed by detailed proofs, refused to speak the truth.

"It was M. de Rohan who stole the necklace. It was by your orders that my husband and myself had the diamonds from it mounted or sold."

When she was urged to give up this ridiculous line of defence, she declared: "There is a secret which I shall confide only in private to the Minister of the King's Household." But when she felt that Breteuil might well decide to accept this interview she simulated madness and also indulged in exhibitionism by remaining naked in her cell for hours on end.

Finally she grew tired, and at her last interview burst into tears. But she would admit only to having instigated the scene in the grove. As for everything else, Jeanne declared that she "threw herself into the arms of Providence."

Before the Cardinal took up residence in the Bastille he had worn secular clothes as often as possible. Now he never put off his ceremonial robes. He appeared in a rochet of Malines lace and a purple cape. While he confessed his error his slender hand on which the ring sparkled played with the pale blue ribbon of the Order of the Holy Ghost. His attitude was noble, dignified and even humble when necessary. His greatest anxiety was to absolve Cagliostro and his wife. We possess the secret correspondence he managed to keep up with his lawyer, Maître Target. Only twice did he ask for news of Marie Antoinette. "Tell me if it is true that the Queen continues to be sad," he wrote.

When the preliminary investigation was over Maître Target, according to custom, published a voluminous "Memorial," showing his client's defence. And the rhymers said:

> Target in his Memorial
> Has told as best he can
> The story of the Cardinal,
> That most unhappy man.
> And all his arguments set out,
> His wordy eloquence,
> Prove clearly without any doubt
> His client's innocence.

Rohan then sent a letter to the King asking if he might appear before Parliament to be judged, but he added these very important lines: "However, if I might hope that the explanations which may have been given, and of which I know nothing, might have led Your Majesty to judge that I am guilty only of having been deceived, I should venture to beg you, Sire, to pronounce sentence in accordance with your justice and your goodness."

In other words, Louis XVI need only declare that the Cardinal was completely innocent and send him, by means of a *lettre de cachet,* to a house where he would be kept under surveillance. A public trial would thus be avoided. But Marie Antoinette had other views. "I want this horror and all its details to be brought into the open before the eyes of all the world." Blinded by a desire for vengeance, she thought the Cardinal was guilty, if not of having stolen the necklace at least of having dared to believe she loved him, and she urged the King to send the affair to the Parliament. By so doing she was to make everyone believe that she was guilty.

So the Queen did not hesitate to entrust her honour to the discontented gentlemen of the robe, who detested her and whose only aim was to humiliate the crown and abase the Queen. It was no longer the Cardinal's trial which was about to begin, but Marie Antoinette's. In Goethe's words, the affair of the necklace was in fact to become the preface to the Revolution.

Being innocent of the theft for which he had been arrested, the Prince de Rohan was to be judged on one point only: was the Grand Almoner of France justified or not in believing that the Queen could give him an amatory interview, write him passionate letters and commission him, without the King's knowledge, to buy a necklace worth 1,600,000 livres?

But could a Prince of the Church be brought before a tribunal? Some people went so far as to evoke the Councils of Antioch and Nicaea, where "it was laid down that Bishops were the sole judges of Bishops."

"No doubt," replied the supporters of a trial, "but at that time Gaul was not Christian."

"But from the time of Clovis to the 10th century one can find judgments proving that the Bishops were judged by Councils." And they recalled the case of the Cardinal de la Balue, whom Louis XI had had arrested and condemned on his own authority.

"But His Holiness censured King Louis XI, who acknowledged his error and asked for a Bull of absolution."

"Did not Henri III have Cardinal de Guise assassinated?"

"Yes, but he was excommunicated."

A decision had to be made, and so "ancient Bulls" were evoked, without any more specific detail, which had formerly warned Bishops and Cardinals "that in temporal matters even their souls were subject to the laws of the sovereign princes." And the trial was fixed for 22 May 1786.

> Oliva says that he was victimised.
> Lamotte says that his crime is undisguised.
> He says himself that he was mesmerised.
>   Alleluia!

> The Holy Father dressed him up in red.
> The King and Queen have blackened him instead.
> The Court will sprinkle whitewash on his head.
>   Alleluia!

The Cardinal whitewashed? It was impossible that the Government would allow such a verdict, which would be an affront to the Queen.

Before the pleadings had been opened the battle had started. The women were the most enthusiastic. The Prelate's supporters wore head-dresses in which sparkled a rivière of diamonds fastened by red ribbons lined with yellow: this was called "Cardinal on the straw." Even in the Polignac clan Marie Antoinette found partisans of her enemy, for example Vaudreuil. "The great ladies of the court," wrote Hardy in his *Journal*, "undertook the defence of the Cardinal with great warmth, for they were greatly touched by and grateful for the delicacy he had displayed at the moment of his arrest in ordering the Abbé Georgel, his confidential agent, to destroy or hide from general view his corre-spondence with a great many of them."

On 22 May 1786 the Parliament assembled, without the Princes of the Blood and the Peers. The judges—the *Grand'Chambre* and the *Tournelle* together—numbered 64. It took six days to read the docu-ments, and then the Procureur Général, Joly de Fleury, was called on. He asked "that the document signed *Marie Antoinette de France*" should be "declared fraudulently falsified." According to him, the Cardinal ought to come "to the *Grand'Chambre* to declare out loud that he had audaciously believed in the meeting in the grove, that he had helped to deceive the merchants by giving them to believe that the Queen knew of the transaction, to declare that he repented and to ask pardon of the King and the Queen; and that furthermore he should be condemned to resign his positions, to give alms to the poor, to spend his whole life at a distance from the royal residences and finally to remain in prison until the execution of the judgement."

And the Procureur concluded: "The Cardinal puts forward what happened in the garden at Versailles as being of a nature to encourage his delusion. But could he allow himself to believe in a false and pretended meeting at night on the terrace at Versailles, could he allow himself to go there, and in going there did he not commit an offence towards the Queen worthy of the highest punishment?"

Hatred for Marie Antoinette was so lively among the lawyers that this wise and just peroration touched off a violent scene. Séguier, the Advocate-General, rose, red with anger. He exclaimed loudly: "The Cardinal should be acquitted!" and turning to Joly de Fleury, he cried: "You are about to descend into the tomb and will leave your ashes covered with ignominy which will be shared by the magistrates!"

"Your anger does not surprise me, Monsieur," replied the Procureur Général calmly. "A man as devoted to licentiousness as yourself was bound to defend the Cardinal's cause."

"I sometimes visit prostitutes," Séguier admitted, amid smiles. "I even leave my carriage at their door. That is my affair. But no one has ever known me basely sell my opinion to fortune."

On 30 August the examination began. Rétaux de Villette, who came first, extricated himself very well, "even anticipating the questions before they were finished, with an air and tone of the greatest precision."

When Mme de la Motte, who came next, saw the ignominious seat she recoiled. "Sit there, Madame," said the usher coldly.

"In less than two minutes," related an observer, "she managed things so well, and her countenance was so assured that she seemed to be in her own apartments seated in her best armchair."

With "intrepidity" and "without the least appearance of embarrassment," "she replied to the questions," we are told, "making herself heard and paying more attention to probabilities than to facts and fastening particularly on the court's inability to show any of the letters, writings and material proofs they would have liked to see." When the alleged letters from Marie Antoinette to Rohan were mentioned she refused to reply "so as not to offend the Queen." But the President insisted, and she went so far as to declare that the Cardinal had shown her "two hundred letters written by the Queen in which she called him *tu*."

There was an uproar. In private all these gentlemen were willing to speak every possible ill of "the Austrian," but in public they owed it to themselves to be scandalised by such ignominy.

When Jeanne had left, President d'Aligre sent word to the Cardinal "that as the accused's stool had been removed he could now come into court." Rohan entered wearing violet robes—the mourning of Cardinals. He looked so pale, as he had just had an attack of food poisoning in the Bastille from drinking whey prepared in a verdigrised pot, and he trembled so much that the President said: "M. le Cardinal is at liberty to sit, if he wishes."

Rohan obeyed, recovered himself and for half-an-hour "spoke from the fullness of his heart," telling his pitiable tale and succeeding perfectly in making himself appear even more stupid than he had been. On ending his speech "he saluted the chief bench and the other magistrates." All returned his salute and the chief bench even rose, "which was a marked distinction."

Oliva made the judges wait, which touched them, for she was occupied in suckling her child by her future husband, the Sieur de Beausire; it had been born in the Bastille. "Rousseaumania" was then prevalent and the occurrence seemed charming. Pathos was followed by laughter with Cagliostro, who expressed himself in a jargon composed of Latin, Greek, Italian and Arabic. The court relaxed.

"Who are you?" asked the President.

"A noble voyager!"

On Wednesday 31 May, judgement was given.

It was five o'clock in the morning. All the Rohans, Brionnes, Soubises, Montlasons and Marsans stationed themselves in deep mourning at the entrance to the *Grand'Chambre* and bowed as the 62 magistrates passed in slow procession before them.

"At two o'clock the voting magistrates interrupted their work to dine at a table laid for forty which the First President had had set up in the Salle Saint-Louis, but most of them ate standing and at half-past three they were in session again."

Two magistrates asked for the death sentence. This was a manoeuvre, for a punishment involving death obliged the thirteen *conseillers-clercs*, who were churchmen, to retire. Among them were eleven of the Cardinal's enemies. Once the priests had left the battle began. There was no question of inflicting a penalty on Rohan, since there had not even been "the beginning of any proof," but according to the friends of the court a formula must be found to punish the "offence."

The President proposed that at least "the Cardinal should be obliged to abstain from carrying out the functions pertaining to the post of Grand Almoner until it should be otherwise ordered by the King." In fact, this judgement would have recalled the fact that "one did not leave the Bastille without being exiled." Other magistrates were in favour of making the accused publicly admit "that he had, as a result of an abuse of the Queen's name, made to the said Böhmer and Bassenge a payment of 30,000 livres for which he received a receipt in the name of the Queen; that he had dared to be lacking in respect for the sacred persons of the King and the Queen; that it was from audacity that he had permitted himself to believe in an alleged nocturnal meeting on the terrace at Versailles; that it was from audacity that, unbeknown to the King and Queen and without having himself made sure of their intentions, he opened and carried on negotiations with the said Böhmer and Bassenge."

Fifteen councillors agreed with these stern but just conclusions. Others, who were wiser, felt that the majority would never come round to this point of view, and simply suggested a nonsuit, which did not completely whitewash an accused, holding him responsible but not guilty of the facts as indicted. This sentence would also have given the Queen some slight satisfaction.

But the majority was stronger. By 26 votes to 22 the Cardinal was entirely "discharged from every species of accusation." Cagliostro was similarly treated and Oliva's case was nonsuited, Rétaux was banished from the realm and Jeanne de la Motte was condemned to perpetual imprisonment after being marked on both shoulders with the letter V given to thieves.

Paris wanted illuminations, but the police intervened. That evening 10,000 people gathered round the Bastille to shout their enthusiasm and in acclaiming the Cardinal demonstrated their joy at seeing the Austrian humiliated. It was in fact the Queen's defeat which was being celebrated.

At Versailles Marie Antoinette wept long and bitterly. "Condole with me," she said to Mme Campan. "The intriguer who wanted to ruin me or to get money by making use of my name and my signature has just been completely acquitted."

The King, too, still considered Rohan guilty both of the "offence" and of swindling. Instead of bowing to the judgement, which would have been the more sensible course, he wrote to Breteuil: "The Keeper of the Seals has informed me of the judgement by which all the indictments are withdrawn. In consequence you will give orders to M. de Launay to let Cardinal de Rohan and Cagliostro leave the Bastille, but as the Queen has been particularly compromised by the affair of the necklace and the diamonds, in which he was greatly involved, you will order the Cardinal to hand in his resignation from his position as First Almoner and the decoration attached to it. You will order him to leave Paris in three days, to see only his family and his advisers, to betake himself to his abbey at Chaise-Dieu, where I hope he will receive only a few persons. You will order Cagliostro to leave Paris in eight days and the kingdom in three weeks."

Mme de Marsan threw herself at the Queen's feet to implore pardon for her cousin. Marie Antoinette looked at her coldly. "The Cardinal must submit to the King's orders."

"This refusal makes me realise how disagreeable my presence must be to Your Majesty. This is the last time I shall have the honour of presenting myself to her."

"Madame, I shall be very sorry."

And the affair ended with the inevitable pun, just as the Archduke Leopold had foretold on the day after the arrest:

> *Le Parlement l'a purgé*
> *Le Roi l'a envoyé à la Chaise!*

The execution on Wednesday 21 June of the sentence pronounced on Jeanne de Valois was a dreadful scene. In the Cour de Mai six executioners were needed to hold her down on her knees while the clerk read the sentence. She struggled, bit, shrieked, howled. Then she refused to undress. "She fought like a tigress with her feet, hands and teeth, in such a way that they were obliged to cut her garments right down to the chemise, which was of the greatest indecency before all the spectators."

She rolled on the ground and reached the foot of the great staircase, pursued by the executioners. She was held down, face to the ground, with her skirts turned up. The red-hot iron was applied to her shoulder and sizzled on the skin. The condemned woman made such a sudden bound that she turned over and the second V was applied on her breast. Before falling in the faint she had time to bite one of the executioners right through his jacket.

A minute later a cab left the courtyard and set off for the prison of the Salpêtrière. The two watchmen "in short robes" who accompanied Mme de la Motte had great difficulty in preventing her from throwing herself out of the window.

Ten months later she managed to escape and of course it was said, as an added calumny, that the Queen had facilitated her flight, for La Motte, who was still in London, was threatening to publish "documents whose publication was feared, unless his wife were restored to him."

"Goodbye, Madame," the nun who opened the secret door for her was supposed to have said. "Take care that nobody *remarks* you."

In three years the storm was to break, but the first thunderclap had already been heard. "This event fills me with as much terror as the head of the Medusa," wrote Goethe.

11

❖

Madame Deficit

ON 1 JUNE 1786, the day after the Parliament's judgement, Marie
Antoinette wrote to Mme de Polignac: "Come and weep with me,
come and console your friend. The judgement that has just been pronounced is an atrocious insult. I am bathed in tears of grief and despair.
. . . Come to me, my dear heart."

The Duchesse must have found the right words to say, for on 4 June
the Queen, who had to write to Mercy to tell him about a dinner at
Trianon, added, merely as a postscript: "What do you think of the
judgement?" Mercy wrote to Kaunitz that the Queen had been
"affected" by the judgement but that she had soon regained her "calm."

A few years earlier Marie Antoinette would have hurried to Mme de
Polignac's house, instead of asking her to come and weep with her.
But she no longer cared very much for her friend's home, where
Vaudreuil was always lolling about on the sofas. During this painful
year he had openly displayed his sympathy for Cardinal de Rohan.
"Four years before the Revolution," an observer remarks, "matters had
come to the point where before leaving her apartments to go to Mme de
Polignac the Queen would always send one of her valets de chambre
to find out the names of the people there, and on receiving the reply
she often stayed away." The former Comtesse Jules was in no hurry to
change the list of her guests. She went so far as to exclaim: "I think
that because Your Majesty is kind enough to come to my drawing room
that is no reason for her to try to exclude my friends."

Marie Antoinette sighed, but bore her no grudge for her boldness.
"I am not angry with Mme de Polignac on that account," she said one

day to La Marck. "At bottom she is good and she loves me, but her associates have subjugated her."

After the affair of the necklace the monarchy was rapidly approaching the abyss, but there was a short period of calm during the last six months of 1786. Astonished by their unbelievable victory, the Queen's enemies seemed to have paused to take breath, and at Trianon the summer had never seemed so pleasant.

At the beginning of June Marie Antoinette, who was now eight months pregnant, went in her carriage to visit the hamlet, which was now finished. In spite of the artificial cracks, the artificially crumbled stones and the artificial old bricks, it really was a village. There were sheep which were sheared, cows which were milked and hens whose eggs were carefully collected. In the porcelain churns and milk pails bearing Marie Antoinette's cipher, and on the marble tables of the clean dairy, butter and cheese were made—the best in the Ile de France, it was asserted, particularly when the Queen and her friends amused themselves at making them under the somewhat anxious eye of the farmer's wife. For there were a farmer and his wife, the Valy-Busard, who came from Touraine and had a small staff under their command.

The Queen had had a little house built, whose walls are still standing and where the floors were made of straw coloured to imitate marquetry work. From the windows of the "Queen's house" Marie Antoinette, exhausted by her advanced pregnancy, could, as she drank milk from one of the famous breast-bowls (but were they ever really used at Trianon?), watch the farmer's wife and her servant washing their linen at the edge of the lake, or follow the work of the gardener's boys as they picked vegetables in the little gardens surrounding each house. On the lawn the hens scuttled about in their enclosure; the cowman led his troop out to pasture; and the farmer fished in the little lake into which 27 pike and 2,000 carp had been placed.

Surrounded by what she thought of as, if not "an agricultural enterprise," at least the "happy village" demanded by Bernardin de Saint-Pierre, Marie Antoinette forgot the lawyers' insult during this month of June, but the King's journey to Cherbourg helped especially to bring a little comfort to her heart.

On Tuesday, 20 June, Louis XVI had left Trianon for Rambouillet and at the end of the week he wrote to Marie Antoinette from Cherbourg to tell her how happy he was. He had been wildly acclaimed.

"My people's love for me found its echo in my heart. You may think of me as the happiest King in the world."

Marie Antoinette began to hope again; perhaps the monarchy was not detested after all. But when the King left Normandy the acclamations diminished. "I can see I am approaching Versailles!" he sighed. Paris's hate for Marie Antoinette was reflected on the "poor man," whom everyone considered too tolerant a husband,

> Who's never jealous.
> He's indifferent. The thing at which he's able
> Is stuffing himself like a swine
> And swilling down his wine
> With his elbows on the table.

When Marie Antoinette gave birth to her fourth child, Princesse Sophie, on 9 July 1786, the only people who rejoiced were those Parisians who had free drinks at the expense of the "Gentlemen."

The people often suffered from hunger and knew that at Versailles the money was still flying. Calonne was reigning as Minister. During this year—the year of the necklace—Marie Antoinette spent 272,000 livres on dress, 60 million present-day francs and 150,000 livres in excess of her budget. And yet the Queen was wearing so-called "milkmaids" or "shirt" dresses. Admittedly Mlle Bertin made up for it with the hats, which were enormous bonnets, big enough for ten heads, or hats resembling by their size hatters' shop signs and costing a small fortune.

Since the beginning of the reign Monsieur had extracted 3,000 million present-day francs and the Comte d'Artois 2,400 million. When these figures were shown to M. de Calonne he was delighted. He borrowed "to spend," he borrowed again, he went on borrowing. He was called "The Wizard."

"How could I have suspected that the finances were in such a bad state?" Marie Antoinette was later to ask. "When I asked for 50,000 livres I was brought 100,000."

> 'Tis not Calonne himself I love,
> But gold, which he's not sparing of.
> If there's no more for me
> I quickly send to him by name,
> My favourite does just the same,
> And then we laugh with glee.

At the end of 1786 the "Wizard," who had come to the end of his tricks, collapsed. There was only one solution left—to summon an assembly of notables and ask them to find a way to fill the coffers without spending other people's money. The monarchy had gone bankrupt and filed its petition.

Calonne showed his books to all the Marshals, Dukes, Peers, magistrates and Princes, and now all France knew what Versailles was costing the nation. Poor devils who earned barely one livre a day learned that Madame Elisabeth alone ate each year 100 million francs' worth of meat and fish. A scapegoat was needed. It could not be the King, who was so good natured and so simple. It was not the costly and outdated ceremonial demanded by etiquette, nor the posts surviving from another age, the 2,111 servants and 4,000 members of the King's Household. One person alone, it was shouted and written, was responsible—the Queen. The deficit was due to her wild expenditure, her pleasures, her reckless gambling, the greed and thefts of her favourites. Already Marie Antoinette's enemies—and she had made a great many—were covertly accusing her "of having in a shocking manner squandered the finances of France, fruit of the people's sweat, to satisfy her irregular pleasures." Now it was merely whispered, but soon a magistrate would cry it aloud from the floor of the court, for the sentence is an extract from Fouquier-Tinville's indictment.

Henceforth she was always known as "Madame Deficit." In her own person she was held to be the incarnation of the bankruptcy of the monarchy. In February 1787, the month in which the Notables met, Marie Antoinette went to the Comédie, where *Athalie* was being given. Joad's speech was madly applauded:

> *Confonds dans ses conseils cette reine cruelle;*
> *Daigne, daigne, mon Dieu, sur Mathan et sur elle*
> *Répandre cet esprit d'imprudence et d'erreur*
> *De la chute des rois funeste avant-coureur.*

At this applause the Queen left her box. A few days earlier she had been hissed at the Opera.

She admitted only one responsibility—her friendship for Mme de Polignac, "who had made herself loathed by her rapacity," as Mercy said on 14 August 1787. In the Queen's mind her favourite was the only reason for this "odious and unjust outburst in which the public obstinately persists." And yet she continued to be friends with the Duchesse merely "from habit, from fear of boredom and from the need for dissipation," as Mercy, not without satisfaction, announced to Vienna.

Marie Antoinette retained her incomprehension in the face of the tide of hatred she felt rising towards her, and which was soon to engulf her. "I shall conquer the malicious by trebling the good I have always tried to do," she sighed.

As Louis XVI had been obliged to let Calonne go, Marie Antoinette suggested the Archbishop of Toulouse, Loménie de Brienne, who was supported by Vermond. The Abbé had first of all wanted to have him made Archbishop of Paris, but the King had opposed it. "The Archbishop of Paris ought at least to believe in God!"

This might also have been a condition for a Controller of Finances in 1787, who needed a miracle to save him!

Louis XVI gave way and accepted Loménie de Brienne. The Queen rejoiced. "Make no mistake, Messieurs," she said as she left the Council Chamber, "he is a real Prime Minister."

Those with privileges were soon to be aware of it, but to their cost. As Brienne had not been able to obtain from the 144 Notables permission to reform the financial structure of the country completely, and consequently to increase certain taxes, he fell back on the court and decided to make economies. It was decided to abolish for the next year 173 posts in the Queen's Household alone. The serving gentlemen, sergeants and their assistants and ordinary messengers said nothing, but those with high posts protested. The Duc de Coigny, who had to give up his title of Grand Equerry—the Great Stable being amalgamated with the Little Stable—made a scene to the King, although his salary still remained. Vaudreuil resigned himself to giving up his post as chief falconer, but Besenval, although he kept his Swiss Guards, was deeply wounded.

"Madame," he dared to say to Marie Antoinette, "it is terrible to live in a country where one is not sure of possessing one day what one had the day before. That used to happen only in Turkey!"

The Duc de Polignac was one of the few to keep quiet when the post of director general of the post-horses was taken away from him, but then he still kept the reversion of the Little Stable.

Marie Antoinette cut down her style of living; there were few feasts or balls. In any case she had no heart for dancing, for in the summer of 1787 she was in mourning. Princesse Sophie was dead, "the pulmonary organ being in a very bad state," according to the "report of the opening" made at Trianon.

In spite of the dismissal of 600 guards and light horse, these economies did not fill the gap and Loménie de Brienne was obliged to come before the Parliament. But the lawyers revolted and refused to register two edicts concerned with the imposition of a stamp duty and making all nobles and commoners who owned property pay the King a land tax. According to the magistrates only the States General could avert bankruptcy and they began to set in motion their customary procedure of "remonstrances," "protests" and "reiterated remonstrances." Urged on by Marie Antoinette, Loménie de Brienne had the two edicts registered at a *Lit de Justice* held at Versailles on 6 August, and the King exiled the Parliament to Troyes.

Paris flared up at once. The carriages were stopped, processions were held and Loménie de Brienne was burned in effigy. Paris was practising for the great combat. The capital was aware that since the death of Vergennes the Queen was taking an active part in the Government and in exiling "the Fathers of the country." If the police had not intervened they would have burned her in effigy too. The lieutenant of police advised the Queen not to show herself in Paris.

The situation was becoming worse, the coffers were empty and a compromise had to be made. The Parliamentarians grew tired of Champagne and agreed to vote a "twentieth part." But on 19 November the conflict started again. The King held another *Lit de Justice* in the great chamber of the Palais de Justice in order to register another edict permitting him to issue successive loans of 420 million. "I order that the edict be transcribed in the registers of my Parliament to be executed according to its form and purport."

In order to spare the magistrates' susceptibility Louis XVI had omitted to add "by my express command," which was the obligatory formula for *Lits de Justice*. On this occasion, therefore, Justice was only half asleep on the bed and it was not forbidden to express an opinion. The tumult grew louder. Through the noise new words were heard for the first time: "arbitrary power," "despotism." The uproar increased, and then suddenly died down. The former Duc de Chartres, who had been Duc d'Orléans for two years now, rose. The head of the younger branch stood up before Louis XVI for the first time. He was heard to say calmly: "If the King is holding a session of Parliament the votes should be collected and counted; if it is a *Lit de Justice* we should be silent." He then added: "This registration is illegal."

This remark does not seem very unpleasant to us, but in the 18th century it constituted an "insolence" which made the King stammer: "Yes, it is legal! It is legal because I wish it!"

While the future Philippe-Egalité was being applauded the King returned to Versailles. Marie Antoinette had a great deal to do with the measures which were now to be taken and which ended in the virtual suppression of the Parliaments. It would appear that until the return of Necker hardly anything was done without her consent. Moreover, after the arrest of the two ringleaders, d'Eprémesnil and Monsabert, and after the Duc d'Orléans had been sent to Villers-Cotterets, the magistrates wrote to the King, assuring him that "such steps are not in his nature, such examples do not stem from his principles: *they have another source.*" They could not have indicated the Queen more clearly.

For his part Fersen wrote to King Gustavus on 27 December 1787: "The King is still weak and suspicious. He trusts only the Queen and it appears that it is she who does everything. The Ministers often go to see her and keep her informed of all business. It was often said by the public that the King was beginning to drink, that the Queen encouraged this passion and took advantage of his condition to make him sign anything she wanted. Nothing could be more untrue. He has no liking for drink and, granting the general supposition, it would be far too dangerous a vice by its consequences, since other people besides the Queen could extract a signature."

If anyone was well informed it was Axel Fersen. According to Saint-Priest, Fersen used to go "on horseback in the park, near the Trianon, three or four times a week; on her side the Queen did the same alone, and these meetings caused a great deal of public scandal, in spite of the favourite's modesty and restraint, for he never showed anything outwardly and was the most discreet of all the Queen's friends."

Axel was obliged to leave for Sweden, since Gustavus III was at war with Russia. During his absence Louis XVI received a packet of letters one day, while he was hunting. He sat down on the grass to read them and his equerries went away. On their return they found the King weeping bitterly. So great was his grief that he could not mount his horse and was brought back to Versailles in a carriage. He revealed to Marie Antoinette that the letter contained horrible accusations concerning the Queen and Fersen.

"They want to take from us the only friend we can rely on," sighed Marie Antoinette, and she proposed to her husband that they should not receive the Swede when he returned. The King dissuaded her, however, and when Fersen came back to France he resumed his almost daily visits to the château.

In spite of the ominous rumbling of the thunder the sky was still clear. The storm might have rolled away, but by an irremediable error the monarchy declared itself powerless: it called on the help of the Nation and set in motion the formidable machine which was to crush everything in its way. The initiative would pass to Moloch.

At the time of the suppression of the Parliaments a few disturbances had broken out here and there and degenerated into riots. At Grenoble the royal troops had been beaten back with a shower of tiles. In all France there was but one cry: "The States General and the return of Necker!" Louis XVI vacillated for six months and finally, realising that the Notables had also failed, he yielded and promised to summon the deputies of the States in the following year at Versailles. An inevitable consequence was that on 26 August 1788—check to the Queen—he dismissed the Archbishop, to whom Marie Antoinette had a Cardinal's hat given in compensation. Loménie de Birenne was replaced by Necker. "I tremble—excuse this weakness," wrote Marie Antoinette to Mercy on the same day, "because it is I who have caused him to be recalled. My fate is to bring misfortune. And if as a result of devilish schemes he fails again or if he extends the King's authority I shall be even more detested." She was seeing clearly now, but it was too late.

Necker no doubt did what he could—he even lent the Treasury two millions of his own money—but he, too, trembled. "I can see the great wave advancing. Will it engulf me?"

The "great wave" was the States General. The public was so occupied by the convening of the deputies that the deficit took second place. Thousands of pamphlets appeared. Public opinion was at fever-heat. The women were the most impassioned. "You know as well as I do," Fersen wrote to a friend, "to what extent women set the tone here and how they like to take part in everything. At present they are only interested in the constitution and to please them, and to be in the swim, the young men talk of nothing but States General and Governments, although their waistcoats, cabriolets and jackets often cause a diversion. I do not know if the kingdom will profit by all these changes, but society is the loser." If Mercy is to be believed, Marie Antoinette was also the loser. "H.M. now seems entirely occupied with the arrangements regarding the interior, the economies, the reforms, the parliamentary discussions. All these affairs are treated without any method or prearranged plan . . . and the result is a confusion which aggravates the evil instead of lessening it. Complaints and disgust follow, and the resulting ill-will falls partly on the Queen, who is so acutely distressed that her temperament is much affected by it."

The Ambassador was not very indulgent towards the woman who at the same time was writing to him: "My confidence in you does not permit me to let you remain in ignorance, Monsieur, of the result of the conversations I have had with several of the Ministers."

On 1 January 1788 Paris learned that the Third Estate was to have as many deputies as the two others put together. The houses were illuminated.

The last day of the Versailles year unfolded with the ceremonies unchanged since the time of the Roi Soleil. It had never been so cold. All the windows were covered with a thick layer of ice. The wood smoked, but did not burn. It was impossible to find in the whole château a log that was not damp, but the *lever* went on at its customary deliberate pace. Indeed, it was slower than usual for the "Gentlemen" of the town had come in a grand procession to present the King with their traditional gift of silver coins. It was so icy in the chapel that the Mass was shortened. During the formal dinner the water froze in the jugs, but that did not prevent the Duchesses *à tabouret* in their low-cut dresses and the crowd of courtiers from watching the King eat. He was the only one to swallow anything. Marie Antoinette did not even unfold her napkin and sat stoically through the interminable procession of fifty dishes.

Her political anxieties were coupled with a great personal grief: the ill-health of her elder son. The Dauphin, who had grown very thin, had a fever every evening. His vertebrae were "displaced and projecting." At that time the good effects of mountain air were unknown and, faced with the child's "state of weakness and languor," the doctors argued fiercely about the salubriousness of the air of La Muette compared with that of Versailles.

"The air at La Muette has more motion than that at Versailles," declared Le Monier. "The river which washes it helps to provide this motion."

"Neither Mont Valérien nor the heights of Montmartre protect La Muette from the cold winds," replied Portal, "and besides, the garden faces due north."

"But the north wind sweeps the air clean!"

Dessaut was in favour of Versailles. "The soil is fertile and suitable for vegetation, whereas the soil at La Muette is sandy. Moreover, Versailles is Monseigneur's native air!"

"But Monseigneur's apartment at Versailles is damp and unhealthy," declared Sabatier. "The walls drink water like a sponge. One of the windows looks on to the Swiss lake, which is stagnant, and the other looks on to the grand canal, which has no outlet."

"Not at all," replied Dessaut. "The air is healthy there and the marshes have been drained! I have lived in Versailles for forty years and I am convinced there are no epidemics there. It is sheltered from the north, whereas the Bois de Boulogne is damp."

There was no end to it! In order to prevent the medical staff from coming to blows the little Dauphin was sent to the château of Meudon. When Louis XVI was a child he too had been sickly and the air at Meudon had done him good; one had only to look at him now. But the invalid's condition grew daily worse. "It is heartrending," wrote the young Comtesse de Laage, who visited the little Prince with the Princess de Lamballe. "His suffering, reasonableness and patience are touching! When we arrived he was being read to. He had taken a whim to lie on a billiard table and a mattress had been put there for him. The Princesse and I watched him, and it occurred to both of us that it looked like a lying-in-state. Mme de Lamballe asked him what he was reading.

" 'A very interesting period of our history, Madame, the reign of Charles VII. There are a great many heroes.'

"I took the liberty of asking if Monseigneur read continuously or merely the most striking passages.

" 'Continuously, Madame. I do not know enough about it to choose, and it is all interesting.'

"He turned his beautiful, dying eyes to me as he spoke."

Marie Antoinette often went to see her son. "Everything the poor little child says is amazing; he breaks the Queen's heart. He shows the greatest affection for her. The other day he begged her to dine in his room. Alas! she swallowed more tears than bread."

The Queen remembered the day he had amused her so much as he sat on his father's knee during a performance in the little theatre at Trianon. She had dried up during a scene and Campan, in his prompter's box, tried to find the page, but in spite of his large spectacles did not succeed. The Dauphin's little voice was heard in the tense silence: "Monsieur Campan, take off your large spectacles, Mamma cannot hear you."

She remembered too the child's joy when, on 22 August of the preceding year, the "Gentlemen" of the town had brought him two pistols, a gold sword and a gun whose stock was charmingly decorated with little dolphins and lilies—a gun he would never shoulder.

He left his bed on 4 May 1789 to lie on the balcony of the Little Stable at Versailles and watch the procession of the States General going from the church of Notre Dame to the church of Saint-Louis.

The Revolution started with a procession.

And what a procession! A procession in which walked the last Kings of France: Louis XVI, Louis XVIII, Charles X, Louis-Philippe, then Duc de Chartres, and the young Duc d'Angoulême who, one day at Rambouillet in 1830, was for three minutes to be the King least known to schoolboys of the future—King Louis XIX of France.

The Duc d'Orléans, who was to send Louis XVI to the scaffold, and whose son would at one blow dethrone Charles X, Louis XIX and Henri V, walked with the deputies of the Nobility. He was the hero of the day. And among all the deputies of the Third Estate there was even the future master of France, M. Maximilien de Robespierre, in a black woollen suit with a black silk cloak and a white muslin cravat.

Everyone carried a candle, except for the standard bearers and the King's falconers, who carried their birds on their fists.

The King, in full dress, wearing a mantle of cloth of gold and with the "Regent" diamond in his hat, was surrounded by the high officers of the crown. He was wildly applauded. But when Marie Antoinette appeared in her dress sprinkled with gold and silver there was silence, a contemptuous silence. In the Place d'Armes, just as she was passing under the balcony where her little Dauphin was dying, a single cry stung her: "Long live the Duc d'Orléans!"

She tottered and grew pale. Would she fall on having the name of the former companion of her pleasures, now her enemy, thus thrown into her face? She wavered, and the Princesse de Lamballe hurried up, but the Queen raised her head, with its bunch of white feathers, and murmured: "It is nothing . . . nothing."

A few minutes later, in the church of Saint-Louis, the Bishop of Nancy, Mgr de la Fare, mounted into the pulpit and dared to say: "Sire, the people over whom you rule have given clear proofs of their patience. They are a martyred people, whose life seems to have been spared only that they may suffer the longer."

The deputies of the Third Estate, who up to this moment imagined that they merely represented over-harassed taxpayers, raised their heads. They would not lower them again.

The Bishop now attacked the luxury of the court. All eyes turned towards the Queen.

"It is in the name of a good King, a just and feeling monarch, that these wretched people practise their barbarities."

For the first time in a French church, and with the Blessed Sacrament exposed, there was applause. On returning to the château Marie Antoinette had such a violent attack of nerves that she broke her diamond bracelets.

At the formal session on the next day the Queen listened to Necker's interminable and blundering speech and anxiously watched the 1,165 deputies. They were taken aback, to say the least, on learning that "it is not to the absolute necessity for pecuniary assistance" that they owed "the great privilege of being summoned by His Majesty as the States General." In his monotonous voice Necker declared that the regular deficit was no more than 56 million. Nothing was easier than to cover it: for example, could not "the sale of ground tobacco be extended to Brittany"?

"What a country is this, where without taxes and with the aid of everyday, insignificant objects one can dispose of a deficit which has made such a stir in Europe!"

Such was the conclusion of the "Magician." The deputies looked at each other, stupefied. It was hardly worth while to have come so far to learn that henceforth, by taking snuff instead of chewing, the Bretons would save France. If the deficit could be covered by "insignificant objects," why could they not turn their attention to uniting the kingdom so that, in Voltaire's phrase, one did not have a change of laws with each change of horses? This was not what Louis XVI had summoned them for, but the King seemed full of good intentions—he had just called himself "the first friend of his peoples"—and he would certainly be glad to see a little order and unity brought about in the patchwork of his *pays d'état* and *pays d'élection*, or even in such provinces as Alsace and Trois-Evêchés, which, although part of France, were not able to trade freely with her.

"The battle is on," wrote a deputy of the Third Estate that evening, and by that he meant not the battle against the King, but with the King to save the kingdom. It was significant that when the King rose he was greeted with applause. To please him they also shouted "Long live the Queen!" They were rather sorry for her "look of sadness and depression." Startled, Marie Antoinette gave a pale smile and sank to the ground in one of the graceful curtseys of which she held the secret and which earned her an immense ovation.

It was with a slight smile on her lips that she returned to the château. As soon as the King had taken off his heavy ceremonial cloak they both hurried to a carriage and went to Meudon, where the Dauphin's condition was growing steadily worse.

It is painful to read the laconic entries in the King's private journal during the next few months. The three words, "Visit to Meudon," appear nearly every day like a *leitmotiv*. Between two audiences given to the deputies, between two hunts, the King hastened to join Marie Antoinette, who hardly left the dying boy's bedside.

On 2 June, at 10 o'clock in the evening, the great bell of Notre Dame sounded for the Forty Hours' Prayer. On the 3rd the Blessed Sacrament was exposed in all the churches in Paris. The King arrived at Meudon at four o'clock and left in his carriage at 10 o'clock in the evening. The Queen remained at her son's bedside. At one o'clock in the morning the child breathed his last. But, in accordance with etiquette, Marie Antoinette had not the right to weep by the little corpse, which was already surrounded by twelve candles. She had to return to Versailles.

The autopsy, which was carried out at once, showed that the child's "vertebrae were decayed, bulging and out of place, the ribs curved and the lungs adhering."

It was not the Queen who placed the body in its white velvet coffin with silver nails, but her "service"; it was not the King who accompanied his son to Saint-Denis, but the Prince de Condé, flanked by bodyguards, soldiers of the Hundred-Swiss and valets bearing torches. As for the little boy's heart, it was the Duc d'Orléans's son, the future Louis-Philippe, who conveyed it by coach to Val-de-Grâce. Slaves of ceremonial, the parents remained at Versailles. "Mass at eight o'clock," wrote the King. "Benediction. I saw no one. My son's funeral." They were allowed one thing: they went to spend a week at Marly—the last Marly —and asked the Archbishop of Paris to have a thousand masses said. Before giving the order the Archbishop made inquiries. How would payment be made, since the State coffers were empty? What was His Majesty's decision? Louis XVI replied: "Have the sum paid by M. de la Ferté and recover it from the expenses on the silver plate." Matters had reached this point.

It was at Marly, on 19 June, that the King received "his councils." It was a crucial moment. Two days earlier the deputies of the Third Estate, together with a few members of the Clergy, had set themselves up as a "national assembly," as they represented "ninety-six per cent of the nation." Without further delay they pronounced illegal any tax raised without their consent, and they invited the two other Orders to take counsel with them. On 18 June part of the Clergy joined them. The "advanced" nobles had not been able to win over the Nobility, who still wished to discuss by themselves—but for how long? The Archbishop of Paris, Cardinal de la Rochefoucauld, and the Duc de Luxembourg, who was President of the Nobility, exhorted the King to resistance. His crown was in peril; he should dissolve the States General, who were exceeding their rights.

Necker arrived at Marly. Received first of all by Marie Antoinette, who called the deputies "a pack of madmen," the Genevan tried to advocate conciliation. The Privy Council began its meeting and the Minister outlined his plan, which was that the King should allow the three Orders to join together and should authorise modifications to the constitution of the kingdom, but on condition that two Chambers were formed. Necker was also in favour of allowing all Frenchmen to have access to all civil and military posts.

After two hours of discussion in the Council Louis XVI began to be influenced by Necker's arguments. Suddenly the door opened and an officer came and spoke in a low voice to the King, who hurried out.

"The Queen has sent for him," murmured Necker. "We've got nowhere!" He was quite right. When Louis XVI came back into the council room he had changed his mind. Marie Antoinette had won her point. There must be no treating with the "rebels."

But on the next day, 20 June, while the King was hunting the stag at Le Butard, the "rebels," finding the Salle des Menus Plaisirs shut, assembled in the Jeu de Paume and the famous Oath followed. As Mirabeau's secretary, Dumont, wrote later, the Third Estate was henceforth "in league against the power of the Throne."

The King and Queen returned to Versailles. Necker, Saint-Priest and Montmorin begged them not to "embitter the Third Estate, the mouthpiece of public opinion." But Marie Antoinette, backed up by Provence, Artois and three Ministers out of six, advocated the use of authority. Louis XVI, only a sawdust puppet who could be made to take up any position, agreed to play the authoritarian. The three Orders would deliberate separately; he had not summoned a national assembly but the States General, and these gentlemen should hold no meeting apart from the royal sessions just as their predecessors of 1588 had done when they had been neatly drawn up at Blois by the Baron d'Oignon.

On 22 June the order of deputies was not made according to the *"rang d'oignon."* Young Dreux-Brézé, all rustling with plumes, introduced the members of the Nobility and Clergy by the main door, while the deputies of the Third Estate floundered in the mud (for it was pouring with rain) while awaiting their turn to enter the hall by the side door conceded to them.

Necker, who had made his opinions publicly known, did not attend the session. Surrounded by his wife and the Princes, Louis XVI played the part of a blind despot. The decrees on taxes of 17 June had no force; the manorial tithes and rights would be maintained.

"If, by a misfortune far from my mind," the King concluded, "you were to forsake me in such a great enterprise, I should work alone for the good of the people and I should consider myself as being its only true representative." In other words: I should not hesitate to dissolve the States General.

Before leaving the hall, followed by the triumphant Queen, Louis XVI commanded the three Orders to separate and take counsel in their respective rooms, but no one moved. The Marquis de Dreux-Brézé, putting on his hat, went over to Bailly and said: "Did you hear the King's orders?"

Most historic remarks have been made up after the event. Mirabeau doubtless refused to leave his place and doubtless spoke of the bayonets which alone could make him rise, but very probably did not utter his famous exclamation which has made the fortune of generations of print-sellers.

When Dreux-Brézé reported his failure to the King, Louis XVI sighed: "They want to stay? Well, to hell with them, let them stay!"

The King seemed to take no interest in the matter. His private Journal reveals what may have been one of the reasons for this strange attitude. On 23 June, after the "royal session with the States," one can read these unexpected and incomprehensible words: "Journey to Marly at quarter-past seven to do the packing." Had the King, then, left possessions and papers at Marly which he was anxious to pack up on that day? It would seem hardly worth while having several hundred servants!

While the King was busy with his "packing" Mirabeau had had the immunity of the representatives decreed. Henceforth to arrest a deputy —such as d'Eprémesnil—would be a "capital crime" for the King. The deputies looked on the royal message as a "challenge" and Mirabeau talked of "denouncing the Queen," who according to him was the cause of all the evil.

"What, the Queen?" asked the youngest son of the Duc d'Orléans.

"And why not?" exclaimed his brother, the future Louis-Philippe. Absolute monarchy, so many centuries old, was dying.

During the days that followed Louis XVI wrote his famous "Nothing" each day in his Journal. On 25 June "Nothing" was accompanied by this sigh: "The stag was hunted at Saint-Appoline," the implication being: "and I was not there." He no longer galloped with the hunt, for he was trying to win the race for the revolution. Having forbidden the Three Orders to meet together, he now commanded them to. The Nobles thereupon declared "that the monarchy must be protected from the King." Marie Antoinette was of the same opinion, but, overwhelmed, she wept and let her husband act.

"Monsieur," the King declared to the President of the Nobility, "I beg your Order to join with the two others. If begging is not enough, I wish it!"

On 27 June "the family was complete," in Bailly's words, and Paris was illuminated. Marie Antoinette could not understand this popular rejoicing. How could France be happy when the monarchy had been degraded by a pack of clodhoppers and lawyers? They must regain the power snatched from them. Louis XVI, who like a bubble obeyed the least breath, hastened to resume his rôle of despot, which he had abandoned on 23 June. He approved the idea of a *coup d'état*. But to dissolve the Assembly he needed troops. The regiments converged on Paris by forced marches. Soon the *Royal-Cravate* was garrisoned at Charenton, *Salis-Samade* at Issy, the Hussars at the Ecole Militaire and the Royal German at La Muette. Besenval, whose job was to "control" Paris, was responsible for them all.

The Assembly was frightened and on 9 July sent a deputation to the King, who replied on the following day: "Only the ill-disposed could mislead my people about the precautionary measures I am taking."

What followed is well known: on 11 July Necker's dismissal was like the crack of a whip. It became known in the town on 12 July and Camille Desmoulins at the Palais Royal cried: "I have just come from Versailles. M. Necker is dismissed. This is the signal for a St. Bartholomew's Day of the patriots. This evening the Swiss and German battalions will cut our throats. We have but one resource—to take to arms."

And two days later, in "searching for arms," they were to take the Bastille.

That evening the King went to bed, after writing in his notebook: "14, nothing." And yet that afternoon a deputation had again come from the Assembly to ask him to withdraw the troops encamped in the Champ de Mars, so as to calm Paris. He had agreed. He risked nothing, for Versailles and the suburbs of Paris were full of soldiers, and the bodyguards had been ready for two days. That very afternoon Mme de Polignac had taken biscuits to the two German regiments encamped in the Orangerie. The deputation had also announced that the Parisians were marching on the Bastille. All right, it would defend itself. After all, M. de Launay had cannons and at the first shot the attackers would disappear. Tomorrow he would go to the Assembly and dissolve the States General.

The King fell peacefully asleep. He awoke with a start. The Grand Master of the Wardrobe, the Duc de la Rochefoucauld-Liancourt, was at his bedside.

"The Bastille has been taken! The governor has been assassinated! His head is being borne on a pike through the town."

The King was now wide awake.

"But . . . but then it is a revolt?"

"No, Sire, it is a revolution."

They consulted together. Should they go to Metz, as Marie Antoinette advised? Maréchal de Broglie remarked sensibly: "It is easy to go to Metz, but what should we do when we got there?"

The King decided to abdicate. Just when nothing prevented him from carrying out his *coup d'état,* for which he now had an excuse, he preferred to change his mind again. On the next day he went to the Assembly with his brothers and announced to the deputies the withdrawal of all troops. But although a weathercock he was none the less a worthy man and he uttered from his heart a sentence which provoked enthusiasm: "I am one with the Nation, I entrust myself to you."

There was wild applause. Hand in hand the deputies accompanied the King, who returned slowly on foot to the château. The crowd which had gathered followed them, crying: "Long live the King!" And one of them added, looking at the Comte d'Artois: "In spite of you, Monseigneur, and your opinions."

The courtyards of the château were filled with an immense crowd who called for the King, the Queen and the new Dauphin to appear on the balcony. Marie Antoinette told Mme Campan to go and find the future Louis XVII and to ask Mme de Polignac not to accompany the little Prince.

"Ah! Madame," said the Duchesse when she heard the Queen's order, "what a blow this is!"

Having carried out her orders, Mme Campan went down into the courtyard just as the King and Queen, with Mme Royale and the Dauphin, appeared on the balcony.

"Ah!" said one woman, disappointed, "the Duchesse is not with her."

"No," a man replied, "but she is still at Versailles. She is like a mole! She is working underground, but we shall be able to dig her out."

Terrified, Mme Campan reported this conversation to Marie Antoinette. The Queen had received many warnings of the same kind that morning and she summoned the Duchesse.

"I fear the worst. In the name of our friendship leave me. You still have time to avoid the fury of my enemies. When they attack you they are more incensed against me than against you."

Mme de Polignac resisted. How could she leave her whole life?

"Do not become a victim to your affection and my friendship."

At that moment Louis XVI entered the room.

"Come, Monsieur," the Queen exclaimed, "come and help me persuade these faithful subjects that they must leave us."

Louis XVI, who had just decided to recall Necker, sighed.

"My cruel fate forces me to send from me all those I love and esteem. I have just ordered the Comte d'Artois to leave, and I give you the same order. Pity me, but do not lose a single moment."

The Duc and Duchesse yielded. At midnight, just as Mme de Polignac, her husband, daughter and sister-in-law were entering their carriage, the Duchesse was handed a note from the Queen: "Farewell, dearest of friends, the word is a dreadful one. Here is the order for the horses. Farewell, I have only the strength to embrace you."

Not without difficulty, for at Sens they were nearly recognised, M. and Mme de Polignac arrived at Basle. Soon they received a letter from Marie Antoinette: "I can only venture to write a word, my dear love . . . I cannot express all my regret at being separated from you; I hope you feel as I do. We are surrounded with nothing but grief, misfortune and unfortunates . . . Everyone is fleeing and I am only too happy to think that all those I care for are far from me."

Fersen was at Valenciennes, where he saw passing through the Comte d'Artois, the Prince de Condé, the Duc de Bourbon, the Duc d'Enghien, Vaudreuil and the Marquis de Polignac. All the Queen's friends left Versailles: Coigny, Calonne, Lambesq, Luxembourg, the Marsans, the Rohans, the Castries, Breteuil, and even the Abbé de Vermond. They left her to face the storm alone.

"My sole resource is in my children," she wrote to Mme de Polignac. "I have them with me as much as possible. You have certainly heard of the appointment of Mme de Tourzel. It gave me great pain."

Mme de Tourzel, indeed, had been appointed Governess to the two Children of France and it was for her benefit that, while the tempest raged and grumbled, the Queen prepared a report on 24 July. It is worth reading some extracts from it, for it shows us an unknown Marie Antoinette, hitherto concealed from us by her frivolity.

"My son is four years and four months old, less two days," Marie Antoinette wrote to Mme de Tourzel. "I will not speak of his build or appearance, for you have only to see him. His health has always been good, but even when he was in the cradle it was noticed that his nerves were very delicate and that the slightest unexpected noise affected him. He was late with his first teeth, but they came through without illness or accident. It was only with the last, and I think with the sixth, that he had a convulsion at Fontainebleau. He has had two since, one in the winter of '87 or '88 and the other after his inoculation, but the latter was very slight. As a result of his delicate nerves he is always frightened by any noise to which he is not accustomed, for example, he is frightened of dogs because he heard one bark near him. I have never forced him to see them because I think that as he gains in reasoning power his fears will disappear. Like all strong, healthy children, he is very thoughtless, very frivolous and violent in his anger, but he is good-natured, gentle and even affectionate when he is not carried away by his thoughtlessness. He has an exaggerated sense of self-esteem which, by good guidance, might one day be turned to his advantage. Until he is at ease with anyone, he knows how to control himself and even conquer his impatience and anger so as to appear gentle and amiable. He keeps his word faithfully once he has given it, but he is very indiscreet and easily repeats what he has heard and often, without meaning to lie, he adds things suggested by his own imagination. This is his greatest fault and it must be firmly corrected. Apart from that, I repeat, he is good-natured and by using kindness and firmness, but without being too severe, one can do what one likes with him, but severity would make him rebel, for he has a strong character for his age. For example, even when he was very small, the word "Pardon" always shocked him. He will do and say whatever one likes when he is in the wrong but he will pronounce the word "Pardon" only with great difficulty and many tears. My children have always been taught to have complete trust in me and when they have done wrong to tell me so themselves. By this means, when I scold them, I appear more hurt and sorry at what they have done than angry. I have accustomed them to accepting a yes or no from me as being irrevocable, but I always give them a reason suited to their age, so that they do not think it is merely a whim on my part. My son cannot read and has great difficulty in learning, but he is too scatterbrained to concentrate. He has no ideas of grandeur and I should wish that to continue. Our children learn only too quickly what they are.

"He is very fond of his sister and has a good heart. Every time something pleases him, like going somewhere, or if someone gives him something, his first impulse is to ask for the same thing for his sister. He was born gay. His health requires plenty of air and I think the best thing is to let him play and work outside on the terrace rather than take him farther. The exercise taken by little children as they run and play in the open air is much healthier for them than being made to take walks, which often tires their backs."

The tragic events of this first month of the Revolution were to bring Marie Antoinette closer to her husband. When the Assembly and the town of Paris, wishing simultaneously to humiliate Louis XVI and make him sanction the massacre, asked him to visit his "good town," Louis XVI agreed. Marie Antoinette protested that it was folly. But the King, having been to communion and appointed Provence Lieutenant General of the kingdom "in the event of his not returning," left for Paris like a man going to the scaffold. The Queen trembled for him. This poor man, this cork on the water, had at last moved her. She suppressed her tears and retired to her private rooms with her children. "A silence of death reigns over all the palace," wrote Mme Campan. Marie Antoinette was convinced that her husband would not return, and she ordered the stables to get horses ready, not for flight, but to go as a sovereign to the Assembly. She even wrote out a declaration:

"Gentlemen, I come to deliver to you the wife and family of your sovereign. Do not permit what was joined in heaven to be sundered on earth."

"As she repeated this speech," wrote Mme Campan, "her voice was broken by tears and by these sorrowing words: 'They will never let him return!'"

When he came back, after being humiliated and wearing in his hat the tricolour cockade he had been forced to display, Marie Antoinette threw herself in his arms, weeping with joy. It cannot be true that, as Mercy asserted, she then drew away from him, on seeing the three colours he wore, and said: "I did not know I had married a commoner." The insult is not in keeping with this day of tears and anguish and one finds it difficult to believe in it.

Versailles then resumed its calm. Mercy, who went to the château on 23 July, saw "nothing but confusion." "Chance is relied on for everything," he wrote. He returned to Versailles on 11 August and reported: "The Queen bears her troubles with the greatest courage, and a great deal is needed not to be overwhelmed or revolted by the injustice and the horrors against which this noble Princess has to fight." Marie Antoinette even began to hope. "These last few days things seem to have taken a better turn," she wrote to Mme de Polignac at the end of the month, "but one cannot rely on anything. The wicked have great power and the means to frustrate or prevent the most just actions . . . But you can always be sure that adversity has not lessened my strength and my courage." True devotion was being revealed. "I am discovering all kinds of truly and sincerely attached people of whom I had never even thought." Such a one was Grétry, who one day came to present to Marie Antoinette his future son-in-law, Bouilly, author of the libretto of *Peter the Great,* an opera by Grétry which had just been performed.

The young dramatist, incidentally, wore a sword knot embroidered by his beloved Antoinette Grétry, the Queen's goddaughter. But let the charming and simple Jean-Nicolas Bouilly speak for himself.

"About half-past twelve we were shown into the Queen's private apartments. She had just been hearing mass in the chapel and as she entered her music-room she took off the black velvet *pouf* she was wearing on her head and her large black lace mantilla and called us forward. Grétry had not finished introducing me when Marie Antoinette, trying to account for the surprise my face occasioned her, suddenly exclaimed: 'I am not mistaken, Monsieur. This is not the first time I have seen you.'

"I replied smiling: 'Your Majesty, I see, deigns to remember the young scamp who on the terrace of the Orangerie dared to take a seat. . . .'

" 'Yes, yes, on one of the marble benches where I was sitting. I remember you perfectly. Grétry,' she added very graciously, 'you can congratulate yourself on having for a colleague a most faithful champion of ladies.'

"So saying, she congratulated us on our success and, looking keenly at me, she deigned to thank me for the devotion I had displayed in the King's cause.

" 'I was all the more delighted,' she added with a slightly mischievous smile, 'as I hear, Monsieur, that you are the son of a deputy of the Third Estate.'

"In this tone of enchanting gaiety and displaying her patronage for the arts and letters, she put several questions to me full of charm and interest on the sweet illusions of a first success. I replied that it was not enough to gain it, one must also be able to deserve it. She again examined me with close attention and I distinctly heard her say to Grétry, who was standing near her sofa: 'He is very pleasing, your collaborator, very pleasing indeed.'

"I was intoxicated. I shook the chains which were already beginning to bind me.

"Marie Antoinette produced a particularly strong impression on me as she spoke of Antoinette Grétry with the affectionate interest of a godmother. Oh! how those kindly words which escaped her lips penetrated deep into my heart! Until then she had dazzled me by her beauty and charmed me by her grace. How moved I was by that penetrating goodness, by that encouraging and majestic familiarity which conquered all who heard it!

" 'How old is my goddaughter now?' she asked her father in truly maternal accents.

" 'Seventeen,' replied Grétry, 'and since then she has been clothed and adorned only with Your Majesty's gifts.'

" 'I hope,' the Queen added, 'that she will always be so. She has everything that will one day make of her a distinguished and accomplished woman, and I shall take it on myself to choose her a husband.'

" 'I think,' replied Grétry, with his accustomed subtle smile, 'that we would do better to let her choose for herself.'

" 'I am strongly in favour of that system,' replied Marie Antoinette.

"Thus speaking, she held out her beautiful hand to the celebrated composer and he hastened to impress a most respectful kiss on it. Involuntarily I exclaimed with enthusiasm: 'Ah! who would not envy the prerogatives of fame?'

" 'Yours is just beginning, Monsieur, under such favourable auspices that I must be eager to encourage it.'

"So saying, Marie Antoinette held out her royal hand to me also. Surprised and confused, I sank on one knee and brushed that noble hand with my trembling lips.

" 'Your Majesty must excuse him,' said Grétry, pressing my arm and signing to me to take hold of myself, 'it is the first time he has drunk ambrosia.'

"This charming remark completely restored me."

It is a pretty scene. And before the collapse of this delightful epoch—

so delightful that for many years it concealed the stench rising from the decaying heart of the age—before this whole world crumbles for ever, let us evoke one last image of the Queen of Trianon.

During these months of August and September she often went to her beloved Trianon, which was visited nearly every day by the deputies of the Assembly, who were quite surprised not to find the famous drawing-room carpeted with precious stones, which was mentioned in the pamphlets. They seemed almost disappointed when they were told that it was only a stage setting and that the jewels were nothing but glass.

After dining in the little château Marie Antoinette went to her musical-comedy dairy. It was there that one day she was nearly taken unawares by three young Lorrainers, who were visiting Trianon. One of them, François Cognel, has given a description which affords us yet another, and very charming, picture of the Queen. "Just as we were about to leave, Marie Antoinette's arrival was announced and as we had no time to reach the garden gate our guide made us go into the stable. The Queen, who was accompanied by a lady of the court, then dismissed her and came on alone towards the dairy. She was wearing a plain linen dress with a scarf and a lace cap. In these simple clothes she seemed more full of majesty than in the grand robes in which we had seen her at Versailles. Her way of walking is peculiar to her. One cannot distinguish her steps; she glides with incomparable grace. She bears her head much more proudly when, as when we were watching her, she believes herself to be alone. Our Queen passed quite close to where we were standing and all three of us had an impulse to bend the knee as she passed."

Her walk was still "caressing," in spite of her generous proportions. Thanks to the journal of Mme Eloff, her dressmaker, we know that at that time the Queen measured about $23\frac{1}{2}''$ round the waist and $43\frac{1}{2}''$ round the bust. This latter figure may seem somewhat large, but was admirably suited to the fashion of the time.

Very often, in the morning, when she had drunk a glass of milk from "her" cows, she would rest on the bed of dry moss arranged in the little grotto behind the box-covered hill. Lulled by the sound of the little spring which rose out of the sand of the grotto, she would fall to musing.

She was musing thus on the afternoon of 5 October.

For the last few days things seemed to have been going better. Of course the taxes were still not coming in, but the King had sent to the Mint 13,000 livres' weight of silver plate, and on her side the Queen had sent 386 dishes, a large quantity of torches and cutlery in silver gilt and silver. She had even wished to make a personal sacrifice and had deprived herself of her patch-boxes, her *crachoirs à manche*, her toothpick cases and the large silver bucket in which she was accustomed to wash her feet.

On Monday 5 October, Marie Antoinette plucked up courage.

"I was delighted with my day on Thursday," she had once more told a deputation the evening before.

Thursday had been the banquet given by the officers of the Versailles garrison on 1 October to their comrades of the Flanders regiment, which had just arrived from Douai to protect the royal family. The latter, indeed, were somewhat isolated since the desertion of the French Guards, who had left for Paris during the night of 30-31 July with all their arms and baggage. Admittedly a National Guard had been formed at Versailles, but there was not much to be said for these shopkeepers disguised as soldiers and commanded by an Admiral, the Comte d'Estaing. "Flanders," of course, had hardly 1,100 men, but they could still count on the Provost of the King's Household and on the detachment of Chasseurs Lorrains encamped at Rambouillet. Moreover the 300 bodyguards of the "July barracks" had been retained, thus doubling the usual numbers of that somewhat undisciplined troop composed undoubtedly of "warm partisans of the Third Estate"—who on the preceding Thursday, however, had demonstrated their warm loyalty to the crown.

At first Marie Antoinette had not wished to attend the banquet given in the Opera Theatre, but one of her ladies, Mme de Tessé, came to ask her at least to have a look. The guests, numbering 206, ate at a horseshoe-shaped table on the stage. After the second service the Duc de Villeroi, Captain of the first company of guards, had invited all the grenadiers, cavalrymen and Swiss Guards who were drinking in the pit to bring their glasses up to the horseshoe and drink four healths: to the King, to the Queen, to the Dauphin and to the royal family. As each health was drunk the trumpets sounded the charge. One of the guests, it appeared, had murmured "To the health of the Nation," but no one had paid any attention. On hearing this report

Marie Antoinette hesitated, but at that moment the King came back from the hunt and the Queen bore him off with their two children to the railed-in box facing the stage. The guests had already done justice to the wines and the meal prepared by the chef Deharmes, and when the royal family appeared they were given a wildly enthusiastic reception. The applause and the welcoming cries still rang in the Queen's ears after five days. She had entrusted the Dauphin to an officer of the Swiss Guards and the smiling child, who was placed on the table, walked all round the horseshoe without upsetting a glass. The orchestra had played Grétry's *O Richard, ô mon Roi*, and everyone sang together:

> *O Richard, ô mon Roi*
> *L'univers t'abandonne.*
> *Sur la terre il n'est donc que moi*
> *Qui m'intéresse à ta personne.*

This was followed by one of Sedaine's songs: *Peut-on affliger ce qu'on aime?* The applause grew so loud that the royal family came down on to the stage. Marie Antoinette had found the subsequent cries, dances and applause in the marble hall somewhat excessive and she doubtless disapproved of M. d'Estaing's aide-de-camp, a certain Perceval, who went so far as to climb up on to the balcony, shouting: "The posts are ours. From now on we must be called the royal guards." But these young hotheads could be forgiven some excesses due to the wine.

As was to be expected, however, on Sunday the Paris pamphleteers— the Marats, Desmoulins and Loustalots—had transformed this happy evening into an orgy. They had actually written that the guests had drunkenly trampled on the tricolour cockade. The Queen had seen nothing of the sort. At the most, perhaps, some young men of the Versailles National Guard had reversed their tricolour cockades, thus displaying the white worn by "Flanders" and the Chasseurs. Perhaps, too, white cockades had been given to some of the guests at the horseshoe and they had taken them. Perhaps, again, when the evening was well advanced, some young men excited by drink had cried: "Down with the Assembly!" under the Queen's windows. So it was said, but Marie Antoinette had heard nothing.

Besides, all these imaginative and exaggerated details came from absentees, such as Lecointre, the Lieutenant General of the Notre Dame barracks of the National Guard, who had not been invited to the banquet. Eye-witnesses were either unaware of them or denied them.

During the meal the guests had shouted so much that many of the dishes and nearly 400 bottles were left over. And so on Saturday the leavings had been finished off at the royal riding-school, and there were fresh cries of "Long live the King!" and "Long live the Queen!" but this time the Nation and the Assembly were not forgotten.

Marie Antoinette thought the trouble would die down. In the words of a contemporary: "the moment there was a lull and an appearance of security she quickly resumed all her illusions." And now, on Monday 5 October, her illusions prevented her from realising that since Thursday's "orgy" Paris was in a ferment. There was no bread in Paris, whereas, according to the pamphleteers, flour was being hoarded at Versailles, where, to make matters worse, they were insulting the Nation. In the streets there were cries of: "It is time to cut the Queen's throat."

How far away all this seemed at Trianon! Through the narrow crack in the rock the Queen gazed at the ravine, where the trees were already changing colour. The sky was dark and the rain began to fall. Suddenly Marie Antoinette saw a page hurrying towards the grotto. In a moment he was before her, panting.

He was sent by M. de Saint-Priest. Paris was marching on Versailles.

12

✤

The Entry into History

IT WAS POURING with rain. The first horde of 6,000 women marched towards Versailles preceded by ten drummers, four cannon and Maillard, the conqueror of the Bastille. Covered with mud and soaked to the skin, they called to the onlookers: "See what a state we are in, but the jade will pay us dearly!"

They were armed with broom handles, pitchforks, swords, skewers and old pistols. There were even some enormous kitchen knives, which the termagants sharpened on the milestones.

"How glad I should be if I could open her belly with this knife and tear out her heart by thrusting my arm in up to the elbow!"

"We each want to bring back part of Marie Antoinette."

"I shall have a thigh!"

"I shall have the entrails!"

"As they said these things," reports a witness, the lawyer Antoine Périn, "many of them held out their aprons, as though they already carried in them what they had promised themselves, and in that attitude they danced." The lawyer also reported other remarks and revolting gestures relating to Mme de Polignac and the Queen which it is impossible to repeat.

Here and there a few muskets were seen, but they were carried by men disguised as women. This is not a legend; there exist 392 depositions for these two days in October which are unanimous on the point. A contemporary observer gives us the reason for this masquerade: "They were less likely to decide to repel women by force of arms." So the men who wanted to follow had had to place themselves at the rear of the column or wear a disguise. However, they were not behind in crying: "We will take the Queen dead or alive!"

And the women replied: "You will take charge of the King! It is we who will take the Queen dead or alive!"

"Her throat must be cut! We will make cockades of her guts!"

At half-past three the van of the terrifying crowd reached Versailles. At the entrance of the Avenue de Paris some of the women were almost knocked down by a group of riders. It was the King, who having heard of the march from Paris was returning hurriedly from the hunt. When he arrived at the château the tocsin sounded and the gates, which had not moved on their hinges since the time of the Roi Soleil, were closed. The bodyguards, the Flanders regiment and 200 men of the Versailles National Guard were drawn up in battle array in the Place d'Armes. Not a single cartridge had been distributed.

Behind the hedge of troops the château was seething. The King was in council with the Queen. What was to be done? The Captain of the Guards came to ask for orders.

"What! For a crowd of women? You are jesting!"

Marie Antoinette was quite calm. Saint-Priest explained his plan. "I described the danger of awaiting this multitude at Versailles and I suggested measures to be taken in this event. They consisted in having the bridges over the Seine guarded by a battalion of the Flanders regiment at Sèvres, by another at Saint Cloud, and by the Swiss Guards at Neuilly, and finally in the King's sending the Queen and the royal family to Rambouillet, where the Chasseurs of the Lorraine regiment were stationed, while His Majesty went to meet the Parisians with 200 Chasseurs des Evêchés and his 800 bodyguards. Once the thousand horse were drawn up on the other side of the Pont de Sèvres the King would order the crowd from Paris to retire and, if they did not obey, would order several cavalry charges to disperse them. Finally, if this did not succeed, the King would have time to regain Versailles at the head of his troops and then to march to Rambouillet."

Louis XVI was tempted, but Marie Antoinette did not want to be separated from her husband.

"I do not wish the King to incur a danger which I cannot share."

While hours went by in waiting and inaction at the château the fishwives, covered with mud from head to foot, infiltrated into Versailles. Maillard, at the head of a group, invaded the Assembly.

"The people have no bread," he cried. "They are in despair, their arms are raised and they will certainly be led into some excesses. We ask permission to search the houses suspected of holding flour. It is for the Assembly to avert the shedding of blood, but the Assembly contains enemies of the people, who are the cause of the famine. Wicked men are giving money and bonds to the millers to ensure that they do not grind."

"The names? The names? Name them!" was cried on all sides.

In all seriousness Maillard replied: "The Archbishop of Paris has given 200 livres to a miller to stop him grinding!"

Those on the right were angry, but Robespierre, in one of his first interventions, approved this absurdity. Disorder crept in, grew and became indescribable. The women howled: "Bread, bread, bread!"

They climbed over the benches, embraced the President—the Bishop of Langres—took off their skirts to dry, booed the deputies, and soon "the most indecent joy filled the sanctuary of the representatives of the leading people of the world."

One harridan, with a "sharpened dagger" in her hand, went up to Maître Thomas de Frondeville, *Président à mortier* of the Normandy Parliament, and asked him in a low voice: "Is the Queen's apartment as well guarded as they say? Isn't there some way of getting in?"

A fishwife brandished a piece of black bread: "I want to make the Austrian woman swallow it before I wring her neck!"

Other women came up against the troops who were still arrayed in the Place d'Armes. Some of them "offered to pull up their skirts in front of the cavalry." The same theme recurred incessantly: "Ah! The bitch! If I could get hold of her I would tear her apart!"

A thick mist fell on the town. Behind the cavalry gleaming with rain a few windows in the château lit up. The King was receiving a delegation of five women of Paris escorted by several deputies. One of them, Louison Chabry, a "worker in sculpture," aged twenty, fainted with emotion on finding herself in Louis XVI's presence and the King made her smell spirits. While he was speaking kindly to the delegation the cries of the viragos reached the *Œil-de-Bœuf* and could be distinctly heard: "We will bring back the Queen's head on the end of a pike."

The King sighed and asked Louison: "Have you come to harm my wife?"

But one of Lafayette's aides-de-camp brought serious news. The commanding officer of the Paris National Guards was marching on Versailles with 30,000 men, including the former French Guards. Saint-Priest immediately recommended a general removal to Rambouillet and even Normandy. The King would not decide before taking Marie Antoinette's advice. She agreed, since there was no longer any question of leaving her husband, and hurried into the children's apartments, where she informed the sub-governesses: "We are leaving in a quarter-of-an-hour, get your things together and hurry!"

But it was too late. What had been possible at four o'clock was no longer possible at eight. The crowd prevented the carriage from leaving the Stables. Force would have been needed and the King refused to employ it. Marie Antoinette sighed: "Go and tell those ladies that everything is changed. We are staying."

There was consternation in the whole court, but Marie Antoinette reassured those about her. During this night of 5 to 6 October she remained astonishingly calm. She entered into history. "Her countenance was noble and dignified," reports an observer, "and her face was calm, and although she could have had no illusions as to what there was to fear, no one could perceive the least trace of anxiety. She reassured everyone, thought of everything and was far more preoccupied by all that was dear to her than with her own person. During this evening of 5 October she was seen to receive a great many people in her drawing-room, to speak with firmness and dignity to all who came near her and to communicate her confidence to those who could not conceal their alarm."

"I know they have come from Paris to demand my head, but I learned from my mother not to fear death and I shall await it with firmness."

This evening, for the first time, she seemed to realise her terrible responsibilities.

A few gentlemen and a handful of officers surrounded her. Among them was Fersen. They begged for an order authorising them to take horses from the stable, so that they might defend the royal family if it were attacked.

"I shall consent to give the order on one condition," replied Marie Antoinette. "If the King's life is in danger you will use it promptly; if I alone am in danger you will not use it."

Meanwhile, Louis XVI, at the urging of the deputy Mounier, gave, weeping, his "pure and simple" consent to the Declaration of the Rights of Man. Still weeping he ordered the bodyguards and the Flanders Regiment to leave their posts and to bivouac, the former in the park, on the "Green Carpet," and the latter in the courtyard of the Little Stables. As Louis XVI no longer wanted these men as defenders he could not let them become victims. Only the Versailles National Guard remained on parade.

"As wet as ducks, floundering and stumbling in the mud," the army of Parisians arrived half-an-hour after midnight. Lafayette left his men in the Place d'Armes and entered the château. The General always seemed to be taking part in a scene intended for coloured reproduction. With a telling gesture of his arm he exclaimed: "Sire, I bring you my head to save that of Your Majesty. If my blood must flow, let it be in the service of my King rather than in the shameful light of the torches of the Place de la Grève."

"Monsieur de Lafayette," replied Louis XVI, "you must never doubt that I always have pleasure in seeing you and your good Parisians. Go and let them know my feelings."

In words that have not come down to us, Lafayette then asked the King to let the former French Guards take over the posts they had deserted a month before and to be entrusted with guarding the château. Louis XVI—in his second abdication of the evening—accepted, "trusting in *everything* a General who was sure of *nothing*," in Rivarol's words.

"Go to the Queen," he ordered his valet. "Tell her to go to bed. I shall do so also."

It was then two o'clock in the morning. Marie Antoinette dismissed her servants, refused the protection of several gentlemen who wished to spend the night outside her door, and went to bed. The sound of drums mounted from the courtyard. It was the Versailles National Guard handing over the passwords to the French Guards. In the distance the Queen heard horses' hooves dying away in the night. The bodyguard were retiring to Rambouillet, while the Swiss Guards regained their barracks at Rueil.

Only a handful of bodyguards were guarding the inner doors. The French Guards were at their posts—the gates and openings on to the park—but in accordance with old orders they left all the doors open to facilitate the changing of sentries.

The Queen slept. Lafayette retired to the Hôtel de Noailles, a short distance from the chapel gate, went to bed and sank into slumber.

"I had no anxiety," this heroic donkey was to say later. "The people had promised me they would remain calm."

Tuesday, 6 October, dawned. The Queen's wonderful musical clock tinkled delicately the notes of "*Il pleut, bergère.*" It was six o'clock. At that moment Marie Antoinette heard a noise under her windows. She rang. Her first waiting-woman, Marie Elisabeth Nolle, informed her that it was "the women of Paris who, not having found anywhere to sleep, were walking on the terrace." Relieved, Marie Antoinette dozed off. A quarter of an hour later she was suddenly awakened. Two of her women, Mmes Thiébaut and Augié, were before her. The château was invaded, and some of the guards had been massacred. Not far off Marie Antoinette heard the immense clamour of the people looking for the entrance to her apartments. They caught phrases: "This way! This way! . . . Kill! Kill! . . . No quarter! . . . Death . . . We must have the Queen's heart! . . . Where is the damned bitch?"

Aided by her two women, Marie Antoinette put on her stockings and a petticoat and fled by the little corridor behind her bed. But the door leading to the *Œil-de-Bœuf* was closed. Behind her Marie Antoinette heard the rioters enter her bedroom. With all the shouts filling the palace it was several minutes before a boy heard the fugitives. Weeping, the Queen ran across the room to get to the King's apartments. They heard her beg: "My friends, my dear friends, save me!"

She took breath again in the old dining room, but the King was not there. A minute before he had left by the secret passage to help the Queen. Learning from a guard that she was in safety, he went to find the Dauphin, while Marie Antoinette hurried to little Madame Royale. Finally, five minutes later, they were all four reunited in Louis XVI's bedroom. They could hear the attackers' axes on the very door of the *Œil-de-Bœuf*. The panels flew in pieces. Suddenly the noise was stilled. What was happening? The French Guards charged and cleared the château.

But the Cour de Marbre and the Cour Royale were black with people. "A crowd of almost naked women," reports an observer, "and men armed with pikes threatened the windows with terrifying cries." Marie Antoinette looked out.

"There she is, the damned whore!"

"We don't need her body, we only want to take her head to Paris!"

"The trollop!" yelled a tall, red-headed woman, showing a sickle held by one of her companions. "This will take her head off!"

Another cry kept on recurring: "Long live the Duc d'Orléans!"

The future Philippe-Egalité arrived at Versailles when everything was over, but in the opinion of the people and the royal family, as well as the historians, it was he who had decided, planned and organised everything. Some people were even to claim to have seen him at the head of the marble staircase showing the attackers the way to the Queen's apartments. But at that time he was still at the Palais Royal.[1]

"They will kill my son!"

Marie Antoinette did not retire from the window embrasure. Madame Elisabeth was at her side, Madame Royale in front of her and standing on a chair, the Dauphin watched uncomprehendingly.

"Mamma, I'm hungry!"

The Queen kissed him with tears in her eyes.

"Be patient."

Other shouts now came from the courtyard.

"Let the King come to the balcony!"

Lafayette, who had finally been got out of bed, retained his disarming optimism and dragged Louis XVI to the casement of the state bedroom.

"To Paris! To Paris!"

Lafayette incessantly begged the crowd to retire. Not a man moved. Suddenly a voice demanded: "The Queen on the balcony!"

All went pale and begged Marie Antoinette not to expose herself. Maria Theresa's daughter looked at the surging crowd brandishing its arms.

"I shall appear."

She came forward, holding by the hand her children, who burst into tears.

"No children!"

"The Queen alone!"

With a movement of her arms she pushed back the Dauphin and Madame Royale and appeared alone on the balcony. Thousands of

[1] On this subject see the author's *Philippe-Egalité, le Prince rouge* (Amiot-Dumont).

eyes gazed at this woman, with her hair disordered, who crossed her hands on her yellow and white striped wrapper.

"Shoot! Shoot!"

Marie Antoinette bowed her head and curtsied.

At this gallantry a great shout of "Long live the Queen!" rang from end to end of the great parade ground.

The Queen re-entered her bedroom, covering her children with tears and kisses. But the cries of "To Paris! To Paris!" grew louder, swelled and became so menacing that there was no drawing back. For the tenth time Louis XVI returned to the balcony with Lafayette. Not without difficulty they obtained a moment of silence.

"My friends," cried the King in a loud voice, "I shall go to Paris with my wife and children. I entrust what is most precious to me to the love of my good and faithful subjects."

There was a thunder of applause, punctuated with shots and even cannon-fire.

"Madame," Lafayette asked Marie Antoinette, "what are the Queen's personal intentions?"

"I know the fate that awaits me, but my duty is to die at the King's feet and in the arms of my children."

"All right, Madame. Come with me."

He led her on to the balcony. But there were such howls that at first Lafayette could not make himself heard. He kissed the Queen's hand. There was applause, and shouts of "Long live the General, long live the Queen!"

Lafayette then made this extraordinary speech: "The Queen has been deceived. She promises that she will be so no longer. She promises to love her people, to be attached to them, like Jesus Christ to his Church!"

Through her tears—tears of shame—she looked at the crowd which was now applauding her loudly.

At twenty-five past one the procession of the fallen monarchy left Versailles for ever, on their first stage towards the scaffold.

As the great guardroom was full of blood the royal family went down by a small staircase and entered their carriages with the Comte and Comtesse of Provence and Mme de Tourzel. After waiting for half an hour the long procession set off, preceded by a vanguard carrying the bloody heads of the two bodyguards massacred at the invasion of the château. The weather was mild and clear.

After the "tragic masquerade of the soldiers," after the troupe of "drunken women astride the cannons," came the royal coach. Marie Antoinette bore in her face "the marks of violent grief." From time to time the King covered his face with his handkerchief "to hide his tears." Women danced around the coach, crying: "We are bringing back the baker, the baker's wife and the little baker's boy. They'll give us bread or we'll know why!"

Some of Lafayette's officers also uttered remarks which an observer held to be "hardly proper."

Behind the royal coach marched the disarmed guards, then 2,000 court carriages. In one of them was Fersen.

The journey lasted seven hours, and the Dauphin wept with hunger. At the Chaillot barrier Bailly, the Mayor of Paris who had succeeded the *Prévôt des marchands,* made so bold as to say to the King: "What a wonderful day, Sire, on which the Parisians hold Your Majesty and his family in their city."

But the "wonderful day" was not yet over. Bailly led his prisoners to the Hôtel de Ville. "As the National Guard were not sufficient to line the whole of the processional route," relates Dom Leclercq, "a battalion had been made up of Franciscans, Recollects, Capuchins, Picpusians, etc. It was a battalion of mendicant friars commanded with jealous care and irreproachable skill by a certain Corbeau, captain of artillery. With a large tricolour tassel on their chests by way of a cockade and a naked sabre on their shoulders these reverend gentlemen affected a martial bearing behind their chief, who in his regimentals displayed a conquering air. Passing before this group, which did its best to present arms and attract his attention, Louis XVI turned away his head and furtively wiped away a tear."

In the Place de l'Hôtel de Ville a dense crowd greeted the sovereigns. These were no riff-raff or fishwives but honest folk who were glad to cry: "Long live the King, long live the Queen, long live the Dauphin, long live us all!" Everyone wept with joy and embraced. The Revolution was over!

Fersen had gone to await Marie Antoinette at the Tuileries, but Saint-Priest asked him to withdraw. "His liaison with the Queen being well known," he might put Marie Antoinette in danger merely by his presence. Axel obeyed.

It was nearly ten o'clock when the royal family finally arrived at the Tuileries, which had been abandoned by the monarchy since Louis

XV's minority. The château was unfurnished and since noon a crowd of people who had installed themselves there of their own accord had been chased away. The court camped as well as it could in this lumber room. The Dauphin's door would not shut and Mme de Tourzel, not daring to go to bed, watched all night by the child's little bed.

In the morning there was a ray of hope. A good-humoured crowd surrounded the castle, continually acclaiming the King, the Dauphin and even the Queen. Marie Antoinette appeared at a window and declared "that she loved the inhabitants of her good city of Paris."

"Yes, yes," cried a voice, "but on 14 July you wanted to besiege the city and bombard it and on 5 October you were going to flee to the frontier."

This was no more than a laughing reproach and the applause thundered again. "If we forget where we are and how we came here," Marie Antoinette wrote to Mercy, who had been advised not to show himself too much, "we should be pleased with the people's mood, particularly this morning. I hope that if there is no lack of bread a great many things will settle down. I speak to the people. The militia, the fishwives—all give me their hand and I give them mine. . . . No one would believe all that has happened in the last 24 hours and yet whatever one imagined would be less than what we have had to endure."

"All hate must cease," she had said that morning to the fishwives. But with her, in spite of her good intentions, hate did not leave her heart. Marie Antoinette had difficulty in not feeling some contempt for her husband, who waddled about being hearty. It would be impossible for Maria Theresa's daughter to forget the terrible awakening of 6 October and the insults thrown in her face. Although she was to claim to have "known everything, seen everything, forgotten everything," there would always be present to her memory those two heads stuck on two pikes, the shameful trophies dripping with blood which had preceded her carriage. She would always hear the cries of the dregs of humanity who had come to tear her from her palace. Like her son she would pronounce "the word Pardon only with great difficulty and many tears." Even more, she would never pronounce it with sincerity. Lafayette was to observe very justly: "She has all that is needed to win the hearts of the Parisians, but an ingrained arrogance and a temper which she is not able sufficiently to conceal more often alienates them. I wish she would bring more good will to it."

Even if Marie Antoinette wished it, and perhaps she did, she would never succeed. It is enough to spend a few hours in the "Inferno" of the Bibliothèque Nationale, where they keep the nauseating pamphlets illustrated with licentious engravings which were written to attack Marie Antoinette from 1788 to 1793, to be no longer able to reproach her with her attitude. The Queen was probably aware of only a small part of this heap of filth and obscenity, but what had come to her eyes had wounded her "pure soul" as much as the people's cries for her death.

"Calumny kills people better than anything," she said to Mme Campan, "and it is by calumny that they will kill me."

Her whole energy was bent to a single end. Once more Lafayette revealed it: "To think how to be beautiful in the midst of danger rather than try to avert it."

Marie Antoinette received the Parliament of Paris in her private apartments. "Her grief had acquired a shade of firmness and her indignation could be seen. She held her son on her knees and, in spite of the courage of which she had given so many heroic proofs, one could not help feeling that her son was a bodyguard whose protection she accepted."

Her children—*Mousseline* and *Chou d'amour*, as she called them— were now her only joy. "We lodge all three in the same apartment," she wrote to Mme de Polignac. "They are nearly always with me and are my consolation. If I could be happy I should be so by reason of these two little creatures. *Chou d'amour* is charming and I love him madly. He loves me very much, too, in his way. . . . He is well, grows strong and no longer becomes angry. He goes for a walk every day, which does him much good."

Axel also brought her consolation. For the first time, as we learn from one of the letters Fersen wrote to his sister at the end of 1789, he spent "a whole day with Her." "Imagine my joy!" he added.

During the whole of the spring of 1790 he was to see Marie Antoinette "freely in her own house" and he sighed, touched: "Poor woman, she is like an angel in her behaviour, courage and feeling. No one has ever been able to love like that." A few days later he wrote: "She is extremely unhappy, but very brave. I try to console her as best I can. I owe her that; she has been so perfect to me!"

It seems that without his dear presence Marie Antoinette would not have been able to bear her burdens. There was nothing to be got from the King. Admittedly, when Louis XVI spoke to her "he revealed in his eyes and behaviour a devotion rarely inspired by the most beloved mistress"; admittedly he constantly consulted her and asked her advice, but the poor man, victim of his perpetual hesitations, was no help or support. He had been completely overtaken by events and by the total disruption of his life.

"When one discusses business with him," said one of his Ministers, "one feels as if one were talking of matters concerning the Emperor of China."

By an outstanding error he let the *Moniteur* publish the famous "red book" showing the expenses of the court. Needless to say, all that was noticed was the sums squandered by the Queen on her protégés. There was not a single village in France that did not know now how much the Polignacs and Marie Antoinette's friends had received.

During this twilight of the monarchy Marie Antoinette, deeply offended, refused to take part in any business at all.

"I am not interfering!"

"The vessel of State is buffeted by a violent storm and there is no one at the helm," Mirabeau was to say.

Gradually, urged by Mercy, Marie Antoinette agreed to alter her decision and soon the tribune exclaimed, not without admiration: "The King has only one man with him—his wife!"

It was of Mirabeau that Mercy was thinking. He was the only man who could restrain the Revolution. At the Ambassador's request La Marck undertook to persuade Marie Antoinette. It was not easy. The Queen had too many memories.

"I think we shall never be so unfortunate as to be reduced to the painful extremity of having recourse to Mirabeau," Marie Antoinette had exclaimed after those days in October.

Mirabeau, to whom this remark was reported, had prophesied: "The King and Queen will perish and the populace will batter their corpses!"

Marie Antoinette felt that the tribune was in the right and so she gave way. Mercy and La Marck could try to win over Mirabeau. This was not very difficult. The plebeian Count, now disillusioned, had veered strongly to the right and he accepted the offers of the court. As Lafayette, who was sometimes witty, remarked: "He is only betraying in the direction of his convictions." Besides, Mirabeau saw that his "treachery" was well paid for—6,000 livres a month (1,200,000 francs), plus the payment of his 208,000 livres of debts and, as a "premium," one million payable on the closure of the Assembly. On 10 May he sent Louis XVI an actual undertaking: "I promise the King loyalty, zeal, activity, energy and a courage which, perhaps, no one can really imagine. Indeed I promise him everything except the success which never depends on one person alone and which only a rash presumption would guarantee amid the terrible sickness which undermines the State and threatens its head."

"When one undertakes to direct a Revolution," said Mirabeau on 10 October 1789, "the difficulty is not to spur it on but to restrain it."

Six months later this observation had never been more accurate. Mirabeau, who on concluding his agreement tried to give back to Louis XVI a few scraps of the power the King's clumsy hands had let slip, came up against the triumvirate of the left: Barnave, Lameth and Duport. He was only partly successful. He might perhaps have succeeded better if he had been willing to join with Lafayette, but the two men hated each other.

Marie Antoinette had not yet received Mirabeau. Like Axel she thought he was a "fine rascal" and that he was "not to be trusted." However, she finally agreed to receive him in the park at Saint Cloud, where the royal family had "permission" to spend the summer. He saw the Queen's eyes veiled with tears, he guessed at the suffering concealed by her pride, and he was conquered. He was so humble, so respectful, and seemed so sincere in regretting his excesses—the thousands of livres had something to do with it—that the Queen, too, was moved and gave him her hand, which he kissed kneeling.

"Madame," said the Comte as he rose, "the monarchy is saved!"

And he wrote to La Marck: "Nothing can stop me. I would die rather than not fulfil my promises!"

This interview was on 3 July 1790. Marie Antoinette was to have a month of hope. The monarchy's last "holidays" were for her an almost happy pause. Axel was staying with friends at Auteuil and "in the gloaming" went to Saint Cloud. He spent his days there. "I write to you from Her house," he told his sister. "My only grief is not to be able completely to console her for all her misfortunes and not to be able to make her as happy as She deserves."

There was gossip, of course, but Marie Antoinette did not mind. "I was informed," wrote Saint-Priest, "that a soldier of the French

Guards, then paid guards, meeting Fersen coming out of the château at three in the morning, was about to arrest him. I thought I ought to speak of it to the Queen and mention that Comte de Fersen's presence and his visits to the château might put her in some danger. 'Tell him, if you think it necessary,' she replied. 'For myself I do not care.' And, in fact, the visits went on just as usual."

This state of well-being—the calm between two storms—was prolonged by the feast of the Federation, one of the finest days in the history of France. At the Champ de Mars, in front of the Ecole Militaire, the Queen attended this first, extraordinary "Fourteenth of July," wearing tricolour ribbons in her hair. In front of her 400,000 people she heard Mass celebrated by Talleyrand to the sound of trumpets and drums. This vast crowd was seated on stands which 200,000 Parisians had built themselves to receive the delegations from the National Guards from all over France. This communal work, carried out in an atmosphere of good humour, had created an amazing feeling of fraternity, which increased after the oath taken by the King. The hearts of all the French seemed to beat in unison. The Queen was carried away by the enthusiasm; her sad face lit up and she lifted the little Dauphin in her arms. For several minutes the air was filled with cries of "Long live the Queen!" and "Long live the Dauphin!"

In the evening everyone danced and embraced. The Revolution was over! As Octave Aubry has so justly remarked; this 14 July was "the first day of patriotism!"

"If Louis XVI had known how to take advantage of the Federation, we would have been lost," Barnave was to admit.

When they returned to Saint Cloud life resumed its slow course. The epoch of the jewellers, of Rose Bertin, of Léonard, of the happy bursts of laughter was now only a pleasant memory. Marie Antoinette now stayed for hours in her room, embroidering or watching her children play. "When I am sad I have my little boy with me." A game of billiards with the King, a walk in the Bois de Boulogne or to the Chaussée d'Antin and the evening suppers were her only distractions.

But the Jacobin revolt of the garrison at Nancy, which was followed by the harsh repression of the General Marquis de Bouillé, set the Revolution moving again. Paris accused the Queen of having encouraged the executions ordered by the General. She certainly approved them, and at the Opera the chorus from *Iphigenia*, "Let us praise our Queen," was booed.

13

✣

Varennes...or the Hand of Fate!

WITH A HEARTBROKEN sigh Louis XVI had brought himself to sign the decree concerning the civil constitution of the clergy. "I would rather be King of Metz," he had said to Fersen, "than remain King of France in such conditions."

When on 10 March 1791, after several months' delay, the Pope finally condemned the civil constitution of the clergy voted by the Assembly, the Queen realised that there remained only one solution for the King—flight. They could reach Montmédy, the headquarters of M. de Bouillé. There Louis XVI could assemble troops "and those of his subjects who were still faithful to him, and could try to win back the rest of his people led astray by seditious leaders." If order could not be re-established, the King would rely on "the help of his allies," that is, on Austria. For six months Marie Antoinette's one idea had been flight. Mirabeau himself was of the same opinion.

"But what are these people thinking of?" he exclaimed. "Cannot they see the abyss opening before their feet?"

According to him, as we learn from La Marck, "the King had only to announce *quite firmly* that he wished to leave Paris, fix the day for leaving and persist energetically in his decision. They would have to let him do what he wanted."

Mirabeau was deceiving himself, and a serious incident proved it. On 25 February, under the pretext of a popular rising at Vincennes, five or six hundred nobles armed with sword-sticks and hunting-knives gathered at the Tuileries, apparently to protect the King and the Queen, but in fact to try to "surround them" and carry them off to Metz. Warned in time, Lafayette hurried from Vincennes and forced the King to order the gentlemen to lay down their arms. Amid a dead silence the "knights of the poniard," as they had been called, placed their inadequate weapons on the chests and tables in the antechamber and left the château between two rows of National Guards, some of them never to return.

After this painful scene Louis XVI was overcome and was still more so when at the end of March Mirabeau took to his bed to die. "In my heart I wear mourning for the monarchy, whose remnants will become the prey of the factious," he sighed. On 2 April he was dead.

To convince her husband of the necessity for leaving was a difficult task for Marie Antoinette, all the more difficult since on 19 February 1791 Louis XV's daughters, Mesdames Adelaide and Victoire, had secretly left Paris. They were arrested at Moret, then at Saulieu and finally at Arnay-le-Duc, and a decree of the Assembly was needed to allow the King's aunts to proceed. The various National Guards had shown themselves the most eager in pursuit all along the route taken by the two old maids' berlin.

This near-failure was not very encouraging. But 15 days later a serious event, which assailed Louis XVI both in his conscience and in his Christian faith, was to force him to decide. Would the King agree to receive Easter communion from the hands of a constitutional curé of St. Germain l'Auxerrois?

Louis XVI adopted a plan which succeeded in putting everyone against him. On Palm Sunday he heard Mass said by Cardinal de Montmorency, a non-juring priest, but refrained from receiving communion. The reply was not long in coming. On his return from the chapel the grenadiers of the National Guard refused to line the King's route. The city immediately became stormy. On the next day, 18 April, Louis XVI decided to leave for Saint Cloud, as he had done the year before. At once the Revolution began to rumble. The King was undoubtedly leaving Paris to fulfil his Easter duties *unconstitutionally!*

Towards noon the King, the Queen, Madame Royale, Madame Elisabeth and the Dauphin entered their coach. The Place du Carrousel was packed with people. The carriages had barely left the courtyard of the Tuileries when men seized the bridles. The National Guard made no attempt to interfere, in fact the grenadiers threatened the postillions with their sabres. The coaches were surrounded by a howling mob. Lafayette and Bailly ordered the National Guards to clear a passage.

"We do not want him to leave!" they replied. "We swear that he shall not leave!"

The King put his head through the window and exclaimed: "It would be extraordinary if, having given the Nation its liberty, I should not be free myself!"

The shouts were like a slap in the face: "F—ing aristocrat! Fat pig!"

Lafayette suggested that Louis XVI should proclaim martial law and resort to force.

"I do not wish blood to be shed for me."

For two terrible hours the royal family remained thus besieged. Finally the carriage door opened and Louis XVI descended calmly.

"So you do not wish me to leave?"

There was dead silence. The King's voice resumed: "It is not possible for me to leave? . . . Very well, I shall stay." And with his rolling gait Louis XVI went back to the château.

"You must admit now that we are no longer free," remarked the Queen sharply as she mounted the steps.

This time Louis XVI agreed to leave for Montmédy. "The event which has just taken place," Marie Antoinette wrote two days later to Mercy, who had taken refuge in Brussels, "confirms us more than ever in our plans. . . . We are in a dreadful position! We absolutely must flee from it during the next month. The King wishes this even more strongly than I."

Axel Fersen had undertaken to arrange the departure. At the Queen's request he had ordered, at the end of December, a far too luxurious berlin painted outside in green and yellow and upholstered in white Utrecht velvet. The carriage contained "two iron cooking-stoves, one canteen to hold eight bottles, two chamber pots of tanned leather, two iron-fitted forks to steady the berlin in the mountains. . .," not to mention "precautionary objects," such as "bolts, axle-nuts, clamps for the swingle-bars, buckles, nails, rivets, washers, etc."

During the two months before the great adventure Axel overflowed with activity to save the woman he loved. Nearly every day he entered the Tuileries by an unguarded door, kept Marie Antoinette informed on his steps to obtain a false passport in the name of Mme de Korff and brought her Bouillé's ciphered dispatches.

Gradually the plan became organised. The royal family would leave with Mme Elisabeth, Mme de Tourzel and three bodyguards disguised as couriers. They would also take two waiting-women, who would travel in a cabriolet. With the six occupants of the berlin this would bring the number to eleven. At each stage they would have to order six draught-horses for the berlin, three horses for the cabriolet and two post-horses for the couriers. This was a large number.

Bouillé came himself to Paris and had long discussions with Fersen. "The most difficult point seems to me to be getting out of the Tuileries where all the exits are guarded." How, indeed, were the royal family to leave their caravanserai? In the summer of 1791 the Tuileries resembled a nomads' camp. Indeed, one has only to read the interrogations of the under servants of the palace, who were closely questioned after the escape.

Pierre-Joseph Brown, guard of the apartments, passed the night on two mattresses placed on the floor of the Grand Gallery looking out on the Cour des Princes. "In the gallery where I sleep," he explained, "there also sleep two little boys, whose names I do not know, who are the messengers of the *garçons du château.*" In the evening the latter also set up their beds in the same room, as did the servants of the *garçons de la chambre.* Quite a dormitory!

Pierre Hubert, a *garçon du château,* preferred to place his mattress in the billiard room, because his friend Péradon "usually slept there."

Each night a footman of the guard slept "on a mattress placed across the door" of Madame Elisabeth's bedroom, while a *garçon de la chambre* set up his bed in "a little room on the right of the said apartment."

But it would be tedious to pursue the list. Not only were the state rooms and the royal apartments packed each night with servants sleeping on camp beds, but a whole population of valets, *garçons de chambre,* male and female wardrobe servants and waiting-women were crowded from eleven onwards in the attics and the garrets between floors. Could the royal family leave the château without being noticed by all these people? And once in the courtyard, could they avoid the sentinels and patrols which surrounded the royal home as though Paris were besieging a fortress?

Axel promised Bouillé to "be responsible for this delicate operation." On the evening of the flight it would be impossible to park the berlin near the château, for it would attract the passers-by. Fersen therefore bought a *citadine*—a kind of omnibus—which would take the fugitives to the barrier. He himself, disguised as a hired coachman, would take the reins.

It was decided that the travellers would then be left to themselves until Châlons. After Pont-de-Somme-Vesle, the first post after Châlons, the fugitives would find detachments of cavalry at each post who would escort them to Montmédy by way of Sainte-Menehould, Clermont, Varennes, Dun and Stenay.

Axel agreed to Bouillé's scheme only very reluctantly. He concurred with the General on the precautions to be taken from Paris to Châlons, for, as he wrote, "the best precaution is to take none at all; all must depend on speed and secrecy." But after that? "If you are not very sure of your detachments," the Swede continued wisely, "it would be better not to have any until after Varennes, so as not to arouse notice in the countryside. The King will then get by easily." He frequently came back to this point. "Be quite sure of your detachments, or do not station any until after Varennes," he repeated. If only they had listened to him!

The departure was fixed for the evening of Monday, 20 June. Axel's private Journal enables us to relive the last days before the adventure.

"Thursday, 16. With the Queen at 9.30. Took the things myself; nothing is suspected here or in town."

"Friday, 17. To Bondy and Bourget" (to reconnoitre the first part of the route).

"Saturday, 18. With the Queen from 2.30 until 6."

"Sunday, 19. Took 800 livres and the Seals. Remained in the château from 11 to midnight."

"Monday, 20 June, arrived."

"Monday, 20. Nothing," wrote Louis XVI in the Journal.

It was a quarter-to-ten. Marie Antoinette, the King, Madame Elisabeth, and the Comte and Comtesse de Provence were together in the Queen's reception room on the ground floor of the palace, whose windows led on to the garden. The future Louis XVIII and his wife, each by a different route, were also to escape that night.

"Take care not to make me moved," the Queen had said to her brother-in-law as they sat down at the table. "I do not want anyone to see I have been crying."

Supper was soon over, the ceremonies having for some time been cut down, and since half-past nine the King and his family had been conversing in low tones. Ten o'clock struck.

"Now we are approaching the worst moment," Marie Antoinette sighed in distress.

The Queen left the drawing room, went into her bedroom and passed through the corridor and up the little staircase to the first floor, where Madame Royale's bedroom was. She had to knock for a few moments before Mme Brunier, alerted by little Marie-Thérèse, opened the door to her. The waiting-woman was informed of the situation in a few words: she was to make the journey; she was to leave with Mme de Neuville, the Dauphin's waiting-woman; in a few minutes they would leave the château and wait for the royal family at Claye, the second stage on the road to Metz.

"Someone will take you to the cabriolet which is already waiting at the Pont-Royal."

But she must hurry. The Queen ordered her to get Madame Royale out of bed and dress her in the little dress she had brought. It was a simple cotton dress "with little blue flowers on a gosling-green ground."

The Queen next went to the Dauphin's apartments. On Mme de Tourzel's orders the future Louis XVII had already been awoken by Mme de Neuville.

"We are going to a place of battle, where there will be many soldiers," the Queen told him.

The child, delighted, asked for his boots and sword. "Quick, quick! Hurry up! Let's go!"

But, alas! he was not brought his French Guards' uniform but a girl's dress. He seems to have been quickly consoled, for a few moments later, in the Queen's entresol, when his sister asked him "what he thought they were going to do," he replied happily: "We are going to act a play, for we are in disguise!"

It was already a quarter-to-eleven. Following Fersen's carefully arranged plan it had been decided that the Children of France would leave the château first. The Queen, followed by Madame Royale and Mme de Tourzel carrying the Dauphin, left her apartments, entered the corridor which ran the whole length of the palace and went towards the apartments of M. de Villequier, First Gentleman of the Bedchamber, who had emigrated. Marie Antoinette opened the door with the key she had provided herself with and the little group entered an unfurnished room. They crossed it to reach an antechamber which led on to the Cour des Princes by an unguarded glass door. The Queen first of all looked into the courtyard. A silhouette could be seen behind the window lit by the carriage lamps and the torches in the courtyard. It was Fersen dressed in his coachman's greatcoat.

Axel entered and took the Dauphin's hand. Madame de Tourzel took the hand of Madame Royale and followed, most rashly, by the Queen, the little group went down the steps leading to the courtyard noisy with National Guards, coachmen and servants.

Following the shadows of the carriages of courtiers who had come for the King's *coucher*, the fugitives reached the *citadine*, which was almost in the middle of the courtyard. Mme de Tourzel and the children got in. Fersen climbed on the driver's seat, cracked his whip at the hired nags and quietly drove out of the courtyard. The Queen, whose emotion and anguish may be imagined, watched the departure of the ramshackle vehicle, which after making a detour by the quays and the Place Louis XV, would wait in the Rue de l'Echelle, at the corner of the Place du Petit-Carrousel. By a miracle Marie Antoinette returned unnoticed to the drawing room. The Comte de Provence was saying goodbye. "We embraced tenderly and separated," he related.

While the King, still slave to a persistent etiquette, had now to play his usual part in the ceremony of the *coucher*, Marie Antoinette went to her bedroom and calmly gave her orders for her walk the next day. One can imagine how her heart beat as she thought of her children, from whom she had never been separated, wandering about in a cab at the mercy of suspicious patrols in that dreadful Paris. If Axel had not been with them she would never have agreed to such a dangerous plan. Her women undressed her, while the servants fastened the bolts and the inside shutters. Marie Antoinette went to bed and was left alone.

It was a quarter-past eleven.

A few minutes later Mme Thiébaut, who was in the secret, came to help her mistress put on a grey dress and black mantle and a large hat with a veil falling from it. Marie Antoinette slipped the bolt and opened the door giving on to the long corridor. She drew back, terrified.

There was a sentry pacing up and down. After ten minutes of hesitation and suspense she took advantage of a moment when the man's back was turned, leaped across the passage, reached the staircase and was soon in M. de Villequier's apartment. One of the bodyguards, M. de Malden, was there, disguised as a courier. Marie Antoinette took his arm and they went down into the courtyard, calmly crossing the guard-room, where the National Guards were chatting. As they walked to the Place du Petit-Carrousel Malden soothed the Queen. Everything had gone well. Madame Elisabeth had reached the meeting place first, but they had had to wait for the King. His *coucher,* at which Lafay-ette had been present, had been longer than usual. A carriage escorted by cavalry men bearing torches brushed past the Queen and her com-panion. Marie Antoinette recognised Lafayette's coach and lashed the wheels with her switch. But now Malden had lost his way in the maze of little streets between the Place du Petit-Carrousel and the Louvre and could not find the Rue de l'Echelle. It was midnight before they finally found the *citadine* with Axel pacing up and down before it.

Everyone embraced the latecomer. Fersen whipped up his two horses and they set off.

But suddenly Louis XVI became anxious. Fersen was taking a curious route for the Saint-Martin barrier; he was going in the direction of the Chaussée d'Antin. The King, who knew Paris very well, did not dare put his head out to question the "coachman." Much to the fugitives' astonishment the *citadine* stopped in the Rue de Clichy, where the berlin had been kept. Fersen got down, knocked on the door and asked the porter if the carriage had indeed left. On receiving an affirmative answer, he quickly resumed his seat and at last drove off towards the barrier, doubtless by the boulevards and the Porte Saint Martin.

It was 1.30 in the morning when they finally came in sight of the round customs house. Another half-hour was lost in looking for the berlin, which was stowed away on the lower side of the Metz road. Fersen's coachman and the second guard, M. de Moustier, had hidden it too well. The *citadine* drew up alongside the berlin so that the royal family passed from one carriage to the other without setting foot on the ground. Fersen turned the *citadine* over in the ditch, entangled the two horses in their harness and mounted the box.

It must have been nearly two o'clock. It was the shortest night of the year and day would begin to break in an hour. They galloped along and in less than half-an-hour the berlin reached Bondy. The six draught-horses ordered by the third guard, M. de Valory, were waiting in their harness before the posthouse. While the grooms unharnessed the horses belonging to Fersen, Axel got down from the box. The King had been opposed to the idea of the officer's going any further. Perhaps he did not think it proper to travel under the protection of a man whom everyone thought to be his wife's lover.

Her eyes filled with tears, Marie Antoinette saw the Swede open the door and bow to her.

"Goodbye, Madame de Korff!"

According to Moustier, "the King embraced Fersen with all his heart and thanked him with touching kindness." If one remembers that Axel was disguised as a Parisian coachman, the grooms and postillions, who were already in the saddle, must have been slightly surprised.

The relay was quickly carried out and soon Fersen, standing in the middle of the road, saw the heavy coach disappear, escorted by Malden, who had mounted a post-horse. Valory had already left to get the horses ready at Claye.

The noise of the iron-bound wheels of the berlin faded and died away in the night. Fersen looked at his watch.

The fugitives were already two hours behind their scheduled time.

Specialists say that at the centre of a typhoon, or at the heart of a whirlwind, is a zone where not a breath of wind disturbs the surface of the sea. During the twenty hours' journey separating Bondy and Varennes—the first and last stages—the royal family will always seem to be in this "dead calm," while all about them the storm rose and burst forth.

Six o'clock

The heavy yellow and green berlin, preceded by the cabriolet with the two waiting-women, left Meaux. The relay had gone off without incident. The two carriages drove towards Trilport on a road bordered by four rows of trees. The worst was over! Marie Antoinette plucked up courage and smiled as she heard her husband exclaim: "Believe me, when I have my backside on a saddle I shall be very different from what you have seen hitherto!"

The Argonne was swarming with detachments going to take up their positions. The disposition of troops arranged by Bouillé and Fersen was being put into action.

At Sainte-Menehould, half-way between Châlons and Varennes, the call to boot and saddle was sounded. Forty hussars, who had been stationed in the little town, set off. They were to occupy the stage of Pont-de-Somme-Vesle, which the royal berlin was to reach at about two o'clock. The inhabitants grumbled at this "detachment of aristocrats."

Eight o'clock

The berlin was not going very fast. The fugitives, their appetites sharpened by the previous night's emotions, "attacked the canteen" prepared by Fersen: bœuf à la mode and cold veal. They ate "without plates or forks," Moustier recounted, "like hunters or economical travellers." The Queen called to Malden, who trotted to the carriage, offered him something to eat and drink and said: "Perhaps at this moment M. de Lafayette's head is no longer on his shoulders."

In Paris Lafayette jumped out of bed and put on his uniform. The astonishing news spread from the royal apartments, reached the attics and descended to the kitchens and like a trail of powder ran all through Paris: "The King has left! The Queen has escaped!"

As he buckled on his belt in his room Lafayette could hear an approaching "murmur like the roar of a wave driven by the storm." By the time he reached the château a "stormy sea" greeted him. All Paris, "intoxicated at being for the first time without a master," was filling the streets.

At Clermont-en-Argonne, the last post before Varennes, the population was uneasy at the presence of 180 dragoons. The head of the detachment announced that he was expecting "a convoy of silver," but all through the morning the rumour went round: "This so-called treasure is none other than the Queen!"

Ten o'clock

The berlin changed horses at Vieils-Maisons, a little village in a hollow between La Ferté-sous-Jouarre and Montmirail. Louis XVI got out "to make water." At the following relay station Marie Antoinette was not able to prevent him leaving the carriage again "to talk to the peasants about the harvest."

At Sainte-Menehould the people, who were already made uneasy by the passage of the hussars, watched the arrival of 30 dragoons, commanded by Captain Dandoins, who took over the little town to protect "the passage of the treasure" intended for paying Bouillé's army.

Anxious townsmen stopped the newcomers: "My friends, these troop movements are not natural. Look out for yourselves!"

Indeed, money usually travelled by coach with an escort of two gendarmes.

In Paris the crowd was in a ferment. The Tuileries were invaded. A cherry seller had installed herself on Marie Antoinette's bed and cried: "Come on! Cherries, fine cherries at 6 sous the livre!"

Of his own authority Lafayete sent out volunteer couriers, mostly National Guards, in all directions, with orders to "run down" Louis XVI and Marie Antoinette.

Noon

The royal berlin rolled peacefully towards Fromentières. On arriving at the relay station the King got out once more "to gossip with individuals of the people who came to see the travellers." Moustier, who was rightly anxious, wanted "to shield him with his person from the gaze of the curious," but Louis XVI prevented him.

"Don't bother! I do not think this precaution necessary. . . . I feel my journey is safe from all accident."

At the Saint-Martin barrier one of the messengers sent by Lafayette went by at a gallop. He took the Metz road, not knowing he was going in the right direction. The fugitives were ten hours ahead of him.

At Sainte-Menehould the Municipality, alarmed by the passage of troops, distributed 300 new muskets to the National Guard.

At Clermont the dragoons were ordered to stay in the stables near their saddled horses. The population guessed "something" was happening.

At Pont-de-Somme-Vesle the young Duc de Choiseul, Colonel of the Royal Dragoons, a friend of Marie Antoinette and nephew of the Minister, came to a halt before the post-house isolated in the middle of the chalky plain. He had come from Paris with Léonard, whom Marie Antoinette had sent out travelling so as not to be deprived of her favourite hairdresser. At the same time the 40 hussars who had spent the night at Sainte-Menehould dismounted before the relay station. At their head was Goguelas, another of the Queen's friends. The officers hastened to dine while waiting for the berlin to pass.

One o'clock

The royal excursion was taking on the appearance of a country outing. Before reaching Etoges Marie Antoinette got out of the carriage at the bottom of a hill "in order to refresh herself," took her husband's arm and both followed the berlin, which slowed to walking pace. Madame Royale and her brother, so it is said, chased after butterflies.

In Paris the Jacobin Club voted a resolution: "Louis has abdicated from the monarchy; henceforth Louis is nothing to us. We are now free and without a King. It remains to be seen whether it is worthwhile appointing another."

A second horseman passed the Saint-Martin barrier. This was Romeuf, Lafayette's aide-de-camp, who carried a decree of the Assembly ordering the King's arrest. A second wave of couriers had been sent out on the high roads. At Bondy Romeuf picked up the trail of the fugitives. This officer had a knightly attachment to Marie Antoinette and spurred on his horses merely to catch up Bayon, whom he knew to be before him, and hold up the pursuit.

Two o'clock

The fugitives reached the relay station of Chaintrix, the last halt before Châlons. It was stifling. The low, heavy sky weighed on men and beasts. The post-master came forward. Stupefied, he recognised Louis XVI and Marie Antoinette. There was no need of explanations. All France knew that the King wished to flee to Paris. With emotion and respect he suggested that the travellers should get out "in order to refresh themselves." The children were dead tired. The Queen accepted and they sat down to table in the large room of the post-house. They were now nearly three hours behind their timetable.

Romeuf passed through Claye. Although he urged his horse on he realised that Bayon was going faster.

At Pont-de-Somme-Vesle, Choiseul, Goguelas and Léonard paced up and down the road. They listened. Surely they would soon hear the clatter of hoofs and the crack of whips announcing the arrival of the fugitives.

Twenty-past two

At Chaintrix the carriages left the relay station, but barely a minute later one of the berlin's wheels struck against a little bridge, the horses fell and the harness broke. It would have to be repaired.

At Pont-de-Somme-Vesle, Choiseul and his companions began to be anxious about this prolonged delay.

At Meaux, Bayon, the first pursuer, changed horses. The post-master, Petit, informed him that that morning, about five o'clock, he had provided 11 horses for a large berlin coming from Paris accompanied by a cabriolet and two couriers. A man, three women and two children were in the coach. Bayon gave a shout of joy—he was undoubtedly on the right road.

Three o'clock

At Chaintrix the accident was repaired and the berlin set off, driven fast by the son of the post-master.

At Pont-de-Somme-Vesle the officers became even more anxious as the peasants of the district gathered round the relay station. They had not paid their taxes and imagined that the "hussars had come to take action against them." Their attitude became almost menacing and, in spite of his forty horsemen, Choiseul was frightened.

At Sainte-Menehould the agitation grew. Why did not Dandoins have the horses saddled? The commander of the detachment had definite orders: he was to be warned of the King's imminent arrival by a courier sent by Choiseul from Pont-de-Somme-Vesle. Therefore no order was meanwhile to be given to the horsemen.

In Paris the fleurs-de-lis were scratched off the fronts of buildings and the portraits of Louis XVI and Marie Antoinette in the print sellers' displays were torn up. Some cried: "A King and Queen have been lost. A good reward will be paid to whoever does not find them!"

Four o'clock

The carriage, rapidly driven, entered the suburbs of Châlons. It was to change horses at the other end of the town, and in spite of the crowd assembled at the post-house everything went off without incident.

Bayon, his horse covered with foam, changed mounts at La Ferté. Romeuf had just left Meaux, having covered 11 leagues in two-and-a-half hours.

At Clermont the dragoons were alert. They had received orders to be ready to mount at five o'clock.

At Pont-de-Somme-Vesle, Choiseul, taking as his excuse the King's delay and the excitement around the relay station, decided to abandon his post of "advance sentry." He ordered Léonard to warn the detachments at Sainte-Menehould and Clermont "that there was no sign of the treasure passing today." Then, followed by his horsemen, he went at walking pace by a short cut which would enable him to avoid passing through the towns and would lead him directly to Varennes through the Argonne forest.

Six o'clock

The berlin arrived at Pont-de-Somme-Vesle. Marie Antoinette looked through the window. The plain was deserted; no sign of a horseman. Yet all was calm. Since the detachment had left the peasants had gone back to their villages.

At Chaintrix, Bayon dismounted before the relay station. He learned from the post-master himself—who in three hours had become considerably less royalist—that the fugitives were now only a short way ahead of him. But he was exhausted. He had ridden 35 leagues in six hours and changed horses ten times. Someone—it is not known who—offered to go on in front and the officer scribbled an order: "On behalf of the National Assembly, all good citizens are ordered to stop the berlin with six horses in which the King and Queen are suspected of being . . . I am dispatching the bearer with the recommendation to call on the public force."

At Sainte-Menehould Captain Dandoins, after Léonard had gone through, dismissed his dragoons. The men began wandering through streets "in police caps and stable dress." Some sat down to table with the townsfolk.

Eight o'clock

The berlin went down the main street of Sainte-Menehould. For the first time since they left Marie Antoinette saw horsemen who automatically brought their hand to their police caps and saluted. As though it were a "joyful entry," the Queen bowed her head "with that air of benevolent and majestic kindness which she never loses." The carriages stopped before Drouet's posthouse. The relay went off without incident, in spite of the presence of a few dragoons and of a group of inhabitants who came to look at these travellers going by in "such grand style." Did the fugitives notice the arrival of Drouet, who at that moment came in from the fields and, seeing the heavy coach, ordered his postillions "not to kill the horses"? Ten minutes later the berlin, flanked by its two horsemen and preceded by the cabriolet, entered the forest road.

At Clermont, Léonard left the relay-station. He had just given the commander of the detachment Choiseul's orders. The horsemen were ordered to return to their billets, but to hold themselves ready to mount.

Romeuf arrived, in his turn, at Chaintrix. Bayon, who had taken some rest and refreshment, had left hardly half-an-hour before.

The next two-and-a-half hours were the most tragic of the whole journey. Nothing is more dramatic than the calm of these poor people who thought themselves safe and the ferment which immediately followed their passing.

The pincers were closing.

Nine o'clock

The berlin rolled slowly over the Argonne hills.

At Sainte-Menehould the rumour ran from house to house "that the King and Queen had just passed." The tocsin sounded, the dragoons were disarmed, and when Bayon's messenger arrived Drouet and his friend Guillaume leaped into the saddle. They rushed off down the road taken by the berlin an hour before.

At Châlons Bayon arrived at the Hôtel de Ville, where he showed his orders. The tocsin sounded at Saint-Alpin. Nearly the whole of the population of Châlons crowded into the streets.

Half-past nine

At Clermont the six horses had just been harnessed to the berlin. The town seemed somewhat excited but the travellers were able to pursue their journey without any incident. They left the main Metz road and took the road on the left to Varennes. On leaving the town Marie Antoinette listened. Surely the commander of the detachment would sound to boot and saddle.

At Châlons there was a great clamour: "Room for the messenger from the Assembly!" It was Romeuf. On arriving at the Hôtel de Ville he announced that he wanted to go quickly on his way. Bayon appeared. He had intended to go to bed, but "begged for the honour" of accompanying Lafayette's aide-de-camp. Against his will Romeuf agreed.

At Varennes, in the lower town, Léonard's cabriolet stopped in front of the Hôtel du Grand Monarque, where two young officers, the

Chevalier de Bouillé, son of the General, and Captain de Raigecourt
were guarding the relay horses in the hotel stables. The horses belonged
to the conspirators, for there was no posthouse.

"I am Léonard," he called out to them, without getting down from
his carriage. "I know all! The King has left Paris but there is no sign
of his having continued his journey."

Five minutes later the hairdresser disappeared towards Stenay. The
Chevalier de Bouillé decided not to go and inform Lieutenant Röhrig,
who was commanding the 60 hussars billeted at Varennes. Besides,
he was not in the secret.

Ten o'clock

With its lamps lit, the berlin rolled along the road to Varennes.
Rocked by the slow trot of the horses, and convinced that the detachments of Sainte-Menehould and Clermont were galloping behind the
carriage, Marie Antoinette fell asleep.

Two leagues behind the carriage two horsemen galloped at full speed.
They were Drouet and Guillaume, who, thanks to a short cut, had
avoided the bend at Clermont. Meeting his postillions on their return
journey, the post-master had learned that the large berlin had left the
main road.

At Châlons, Romeuf and Bayon passed through the Porte Saint-
Jacques and rode quickly on to the Metz road.

At Clermont the townspeople opposed the dragoons' departure.

At Varennes young Bouillé and his companion went to bed. Lieutenant Röhrig, not seeing the "treasure" arrive, let his men drink "more
than was reasonable."

In the Argonne forest Choiseul and his exhausted horsemen wandered hopelessly about. They had lost their way and had not yet found
the path leading to Varennes.

Half-past ten

Marie Antoinette was awakened by a "fearful shock." The carriage
had stopped at the first houses of the "upper town" of Varennes. The
road was deserted and not a hussar was to be seen. The relay horses
they had expected to see at the entrance to the town were not there.
Marie Antoinette got out and took a few steps. With the King she
knocked at the door of an isolated house. A sleepy voice replied: "Go
on your way!"

While one of the bodyguards went into the town in search of the horses they got back into the carriage and waited.

Quarter-to-eleven

The berlin was still halted at the top of the little town. The bodyguard who had gone to look for the horses had not yet returned. None of the occupants of the carriage seems to have noticed two horsemen, Drouet and Guillaume, who passed the fugitives and descended into the "lower town." A little farther on, outside the Bras d'Or inn, they dismounted.

Ten minutes later the trap was ready. A cart full of furniture barred the little bridge over the Aire. The *Procureur* of the district, the grocer Sauce, was awakened and with several National Guards took up his position at the end of a vaulted passage, a real death-trap which could even be closed by a carriage-gate. Standing against the walls, they waited for the berlin, which could take no other road.

Eleven o'clock

For thirty minutes the berlin had been waiting by the first houses of the "upper town." They could not stay there for ever. The bodyguard had found nothing. Perhaps Bouillé had got the horses ready on the other side of the river. The Clermont postillions agreed to drive that far. Everything seemed so calm that there was no anxiety in the heart of the fugitives. The heavy coach, with its brakes on for the hill, proceeded towards the vaulted passage which spanned the road.

Suddenly there were cries: "Stop! Stop!"

On the previous evening, at the same time, Marie Antoinette had been pretending to go to bed in her bedroom at the Tuileries.

The escapade had lasted exactly 24 hours.

The Queen and her family were once more prisoners of the Revolution.

The Chevalier de Bouillé and Captain de Raigecourt were the last people in Varennes to hear of the King's arrest. Together with Lieutenant Röhrig, who was horrified at learning what had been the "treasure" he had to protect, they leaped to horse and disappeared in the direction of Montmédy to warn General de Bouillé, who was at Stenay with the Royal German regiment.

The tocsin rang urgently. All Varennes had been awakened and was now in front of the grocery run by the Procureur of the district, a plain wooden house to which the royal family had been conducted. Suddenly the Queen started. She could hear in the distance the sound of a troop of horsemen. They were the 40 hussars from Pont-de-Somme-Vesle, who had finally left their woods and swamps. With Choiseul at their head they galloped quickly down the main street, clearing the approaches to the grocery. But Louis XVI refused to order the use of force to snatch him from the hands of the municipality.

"One must have the soul of a monster to shed the blood of one's subjects."

Marie Antoinette had only one hope: the arrival of General Bouillé, whom his son had gone to warn. She heard the King explain: "There are only eight leagues from here to Stenay. On horseback a man could cover the distance in two-and-a-half hours. M. de Bouillé will be here about four or five in the morning and we shall leave here in safety without any danger or violence."

Meanwhile the National Guard from five leagues around marched on the little town which was making its entry into History. Varennes soon took on the appearance of a vast pleasure-garden or an enormous fair. Everywhere bread was being baked and bacon cooked and wine flowed like water. The crowd pressed so closely against the house that they finally entered. The most daring managed to climb to the first floor and gaze boldly at the "Austrian."

The hours passed, filled with anguish. Seated on cane chairs, the prisoners waited for their rescue, which could come only through Bouillé.

Suddenly, at five in the morning, the door of the little room opened. It was Bayon, with his coat unbuttoned and staggering with exhaustion. He could hardly speak and murmured disconnected phrases: "Sire . . . They are slaughtering each other in Paris! Our wives and children may be threatened. You will go no farther . . ."

Marie Antoinette came forward, took the officer's hand "with a forceful gesture" and pointed to the grocer's bed, where the Dauphin and his sister were sleeping.

"Am I not also a mother?"

Suddenly she saw Romeuf, white with dust. He was holding a paper.

"What, Sir!" cried the Queen, who saw the aide-de-camp every day at the Tuileries. "What! Is it you? Ah! I should never have believed it!"

Weeping, he handed the King the Assembly's decree. Louis XVI read aloud: "Order to all functionaries to arrest all the members of the royal family. . . ."

He looked at the Queen and said dully: "There is no longer a King in France."

Then he put the decree down on the bed. Marie Antoinette lost her self-control. She snatched the sheet of paper and flung it violently to the ground. "I will not have it contaminating my children!"

Ten thousand people had flocked into Varennes and howled under the windows: "To Paris! To Paris!"

They, too, were thinking of Bouillé. The cries grew louder. "We will drag them by the feet into their carriage! To Paris! To Paris!" The King tried to gain time and asked for some supper, but the crowd threatened to invade the house. Marie Antoinette lowered herself so far as to entreat Mme Sauce.

"Well, Madame," replied the grocer's wife, "you are in a very unpleasant position, but my husband is responsible. I don't want any trouble to come to him."

Finally Louis XVI left the little room and gave orders to harness the carriage. The tocsin was still ringing; the steeple of Varennes seemed to be sounding the knell of the monarchy.

"At about half-past seven," wrote an under-officer of dragoons, who was stationed at the entrance to the town, "I saw the royal carriage coming surrounded by a troop of armed men. It passed close to me and moved so slowly that I could see the Queen returning my salute. The King made a gesture which revealed his deep grief and prostration. The Queen appeared even more distressed. . . . I have never in my life experienced such a sensation and this poignant scene was never effaced from my mind."

A quarter-of-an-hour later General de Bouillé arrived at the little town at the head of the Royal German regiment. From the farther side of the river, which was too deep to be forded, he could still see the berlin driving away with its guard of 4,000 men. By a refinement of misfortune he was unaware that a little farther on the road crossed to the right bank of the Aire. The regiment would only have had to gallop for a few minutes in order to overthrow the escort and rescue the King. From the hamlet of Ratantout Bouillé ordered the retreat to be sounded.

The berlin, which seemed to be borne along by a large crowd, rolled slowly along the road to Paris. The procession gave so much the impression of a mob that towards eight o'clock the magistrates of Châlons, who had ridden out to meet the King, could not get near and retired, horrified, to their town.

At half-past eleven, when they had been travelling for 16 hours, Marie Antoinette finally saw at the entrance to Châlons the silhouette against the sky of the triumphal arch erected in her honour when she arrived in France. It was adorned with an inscription:

Aeternum stet, ut amor!
May it stand as long as our love!

It was thus that Châlons had paid honour to the

Princess, whose every charm and grace
Bring new adornment to our race.

Now, on 22 June 1791, Marie Antoinette was not surrounded by a brilliant cavalcade, but by four or five thousand men, dishevelled, yelling, drunk and brandishing the bloody remains of Comte de Dampierre, who had just been massacred for having dared to salute the Queen. Marie Antoinette, "in a state of prostration hardly to be conceived," watched the appalling spectacle. The procession stopped before the former "Intendancy" of Châlons, where the Dauphine had spent the night 21 years before.

It was two o'clock in the morning when the unfortunate people, who had not been to bed since they left the Tuileries, finally retired. But a wild hope kept them awake. Mme de Tourzel informs us that certain of the town's authorities showed the King a secret passage leading from the room where the Dauphin was sleeping and suggested that he should flee and ride to join Bouillé's army. But he would have had to leave the royal family, and Louis XVI refused. Why should they not try to remain at Châlons? The National Guard of Rheims would arrive at dawn and Louis XVI, remembering the cheers at his Coronation, trusted to the feelings of "his good Rémois." Perhaps with their help he could surround himself with defensive forces.

At dawn Marie Antoinette fell asleep. It was the dawn of 23 June, a terrible day for Fersen, who on his arrival at Arlon learnt of the catastrophe from Bouillé himself. "All is lost," he wrote, "and I am in

despair. Imagine my grief and pity me." Marie Antoinette had guessed
what would be the extent of the despair of the man she loved. During
the night at Varennes she had asked Choiseul with tears in her voice:
"Do you think M. de Fersen is safe?"

On Thursday, 23 June, the King and Queen were awakened at nine
o'clock by an immense outcry. It was the "good Rémois" entering
Châlons. As a serenade they shouted under Marie Antoinette's windows: "We will eat her heart and liver!"

The dregs of Rheims now took charge of the procession. There are
no words to describe that appalling day.

A little before four o'clock the inhabitants of Chouilly saw the berlin
slowly descend the slope of Haute-Borne and halt at the entrance to the
village. The heat was suffocating. The National Guards rushed to the
inns to refresh themselves. During this time men crowded round the
carriage and hooted the King and Queen, shaking their fists. One of
them climbed on the step and spat in the face of Louis XVI, who
without saying a word wiped himself with a trembling hand. At half-
past four, having roasted under a burning sun for half-an-hour, the
carriage set off again.

The arrival at Epernay is past belief. An enormous crowd filled the
courtyard in front of the Hôtel de Rohan. A meal had been prepared.
It was impossible to get the berlin as far as the steps. The royal family
hesitated before venturing through all those people armed with pikes
and shouting insults and threats of death. A witness of the scene relates
that he distinctly heard a man say to one of his companions: "Hide me
so that I can fire on the Queen without anyone knowing where the
shot comes from."

They had to get out, however, and all arrived safe and sound in a
room at the inn, where Marie Antoinette, her dress having been torn
by the crowd, asked if anyone could find a seamstress. The innkeeper's
daughter, "a young and very pretty person," knelt down and tried to
repair the damage as best she could.

"That's what you get by travelling!" remarked one of the members of
the Epernay council.

Going back to the berlin was another ordeal. Amid a storm of booing
the Queen, insulted, threatened, jostled, was pushed by the crowd to
the carriage door. "Get along, my girl, you'll get worse than that!" a
Sparnacienne shouted in farewell.

An hour later the mob, drunk with shouts, exhaustion and exasperation, were at a halt before the farm of Chêne-Fendu on the bank of the Marne. A great shout arose. The carriage of three deputies of the Assembly, come to meet the prisoners, was in sight and soon stopped at the head of the procession. Preceded by an usher, the two "advanced" deputies, Pétion and Barnave, together with their colleague of the right, Latour-Maubourg, advanced towards the berlin.

"We came up to the carriage door," Pétion related. "It opened at once. Confused noises could be heard. The Queen and Madame Elisabeth appeared, profoundly moved and in tears.

" 'Gentlemen,' they said, eagerly and breathlessly, with tears in their eyes, 'Gentlemen, ah! Monsieur Maubourg!' taking his hand, 'for pity's sake! Ah! Monsieur!' taking Barnave's hand also, 'Ah! Monsieur! Let there be no misfortune, let not the people who accompanied us be victimised, let no attempt be made on their lives. The King did not wish to leave France.' "

Latour-Maubourg took his seat in the cabriolet with the waiting-women, while Pétion and Barnave squeezed themselves as best they could into the berlin. Barnave, the Dauphinois, who had so often attacked the Queen in the Assembly and who had in the Tribune denounced Mirabeau's "treachery," was at first very embarrassed at finding himself seated between Marie Antoinette and the King. This strict Protestant, although not so far to the "left" as Pétion, hated the monarchy and the nobility. He was quite surprised by the royal family's "air of simplicity." He had pictured royalty in coronation robes and was taken aback by "the easy ways and family good-humour" of the travellers. Marie Antoinette and Madame Elisabeth called each other "my little sister"; the King dandled his son on his knees. The child then installed himself on Barnave's knees. He looked at the young deputy's engraved buttons and spelled out the letters on them. "Look, Mamma, do you see? 'Live free or die!' "

Marie Antoinette did not reply. Barnave felt his convictions weaken. He was moved by the tear-filled eyes of this woman, still young and pretty, who spoke to him with trust and friendship. With the Chevalier de Rougeville, Barnave would be Marie Antoinette's last conquest. He would listen to her, be won over and would soon be scandalised by the cries of the populace, who insulted the King and Marie Antoinette at each town they passed. On his orders, when they left Château-Thierry, the berlin out-distanced its sweating, yelling escort.

The next day saw the last stage. It took 13 hours from Meaux to Paris. All during the journey the heat was dreadful. "The dust raised by the people surrounding the carriage," recounted Mme de Tourzel, "was as thick as the worst fog."

In spite of this stifling atmosphere, the "free, cheerful" conversation, at least at the beginning of the day, went on "with the ease one has with friends." From time to time the King handed out a little tepid orangeade to drink. Marie Antoinette teased Barnave, asking him questions which were very embarrassing for an almost republican deputy. Ill at ease, he turned away his eyes.

"Please tell M. Barnave," she said laughingly to Pétion, "not to keep on looking out of the window when I ask him a question."

And they all laughed. They were very young. Louis XVI was the oldest, and he was only 36. Marie Antoinette was a year younger, Madame Elisabeth was 27, Barnave 30 and Pétion 32.

The first clash with the Parisians who had come to meet the prisoners took place in the forest of Bondy. "A crowd of madmen," in the words of a witness, issued from the wood and threw themselves on the National Guards. "In vain were they driven back, they slipped under the horses and between the wheels," in their attack on the carriage. There were nothing but yells and in all the noise the Queen was the most often attacked. "Harridans uttered dreadful cries: 'The bitch, the slut, the whore!' "

To calm the crowd that besieged the berlin Marie Antoinette lifted up the little Dauphin, who was crying. A voice lashed out: "It's no good her showing us her son, we know very well it's not fat Louis's."

The King heard the insult, turned pale, but said nothing. Tears rolled down from the Queen's eyes. The Dauphin uttered "cries of terror."

The berlin moved forward again, laden with men and *tricoteuses.* They were everywhere, on the seats, on the shaft, on the mudguards and even on the box. It was a "hideous and sinister spectacle." A little farther on there was another incident. The National Guards on horseback, who had accompanied the carriage since Meaux, and the grenadiers on foot, commanded by Captain Lefebvre, the future Marshal, began to fight. Each side claimed that the "post of honour" near the berlin was due to them. "The fray grew lively, and bayonets flashed around the carriage." Mathieu Dumas, who commanded the escort, could no longer make himself heard. Barnave then leant right out of the window, shouting above the tumult: "Remember, Colonel, you must answer with your head for the safety of the royal family!"

Spurred on by the young deputy's voice, Dumas managed to free the carriage.

They skirted Paris by the boulevards. Apart from the sound of drums beating in funereal time there was a crushing, insulting silence. The National Guard lined the road with their muskets reversed, as for a funeral. Still hung with groups of "patriots," the berlin reached the Etoile barrier and went down the Champs-Elysées.

Marie Antoinette seemed to be suffering deeply. The Dauphin "stood at the window, looking at the people," and as for Louis XVI, who seemed to have a mantle of lead on his shoulders, he looked at the multitudes with a dazed eye, "the look of a drunken man," reported a witness. The three bodyguards were chained together on the seat; one of them was weeping. "Before the carriage went eight cannons, and as many behind, with the fuse lit. . . . The only radiant face was that of M. de Lafayette, who was riding a superb battle-horse. A large white plume in his hat marked him out from a distance. He commanded the whole crowd with the dignity of a hero. He really appeared like a demi-god." And the bitter, thick, whirling dust still entered by the lowered windows, covering the women's dresses and the King's brown plush clothes with a layer of white, mingling with the sweat and painting black lines on the faces of those poor people, who were a thousand miles from understanding the reasons for all this hate.

The King entered the Tuileries and Lafayette came forward with "affection and respect," as he himself asserted.

"Sire, Your Majesty knows my attachment to you, but I did not leave you unaware that if you separated your cause from that of the people I would remain on the side of the people."

"It is true," admitted the King. "You have followed your principles. It is a party affair. Now, here I am. I shall tell you frankly I thought I was surrounded by a crowd of people of your opinion whom you had put around me, but that that was not the opinion of France. During this journey I have come to see that I was mistaken and that it is the general opinion."

Lafayette was modest in his triumph. "Has Your Majesty any orders to give me?" he asked, bowing.

The King gave a loud laugh. "It seems to me I am more at your orders than you are at mine!"

The Queen did not conceal her "irritation" and went to her rooms. She took off her hat. Her hair, ash-blonde five days before, was now quite white "like that of a woman of seventy."

Two days later she wrote to Fersen: "I exist. . . . How anxious I have been about you and how I pity you. . . . I shall not be able to write to you again. . . ."

That same day Louis XVI wrote in his Journal: "I took some whey."[1]

[1] For further details on the royal escapade see the author's *Souverains en fuite* (Amiot-Dumont) and *Varennes, le roi trahi* (André Bonne).

14

❦

Lost Opportunities

THE KING AND QUEEN were prisoners. Sentries were posted everywhere, even on the roofs of the château. Marie Antoinette informed Fersen of this and the latter noted in his Journal: "The officers wished to sleep in the Queen's bedroom. The most she could obtain was that they should remain between the two doors. They came two or three times during the night to see if she was in her bed."

The King accepted everything. When a parliamentary committee came to question him on the details of his "abduction"—for they pretended to believe in this childish version—Louis XVI replied politely and then turned to his sister, who at that moment entered the room.

"Elisabeth, go and see if the Queen can receive these gentlemen. See that she does not keep them waiting."

Marie Antoinette sent a message that she "had just entered her bath" and that she would receive the "gentlemen" the following day. Not without irony she then offered them armchairs and herself sat on an ordinary chair.

How was this drifting kingdom to be governed? Louis XVI was less capable than ever of "acting like a King," as he was advised by Rivarol. He took advantage of his enforced leisure to indulge in the pleasures of statistics. "From 1775 to 1791," he wrote in his private Journal, "I went out 2,636 times." This calculation filled him with satisfaction.

Marie Antoinette had probably never been so much aware of the unfortunate man's incapacity as at that time. After the deep prostration into which she had fallen after the insult of her entry into the capital and after the dull despair which had seized her when her dream crumbled, she suddenly took hold of herself. She cast about for the best thing to do. There was no King left in France. She took a decision which was to have unlimited consequences: she decided to replace the sovereign who was no more than a royal ghost. But where could she find support? There was no hope on the right; 256 deputies declared that since the King was a prisoner they would take no further part in the work of the Assembly. This "emigration to the interior," as it were, left the Constitutionals, such as Barnave, facing the Jacobins. A compromise had to be made with the "lukewarm." Through the intermediary of the husband of one of her waiting-women, General de Jarjayes, Marie Antoinette got in touch with Barnave. At the beginning of July she wrote to Jarjayes: "I would like you to try to see 2-1 [a cipher indicating Barnave] on my behalf and tell him that I was struck with his personality, which I recognised during the two days we spent together, and that I should very much like to know from him what there is for us to do in our present position. . . . Having thought a great deal, since my return, about the strength, capacity and intelligence of the man I spoke to, I felt that it could not but be advantageous to begin a kind of correspondence with him, always on condition, however, that I should frankly let him know what was in my mind."

Barnave read the note several times "with delight." He promised to save the Queen with the help of his friends. But Lameth and Duport were more reticent. In their eyes Marie Antoinette was "very frivolous" and incapable "of any continuity of thought." However, events were to force them to give her "her chance." The Republicans—a party born as a result of the catastrophe of Varennes—wanted to depose Louis XVI. The Triumvirs knew that once the King was suppressed the whole edifice built by the Constituent Assembly would crumble. The Moderates would have to stand with the threatened King.

"Once the Nation is free," Barnave declared in the Tribune, "and once all French are equal, to wish for more is to wish the beginning of a cessation of freedom and to become guilty."

There was applause and Robespierre was not even able to get a hearing.

Thanks to Barnave's speech the King was "maintained," but he was "suspended" until he should be presented with the new constitution on which the Assembly was working. Barnave had unfortunately been unable to prevent the arrest of all those who had taken part in the flight, including Mme de Tourzel, who in view of her state of health was allowed to remain at the Tuileries. This outcome was a success, however. The worst might have been feared, for indeed one has only to read the press of the extreme left, which called Marie Antoinette "a criminal prostitute" and demanded that her friends in the Assembly should be "impaled alive."

Barnave ignored these attacks. Moved by the good intentions displayed by Marie Antoinette and with his friends' authorisation, he took up his rôle of teacher. Everything must be altered. "The King has for long been deceived. He has allowed himself to be led into a succession of steps the last of which threatens to lose him his crown." But all could yet be saved if the King and Queen would "take their stand" on what they had seen during their journey. Was not the "general wish" of the country for the new constitution then being discussed article by article? The Queen must let her "present intentions" be publicly known. This could be done by working on her brother Leopold and on the Emigrés, even more numerous, who were stirred up and spoke of invading France and rescuing the prisoners of the Tuileries. It was for Marie Antoinette to make them understand that in all loyalty the King and Queen wished to become constitutional monarchs. Provence—who had crossed the frontier without incident—and Artois must return to the kingdom and the Emperor of Austria must recognise the future constitution. Barnave declared that Marie Antoinette "can neither adopt other ideas nor leave this path without being ruined."

The young deputy saw clearly. Either Louis XVI accepted the constitution without reservations and asked his brother-in-law Leopold not to meddle in his affairs, or he abdicated. By refusing to adopt one or other of these two positions the King and Queen hastened to their doom.

On 9 July Marie Antoinette sent her second secret letter to the Triumvirs. She seemed a little more reticent. Perhaps she had been somewhat ruffled by the clear-cut tone of Barnave's reply. On the same day the Assembly voted a decree against the Emigrés, providing for the sequestration and subsequent seizure of their property if they did not return to the kingdom. Marie Antoinette was therefore in a good position to tell Barnave that it "seemed impossible to her that people who had voluntarily left their country two years before should take part in negotiations at a time when a large part of their fortune had been taken from them." As for the Emperor, although the Queen thought she had no influence on Leopold II she "did not refuse to write to him." But she was anxious on one point: would the constitution declare Louis XVI to be "inviolable"?

On the next day Barnave calmed her fears on this subject. "Success is certain. If the King and Queen have as much confidence as they on their side will have constancy and courage, they will answer for everything." In the lines that follow one can perceive the suspicions of Lameth and de Duport. If the King and Queen are not sincere, if Marie Antoinette should fall under "the influence of any adviser," if the sovereigns should "diverge from the plan of conduct," the Triumvirs "could see safety for themselves and for the public weal only in throwing themselves into a completely opposing party." The problem was set and the threat was definite: Marie Antoinette would have to assume her responsibilities.

On Sunday, 17 July, a serious occurrence showed the path the King and Queen would have to take. The extreme left had summoned their supporters to the altar in the Champ de Mars to sign a Republican petition. The affair began as a farce: two citizens had hidden themselves under the altar and spied on the concealed charms of the petitioning ladies. The two *voyeurs* were taken for spies and with sudden brutality the tragedy began. They were massacred and their heads carried through the city. Bailly, Lafayette and Charles de Lameth, who was the brother of Alexandre and, so to speak, the fourth Triumvir, decided to re-establish order. The troops invaded the Champ de Mars, but by an irreparable stroke, the guards fired as a result of an incident, which remains obscure, and fifty corpses were left on the ground.

The "massacre of the Champ de Mars" dug a trench of blood between the constitutional and the advanced deputies. The latter—Danton, Marat, Desmoulins and Santerre—went into hiding. Louis XVI and Marie Antoinette ought now to have had no hesitation in going forward blindly with the moderates. Barnave's speeches at the Tribune were of prime importance for the monarchy and Marie Antoinette seems to have understood this. "I saw with pleasure the force and courage with which the people to whom I write have supported the monarchy. This force cannot but inspire me with confidence on all other points."

On 20 July, with patent goodwill, she asked for more frequent contacts with the Triumvirs. Feeling "isolated and being unable to see anyone," she even expressed the following wish: "I should like to be given a few points to consider, either concerning present events or concerning those of even more importance in the future, and in my retreat I shall always reply with care and truth."

Full of joy, Barnave wrote on the following day to Marie Antoinette to say: "The Revolution must be ended." He emphasised the rôle which the Queen "can and must play" to make her brother abandon the idea of war and to persuade the Emigrés "to return to the great family of Frenchmen." Barnave declared that these madmen must be left "without help." If the King and Queen and the allies abandoned them, "they will be forced to renounce all their rash ideas."

Marie Antoinette seemed to be entirely in agreement with him and asked both for an interview with the Triumvirs and for the draft of a letter to be sent to the Emperor.

When he sent the draft, Barnave—and here one feels the anxiety of his two colleagues—felt it necessary to repeat once more the point of view of those in whom Marie Antoinette "revealed her confidence." The Queen was now about to act, but before doing so she should "question herself" and "be sure that she will never retreat from or vary the line of conduct she is going to adopt." The advice given by Barnave and his friends was "good" and "success was certain," but Marie Antoinette should *above all be resolved to follow it steadfastly.* She had, of course, "aroused profound resentment against herself, but she had suffered" and the French, who had been moved by this, were ready to forget the past and to love their sovereign. Marie Antoinette could once more become Queen of France. Perhaps she would never more see, "as before, everything bow to her sovereign and absolute will, but she could again see herself surrounded by the attentions of a numerous society and the homage of an immense people." She must, then, hasten to act for the good of the country. And he concluded: "The Queen still has a moment and has no more than a moment."

On 26 July Marie Antoinette replied. One can see that she was somewhat shocked by this summons, although she declared that she was touched by the "frank way" in which he had spoken to her. She thought the draft of the letter to Leopold "very good" and she promised to copy it and to send it to Brussels, where Mercy would send it on to Vienna.

This exchange of letters, Marie Antoinette's good intentions and the noble enthusiasm displayed by Barnave could be very moving. But, unfortunately, only the Triumvirs were sincere. Marie Antoinette was lying to them.

She had not the slightest wish to follow these "exaggerated ideas," which would never "suit her." Furthermore, she had entered into the correspondence merely in order to "temporise." She admitted this to Mercy on 29 July and asked him to warn her brother to pay no attention to the letter dictated by the Triumvirs. In Marie Antoinette's view, as she explained to Mercy, to Breteuil and to the Emperor, it was necessary that "at least for some time to come" *they* should think that she was "of their opinion." For some time to come—until the Allies could intervene and come to save her. "The army is lost," she wrote to Mercy on 4 August. "There is no more money and no bond or hindrance can hold back the armed populace from all sides."

Marie Antoinette was all the more at a loss as, since her return, she was without news of Axel. She wrote to Esterhazy: "If you write to him tell HIM that many miles and many countries can never separate hearts. I feel this truth more strongly every day." She sent the same friend of happier days two rings of a kind which "are sold everywhere here." Outside each ring were engraved three fleurs-de-lis and inside this inscription: *"Lâche qui les abandonne."* "The one wrapped in paper is for HIM. Ask HIM to wear it for me. It is just his size. I wore it for two days before packing it. Tell HIM it comes from me. I do not know where he is. It is torture to have no news and not even to know where the people one loves are living."

Marie Antoinette remained without news until the end of September. Axel certainly wrote to her but the letters went astray. He was then in Vienna trying, not without difficulty, to interest Leopold II in his sister's fate and to prevent the Emigrés from doing harm. Marie Antoinette also feared what might come of that "noisy, confused and inconsiderate" opposition, who, with the King's brothers, were agitating in Coblenz. "You know yourself," she wrote to Mercy, "the Emigrés' evil talk and evil intentions. After abandoning us, the cowards want to insist that we alone should expose ourselves and that we alone should serve their interests." She constantly spoke of "that wicked race of men, who profess themselves attached to us and do us nothing but harm." Without the assistance of the Allies they could do nothing. The Queen reiterated this to Esterhazy: "Their arrival in this country would mean the loss of everything."

The heroics of the Emigrés were all the more dangerous as during

August the Assembly was occupied with the future constitution. Only Barnave and his friends could make what the Queen called "the charter" acceptable, and so she continued her "double game." "The moment has now come," she wrote to Barnave on 4 August, "when I can fully judge those who have bravely come out in favour of the monarchy. It is not words that are needed, but the preservation of the monarch's real rights, giving him the necessary dignity, in a word, giving him the strength and the means to govern." Finally she threatened the Triumvirs that she would "withdraw" if they did not maintain "with all their courage the monarch's just and lawful rights."

Barnave, Duport and Lameth were stupefied. Why did she speak to them in that tone "when for the past month we have influenced opinion and the direction of affairs in a way that no one but us would even have dared to try?" Besides, was it not the Queen who had sought them out?

Marie Antoinette realised that she had been unjust and hastened to retreat. Finally, thanks to Barnave and his friends, the constitution was voted. It gave the King powers which were undoubtedly limited but which were infinitely more extensive than the practically non-existent powers which the extreme left wished to grant him. Louis XVI could exercise his "veto" if he did not like a law. He would continue to nominate the Ministers, the Ambassadors and the military chiefs. He no longer had the right to make war, but the future legislative assembly could start a conflict only if the King asked it of them. Elsewhere it was laid down that only those could vote who had a landed revenue of 200 francs in the towns and 75 francs in the country. It was the triumph of the bourgeoisie.

But what was considered by the advanced deputies as "a step backwards" and resulted in Barnave's being described by Robespierre and Pétion as "an infamous cheat sold to the Austrian party," what seems to us today extremely moderate, appeared to Marie Antoinette, as she wrote to Mercy on 7 August, "a tissue of insolence and impractical absurdities." Now Barnave and his friends saw in this "absurdity," which they considered "very monarchical," the only means of saving the royalty. Louis XVI would have the title of "representative of the Nation, the most majestic that the King can bear." Marie Antoinette pretended to be convinced by Barnave's arguments. "Certainly," she wrote on 31 August, "there are advantages to be gained from the constitution both for the King and for the monarchy. . . . My trust in the courage, firmness and intelligence of those who wish for what is good reassures me." But three days before she had written to Mercy: "It is not possible to go on existing like this. All we have to do is to hoodwink them and make them trust us so as better to defeat them afterwards."

One would very much like to be able to tear this page from the Queen's life!

"Our only resource now is in the foreign powers," wrote the Queen on 26 August. "At all costs they must come to our aid."

Like most rulers of the time, Marie Antoinette had no feeling of "patriotism." For them the country was a possession, just as a landowner possesses farms. In their eyes all sovereigns formed one large family and it was not betraying the nation to want to correct it when it was unfaithful. After all, a family council was summoned when a child needed to be set on the right path.

Marie Antoinette was more excusable in calling on the help of foreigners than in deceiving loyal, honest, and sincere people who because they had believed in her and had tried to save her would one day mount Sanson's ladder.

The comedy went on. In order to give his consent Louis XVI had to make a speech to the Assembly, which was soon to disperse. "We will answer for everything," Barnave wrote, "if the King's speech is as it should be," and Marie Antoinette hastily asked her "friends" to revise the text carefully. They worked on it and one can imagine Marie Antoinette's feelings once the speech was drawn up. "I would have liked the acceptation to have been simpler and shorter," she wrote to Axel, from whom she had at last heard, "but it is our misfortune to be surrounded only by villains."

The session of 14 September was a series of rebuffs for Louis XVI. From one of the benches Marie Antoinette could see the Assembly sit down when the King pronounced his oath. The deputies did not rise either when Louis XVI began his speech and "disconcerted and annoyed," he sat down in his turn. On his return to the Tuileries he sank into an armchair and burst into tears.

"And you were a witness to this humiliation!" he sighed to Marie Antoinette. "You came to France to see that!"

The Queen knelt down and folded him in her arms and the husband

and wife, brought closer to each other by misfortune, embraced weeping.

The orders which had turned the château into a citadel were lifted, the "artisans of the flight" were liberated and on 18 September Marie Antoinette was applauded at the Opera, where *Psyché* was being performed. She smiled. Amid acclamations the sovereigns drove to the Champs-Elysées in their carriage.

The deputies dispersed to their provinces, convinced yet again that the Revolution was over. Barnave was triumphant. "The King is reestablished, and the most difficult, the most critical and, we may even say, the most painful times are over." Marie Antoinette agreed and received the Triumvirs in the Tuileries, but she wrote to Axel: "You would never believe how much it costs me to do all I have to at present!"

As one reads the letters of Barnave and his friends one can perceive the latent drama and feel these honest men's weariness when faced with "the langour and apathy" of Louis XVI and with what they called "the Queen's uncertain and irresolute conduct." It is quite certain that Marie Antoinette's double game created an indefinable state of uneasiness. Marie Antoinette confirmed her good intentions by writing a letter to Barnave on 20 October which, for the sake of the Queen's memory, one would prefer not to have survived. "When I began my correspondence with those gentlemen I was completely frank and I always shall be in everything, for such is my character. I have always sacrificed my prejudices. . . . My approaches were made without any mental reservations. I said to myself 'This is my duty,' and that idea was enough for me."

The day before she had written to Axel: "Set your mind at rest, I am not going over to the madmen, and if I have relations with some of them it is merely to make use of them. They revolt me too much for me ever to go over to their side."

Axel calmed down and approved. Presumably before receiving this letter he had been somewhat anxious. He doubted whether the Queen would ever succeed in "winning over the factious." "You would be disgraced in the eyes of Europe," he wrote. But a few days later he was quite reassured on receiving a note from Marie Antoinette: "How wonderful if I could one day be again [powerful] enough to show all these wretches that I was not their dupe."

One cannot read these lines without feeling uncomfortable.

Every day, with the help of invisible ink and lemon juice, she wrote letters, sometimes 30 pages long, which were sent to Brussels hidden in hats or biscuit boxes. "I am exhausted with writing," she sighed. "I have never worked so hard!"

To start off with, the new Legislative Assembly, a somewhat mediocre gathering, voted two decrees, one demanding the famous civic oath for priests, in default of which they would be imprisoned, and the other condemning the Emigrés to death if they did not return to France within two months.

Encouraged by Marie Antoinette and Barnave, who was no longer a deputy, the King refused to approve the two decrees.

"I do what everyone desires often enough for them to do what I want for once," he declared. And he persisted in his veto. This unaccustomed obstinacy amazed everyone. The "poor man's" obduracy is in keeping with Louis XVI's character, however. When a weak man is given the means to be strong he becomes wilful. For the King this right of veto granted by the Assembly was the plank to which he clung and from which, as he thought, he could peacefully manifest his wishes in virtue of the very principles of his adversaries. The latter took it badly and were already thinking of stirring up the people so that "Monsieur Veto" would be forced to yield. The calm of September was forgotten, the gulf yawned again and the Revolution began to move once more.

At the end of 1791 the Duc d'Orléans came to offer himself to help save the monarchy.

"He returns to us in all sincerity," admitted Louis XVI after receiving his cousin, "and he will do all he can to repair the evil done in his name and in which his share may not have been as great as we imagined."

Marie Antoinette was not so easily convinced and in the Queen's drawing-room Philippe was insulted by the sovereign's remaining supporters. Some of them spat in his face. Convinced that Marie Antoinette had inspired the indignities he received, he left the château never to return. The Queen, who had never known how to make friends with those whose help she needed, did not recall him and threw him back on the mob.

At Coblenz, Provence and Artois were still agitating. They had but one aim: to return to the old régime. In Paris they were supported by Madame Elisabeth, who dreamed of absolutism. Louis XVI knew that such a plan could be realised "only by shedding seas of blood." "You make me shudder with horror," he is said to have written to his brothers on learning of their wild talk. "I would rather the monarchy crumbled than that it should ever agree to such schemes!" The letter may not be authentic, but those were certainly the King's feelings. In his will he was to speak of those who by their "false zeal," or by "misunderstood zeal," had done him "much harm." Marie Antoinette was of the same opinion.

"Cain! Cain!" she was to call her brothers-in-law.

While, in spite of his veto, Louis XVI honestly imagined he could become King of the Revolution, Marie Antoinette had only one hope—Austria.

And yet Leopold repeated: "There can be no question of expending our gold and our blood in order to re-establish France in its former powerful state."

What did Marie Antoinette, in whom the Archduchess was always latent, care if France was diminished by her liberation in the future? Louis XVI, on the other hand, knew his brother-in-law's greedy disposition. These ideas were constantly in conflict and the Queen, her husband and her sister-in-law were constantly opposed in violent arguments. "Our home is a hell," Marie Antoinette wrote to Axel.

Fersen knew that the interests of the Emigrés, the Austrians and the Fanatics were irreconcilable, and he therefore suggested a fourth solution—flight. In order to defend his proposition he decided to come to Paris. It was madness, for as a foreigner, with a warrant out for his arrest, he risked his life in order to rescue Marie Antoinette from her agony. Furnished with forged papers and disguised as a courier, he managed to enter Paris on Monday, 13 February 1792.

Without being recognised he entered the château "by his usual route" and did not leave the Queen's apartment during the whole of the following day. At six o'clock in the evening he finally saw Louis XVI. The delay of a day may have been due to the Queen concealing Axel's presence from her husband in order to remain alone with him.

The King refused to repeat the Varennes adventure. The National Guards were closely stationed not only round the château but also round the apartments. "In fact," wrote Axel, "he feels scrupulous about it, having so often promised to remain, for he is an honest man."

"Well now," continued the King, "among ourselves we can speak frankly. I know I am taxed with weakness and irresolution, but no one has ever been in my position. I know I missed the right moment. I missed it on 15 July. Then was the time to go. . . . Since then I have never found it. I have been deserted by everyone."

At half-past nine, without arousing attention, Axel slipped out of the Tuileries. For a whole week he lived in hiding at the house of one of his mistresses, Eleonore Sullivan, without her official lover, Craufurd, ever noticing. In the evening, when the Englishman was out, Eleonore ordered supper as though it were for herself. Half-an-hour after midnight Craufurd returned and, wrote Fersen in his Journal, "ate what I had left, believing that it was she who had been eating."

On 23 February Axel left Paris, apparently without having seen Marie Antoinette again. During the following night, in extremely cold weather—"the wheels crunched as they do in Sweden"—he crossed the frontier without trouble. Would he succeed in persuading the Allies to fly to the help of the prisoners of the Tuileries? Unfortunately his strongest supports gave way: King Gustavus was wounded by Captain Anckarström during a ball at the Stockholm Opera House and died a fortnight later on 30 March.

"This blow will rejoice your Jacobins in Paris," sighed the dying man.

Deprived of Sweden's help, would Austria and Prussia still enter into a war with France? It was France which took the first step.

At that time Louis XVI had a constitutional Ministry, the Feuillant Ministry, as the moderate deputies were called. They wanted peace, whereas the Girondins wanted to fight Austria. Lessart, the Minister for War, concealed from the Assembly certain news which might have touched off a conflict. He was impeached and the Ministry fell.

The monarchy now had only four more months to live, and these four months would see the birth and death of the last of the lost opportunities—that of Dumouriez. The Gironde had forced Louis XVI to have the General as Prime Minister. Dumouriez wanted to be a second Mirabeau and save the monarchy. This was reckoning without Marie Antoinette, who could not bring herself to consent to the monarchy's being put under guardianship. He had asked for an audience, but the Queen did not give him a good reception.

"Monsieur, at present you are all-powerful, but this is through the favour of the people, who soon break their idols. Your existence is dependent on your conduct."

And as Dumouriez seemed somewhat abashed by this reception, she added: "Neither the King nor I can bear all these innovations in the constitution. I tell you frankly: you must make the best of it!"

At least this was frank. Dumouriez would not be put off and tried persuasion.

"Believe me, Madame, I detest anarchy and crime as much as you do. I am in a better position than Your Majesty to judge events. This is not a passing popular movement, but the almost unanimous insurrection of a great nation against inveterate abuses. Everything that tends to separate the King from the Nation leads to the ruin of both. I am working to reunite them; it is for you to help me."

Like Mirabeau 18 months before, he threw himself at her feet and kissed her hand. "Allow yourself to be saved!"

Would she faithfully trust the man who was bringing her her last chance? No.

"One cannot believe in the protestations of a traitor," she was to say to Madame Campan.

She had let the last opportunity slip. Henceforth, with her eyes bandaged, the poor woman walked towards the scaffold.

For her, help could come only from abroad. In any case, everyone wanted war, but for different reasons, from the Girondins and Marie Antoinette to Francis of Austria, son of Leopold, who had just succeeded his father and saw in the Revolution an enemy to be struck down.

There was a pretext ready, for Austria had authorised Condé's army to assemble on its territory.

War—a war which, with truces, was to last for 23 years—was imminent. Dumouriez explained his clever plan to the Council held at the Tuileries on 25 March. Marie Antoinette wrote to Mercy the next day: "M. Dumouriez, no longer in doubt as to the agreement between the Powers, owing to the troop movements, has formed the scheme of being the first to start with an attack in Savoy and another by the Liége country. M. de Lafayette's army would be used in the second attack. This is the result of yesterday's Council."

One cannot help starting as one reads what for us is clear and definite treachery. But we should try to understand. Marie Antoinette did not in any way consider herself to be Queen of the France of 1792. Admittedly, when she formerly busied herself with the affairs of Bavaria, so dear to Marie Theresa, or the problem of the Mouths of the Scheldt, in which Joseph II was so interested, Marie Antoinette had behaved more like an Austrian Archduchess than the wife of Louis XVI. But would she, in the event of war, have gone so far as to communicate to her mother or brother the French army's plans of campaign? Nothing is less certain! But now she felt she was in danger. The woman who, to save her life and that of her children, calls her family to help her has the right to plead extenuating circumstances, especially if she has not the soul of a Camilla. Let us not forget that in the Tribune Vergniaud had just threatened Marie Antoinette with the gallows, with a violence that sent a shudder of terror over the Assembly: "From here I can see the windows of a palace where counter-revolution is being plotted, where they are working out ways to plunge us once more into the horrors of slavery. . . . Let all those who live there know that our Constitution grants inviolability only to the King. Let them know that the law will reach without distinction all who are guilty, and that there is not *one single head* which, once convicted, can escape its sword!"

The speech terrified Marie Antoinette. There must be a war, as she wrote to Mercy, "so that one may finally be revenged for all the outrages inflicted in this country."

Finally, on 20 April, Louis XVI "formally proposed" to the Assembly "a war against the King of Hungary and Bohemia." Five days later Marie Antoinette revealed to Brussels the negotiations begun by Dumouriez in an attempt to detach Prussia from Austria.

As was to be expected, when the French offensive began—the offensive whose plans the Queen had sent to Austria and Prussia—there was a rout. Naturally, Marie Antoinette and "the Austrian committee" were accused.

This accusation enabled the Girondins to pass a series of important measures. The constitutional guard given to Louis XVI some months before was dismissed; the non-juring priests were to be deported; and a camp of 20,000 Federates was set up in front of the walls of Paris. The King yielded only on the first measure, although the monarchy was henceforth practically undefended, but exercised his veto with regard to the two others, in spite of Dumouriez's urging. No longer in agreement with his Girondin Ministers, Louis XVI dismissed them, with the exception of Dumouriez, whom he tried to keep. But on 16

June, being unable to persuade the King to give way, the General preferred to resign. Louis XVI and Marie Antoinette did nothing to hold him back, not realising that their last defender went with him— the only man who might have been able to prevent the Girondins from launching Paris on the attack against the château.

15

❧

Madame Veto

ON THE EVENING of Tuesday, 19 June, Paris was in a ferment. On the next day it was to celebrate the anniversary of the oath of the Jeu de Paume (it was also a year since the King had tried to escape), and Louis XVI had chosen the eve of the Republican festivities to declare to the Assembly that he definitely opposed his veto to the decrees. The suburbs seethed with faces only seen in Paris on sinister occasions. Here and there armed groups formed. There was a rumour that 18,000 "knights of the poniard" had gathered at the château and that the King "had been to confession and made his will." There was one dominating cry: they must go to the Assembly and insist on the suppression of the vetoes. The Directory of the Department—a body somewhat like the present Prefecture of the Seine—had pronounced "all assemblies against the law." Roederer, the *Procureur Général Syndic* (or Prefect), reminded the municipal officers of this, but they, being completely overtaken by events, "agreed in saying that the citizens seemed to them to have the most peaceful intentions, but that they insisted with the greatest stubbornness in going armed" (to the Assembly).

Pétion, who was still Mayor of Paris, alleged that he had "insisted" to the municipality. "They replied," he told his friend Roederer, "that they thought it impossible to overcome the general feeling on this matter. As you see, it is a very delicate position." It was so delicate that at the Hôtel de Ville, Pétion confined himself to ordering "the doors to be held," but paid no attention to the dangers to which the capital might be exposed by the "seditious gathering." Neither did he think of requisitioning troops, as he was allowed to do by law and as the Directory advised him. Moreover, at midnight he wanted to "legalise the movement" which he could not check, and authorised the "gathering to march and to unite under its flags and under the command of its chiefs."

The Directory rejected this proposal and at five o'clock Pétion still persisted in his resolve. The gathering grew larger.

At eight o'clock on the Wednesday morning the Minister of the Interior, Terrier, asserted that "the night's news was not alarming," but at nine o'clock, his eyes having been opened, he sent a cry of alarm to the Directory, asking them "without delay" to "give the order to the troops to march to defend the château." Apparently no order was given and only the usual posts of the National Guard protected the Tuileries. All that was done was to close the gates.

An hour later the crowd began to gather. It did not approach the gates of the Tuileries, fearing "the treachery" of the court. The intention of the *"Piques,"* as they were called, was still merely to march to the Assembly. The meeting hall was the former riding school of the Tuileries, on the site of the present Rue de Rivoli, near the Place Vendôme. The hall abutted on the former Convent of the Feuillants.

Marie Antoinette was listening. The Princesse de Lamballe, who had come back to France now that her former friend was in danger, was standing near her. The two women could hear the murmuring of the petitioners moving about in front of the Manège as they waited for the deputies' decision. Would the "armed citizens" march up to the bar? In the Assembly they first of all heard "the orator of the troupe," who had come to present the wishes of the petitioners.

"We ask you to inquire into the causes of the inaction of our armies. If it results from the executive power then the latter should be abolished. The blood of patriots must not flow to satisfy the pride and ambition of the perfidious château of the Tuileries."

The results of a deliberation with 20,000 armed men at the door may be foreseen. At two o'clock, preceded by about ten musicians, according to an eye-witness, there began the procession "of citizens from all sections, mingled with detachments of the National Guard and led by Santerre and Saint-Huruge, who was half mad. The men were armed with pikes, axes, paring-knives, knives and sticks; some of the women carried sabres. Various emblems were displayed, on which could be read menacing inscriptions, such as 'Down with the veto! Warning to Louis

XVI: The people are tired of suffering. Liberty or death!' An old pair of black breeches was seen on the end of a pike, and above it the words: 'Long live the SANS-CULOTTES! Down with the veto.' "

The crowd penetrated into the Manège by what is now the Rue de Castiglione and flowed on through the Passage des Feuillants towards the Tuileries. From the windows of the château the Queen could see the *Piques* assembling outside the garden gates. As the crowd marched up the pressure against the gates grew stronger.

Three municipal officers were received by the King. "My colleagues and I, Sire, observed *with sorrow* that the Tuileries were closed just as the procession arrived. The people, confined in the Passage des Feuillants, are all the more annoyed as through the wicket they could see people in the garden. We ourselves, Sire, *were very strongly affected* on seeing cannon pointed against the people. Such steps *are more likely to irritate than to satisfy them.* It is urgently necessary that Your Majesty should give the order for the Tuileries gates to be opened."

"I agree to their being opened, but on condition that you make the procession move along the terrace and out by the door of the courtyard of the Manège, without going down into the garden."

At that moment there was a shout from the garden; the gates had given way. The tide of people rushed in across the garden, confining itself to yelling the usual threats. On arriving at the terrace, the head of the procession turned left and passing through the Louvre gates reached the Carrousel in front of the entrance to the château. It was four o'clock. Santerre, who had been the last to leave the Assembly, stood in front of the great door.

"Why have you not entered the château? We must enter; that is all we came for."

Behind him a group of citizens from the Val-de-Grâce section were dragging a cannon. Turning to the National Guards of the Petits-Pères battalion, who were drawn up in the Cour Royale, the "General" shouted: "If you refuse to open the doors we shall break them down with shot!"

"Then everything moved at once. . . ."

Marie Antoinette heard the clamour growing nearer. This time she was not the only one to be attacked. "To hell with the veto! Down with Monsieur Veto!"

There was a dull sound—the tramp of feet on the steps of the great staircase, then a crashing noise—the cannon being hoisted to the first floor. The rioters were massed in the great vestibule which took up the whole of the first floor of the central wing of the château, from the "courtyard side" of the Carrousel to the "garden side" of the Tuileries, in the phraseology of the actors of the King's theatre, whose stage ran the width of the château. Marie Antoinette, whose apartments were on the ground floor, could hear a door overhead being broken down with an axe. The rioters had just burst into an enormous room whose windows also looked out on to the "courtyard side" and the "garden side" and which, since it was used as an antechamber to the state bedroom, was called the *Œil-de-Bœuf*, as at Versailles. After this room, where the bed was, there were rooms on both sides of the château. Looking on the courtyard there were successively the Council Room and the Galerie de Diane, and looking on to the garden were the apartments of the King and the Children of France.

Other *Piques* had remained on the ground floor and were trying to find an entry into the Queen's apartments. A small band of National Guards were on duty in the antechamber, but they let the crowd pass in. One of them, the volunteer Jaladon, admitted that their muskets were not even taken from the racks. A man reached a door and broke down the panels with an axe. Marie Antoinette was only a step away and heard: "I shall take the Queen dead or alive."

The unhappy woman wanted to seek refuge with the King, who on the first floor had gone to meet the raging crowd, but the Princesse de Lamballe stopped her.

"What have I to fear? The worst would be to be killed!"

Her women dragged her in haste to the Dauphin's apartments. The child was no longer there, for his valet had taken him to Madame Royale. At last Marie Antoinette was able to press her two children in her arms. All three hid in a little passage separating the Dauphin's bedroom from the King's, the door of which was hidden in the woodwork and could not easily be seen. It was by this corridor that the King had escaped a year before.

They had to wait a long time. The tumult about them grew louder and the threats of death fiercer. "Marie Antoinette stifled her sobs," relates Mme de Tourzel. For a quarter-of-an-hour she knew nothing of the King's fate. Finally, someone came to tell her that Louis XVI and his sister, hemmed in by the rioters who milled about them, were in the

Œil-de-Bœuf. A "Chevalier de Saint-Louis" held the King's left hand and his right was grasped by Garland de Saint-Farre, director of the Théâtre de Minerve, formerly "Les Enfants Comiques."

The *Piques* were still looking for the Queen. The noise of doors being shattered by axes drew nearer. The first room of the Dauphin's apartments was forced open. Marie Antoinette had to leave her hiding-place.

"Let me go to the King, my duty calls me there!"

Weeping, she advanced towards the mass of armed men, who were coming to seek the coffer on which the King had finally taken refuge. Its appearance in the antechamber was apparently the signal for the rush for spoils. An habitué of the Tuileries, the Chevalier de Rougeville, one of the "knights of the poniard," stopped her.

"Where are you going, Madame?"

"To the King. I count on you, Monsieur, to help me to reach him."

The Chevalier would not allow her to pass.

"It is only with me that the people are angry," begged Marie Antoinette. "I am going to offer them their victim."

But Rougeville, paying no attention to the Queen, bore her off to the Council Room, which had not yet been invaded. The Chevalier asked Marie Antoinette to sit with her children and her ladies behind a heavy table, which was pushed into a corner of the room. The grenadiers of the royalist section of the *Filles Saint-Thomas* were drawn up in three rows in front of the table.

Meanwhile, the crowd was still pressing round the King, demanding that he withdraw his veto and threatening "to come back every day."

"Force will have no effect on me and I am above terror."

He was handed a red bonnet; he put it on, accepted everything, but refused to yield.

The butcher Legendre managed to make himself heard.

"Monsieur, listen to us. It is your business to listen to us. You are a traitor. You have always deceived us and you are still deceiving us. But take care; the measure is full to overflowing and the people are tired of being your plaything."

The deputies who were deliberating in the Manège did not go to the help of the "executive power."

"The King cannot be in danger, he is surrounded by the people," cried Thuriot.

"They are not the people, they are brigands!" retorted Beugnot.

Pétion finally appeared at the Tuileries. It was six o'clock. Since early afternoon he had been at the Hôtel de Ville, watching the crowd go by and sighing: "What a fine sight!"

He advanced towards the King.

"Sire, I have *this moment* heard of the situation you are in."

"That is very surprising," Louis XVI replied calmly. "This has been going on for two hours."

Pétion was hoisted on to the shoulders of two grenadiers. The King rang a bell and the Mayor began his speech.

"The people have done what they should. You have acted with the pride and dignity of free men. But this is enough. Let each man retire."

Louis XVI put forward a suggestion: "I have had the state apartments opened. If the people file past on the gallery side they will enjoy seeing them."

It was not easy to change the rioters into peaceful visitors, but curiosity won, and the crowd passed through the state bedroom. The door of the Council Room was then opened. Everyone halted, astonished. Marie Antoinette, whom they had been looking for everywhere, was there behind the table, on which the Dauphin was standing. Santerre came forward the first, calling to the grenadiers who were protecting the Queen and the little group of women around her.

"Make way for the people to enter and see the Queen!"

The soldiers obeyed. A certain M. de Wittergoff, Lieutenant-General of the 17th Division (some eye-witnesses also refer to him as M. de Wisquichef), placed a red bonnet on Marie Antoinette's head. The Queen took it off and put it on her son's head.

With anguish Marie Antoinette now saw Santerre approach the table and lean on it. "Fear nothing, Madame, I do not want to hurt you, but remember that you are in the wrong and that it is dangerous to deceive and try to dominate the people. However, I shall answer for everything and I shall make them file past."

He turned back towards the crowd, which, somewhat intimidated, had remained in the doorway, and shouted like a barker: "See the Queen and the Royal Prince!"

The people slowly walked past the table. Very pale and with blood-shot eyes, but holding her head erect, Marie Antoinette watched these men and women brandishing whips and carrying placards: "To the lantern with Marie Antoinette!" Did she also notice the man who, as he passed in front of the table, shook a gibbet with a cord from which hung a female doll?

One harridan shrieked: "You're a vile woman!"

"Have I ever done you any harm?" the Queen murmured quietly.

The crowd pressed in from the courtyards and the neighbouring streets, mounted the staircase and filed through. Gradually they became simply sightseers, following their leaders. One woman looked at Marie Antoinette and her two children and the group of frightened ladies. She burst into tears.

"She is drunk," explained Santerre.

In order to reach her sister-in-law Madame Elisabeth had to join the line. On arriving at the table she calmed the Queen, saying in a low voice: "The King is safe."

"Next time they will kill me," murmured Marie Antoinette, "and what will become of my children?"

At eight o'clock in the evening the masquerade was over. Shattered doors lay on the ground, and there was broken glass under foot. The cannon had staved in the floor-boards. Louis XVI was at last able to rejoin his wife. His sister and children threw themselves in his arms. The Queen looked at him, horrified. He had forgotten to take off the red bonnet the rioters had put on his head.

"I still exist, but it is by a miracle," wrote Marie Antoinette to Fersen. "The 20th was an appalling day. It is no longer against me that they are most enraged, but against my husband's very life, and they do not conceal it." The next day she again called for help. "Your friend is in the greatest danger. . . . Let his relatives know of his unhappy position."

Louis XVI had not yielded. He now seemed to have lost his apathy and did not hesitate to read a violent lecture to the Mayor of Paris. His manifesto of 22 June held a tone which the King was not to quit right up to the scaffold and which would have had its effect if the monarchy had not reached the end of its resources. "The French will learn not without grief that a mob, misled by a few malcontents, entered with arms into the King's dwelling. . . . He replied to threats and insults only with his conscience and his love for the public weal. . . . If those who wish to overthrow the monarchy need yet another crime they may commit it."

When Pétion's house was searched, later on, letters were found which are now preserved in the Archives and enable us to realise how terrified Roederer and the Mayor were at the serious situation which had arisen from their inertia and weakness. Pétion wrote to Santerre on 22 June, begging him "for pity's sake to calm the people's minds." There was already talk of another uprising and the Mayor, a veritable sorcerer's apprentice, implored the "General" to intervene. Into what "an abyss of evil a further and illegal action by the citizens of Paris" might plunge the city! As far as Pétion was concerned the principal evil would be to be dismissed for not having been able to keep order, and this soon happened. On 8 July he received a note from Roederer, addressed to "M. Pétion himself," and dated four o'clock in the morning, informing him of his dismissal, embracing him and congratulating him: "May I also find someone to suspend me, until they hang us!"

Lafayette would have liked to hang the members of the Paris Commune and of the Directory who cried with the pack. On learning of the behaviour of the Paris magistrates on 20 June, Lafayette left the army and hastened to the Tuileries. He was full of schemes for saving the King, but Marie Antoinette remarked sarcastically: "I can see that M. de Lafayette wishes to save us, but who will save us from M. de Lafayette?"

The château was no more than a tempest-tossed wreck. Louis XVI and Marie Antoinette lived there like castaways, their ears open to the sinister rumours that reached them. "The band of assassins grows constantly larger," wrote Marie Antoinette, whose tortures increased. Mme Campan had a bodice made for her mistress which would "resist knife-thrusts and bullets." Marie Antoinette refused to wear it.

"If the insurgents assassinate me it will be a blessing for me; they will deliver me from a most miserable existence."

The Queen sometimes longed for the final and immediate catastrophe. Anything seemed preferable to this protracted agony. In the galleries, as the sovereigns passed by, the National Guards cried: "Down with Veto!" The chapel orchestra played the *"Ça ira!"* when the King and Queen entered. The gardens were full of fanatics, who yelled when they saw a curtain drawn aside. Under the Queen's windows hawkers sold passers-by indecent engravings showing Marie Antoinette lying in the arms of Mme de Polignac, the Princesse de Lamballe, or the Comte d'Artois.

"They have taken everything, except my heart," the unhappy woman sighed.

One morning the château was alerted: the suburbs, it was said, were marching on the Tuileries. Mme Campan refused to wake the Queen, who had not fallen asleep until dawn. The King agreed with the waiting-woman.

"It is good to see her take a little rest. Her sufferings increase my own."

When the danger had passed the Queen awoke and "wept bitterly with regret."

"Elisabeth was with the King and I was sleeping, I, who wish to die at his side! I am his wife, I do not wish him to incur any danger without me."

Soon the poor woman did not even sleep. "She insisted that the shutters and blinds should not be closed," wrote Mme Campan, "so that her long, sleepless nights might be less trying."

Occasionally she had a moment of hope. It was not possible that her nephew Francis should leave her in this terrible situation and not do everything he could to overthrow the French troops and reach Paris. She constantly urged Fersen: "Ours is a dreadful situation . . . time presses and it is impossible to wait longer." And on 24 July: "Tell M. de Mercy that the lives of the King and Queen are in the greatest danger, that one day's delay may produce incalculable misfortune, that the manifesto must be sent at once, that it is awaited with extreme impatience."

It was on 25 July that the Duke of Brunswick proclaimed the Manifesto at Coblenz, threatening Paris with military force "if the least violence or the least outrage is committed against Their Majesties the King and Queen." The text was soon all over Paris and caused an explosion. The arrival on 30 July of the Confederates from Marseilles increased the tension. The final attack was imminent. The remaining adherents never left the Tuileries, which they tried, as well as they could, to prepare for resistance, for it must not be thought—following the example of some over-royalist historians—that those of the right prepared meekly to have their throats cut. Police reports and letters found in the Tuileries the day after the 10 August (documents which have remained for the most part unused and are preserved in the Archives) prove that the defenders armed and organised themselves.

It was hoped that the émigré bodyguards would return from Coblenz— their money was still being paid; it was said that barges brought arms and powder; the Swiss were dismissed to their barracks. On 25 July eight witnesses claimed to have seen pages of the King's Household, disguised as National Guards, mounting guard around the château. The son of a miller of Montmartre was sure he had noticed "three Knights of Saint-Louis" pacing the heights of the *Butte* in order to find the best place to set up the artillery. Other witnesses asserted that powder and arms were stored at Meudon and Montrouge.

"The King and Queen are preparing a counter-revolution," the agitators repeated.

In the King's mind it was only a question of defending himself; in that of the people it was a question of attacking the "patriots" once the Royalists had gathered strength.

Curiously enough, Pétion himself no longer believed in the danger. In a letter to Roederer on 1 August he asserted "that an attack on the château" was a "completely false and absurd rumour."

In spite of what many historians have said, there were no misgivings in the Tuileries on the evening of 9 August. To be convinced of this one has only to read the fragment of the unpublished diary written by the Abbé Gallois, the chapel sacristan, a diary which the revolutionaries found on 10 August on the table in his little bedroom in the attics of the Tuileries.

"It is nine o'clock and have just got ready for the night," wrote the Abbé before going to bed. In a neighbouring room François de la Rochefoucauld, who had been to the theatre, was drinking punch with his friend Tourzel, son of the governess. The latter was always well-informed through his mother.

"Nothing will happen, or at least not much."

The two young men gossiped peacefully, but at 11 o'clock they were disturbed by a message from Mme de Tourzel. There was to be no King's *coucher* that evening. Until now etiquette had been preserved aboard this leaking wreck. La Rochefoucauld and Tourzel were worried by the news. Undoubtedly His Majesty was going to try to reach Fontainebleau on horseback, and the two young men hurried to put on their boots.

The Abbé was still sleeping. At half-past two he awoke and wrote:

"I can hear the tocsin sounding and the alarm being beaten, which indicates that vigorous action is being prepared." The sacristan went to find out what was happening. On being told, he returned to his room and wrote: "The Confederates are assembling in the Champs-Elysées. Are they waiting for the Marseillais and the other *sansculottes*? I do not know. . . . All I know is that they are planning an attack on the château."

In fact the bells of Paris were giving the signal not for an attack on the château, but for an attack on the Hôtel de Ville. Commissioners appointed by the sections of Paris were occupied in dismissing a municipality which was too respectful of formalities and in replacing it by a "revolutionary *commune*."

The Abbé was a sound sleeper, for the tocsin had begun to sound just before one o'clock at the church of the Cordeliers. By half-past two all the churches in Paris were answering the signal given by Danton. Marie Antoinette, who had not gone to bed, listened to the alarming sound of the bells ringing through the stifling night. At that moment Paris was taking over power, but she did not know this. Standing at the windows, each one named the church whose bell he recognised. The abolition of the *coucher* had disorganised the life of the château. The bewildered court encamped in the drawing-rooms, to the despair of the ushers, who were horrified by these crimes of *lèse-etiquette*.

Roederer brought reassuring news. Undoubtedly, as Pétion had announced at midnight, the suburb of Saint-Antoine was "in a ferment"; "the citizens are stationed before their houses, armed and ready to march," but there were only 1,500 to 2,000 men assembled.

"The tocsin is having no results," someone came to inform them.

They were all the more reassured since this time the Swiss regiment of 900 men had been summoned from Courbevoie and was guarding the château. There was also the National Guard, not very reliable, it is true, but the royalist battalion of the Filles Saint-Thomas was also on guard. They could count on 1,500 faithful men, together with two or three hundred gentlemen who had arrived at the château.

The King went to lie down in his room fully clothed, but Marie Antoinette, followed by the Princesse de Lamballe, wandered from room to room. She was determined to face the rioters. Madame Elisabeth called her.

"My sister, come and watch the dawn break."

The sky was blood red. It was four o'clock.

Suddenly the tocsin ceased and everyone felt relieved. "I conclude that no one is coming," wrote the Abbé. In front of the window Marie Antoinette continued to look out over Paris. The heavy silence which followed the sound of the bells seemed even more menacing. Her presentiments had not deceived her; the Marquis de Mandat, commander of the National Guard, had been summoned to the Municipality and cut down on the steps of the Hôtel de Ville. His body was thrown into the Seine. In him the Tuileries lost its only defender.

Marie Antoinette went to look for Louis XVI. Woken from a heavy sleep he staggered into the *Œil-de-Bœuf*. His wig was flattened and unpowdered from where he had slept on it. Roederer proposed taking refuge in the Assembly. Marie Antoinette raised her head.

"Monsieur, there are troops here. It is time to find out who will be the stronger, the King and the Constitution or the factions."

And she ordered drinks to be taken to the Swiss Guards. Marie Antoinette was calm. There was no excitement, no anger, no despair, and no useless bravado either. Roederer was to say: "During this fatal night the Queen made no show of masculinity or heroics, was neither affected nor romantic; I saw no rage or despair in her, nor any spirit of revenge. She was a woman, a mother and a wife in danger. She feared, hoped, sorrowed and was reassured."

The suburb began to make its way towards the Tuileries. In the gardens and courtyards the troops who were to defend the château lined up. Three cannons were placed facing the Carrousel. Two more were put on the terrace. Urged by his wife, Louis XVI went down to review the defenders. The drums beat the general salute. From a window Marie Antoinette watched the scene. Nothing less royal could be imagined than the fat man in a grey suit and flattened wig, who with a gloomy look passed silently in front of the men who were to die for him. A great shout of "Long live the Nation!" drowned the applause of the Swiss Guards and royalist companies of the National Guards. Some gunners left their cannon and came to insult the King. Marie Antoinette could hear their cries: "Down with the veto! Down with the fat pig!"

The poor man stammered: "I love the National Guard."

Pale, "as though he had ceased to exist," according to a witness, he returned to the château. Some of the gunners were already leaving their posts to join the vanguard of the *Piques* approaching the château.

The Queen waited in the state bedroom for the King to return. She wept "without a groan, without a sigh, without a word." When she came back into the Council Room, where Roederer was, "the redness of her eyes and cheeks had passed" and she appeared "calm and even detached." Around her all were preparing to die. M. de Saint-Souplet, the King's Equerry, and a page were seen solemnly shouldering the fire-tongs which they had broken in two to use as weapons in place of muskets.

"Half-past seven," wrote the Abbé in his attic. "Word has just come that they have arrived and are at present in the Carrousel."

"Sire," said Roederer at the same moment, "Your Majesty has not five minutes to lose. You will find safety only in the National Assembly."

"But I did not see many people in the Carrousel," the unhappy man stammered.

"But Monsieur," asserted Marie Antoinette, "we have troops."

"Madame, all Paris is marching."

And turning to the bewildered Louis XVI, he added: "Sire, time presses. We are no longer begging you, we no longer take the liberty of giving you advice. There is only one thing for us to do at this moment; we ask your permission to take you away."

"What!" said Marie Antoinette, "are we alone, can no one do anything?"

"Yes, Madame, alone. Action is useless, resistance impossible."

"The King raised his head," wrote Roederer, "looked fixedly at me for a few seconds, then, turning to the Queen, he said: 'Let us go,' and rose."

At the top of the staircase Roederer cried: "The King and his family are going to the Assembly alone, with no other accompaniment than the Ministers and a guard. Make way for them!"

"But, Monsieur," replied Marie Antoinette, "we cannot abandon all these brave people who have come to the château to defend the King."

"If you oppose this move," Roederer declared, "you will have to answer for the King's life and those of your children."

Marie Antoinette gave way.

Surrounded by a body of National Guards, the King, who had put on the hat of one of the guards marching beside him, preceded the Queen, who, "red and weeping," held her son by the hand. Behind her came Madame Royale, Madame Elisabeth, the Princesse de Lamballe, Mme de Tourzel, the Ministers and a handful of faithful supporters.

Marie Antoinette called to M. de Jarjayes: "We shall soon be back."

And the little group moved slowly towards the garden sparkling in the sunshine.

"It seems as though it would end there," wrote the Abbé, but he resumed: "I am wrong. Voices from outside announce perseverance in the plan to attack . . ."

There, without a full stop, the sacristan's log-book ends. The defenders were also persevering. Now that the King had gone, the best thing for them would have been to go too, but old Maréchal de Mailly, who was 84, considered that for him the finest end would be to die with his sword in his hand and, taking the command on himself, he proceeded to transform the château into a fortress.

During the remaining fourteen months of her life Marie Antoinette was to hear herself accused of having, on that morning, "caused the people to be fired upon."

The Assembly, which had been in session since two o'clock in the morning—under the Revolution one slept when one had the time—was occupied with the report "concerning the gradual abolition of the slave trade," when it was announced that the Revolutionary Commune of Paris had arisen in opposition to them. Without being greatly disturbed the deputies referred "these details" to a committee and were about to go back to their negroes when the royal family entered the hall.

Did the King utter those dignified words attributed to him by the *Moniteur*? "I have come here to avoid a great crime and I believe that I cannot be safer than among you."

The President replied cautiously: "Sire, you may count on the firmness of the National Assembly."

This "firmness" consisted first of all in shutting the King and his family up in a little office behind the President's chair, which was used by the editors of the *Logographe*. They stayed squashed together in this tiny box until ten o'clock in the evening.

Whereas the King had recovered his good-humour and chatted with various deputies, Marie Antoinette, her head held high and wearing a fixed expression, watched the endless session without uttering one word. From this cupboard, which was unbearably hot, the Queen saw her last hopes crumble. Near by, the cannon and musket fire raged. Would the Swiss Guards succeed in holding the château, in spite of the order sent by Louis XVI to cease firing? Participants in the battle were constantly arriving to give news of its progress and of the "treachery" of the Swiss, who had greeted the assailants with shots.

"Is this how French citizens should be received in the palace of their King?" demanded a powder-blackened patriot.

But were the French citizens in the habit of presenting themselves with arms and munitions at the palace of their King?

The gunfire died away, and soon only a few shots could be heard. Finally there was silence: the château had surrendered.

Then, like a wreck thrown up on the shore after a tempest, the victorious rioters carried their trophies to the Manège. Marie Antoinette saw brought into the hall her jewels, her silver, letters found on her table, boxes of correspondence and even fragments of trunks found in her apartments. The looters interrupted their unpacking only to give way to the unfortunate and terrified Swiss Guards, who were being exhibited before being sent to the Abbaye Prison. There was a farcical interlude: a petitioner, "his heart wrung with anguish, all covered with blood and dust," in his own words, came to show a Swiss he had captured and for whom he had conceived a sudden affection. He embraced him and fainted with emotion. On being revived his first words were to ask that he be authorised to take the Swiss to his home "to have the honour of feeding him."

"That is how I wish to avenge myself on him."

The deputies were no longer the masters, in spite of their "firmness." The Commune, Robespierre, Marat and Danton were in command and insisted that matters be settled. At the beginning of the afternoon Marie Antoinette saw Vergniaud rise, refer to the "grief" with which his colleagues were filled and ask for the immediate adoption of two measures:

"The French people is invited to form a National Convention . . .

"The head of the Executive Power is provisionally suspended from his functions."

But there was still no question of the Temple prison. Once calm was re-established the royal family would be allowed to reside in the Luxembourg. Gradually the tone changed. By the end of the day no one paid any attention to "the grief of the colleagues." The Assembly was a passive herd, harassed by the delegations, who, incited by the Commune, continually demanded the deposition of the monarchy.

"It has been rendered incapable of doing any harm," Vergniaud promised. "The future Convention will make the decision."

Dazed, overcome with exhaustion and thirst, her fichu and handkerchief "wet with tears and sweat," supporting her son's nodding head in her hands, Marie Antoinette, apparently unmoved, received these rebuffs.

In the evening the royal family, the Princesse de Lamballe, Mme de Tourzel and one of the Queen's women, Mme Augié, were placed in the little cells of the Feuillants convent next to the Manège. For Marie Antoinette it was another sleepless night. At the end of the corridor, behind a grille, a mad crowd shouted threats of death. "When one of the ladies appeared at the door of the apartment," wrote an eye-witness, "she was obliged by the terrifying cries to return at once. Every time I looked at the grille I thought I was in a menagerie watching the fury of the wild beasts when someone approaches the bars."

The Queen's name constantly recurred in their insults.

"I fear she is lost," sighed Mme de Lamballe.

During the evening a few supporters—Choiseul, Goguelas, Nantouillet, Aubier and young Tourzel—managed to find their way to the "apartments."

"My handkerchief is soaked with tears," murmured Marie Antoinette.

Aubier offered his and the Queen thanked him "with a painful smile which wrung my heart," the officer reported.

At six o'clock in the morning an unknown man—a certain Dufour—managed to prepare a meal, but Marie Antoinette, who was "moaning," could not swallow a mouthful. At half-past seven on Saturday, 11 August, their martyrdom began again and they were once more led to the little press-box.

Throughout the day they were humiliated by speeches in which each man tried to show himself more republican than his neighbour and in which vexatious measures were proposed to prevent the King from being carried off.

On the 11th a traitor had improvised a meal, but on the 12th the service of the *Bouche* was resumed. Dinner consisted of two soups, eight entrées, four roasts and eight desserts and supper of two soups, two entrées (one of which was *noix de veau sauce Menehould*), a fowl, a rabbit, cold chicken and five desserts. In spite of the shouting which continued around the convent, Louis XVI ate heartily. Marie Antoinette, who hardly touched anything, was embarrassed. That morning, in her little green-papered cell in the Feuillants, seated on a poor chair, she had wept in the arms of Mme Campan, who had succeeded with some difficulty in joining her.

On Sunday, 12 August, the prisoners had to listen to long discussions on their future residence. Paris was opposed to the Luxembourg Palace, where "there are several concealed exits." The Assembly suggested the house of the Minister of Justice in the Place Vendôme. Manuel, speaking for the Commune, refused. "It is surrounded by houses through which it would be very easy to escape." Why should the Assembly not entrust the Commune with guarding the prisoners? In the evening Manuel suggested putting "the King with his wife and their sister" in the Temple, where "they will be conducted tomorrow with all the respect due to misfortune."

"All their correspondence will be intercepted, for they have only traitors for friends. The streets they will pass through will be lined with all those soldiers of the Revolution, who will make them blush for having imagined that there could be slaves among them willing to support despotism. Their greatest torture will be to hear the cries of 'Long live the Nation.' 'Long live Liberty!' "

The frightened deputies pretended to think that by the Temple was meant the former palace of the Comte d'Artois and they left "to the Commune of Paris the task of fixing the King's residence and entrusted them with guarding him."

It was the gesture of Pilate. The Queen, too, had no thought of the famous keep with its four towers of medieval appearance, which stood in the gardens of the Temple and which she had often asked her brother-in-law to pull down. But Artois liked this useless and gloomy fortress.

On the next day the prisoners were spared the session of the Assembly. The King argued with the Commune in order to obtain twelve servants. "By dint of insisting" he was allowed no more than two valets and four women. At six o'clock the royal family, the Princesse de Lamballe, Mme de Tourzel, her daughter Pauline, Manuel, the Procureur of the Commune, the magistrate Colonge and Pétion, "once more mayor by the people's choice," squeezed themselves into one of the large court coaches harnessed with only two horses. It took an hour to reach the brilliantly lighted palace by way of the boulevards. The Commune had done things well: the meal prepared by the *Bouche* was worthy of the Tuileries.

In the *Salle des Quatre Glaces*, where the Comte d'Artois had formerly received Marie Antoinette, they had to sit down and make a pretence of eating. This time there were no lackeys in powdered wigs; the table was surrounded by men "dressed in the dirtiest and most disgusting clothes." There was no clavichord, no violas d'amore or de gamba; in the gardens and courtyards the Marseillais attended to the musical side of the evening.

Pétion did not dare tell the King that he was not to reside in the palace but in the tower, which could be seen a hundred yards from the palace in the crude light of the *terrines*. Before the interminable meal was over the Mayor went to the Hôtel de Ville and declared that he "had not thought it right to comply with the decision of the previous day and had authorised residence in the palace." There was an uproar and the municipality decreed that "the decision concerning the tower was to be maintained."

The keep, about 60 feet high, was composed of four identical floors, four halls whose ogival vaults were supported on each floor by a heavy stone shaft. On each side two barred windows were set in embrasures so deep that there was ample room for a bed in them. The walls, in fact, were nearly ten feet thick.

To lodge the prisoners, ceilings would have to be built and the rooms divided by partitions. Meanwhile Manuel decided to confine the royal family in "the little tower," a more modern construction backing on the keep. It was here that the cultivated M. Berthélemy, the archivist of the Order of Templars, lodged. In a few minutes he was expelled from his apartment, in spite of his tears, complaints and vehement protests.

It is not known who had the courage to announce to the King and Queen, at the end of their meal, that they were not to reside in the palace. Towards one o'clock in the morning the municipal officers preceded Marie Antoinette to the medieval keep which was henceforth to be her dwelling. As she crossed the garden her ears were assailed by singing:

> Madame is mounting to her tower,
> Who knows when she'll descend?

Marie Antoinette seemed not to hear the coarse laughter which greeted each repetition of the refrain. She hurried across the damp garden—there had just been a storm—and towards the entrance to the tall tower which led to the Gothic Hall on the ground floor and thus to M. Berthélemy's lodgings. On the first floor she found her son, who had fallen asleep while drinking his soup and whom Mme de Tourzel had carried there a short while before. In front of the little trestle-bed, where her Dauphin was sleeping so peacefully, Marie Antoinette experienced a moment of weakness. Tears filled her eyes.

In the garden, and on each landing of the tower, the sentries continued to yell:

> Madame is mounting to her tower,
> Who knows when she'll descend?

16

✤

The Widow Capet

AFTER DINNER ON 3 September, at about three o'clock, Marie Antoinette and Louis XVI were playing backgammon in the Queen's room on the first floor of the small tower of the Temple. The room, which was upholstered in sky blue, looked almost elegant with its sofa and armchairs *à la reine* "in blue and white lampas." Madame Royale and her brother, seated on heart-shaped stools, watched their parents' game. Were it not for the presence of the two municipal officers in their hats with the tricolour feathers, one might have been in one of the *bourgeois* homes so dear to Chardin.

Marie Antoinette was at last able to breathe freely, after the terrible days of 20 June and 10 August and the anguished nights at the Tuileries and the Feuillants. Protected by a numerous guard, she enjoyed relative tranquillity. There was no risk now of waking with a start, to find her bed surrounded by murderers; the worst seemed to be over. Certainly there were many more humiliations in store for her. Already, during the night of 19-20 August, the Princesse de Lamballe, Mme de Tourzel, her daughter Pauline, the three waiting-women and the King's two valets had been snatched from their beds and taken God knew where.

What fresh danger could she fear? The only penalty contained in the constitution was deposition. But above all, Marie Antoinette clung desperately to the idea of an Austrian victory. Learning from her jailers the capture of Verdun and the threat to Longwy, she found it difficult to conceal her feeling of hope. These defeats had aroused a great deal of excitement around the prison. The alarm gun had been fired and the tocsin had rung sombrely. The day before, Cléry, the Dauphin's valet, had announced "that there was a commotion in Paris" and that "the people were going to the prisons." The municipal guards were shortly to refuse to allow the royal family to walk in the garden. During dinner the drums were still heard beating and a few cries came from the direction of the Rue de Temple.

Now there was calm. Only a confused murmur came from the garden —doubtless from the workmen who were building a wall around the tower.

Suddenly a piercing cry came from the little ground-floor dining room, where Cléry and the Tisons, the servants installed by the Commune, were beginning their dinner. A few seconds later Cléry appeared in the room, haggard, his eyes full of horror. He looked at the Queen and said nothing. He could not speak of what he had just seen on the end of a pike, framed in the window—the severed head of the Princesse de Lamballe. Her long fair hair, still curled, floated in the air. Seeing this appalling picture, Mme Tison gave a cry, which the frenzied crowd answered by "frantic laughter"; they thought they had recognised the Queen's voice.

The Princesse had been murdered during the night in the prison of La Force. She still wore on her finger a ring set with a blue stone and containing some white hairs plaited *"en lac d'amour,"* with the motto: "They were whitened by misfortune." It was the Queen's hair. The horribly mutilated body, cut open to the breast, was dragged by the legs to the Temple by a cabinet-maker of the Faubourg Saint-Antoine, a chess-board maker of the Rue Popincourt, a gunner from the Montreuil section and a young drummer from the Halles. In front of them other men brandished the head, waved a strip from a blood-stained vest and exhibited the head and genitals. The victim's private hair was worn as a moustache by one of the assassins.

The officers of the guard had not been able to prevent this bloody masquerade from yelling at the foot of the tower and shouting for the Queen to come to the window.

"As she doesn't show herself we must go up and make her kiss the head of her whore!"

On the first floor one of the municipal guards drew the blue taffeta curtains. Cléry could still not utter a word and Marie Antoinette did not know what was going on.

"They are spreading the rumour that you and your family are no longer in the tower," one of the officers explained. "They want you to appear at the window, but we will not allow it."

The cries grew louder. Other municipal guards appeared in the room; they were ghastly pale. Marie Antoinette, seized with anguish, asked what was being hidden from her. There was a tall fellow there, whose sword struck against the velvet chairs. Marie Antoinette looked at him and the man explained "in the coarsest possible tones: 'They want to hide from you the head of the Lamballe which has been brought here to show you how the people takes its revenge on tyrants. I advise you to appear.'"

But Marie Antoinette did not hear the end of the sentence. "Frozen with horror," without a cry, she fell in a faint.

Once more the storm moved away. For three months Marie Antoinette was to live in calm.

The Queen had arrived in the Temple with four chemises, four petticoats, a wrapper, a spare coat and a few bodices which had been ordered, on 12 August, from the Feuillants. Very little had been saved from the Tuileries, but the Commune was generous and Marie Antoinette ordered a wardrobe suitable for a pretty woman, who, in spite of her imprisonment, did not intend to abandon all elegance. Thirty dressmakers worked incessantly for "the former Queen," and one is somewhat surprised on reading, in the Archives, the bulky accounts of the tradesmen who delivered to the Temple coats of Florence taffeta in "Paris mud" colour, hundreds of fichus, lawn bonnets, shoes of puce, blue or grey, kerchiefs, *pierrots* of toile de Jouy or pink cambric, lawn sashes for "coat-dresses," Chinese sabots, jockey-caps in black beaver. One of the latter must have been particularly becoming, for Madame Elisabeth ordered for herself "the same as the Queen's." This is apart from the "*pâtes royales* for the use of the tyrants," invoiced by the perfumery of Prevost and Laboulée, whose bill amounted to 110,000 present-day francs.

The Commune was just as generous where food was concerned. The meals, whose menus have been preserved, were sometimes more abundant than at the Tuileries. At dinner there were three soups, four entrées, six roasts, and four or five desserts, not to mention fruits and jams. In the evening two of the entrées were withdrawn, but the number of roasts and desserts was the same.

At the beginning of the imprisonment the officers were often good people, as for example the former inspector of food at the Halles, who from the beginning of his guard duties was surprised and conquered by Marie Antoinette's simplicity.

"Come here, Monsieur," she said to him. "Where we are you will see better to read."

A little later she came to show her jailer the hair of the first Dauphin and of the little Sophie. "The Queen put them back where she had taken them," he related, "and came back to me rubbing scent into her hands and passing them before my face so that I could smell the scent, which had a very sweet perfume."

Thanks to Turgy, a serving-lad who had been in the kitchens at the Tuileries, Marie Antoinette was kept aware of events and the code she gave him shows how much hope she still had. From the way this faithful servant placed his fingers on his face the Queen would know if the Austrian troops had won a victory. "When they are fifteen leagues from Paris, the fingers will be carried to the mouth."

Poor people!

At the end of September the work on the great tower was ending. The Commune had brightened up the building by having blinds placed in the windows which let only a narrow band of light through.

No work of any importance had been done on the two lower rooms. That on the ground floor would be used as a Council Room, where the eight municipal officers, half of whom were relieved every evening, would sit, and the first floor would be a guard room. The second and third floors were each divided into four rooms by means of wooden partitions and false ceilings of canvas. The second floor, for the King and the Dauphin, comprised an antechamber, a bedroom for Louis XVI and his son, a dining room and a room for Cléry. Louis XVI moved in on 26 September. Marie Antoinette's floor, the third, was divided into four rooms and was not finished until 26 October. On that day Marie Antoinette climbed the winding-stair, interrupted by wicket gates, for the first time. There was an opening in the middle of each gate. It was large enough for a man to pass through by bending down and stepping over, but impossible to get through quickly. Such was the purpose of the obstacles, of which there were twelve between the ground floor and the third storey. On each landing two heavy doors, one of iron and the other of wood, covered with bolts, locks and chains, divided the staircase from the "apartments."

The Commune had a bath installed for the Queen—it was a luxury at that time—and hired "bath shirts." Furthermore, a clavichord was placed in Marie Antoinette's bedroom, just above the King's, and every day the Queen sang songs which were "nothing less than sad," as Cléry related. Without the presence of the Tisons, whom it was impossible to soften, life would have been bearable. Escorted by municipal guards, who never left them, the prisoners on the second and third floors met at meal times and for their daily walk. In the afternoon "the Queen and Madame Elisabeth," relates one of the officers, "busied themselves with a little work in their room and with the education of the young princess, as did the King with that of his son, which the Queen did not neglect either, for one day, when the young prince was leaving her to come into the room I had just entered and had passed in front of me, looking at me but not saluting me, the Queen, having noticed it, called him and said sternly: 'My son, go back, and salute Monsieur when you pass in front of him.'"

One morning after breakfast—it was Friday, 7 December—the King remained alone with Marie Antoinette and announced a piece of news which Cléry had learned the day before from his wife, who had come to see him in the parlour. In four days' time his trial before the Convention would begin.

At dawn on Tuesday, 11 December, Marie Antoinette heard the alarm sounded. The whole enclosure of the Temple was full of noise. Cannons were even placed in the garden. The King was fetched to be taken to the Convention. Marie Antoinette was not to see her husband for another six weeks. She tried to convince herself that as the constitution pronounced the King "irresponsible" the outcome of the trial, now that France was a Republic, would merely be to exile Louis and his family. Certain newspapers, indeed, argued: "An exiled King has no partisans; a King who has been killed arouses sympathy . . . Tarquin had no successors; Charles I still has."

Her illusions were short-lived. A few days earlier the "Commune of the 10 August" had been replaced by a "provisional Municipality," whose new officers allowed the guards to cover the walls with graffiti which the Queen could read as she went to take her walk: "The guillotine is permanent and waits for the tyrant Louis XVI. . . . Veto will tread the measure." The prisoner could even see caricatures showing her husband on the scaffold, with the caption: "Louis spitting into the sack." Each time the Queen passed before him the concierge amused himself by blowing smoke into her face, while the guards burst out laughing.

The unhappy woman grew thinner. We learn this from the bills of citizen Roussel, dressmaker, who "unstitched a corset to take it in all round." From 1 January onwards she drank a "medicinal soup" every day.

Through Cléry and Turgy she received news of the accused. Did she know that on Christmas morning, alone in the prison where he had been confined by his subjects, the King seemed to have been touched by Grace? Louis XVI wrote his will: "I commend my children to my wife. I have never doubted her maternal tenderness for them. I charge her particularly to make of them good Christians and honest men, to make them look on the grandeurs of this world (if they should be fated to experience them) merely as dangerous and transitory advantages, and to fix their eyes on the sole reliable and lasting glory of eternity. I beg my sister to continue in her tenderness for my children and to be a mother to them if they have the misfortune to lose their own."

Perhaps he had guessed that when he was gone Marie Antoinette could not hope for a pardon.

"I beg my wife to forgive me all the evil she is suffering for my sake and the grief I may have caused her during the course of our marriage, *as she may be sure that I hold nothing against her, if she should think she had anything with which to reproach herself.*"

The paper-sellers cried the news. One of them, a pedlar with a stentorian voice, had been paid by a friend of the Queen to shout out a summary of his paper in the Rue de la Cordonnerie, not far from the tower. On Sunday, 20 January, Marie Antoinette heard him cry: "The National Convention decrees that Louis Capet shall undergo the death penalty. . . . The execution shall take place within 24 hours of its notification to the prisoner."

The "notification" took place at two o'clock, so the execution was to take place the following day. Marie Antoinette passed the day in sobbing. In the evening, at about eight o'clock, the two landing doors burst open; she and her family had been sent for, as the Convention had given permission for the condemned man to see them.

The scene took place in the dining-room. The Queen appeared first, holding her son by the hand, and then came the two Princesses. All threw themselves into the King's arms. The Abbé Edgeworth de Firmont, who had come to help the condemned man, remained in a little room in one of the small towers. In spite of himself he was a witness of the scene. "No pen can ever describe how heartrending it was. For nearly a quarter-of-an-hour not a word was spoken." There were nothing but "cries so piercing as to be heard outside the tower. The King, the Queen, Madame Elisabeth, Monsieur le Dauphin and Madame lamented together and their voices were mingled. Finally the tears ceased, since no one had strength to shed any more. They spoke in low tones, and fairly calmly."

Louis related his trial at length, the questions put to him, which he had not expected and which had confounded him, and the presence among his "judges" of his cousin Orléans. Unconditional death had been voted for by 361 deputies, and since 361 was an absolute majority the King had been condemned by a majority of one vote. Without the vote of Philippe-Egalité Louis XVI would have escaped the scaffold. The former Duc de Chartres, the friend of Fontainebleau and of the excursions in the forest, the friend of the Opera balls, the man with whom Marie Antoinette had danced at her marriage had voted for the death penalty.

The little Dauphin, who in a few hours would be King, stood between his father's knees.

"My son, promise me never to think of avenging my death."

Taking the child in his arms, he added: "You heard what I just said? Lift your hand and swear that you will fulfill your father's last wishes."

At a quarter-past ten the King rose. When Cléry entered the room he saw Marie Antoinette holding her husband's arm and making a few steps towards the door "uttering cries of the deepest grief."

"I assure you," said the King, "that I shall see you tomorrow at eight o'clock."

"Why not at seven o'clock?" begged the Queen.

"Very well, yes, at seven o'clock," Louis replied.

Madame Royale fell in a faint, and the little Dauphin threw himself on his knees before the officers, begging them to let him go and ask for a pardon "from the gentlemen of the Paris sections, so that his Papa should not die."

After putting her son to bed Marie Antoinette did not herself undress. She threw herself in her clothes on her bed covered with green damask. "We heard her all through the night trembling with cold and grief," wrote Madame Royale.

How far they were now from the time when, in Mme de Polignac's house, the clock was put on so that the spoil-sport would go to bed earlier! Was remorse mingled with those tears? Marie Antoinette, indeed, had often blushed for her husband's blunders and coarseness. Not long ago, at the Feuillants, she had been distressed at seeing the fat man munching away peacefully while behind the bars in the corridor the crowd yelled for his death and insulted him. She could still hear the King's loud laugh, his "simple joy," when on 2 September he watched the houses in the Temple enclosure being pulled down. He had so often embarrassed her. But this King, who was soon to be executed by his subjects, lacked neither goodness nor greatness of soul.

"As long as I reign my first care will be to see that religion is respected and to watch over the maintenance of morality."

Did Marie Antoinette remember the remark of the Maréchal de Richelieu?

"Each of the three branches of the House of Bourbon has a dominating and pronounced taste: the eldest loves hunting, the d'Orléans pictures and the Condés war."

"And Louis XVI?" someone asked.

"Ah! he is different. He loves the people!"

This was meant to be ironical, but it was only too true. Louis XVI did indeed love the common people, whose representatives had voted his death. But all these qualities had been frustrated by his hesitation, his habit of "detaching himself," his perpetual weakness.

How he had loved her, too! He had loved her to the point of deferring to her feelings for Axel. This inadequate lover felt that perhaps he had no right, once the succession was assured, to prevent his wife from enjoying a few moments of happiness.

In default of passion, she gradually came to feel a great tenderness for him. This good man—this "honest man," as Fersen called him—finally moved her by all his "sincere and inert" virtues, in Mirabeau's words.

And now this calm in the face of death, this "martyr's courage," touched her in the very depths of her heart.

Perhaps, during that long night, she believed she loved him.

From Paris came the noise of cannons being continually moved about. In the distance the drums were beating, calling to arms those who were members of the armed sections. Horses' hooves clattered on the damp, greasy roads.

In the distance a clock struck five.

Marie Antoinette sat up—a noise could be heard in the King's room. It was Cléry lighting the fire. There were footsteps on the stone staircase. At six o'clock the heavy doors of the apartment opened noisily. They had not come to fetch her. It was only an officer asking for Madame Elisabeth's missal for the condemned man's Mass. The door shut again and the bolts were pulled to.

A misty day was dawning. Detachments of cavalry entered the enclosure, and then "a great rumour" was heard. "General" Santerre, followed by municipal officers and gendarmes, mounted the staircase. The Queen stood near the door. Why did they not come to take her to her husband?

"It costs me a great deal to go without receiving their last embrace," the King was sighing at that moment.

He then turned to Cléry. "I entrust you with my farewells to them."

Suddenly Marie Antoinette heard trumpets sound under her windows. Surrounded by gendarmes, Louis XVI crossed the garden and turned round twice to look at the keep. In the distance she could now hear a vast muffled beating of drums, which gradually faded away and became indistinct.

It was eight o'clock.

At ten o'clock the door opened. Turgy was bringing dinner: chicken, larks and a rabbit. The Queen wanted to make the Dauphin eat, but the child refused. Marie Antoinette's clock, which represented "Fortune and her wheel," showed half-past ten. In the distance salvos of artillery were heard.

Louis XVI's head had just rolled on the scaffold.

The drums of the Temple guards were beating. Under the windows of the keep the sentries cried: "Long live the Republic!"

The Queen understood. "She choked with grief," related Turgy. "The young Prince burst into tears, Madame Royale uttered piercing cries." Her body shaken with sobs, Marie Antoinette sank on to her bed. Suddenly she rose, went to kneel before her son and saluted him with the title of King.

The "widow Capet" was able to procure "full mourning" dresses, "waxed" shoes, underskirts of *histaly* and even a black taffeta fan.

She refused to go down to the garden, as she did not want to pass Louis XVI's door. She would remain for hours seated in her green and white damask chair and knitting by the window, which was still obstructed by the shutter. She had become "extremely emaciated," according to a witness, and preserved a gloomy silence.

This prostration touched one of the officers on duty, the Toulousain Toulan. This fanatical revolutionary, who had been at the taking of the Tuileries on 10 August, had become profoundly royalist soon after first going on guard at the Temple. It is said that he was in love with Marie Antoinette and it is quite possible. By her charm, her voice and her smile the Queen was always able to arouse extraordinary devotion, and moreover she was now unhappy. Toulan did a few small services for the prisoner, paid the pedlar with the stentorian voice and on 1 January transmitted Louis XVI's good wishes to his family, but on the day after the King's death he made a serious decision—to help Marie Antoinette escape from the Temple.

Was it, as has been affirmed, a mad, unrealisable scheme? Certainly not. The Templars' keep was far from being a model prison. One had only to wear a uniform to be able to reach the tower, and one could even go in. One day the municipal officers found themselves face to face with three gendarmes, who were walking about "from a curiosity to see the building."

The prize for assurance undoubtedly goes to a certain Christophe Va, who was a brother, or so he claimed, of a municipal officer. On 26 September 1792 he entered through the main door of the Temple Palace, declaring that he had come to see his brother, and he was allowed to pass. On the 27th he entered the little tower where Louis XVI was still living, contemplated the royal family at his leisure and then—incredible detail—invited himself to dinner at the officers' table! Having developed a liking for this, he presented himself at the wicket-gate on the 28th just as the prisoners were going for their walk in the garden. He was sent off by the concierge, Mathey, but reappeared a few minutes later with the guard going on duty. He had managed to replace a certain Liemberger of the section of *Cloître Saint-Jacques de la Boucherie*, who had lent him his uniform and musket. With the air of an *habitué* he showed his comrades round the prison and decided to mount guard in the tower from four to six in the evening. "I shall not do it any where else!"

The Commune was not unaware of this state of things and ordered "a visit to the cellars which may exist around the Temple." Then, to reassure its members, it detailed two of Palloy's aides to dig a 12-foot ditch around the keep.

These unpublished details show that at the beginning of the royal family's captivity the Temple tower was not, in spite of what has been said, a fortress completely cut off from the land of the living. One could enter with comparative ease—and consequently leave also.

Marie Antoinette knew this. When Toulan declared he could arrange for her to escape with her children and Madame Elisabeth her heart beat with hope. But she did not want to continue with the scheme before consulting with General de Jarjayes, who, it may be remembered, had been the intermediary between Barnave and the Queen. On the King's orders he had remained in Paris. One may imagine his stupefaction—and his fear—when on 2 February 1793, Toulan, all blazing with the tricolour, came to see him. The Commissaire had a friendly face—bright eyes, a broad forehead and a rather flat nose—but the General remained on the defensive. Toulan was armed with a note from the Queen: "You may trust the man who will speak to you on my behalf and will hand you this note. His sentiments are known to me. During the last five months he has never wavered."

Without wanting to go any further, Jarjayes asked Toulan if he could get him into the Temple. The municipal officer was full of daring and, in spite of the presence of the Tisons, informed the Queen that Jarjayes would very soon be coming to see her. Marie Antoinette became uneasy and wrote: "Now that you have decided to come here, it had better be soon. But, good heavens, take good care not to be recognised and in particular beware of the woman who is shut up here with us."

With all the southerner's power of invention Toulan managed to persuade the "Illuminator," who came every day to look after the lamps in the Temple, to lend him his clothes for a "patriotic" friend who wanted the pleasure of contemplating the Queen "in her fetters." The lamplighter agreed and Jarjayes was able to have his interview with Marie Antoinette without difficulty.

The plan of escape took shape, but for it to succeed Turgy, who was on their side, and a second officer had to be informed of the plot. The municipal officer Lepitre was chosen. He had not a very suitable name for a conspirator, but he took fire at Toulan's first words. This semi-cripple—he limped heavily—was delighted to take part in such a plot and protested his loyalty. Marie Antoinette sent him to Jarjayes. "You will see the new man. His appearance is not prepossessing but he is absolutely necessary and we must have him." In fact Lepitre was betraying the Commune not from royalist conviction but from personal interest. He intended his help to be well paid for, but the main thing was that he agreed to help. The motives did not matter.

Mounting guard at the Temple had become a tiresome job for the municipal officers, and so Toulan and Lepitre frequently proposed replacing their colleagues. In this way the two conspirators managed to be on guard once or twice a week. "To be quite sure we were not separated," Lepitre related, "Toulan invented this scheme: three of us would arrive; generally the same number of tickets were made out, one of which said 'day' and the other two 'night.' Toulan wrote 'day' on all three and drew lots with our colleague, and when the latter opened his ticket with the word 'day' we both threw ours into the fire without looking at them and went to take up our posts. As we hardly ever came with the same person this ruse was always successful."

Toulan and Lepitre appeared very fat when they entered the Temple. Under their coats they concealed two jackets, or sometimes two quilted wraps. On occasion they entered the prison with hats on and left it bare-headed. They and Jarjayes had decided that Marie Antoinette and her sister-in-law should leave the tower dressed as municipal officers. "It was enough to show one's card from a distance not to be stopped by the sentries," Lepitre explained. The little King would be placed in a dirty linen basket covered with cloths such as Turgy regularly took out of the prison each week. As for Madame Royale, she would be dressed in rags like those worn by one of the two little boys who always came with the lamplighter. The royal family would thus escape in four groups after the Tisons had been put to sleep with a powerful narcotic.

Once they were out of the Temple Toulan was in favour of their fleeing in a large berlin, in which Jarjayes and Lepitre would also be seated, while he himself would precede them on horseback in order to arrange for the boat to take them across the Channel. Relays would be set up between Dieppe and Paris. But Marie Antoinette remembered

Varennes and preferred taking three cabriolets.

"Our plans were so laid," wrote Lepitre, "that no one could set out in our pursuit until five hours after we had left. We had calculated everything. First of all, no one went up into the tower until nine o'clock in the evening, to lay the table and serve supper. The Queen was to ask that it should not be served until half-past nine. Knocking several times and being surprised at not seeing the door open; inquiring from the sentry, who having relieved the guard at nine o'clock would not know what had happened; going down to the Council Room and telling the other members of the surprising occurrence; going back with them, knocking again, calling the preceding sentries and getting only vague answers from them; sending for a locksmith to open the doors, whose keys we would have left inside; succeeding only after much time and difficulty, as one of the doors was of oak and covered with large nails, and the other of iron, both with such strong locks that they would either have to be burst inwards or else part of the wall would have to be knocked down; searching the apartments and the towers; shaking Tison and his wife without being able to wake them; going down to the Council Room; drawing up a report and taking it to the Council of the Commune, who, even if they had not separated, would lose more time in futile discussion; sending for the police and the mayor, and to the committees of the Convention to find out what steps to take—all this delay would have helped our flight forward. Our passports were in order, since as a President of the Committee I had drawn them up myself, and gave us no anxiety for our journey, while we would have preserved our advantage in time."

Lepitre recounted all this with cheerful optimism—in 1817. In 1793 he was considerably more indecisive. Having received an advance of 200,000 francs from Jarjayes (20 million nowadays), he was so long in making out the passports that it was already 13 March. After Dunmouriez's treachery a state of semi-siege was proclaimed and the Passport Committee was ordered to deliver no more *laissez-passer*. Jarjayes became anxious and in these conditions thought the successive departure of the whole family a "chimera." The four disguises seemed too risky to him. Only the Queen's escape appeared "practicable."

But Marie Antoinette refused to leave her son. "We dreamed a beautiful dream, no more," she wrote to Jarjayes, "but we have gained much from it, as this occasion has provided further proofs of your total devotion to me. My confidence in you is unbounded. You will always find that I have character and courage but my son's interests are the only ones that guide me. However happy I should have been to escape from here I cannot consent to be separated from him. I could never enjoy anything without my children and this idea leaves me without any regret."

There was nothing more for Jarjayes to do in Paris. Marie Antoinette asked him to take to the "Regent"—the Comte de Provence—the seal with the arms of France and the King's wedding-ring, on which was engraved: "M.A.A.A. 19 aprilis 1770," the wedding-ring which had been blessed in the Augustines' Church in Vienna at the marriage by proxy and which Marie Antoinette had brought with her to France. Louis XVI had given it to Cléry on the morning of 21 January, telling him "to give it to his wife, and to tell her that it grieved him to part with it." Toulan had managed to get hold of these two relics, which were locked up in the Council Room, and to hand them to the Queen. Then he had cried out louder than anyone else when the "theft" was discovered.

With the wedding-ring and the seal, which were intended for the future Louis XVIII, Marie Antoinette sent an impression from a seal, intended for Fersen. "The impression I send is something quite different. I want you to give it to the person whom you know to have come to see me from Brussels last winter and to tell him at the same time that the motto has never been more true." It shows a pigeon in full flight, Axel's emblem which Marie Antoinette had adopted. The bird was surmounted by a motto: *Tutto a te me guida*—Everything leads me to you.

"The motto has never been more true."

A little later Baron de Batz, who had already tried to save the King between the Temple and the scaffold, conceived another plot. Together with 30 royalists he formed a troop of National Guards. With the complicity of the prison administrator, Citizen Michonis, he planned to enter the Temple, give the prisoners military hats and cloaks, put them in the midst of his patrol and so leave the prison. This improbable plot nearly succeeded in the night of 21-22 June. Michonis was already in the Queen's apartment. Batz and his men in the bodyguard, the other band of conspirators, were waiting in the street. Midnight struck.

Suddenly the entrance bell rang. It was the shoemaker Simon, one of the Commissaires of the Commune, who entered in indescribable excitement. He cried: "Call a roll of the men!"

He had just received an anonymous note: "Beware, Michonis will betray you tonight." Batz, who was disguised as a National Guard, managed to slip away into the night, and Michonis, during his interrogation, succeeded in giving the impression that a "joker" had played a trick on the "fool of a shoemaker."

After this fresh setback Marie Antoinette still retained some hope, and at the end of June Turgy was receiving notes in the following style: "Is it thought that we shall still be here in August? If yes, blow your nose without turning round. Are the men of Nantes at Orléans? Two fingers when they reach it."

The days went by, long and depressing. The two women played with "Republican cards," or sometimes the Queen worked at her embroidery. The Commune had not been ungenerous in giving her the silks she asked for.

The Toulan affair was to have its sequel. Furious because one day she had not been allowed to see her daughter, Tison's wife denounced the Toulousain, the terrified Lepitre and all the officers who had "truckled to the widow Capet." Furthermore she indicated that the prisoners were able to correspond with people outside the prison, thanks to Turgy. Having made her denunciation, the unhappy woman became a prey to remorse. It was even worse when, on the evening of 29 June, she learned that the Committee of Public Safety had decided to take the little King from his mother.

"I shall remove him from his family so that he may lose any idea of his rank," promised Chaumette.

Tison's wife was convinced that this terrible step was the result of her declaration. Realising how great the Queen's grief would be, she became frightened and threw herself at the prisoner's feet.

"Madame, I ask Your Majesty's pardon. I am very unhappy. I am the cause of your death and that of Madame Elisabeth."

She shrieked and fell into convulsions. The next day eight men had difficulty in carrying her out of the tower; she had gone mad.

In her ravings she had not revealed anything about the Committee's decision and when Marie Antoinette went to bed on 3 July she had not the slightest suspicion that anything was to happen.

At ten o'clock there was a knock on the door. A group of men with plumes in their hats entered the room. They were the officers of the relieving guard and included a stone-cutter, a painter, a perfumer, a lawyer and a "secretary-reader." The voice of the man who had to read the decree trembled.

Without at first understanding what it was about, Marie Antoinette looked at him. What! They were taking away her son?

"Never!"

The child had woken up. He understood, and uttered "loud cries," throwing himself into his mother's arms. The officers approached the bed and Marie Antoinette stepped between them. She would never consent to give up her child. Madame Royale, the only eye-witness, related: "The officers threatened to use violence and to summon the guard to take him away by force. An hour went by in discussions, in insults and threats from the officers, in pleading and tears from all of us. Finally my mother consented to give up her son. We got him up and when he was dressed my mother handed him over to the officers, bathing him in tears, as though she could see into the future and knew she would never see him again. The poor little boy embraced us all tenderly," concludes Madame Royale, "and went out weeping with the men." The cobbler, Simon, was waiting for him in Louis XVI's bedroom, where he was to live with his "ward."

For an hour Marie Antoinette had defended her son's bed. When, on the following day, she learned who was the "tutor" chosen by the Commune, she was overwhelmed. From her room she could hear her son's sobs, which went on for two days. The child's despair was so great that Simon did not dare take him down into the garden. Surprised at not seeing him, the soldiers of the guard murmured: "He is no longer in the Temple."

The Committee of General Security became alarmed and on 7 July sent four of its members, including Drouet, to the tower. They found the child somewhat calmer. "Capet's son was playing quietly at draughts with his mentor." His tears seemed dried and the members of the Convention decided to take him down into the garden. When they were in the chestnut walk the little boy stood firmly before the men and asked them "to show him the law which commanded that he should be separated from his Mamma."

For hours on end Marie Antoinette watched from a little window in one of the towers "to see her son pass at a distance when his guardian led him to the roof of the tower." She was now no more than a shadow. This time they had taken everything from her, even her heart.

Very soon little Louis would listen without flinching to his "tutor's" advice and would follow his directions with extraordinary diligence. Chaumette and Hébert had advised Simon to turn the "whelp" into a perfect *sans-culotte*. The cobbler was completely successful and in a few weeks the goal was reached. Pleased at behaving "like a man," at making the officers laugh, delighted to be able to indulge in everything he had hitherto been forbidden to do, the little King had become as badly brought-up as the lowest "patriot." With anguish Marie Antoinette heard him utter "dreadful oaths against God, his family and the aristocrats."

The poor woman would never know how far the cobbler's "education" had led her little King. "I was playing a game of bowls with him one day," related Daujon, a municipal officer. "It was after his father's death and he was separated from his mother and aunt by order of the Committee of Public Safety. The room where we were was below one of the family's rooms and we could hear a sound like jumping and chairs being moved over our heads, which made quite a lot of noise. The child thereupon said with an impatient gesture: 'Haven't those damned whores been guillotined yet?'"

Her *chou d'amour!*

17

❧

The Conciergerie

SHORTLY AFTER NOON, on 1 August, through the windows, which were open on account of the stifling heat, the prisoners could hear a noise with which they were now familiar: a murmur interrupted by trumpets and orders being shouted in the palace courtyard.

A few minutes later footsteps sounded on the staircase, sabres clanked against the steps and the walls, the wicket-gates creaked as the jailers opened them loudly, the bolts grated and slid back heavily and all these noises reverberated in the tower as in an organ-pipe.

It was the usual inspection. This time Hanriot, commander of the armed forces of Paris, which were making all the noise, hardly glanced at the prisoners' apartments. He was much more anxious about the "lack of artillery" of the Temple garrison. He therefore ordered fresh measures of surveillance: the commanders of the guard would receive munitions and from that evening the gunners were to stand by their guns.

This decision to order a state of siege at the Temple was a result of the taking of Valenciennes, where Fersen's regiment had formerly been stationed. The road to the capital was open. In Brussels Axel was forming a plan "to drive with a large force of cavalry towards Paris, which would be all the easier since there was no army ahead and all the barns were full of provisions."

Once these security measures were taken the Committee decided, in order to avoid a surprise attack, to make the Allies believe that the Queen was about to be brought to trial. They might then be able to exchange Marie Antoinette's life for an advantageous peace treaty.

Still on 1 August Barère, in reply to the taking of Valenciennes, cried

335

in the Tribune of the Convention: "Is it our forgetfulness of the Austrian woman's crimes, is it our indifference towards the Capet family that have thus deceived our enemies? Well then, it is time to root out every trace of the monarchy!"

Without further hesitation the Convention voted the decree referring "the widow Capet" to the Revolutionary Tribunal.

When the news reached Brussels both Allies and Emigrés were convinced that the Queen's last hour had struck. They simply did not understand that it was merely an offer to negotiate, and from fear of hastening the prisoner's end they even gave up Axel's scheme of invasion.

"There is nothing to do but wait," said Mercy philosophically.

He had never liked his "ward," and so his grief was slight. Fersen, on the other hand, was overcome.

"I am no longer living," he wrote to his sister Sophie, "for it is not living to exist as I do and to suffer such grief. . . . If I could only still act to deliver her I feel that I should suffer less, but to be able to do nothing but entreat is agony for me."

The government did not delay in carrying out its threat. A few hours after the Convention's vote, during the night of 1-2 August, four police administrators, headed by Michonis and surrounded by officers of the guard, read to Marie Antoinette the decree transferring her to the Conciergerie to be sent to the "Tribunal extraordinary." Without a word she rose. Henceforth the poor woman had no strength to react, and "without emotion," as Madame Royale was to relate, helped by her daughter and sister-in-law, she prepared a parcel of her clothes. Then, in the presence of the men who had invaded her room and who refused to leave her by herself, she dressed and on their request "showed her pockets." After searching her the officers left her only a handkerchief and a bottle of smelling-salts, "in case she felt ill." They took possession of the rest, which they packed up.

She was urged to hurry. She embraced her daughter, telling her to "take courage and care of her health," entrusted her children to her sister-in-law, and without looking at Madame Elisabeth and Marie-Thérèse left the room in which she had lived for more than nine months.

Twelve times she bent down and twelve times stepped through the wicket-gates. The procession halted on the ground floor in front of the Council Room. The officers drew up a report "handing over the person of the widow Capet." Marie Antoinette remained standing at the door, carrying her bundle and waiting for the officers and the representatives of the Commune to finish their paper work. Finally everything was completed and the Queen was urged on towards the garden. As she passed through the last wicket-gate, Marie Antoinette forgot to stoop and hit her forehead. Michonis was alarmed. "Did you hurt yourself?"

"Oh, no! Nothing now can hurt me any more."[1]

Half-past two sounded from a near-by clock. Like an automaton she walked towards the palace of the Temple, where she had not been for nearly a year, since the supper of 13 August. At the top of the flight of five steps she may perhaps have turned round to look for the last time at the tall outline of the sinister keep standing out in the bright August night—the keep where, on the second floor, her little King was sleeping and, on the third, her little blonde *Mousseline* was crying in her aunt's arms.

The little group quickly crossed the large salon and the billiard room and descended into the great courtyard by another flight of five steps. There were two or three cabs there, surrounded by about 20 gendarmes on horseback. Followed by Michonis, the Queen took her seat in the first carriage. The procession trotted rapidly through the palace gates, turned to the left and entered the Rue du Temple. Twenty minutes later the cab entered the Cour de Mai and stopped under the arcade, to the right of the main staircase of the Palais de Justice. The Queen went down four or five steps, crossed the little basement courtyard and stopped in front of the prison door. Ignoring the knocker, the soldiers of the guard beat on the door with the butts of their muskets. Larivière, one of the eight turnkeys, still full of sleep, for he had been dozing in the concierge's large winged armchair, opened the door and through the gloom perceived a "tall, beautiful woman," surrounded by men whose gilded uniforms glittered in the night. The prisoner bent down, stepped over the stone threshold between the two wickets and entered the hall, which became filled with lights. Amazed, Larivière then recognised the Queen "dressed in a long, black garment which made

[1] M. André Hurtret, keeper of the Château of Vincennes, has recently informed me that this door is now the entrance door to the keep at Vincennes.

her extraordinary whiteness even more dazzling." He had often seen her at Versailles, where he had been a pastry-cook's apprentice in the King's kitchens.

The prisoner was taken to the record office, a little room on the left, leading off the hall, where the search and the traditional committal were to take place, but Michonis then changed his mind and quickly pushed the Queen towards the third gate leading into "the black corridor." With a few steps the Queen reached her new prison, a cell dripping with damp and lit by a low window almost level with the ground of the women's courtyard. General de Custine had been occupying it a few hours before. During the afternoon the wife of the concierge, Mme Richard, assisted by her servant, pretty Rosalie Lamorlière, had sent to Bertrand, the upholsterer, who lived a short distance away, for a camp-bed, two mattresses, a bolster, a blanket, a cane armchair to put clothes on and a "red leather basin with its spray, all new, for the use of the said widow Capet." Mme Richard had added a table and two cane chairs.

Richard, the concierge, as the director of the prison was then called, put the large register on the table and made a note of the entry of his 280th prisoner "accused of having conspired against France," as the text shows. In August 1793, therefore, there were not thousands of prisoners in the Conciergerie as is usually stated. Then the packet of things taken from the Temple was opened. Richard counted them, noting them down in his stained book.

Still standing, dazed, treated with no more consideration than a thief or a prostitute arrested in the public street, Maria Theresa's daughter watched this degrading scene. It was hot in the small, low room filled with people, and Marie Antoinette frequently wiped the drops of sweat from her face. Richard collected the prisoner's possessions in his coarse hands and made a clumsy packet of them. Wax was heated and the Queen affixed her seal.

Now everything was over. The Queen of France was "committed." The prisoner was now alone with Mme Richard and Rosalie. Her shortsighted eyes took in the dreadful bareness of the cell, which daylight was beginning feebly to light up and whose walls were half covered by "hangings of paper nailed on to frames." In the Temple Berthélemy's furniture, the armchairs in lampas *à la reine*, the chairs of velvet *prune de monsieur* were certainly modest, but never in her life, except perhaps for the night of Varennes, had Marie Antoinette sat on such chairs as these or eaten from such a table. Thanks to Mme Richard the bed was made with fine linen and not coarse cloth. Rosalie had brought from her own room a little tapestry stool. The Queen looked about her. She was looking for somewhere to hang her watch, which had been left to her, the little watch she had brought from Austria twenty-three years before. There was a rusty nail in the wall, rather high up. She stood on Rosalie's stool, hung up her watch and began to undress. The servant came forward shyly and offered to help the prisoner.

"Thank you, my girl, but now that I have no one I serve myself."

The sun was now completely risen. The two women took the torch away.

Early in the morning Richard sent to her the turnkey Larivière's mother, who had formerly been a concierge at the Admiralty. The old woman—she was nearly 80—made a good impression on the Queen. For thirty years she had been attached to the household of the Duc de Penthièvre and "from her youth had lived with the nobility." On this morning she told her son to buy "half an ell of muslin" to patch the prisoner's dress, which was "in holes under the arms and worn at the hem" by contact with the stones of the Temple.

Four days later Michonis decided that the woman Larivière was too old—or at least that was the reason he gave—and replaced her by "Citizen Harel," aged 36, whose husband was a clerk at the town hall. The Queen does not seem to have cared much for her. On the day the woman Harel began her duties the Administrators confiscated the little gold watch from which Marie Antoinette had never been parted since her earliest youth. On being separated from this last remembrance of the Empress, the watch which had for thirty years told so many happy hours, Marie Antoinette wept bitterly.

Two other people were forced on her: Gilbert, a "National Gendarme," and his superior, Sergeant François Dufresne. Until 13 September they lived in the same little room, which was only $11\frac{1}{2}$ feet square. The room was divided into two by a screen, so that the Queen could undress without being seen by her two keepers. They were not bad men—they regularly brought flowers to their prisoner—but they were gendarmes just the same. When they were not sitting in their corner with their sabres and muskets they smoked and drank about four pints of wine a day and 2 livres 5 sols' worth of brandy, which is not bad for a sedentary job.

In the morning the Queen rose at seven, put on her little "turned-down" slippers and drank a cup of coffee or chocolate. She performed her toilet before a little mirror lent to her by Rosalie, which had cost the girl 25 sous. "Her hair was very simply dressed," the servant related. "She parted it in front, after putting on a little scented powder. Mme Harel bound the ends of her hair with a piece of white ribbon, about an ell in length, knotted it firmly and then handed the ends to Madame, who by tying them herself and pinning them on the top of her head arranged her hair in the form of a loose chignon." On top she wore her buckram mourning bonnet, which was so large that she was soon able to divide it "to have two informal bonnets." While Rosalie made the bed the Queen put on one of her two dresses, either the black or the white, and the hours passed by.

A few days after her arrival Marie Antoinette obtained pen and ink and wrote to her daughter. "I want to write to you, my dear child, to tell you that I am well. I am calm and would be at peace if I knew that my poor child was without anxiety. I embrace you and your aunt with all my heart. Send me some silk stockings, a dimity coat and an underskirt."

The letter was confiscated by the Commissioners, but thanks to Michonis Marie Antoinette had sent from the Temple some chemises "trimmed with lace known as *mignonettes*," two pairs of black silk stockings, a mantle, three lawn fichus and, most important, a pair of shoes *à la Saint-Huberty*, of which she was "urgently in need," as she told Michonis. Those she already had were falling to pieces with the damp. She was also able to obtain a bottle of dentifrice, a box of powder and a puff. So that she could keep these treasures from getting dusty Rosalie lent her a cardboard box, which she received "with as much satisfaction as if she had been lent the most beautiful piece of furniture in the world."

Dinner was served at two or half-past two. Mme Richard laid the table, while Rosalie, Mme Harel and the gendarmes looked on. The food was ample: "Soup, boiled beef, a dish of vegetables, chicken or duck—her favourite dish—and a dessert." In the evening her supper comprised cutlets, beef, a fricassée of turkey or pigeon. The cost to the Treasury for the "74 days" was 1,110 livres. The Queen drank only Ville-d'Avray water—*Viledavré*, as Madame Royale wrote—which was sent every day from the Temple. "On account of the recent law Madame Richard had hidden all her silver," Rosalie recounts. "The Queen was served on pewter plates, which I kept as clean and polished as possible. Her Majesty had a fairly good appetite. She cut her fowl into two, that is, to last her two days. She cleaned the bones with incredible ease and care. She rarely left any of the vegetables, which formed the second dish. When she had finished she said her grace in a low voice, then rose and began to walk. That was a signal for us to leave."

After supper her only distraction was to lean on the back of a chair and watch the two gendarmes playing backgammon. "Overcome with boredom," she had asked for the work she had begun—a pair of stockings for her son—to be brought from the Temple, but this had been refused. She might perhaps have tried to kill herself with the needles. So from time to time she pulled out the coarse threads of the cloth covering the walls "and with these threads, which she smoothed with her hand, she made very plain lace, using her knee as a cushion."

She was also given some travel books: "The Travels of Captain Cook," "The Travels of Young Anarcharsis," "A Voyage to Venice," "A History of Famous Shipwrecks." Marie Antoinette confided to Richard "that she read with pleasure the most terrifying adventures."

They had forgotten to take away her two solitaire rings. "Without her realising it," wrote Rosalie, "these two jewels were a kind of toy for her. As she sat and mused she would take them off, put them on again, and pass them from one hand to another several times in one minute."

Motionless and with her gaze vague, she seemed haunted by memories. At the beginning of her imprisonment she saw Larivière enter in his uniform of a National Guard. Marie Antoinette turned to the turnkey's mother.

"Please ask your son, our former servant, not to wear that uniform in my presence as it reminds me of the 6 October and all the misfortunes of my family."

To distract her, Mme Richard one day brought her youngest child, "who was fair and had very pretty eyes." The poor woman, relates Rosalie, "seeing this handsome little boy, started visibly. She took him in her arms, covered him with kisses and caresses and began to cry, while she spoke to us of M. le Dauphin, who was about the same age. She thought of him day and night and constantly spoke of him. . . . Hidden in her bodice she wore the portrait of the young King and a lock of his hair wrapped in a little yellow leather glove, which had belonged to the child, and I noticed that she often concealed herself near her wretched camp-bed to kiss these objects as she wept. One could speak to her of her misfortunes and of her situation without her showing any emotion or depression, but her tears flowed unceasingly at the thought of her deserted children."

Sometimes, too, she spoke of the King.

"He is happy now," she sighed.

At the Conciergerie in 1793 the political prisoners were still mixed with the thieves and murderers awaiting their appearance before the criminal court, and the old lags quickly "initiated" the newcomers. At dawn the vast cells—the *Gaillote*, the *Taillerie*, the *Noviciat* and the *Bonbec*—were opened, and until the evening the prisoners could walk at will in a large covered courtyard. In the central corridor of the prison and in the famous "Rue de Paris" there was a continual coming and going of turnkeys, gendarmes, prisoners going to the registry or coming back, and visitors going to the parlour. In the women's court-yard, on to which the windows of the Queen's cell looked, a railing marked off a narrow strip of ground where the prisoners kept in what was known as the *Quartier des Douze* could walk. Through its bars men and women shared their meals or started romances. The prisoners seemed to have been able to communicate easily with the outside world, for at that time they were even able to have their dinner brought in by the caterer, Citizen Maire, who also furnished the meals for the Queen's gendarmes and "waiting-woman." It was child's play to get anything in or out of the Conciergerie if one is to believe letters written by a prisoner from the prison itself. "If I make my long journey shortly, and as one knows in advance the day one is to appear [before the Tribunal], I shall make up a parcel and have it delivered in town."

No objection can therefore be made to the story of the concierge Richard's protégée, Mlle Fouché, a young woman from Orléans, who in company with the Abbé Charles Magnin, Director of the Little Seminary of Autun, which had moved to Paris, often entered the Conciergerie at that time.

One day in August, probably about the 10th, Mlle Fouché, who had been visiting some prisoners, asked Richard "if it would not be permitted for her to see the Queen." After some persuasion the concierge agreed. At half-an-hour after midnight he showed the visitor into the Queen's cell. Marie Antoinette had not yet gone to bed. She silently gazed at the unknown woman, who bowed to her and placed some linen and "a little food" on the table.

Mlle Fouché's account was written at the end of the Restoration and this last detail seems a little exaggerated. The Queen's diet was more than sufficient, but no doubt in the reign of Charles X it was good form to have prevented the Queen from suffering hunger. The rest of Mlle Fouché's account appears more truthful. Marie Antoinette received the young woman "with icy coldness," refused even to speak to her and confined herself to giving her "an imposing look." The interview was therefore short, and before taking her leave Mlle Fouché asked if "Her Majesty [this was written in 1824] would permit her to return."

"As you will," the Queen replied indifferently.

It would seem that the prisoner must have made some inquiries with Richard, for at a second interview she greeted her visitor with "trust." Mlle Fouché became bolder and proposed "bringing a priest" to the Queen.

"But do you know one who is a non-juror?"

The existence of the Abbé Magnin was revealed and at the third visit Richard allowed the priest to remain with the Queen for an hour-and-a-half.

In order to give some credence to what is about to follow, it must be remembered that not far from the Queen's cell the Abbé Emery was hearing confessions, saying Mass and giving communion. A letter from Barthélemy de la Roche confirms that hosts "were procured from the town." Although the Abbé Emery, Superior of the Saint-Sulpice Seminary, was in prison, other refractory priests were not, and were able to enter the prison regularly to bring "the Almoner of the Conciergerie" the pyx full of hosts. The evidence is incontestable.

When those who had been condemned left the Tribunal, surrounded by gendarmes, and crossed the courtyard to the office, where the executioners were waiting for them, the Abbé did not dare to meet them and give them absolution, for there were always a few members of the Tribunal, judges or jurors, at the windows of the bar on the first floor to enjoy the spectacle. But the jailers could not resist the Abbé and allowed him to spend the night with those who were to die, in the "waiting room," a wretched hovel which can still be seen today.

If the Abbé had not been able to obtain this favour he would let the condemned persons know at what point on the route they would meet one of his former pupils to whom he had sent a message.

The Abbé Magnin helped the Abbé Emery and "continued to bring the prisoners the consecrated hosts in a box hung round his neck." In the light of these incredible, but historically correct, facts, there is no reason not to believe that the Abbé Magnin—as he himself wrote in 1824 and solemnly swore to in the pulpit and before the altar—"had the happiness of twice hearing the confession of the Queen of France and of taking holy communion to her at the time when Richard was still the concierge of the prison of the Conciergerie."

The Abbé Magnin and Mlle Fouché were not alone in being thus able to enter the prison. It is said that Richard also introduced into the Queen's cell a certain Mme Guyot, head nurse of the Archevêché hospital, the wife of the hairdresser Laboullée, who lived at 83 Rue de Richelieu, and even—Fersen tells us in his private Journal—an Englishman, who for 25 louis was able to enter the prisoner's cell "to bring a jug of water."

Why should Richard have minded, when the example was set by the police administrators, who came to see the prisoner "on different occasions with one, two and sometimes three women," according to Gilbert, not to mention the painter Prieur, who was granted several sittings?

Among the administrators the one most frequently seen was undoubtedly Michonis. During the first three weeks of the Queen's imprisonment the "citizen administrator of police in charge of prisons" transformed himself into a guide. Whenever he was asked he agreed to show the Queen. One would hardly believe this without having seen Michonis's interrogations and depositions. The administrator admitted readily having entered to see "the widow Capet."

"I went with several people who were moved by curiosity and whom I could not have refused to take with me."

When the Queen was asked about the faces of these visitors she was able to reply with a shrug: "So many of them come!"

18

❦

The Carnation

ON WEDNESDAY, 28 August, Michonis entered the cell as usual. He was accompanied by a visitor, a man about 36, rather short, with bright eyes and a round face marked with smallpox and framed by curled hair. He was dressed in a striped, somewhat dark suit, the "colour of Paris mud," and was wearing two carnations in his button-hole. The moment the Queen set eyes on him she started and "her face was aflame." She recognised Rougeville, the Chevalier de Saint-Louis, who when the Tuileries were invaded on 20 June of the previous year had prevented her from joining the King and had taken her to the Council Room.

Tears sprang to her eyes. Michonis's companion looked at her earnestly. He had difficulty in recognising the Queen in this old woman who looked like "a deformed spectre." Rougeville stepped forward, took the carnations from his buttonhole and threw them down by the stove. Marie Antoinette looked at him blankly, without understanding. The Chevalier then "gave her a meaning look," but the Queen still did not comprehend. The Chevalier drew closer and in a low voice told her to pick up the note. But Michonis was already moving towards the door.

The two men left the cell. A few seconds later, through the barred window, the prisoner saw Michonis taking his companion to visit the women's courtyard. With astonishing presence of mind she asked Gilbert to take a complaint to Michonis about her food. The gendarme meekly went to the window, called the Administrator and reported the complaint. The moment he turned round the Queen went towards her screen. She had had time to pick up the two flowers and to see that each contained a note. Her heart beat rapidly.

Born on 17 September 1761, Rougeville was really called Alexandre Gousse, or Gonsse, which he did not like at all. He had therefore chosen to adopt the name of a farm belonging to his father and bestowed on himself the more noble title of Chevalier de Rougeville.

Whatever Alexandre Gousse de Rougeville may have written and affirmed, he was never a gendarme of the King's Guard, nor an aide-de-camp to General Lee, nor to Washington, nor a lieutenant-colonel in America, nor a cavalry colonel in France, nor an equerry to Monsieur, the King's brother. Lenotre, carried away by his zeal, even declared that "Marquis" de Rougeville had never been a Chevalier de Saint-Louis and consequently had never worn a sword. Rougeville, who does not appear to have claimed to be a Marquis, was certainly a Chevalier de Saint-Louis, as witness the register of the Archives de la Guerre under the date of 6 October 1791.

Everything Rougeville wrote was not boasting, as some historians have asserted. "The great agitation on the face and in the limbs of the widow of Louis Capet" when she saw Rougeville in the Conciergerie, the tears which came to her eyes, prove that Marie Antoinette knew what the man was worth and what he was capable of. She remembered what he had already done for her. Not for one moment, when she saw him enter the prison with the Administrator, did she think that Rougeville had changed his opinions, as had so many others. If he was there it was to save her.

This rehabilitation is necessary if one is to try to understand this plot of the carnation, which has remained so obscure. If one tries to decipher it by giving some credence to the Chevalier's statements and by checking them with unpublished documents from the Archives,[1] many points, particularly the ending, become clear.

On the evening of 10 August 1792, Rougeville did not reappear at the Hôtel des Tuileries, 75 Rue Saint-Honoré, where he was living. This was not because he was afraid of being arrested as a frequenter of the château. A more serious danger threatened him: a woman with whom he was living, a certain Dame Lacouture, 33-year-old widow of a councillor of the Presidial of Coutances, who found consolation for

[1] See the chapter "Sources," pp. 417-418.

her loss in the arms of our conspirator. Rougeville, deciding that the massacre of the defenders of the monarchy was an excellent pretext, disappeared neatly from the life of Dame Lacouture, who not seeing her consoler reappear thought herself a widow for the second time. But one day, at the beginning of March 1793, the deserted woman learned that far from being dead her Chevalier was consoling in another hotel, in the Rue des Quatre-Fils, another widow called Sophie Dutilleul, who had the undoubted advantage over Dame Lacouture of being ten years younger and a Parisienne. In Rougeville's absence the two widows had a violent scene. The Rue des Quatre-Fils rang with their shrieks. The Norman soon realised that she could not fight her pretty young rival. Her lover being definitely lost to her she decided it would be as well if he were also lost to the seductive Sophie and she denounced the Chevalier de Rougeville to the Municipality as being a friend of the King and a combatant of 10 August.

On 3 June the police were able to lay their hands on the consoler of widows. He was hiding in a cupboard of a country house which Mme Dutilleul owned at Vaugirard.

To be arrested in the middle of the Jacobin uprising, under the accusation of having been a "knight of the poniard," was the equivalent of a ticket for the other world. And yet on 10 June Rougeville cheerfully left the Madelonettes prison. This was thanks to the administrators "whom I had suborned with money," he explained later, adding: "I had particularly noticed the director Michonis."

In reality Rougeville had been recommended to Michonis by a certain citizen Fontaine, who was possibly a friend of Batz. What is more certain is that during Rougeville's absence he had become the protector of the widow Dutilleul after a meeting "on the boulevard." Michonis therefore had the Chevalier released and the two men began to conspire feverishly. Later, in order to save his head, the administrator declared that he had not met Rougeville until 15 August 1793, but we know from the documents preserved in the Archives that the two conspirators met constantly during the months of June, July and August.

In asserting the contrary during his interrogation Michonis was lying, and if he was lying it was because he had something to hide. The administrator was quite simply Rougeville's accomplice. To deny this, as have so many historians, made the conspiracy of the carnation completely meaningless. Besides, Michonis had a previous history. In June 1793 he had helped Baron de Batz in his schemes for Marie Antoinette's escape from the Temple. If one refuses to admit Michonis's complicity how can one explain that a quarter-of-an-hour after throwing the carnations down in the Queen's cell Rougeville was able to come back alone to see the prisoner, while Michonis *was still in the courtyard,* and in spite of the presence of the gendarme? The Queen stated this definitely at her trial.

"He came back twice in the space of a quarter-of-an-hour."

During this quarter-of-an-hour the prisoner had had time to read the note behind her screen. "I shall never forget you, I shall always seek means to demonstrate my zeal. If you have need of three or four hundred louis for those about you I shall bring them next Friday."

As for the other note, which was not mentioned at any inquiry, it contained, according to Rougeville, "a safe and well thought-out plan for her escape, if she wished to lend herself to it."

One can guess at Marie Antoinette's emotion as she looked at her visitor. A rapid exchange took place between them.

"I tremble at your rashness."

"Do not worry about me. I have money, men, administrators, and sure means to get you out of here."

"I am not moved by the danger to my life. My children are the cause of all my anxiety."

"Is your courage low?"

"If I am weak and downcast, my heart is not."

"Take courage, we shall save you. I shall come back on Friday, the day after tomorrow, and shall bring you the money you need for your keepers."

Michonis came to fetch Rougeville. They had hardly left the room when the Queen, with beating heart, drew near to the gendarme Gilbert. They were alone. The woman Harel had gone to fetch water and Sergeant Dufresne had also gone out. Marie Antoinette decided to wait no longer to try to win over her keeper. He often brought her flowers and he had closed his eyes to the Abbé Magnin's visits.

"Monsieur Gilbert, you see how I tremble. The gentleman you have just seen is a Chevalier de Saint-Louis, employed in the army, to whom I owe much for not having abandoned me in trouble."

Through these words, which were related by Gilbert at his interroga-

tion, one can feel the emotion which must have seized the unhappy
woman. If she could move her keeper she was saved. Her voice became
softer and her tone more confiding.

"You would never imagine how he managed to hand me this note.
He gestured to me with his eyes and as I did not understand what he
was trying to say, he came close to me and said in a low voice: 'Pick up
the carnation on the ground which holds my most ardent wishes. I shall
come back on Friday.' You know the rest. I stooped and picked up the
carnation, in which I found the note."

The end of the gendarme's account is false. During this same conversation the Queen is supposed to have shown Gilbert a reply intended
for Rougeville and consisted of a dozen words traced, or rather pricked
with a pin, on a little piece of paper. When could she have done this?
Let us hear from Gilbert.

"Michonis went out with the individual and it was then that she
showed me a note she had pricked, in which the holes formed two or
three lines of writing, saying to me: 'You see I do not need a pen to
write with.' She added that it was her answer, to be given on Friday to
the man who had handed her the note inside the carnation."

Still according to the gendarme, the woman Harel came back to the
cell at precisely that moment. Gilbert alleged that he then snatched the
note from the Queen's hand. "I went out *at once*," Gilbert continued,
"to find the wife of the concierge and to tell her that I had something
to give her. Taking her aside, I handed her the pricked note, relating
what had just taken place."

It was not on Wednesday 28 August, *between Rougeville's two visits*,
that the note was traced. In his report written in the morning of 3 September, the gendarme declared: "As her waiting-woman was playing
a game of cards with me the woman Capet took advantage of this to
write with a pin on paper."

The woman Harel was asked: "While Michonis and this individual
were in the room were you not engaged in playing cards?"

"It was not on that day," she replied, "for on the day Michonis and
the individual you are speaking of came *I was not playing, I was at
work.*"

That is unambiguous!

The woman Richard alleged during her interrogation that "on the
same day" as the gendarme brought her the note she handed it "in the

same moment" to Michonis. The latter declared that the note was given to him *one or two days after the day he had come, Wednesday, the 28th, with the Chevalier*. The note was therefore given to him on the Thursday or, better still, the Friday, the day when Rougeville came back to the Conciergerie with Michonis and brought the money for the Queen. This fact, which seems not to have been noticed up to now, proves that at first Gilbert had readily agreed to enter the conspiracy.

For Gilbert lied in saying that he had taken the concierge's wife aside to give her "the pricked note"; it was the woman Richard who took it from him. Sergeant Dufresne revealed this. "In sport the wife of the concierge put her hands in his pockets and took his papers, among which was the note."

One can guess the Queen's terror. To whom would Mme Richard hand the note? All through the day she "persecuted" Gilbert—the word is his—asking him to go and get back the note which might cause everything to miscarry.

But what was in those three lines? The note—a narrow piece of grey, rather silky paper—is still pinned to the Queen's interrogation in the National Archives. It is completely illegible. An expert, M. Pilinski, claimed to have deciphered these words:

> I am closely watched.
> I speak to no one.
> I trust you. I shall come.

When the Queen was asked "what her writing contained," she declared: "With a pin I tried to write that I was closely watched, that the danger was too great to reappear there [for Rougeville to return] and that I could neither speak nor write."

Not a word, of course, about the last line deciphered by the writing expert. The Queen kept to the same line of defence during the interrogation she underwent on the eve of her trial.

"I tried, with a pin, not to reply to him but to tell him not to come back, in case he should once more present himself."

She could hardly reply otherwise. And it is curious that neither Fouquier-Tinville nor President Hermann replied: "Why incur such danger and run the risk of all being discovered in order to write to the man who wanted to free you what you had just said to him? You are hiding the most important fact!"

And, indeed, "I trust you. I shall come" is undoubtedly the one accurate line of the note. Influenced by the Queen's answers, M. Pilinski may have made a mistake in deciphering the beginning of the riddle. The first line told Rougeville nothing he did not know, and the second was manifestly untrue.

The note, traced by the Queen *after* her conversation with Gilbert, must have informed the conspirators that she had been able to win over the two gendarmes, thanks to the money brought by Rougeville that same day. In the various interrogations this third visit is not mentioned, but it seems probable that the Chevalier was not lying when he asserted that on the 30th, *in another dress,* he was able to return to the prison, bringing the Queen 400 louis d'or and 10,000 livres in promissory notes. "It was during this interview," Rougeville recounted, "that it was decided that, in spite of the Queen's state of extreme weakness, the escape would take place on the night of 2-3 September."

A letter preserved in the Archives shows that the Chevalier was right to speak of the prisoner's "extreme weakness." On the following evening, at ten o'clock, Lieutenant de Busne wrote to Fouquier-Tinville, informing him that the widow Capet had been taken ill twice during the evening. These swoons were certainly a result of the Queen's anguish at the confiscation of the famous note. Mme Richard had indeed handed the note to Michonis and the latter had pretended to treat the matter as unimportant and had advised the concierge's wife not to speak of the incident, but the Queen was unaware of these reassuring details and one may imagine the unhappy woman's anxiety as she waited for the time when Rougeville was to enter her cell. Would the conspirators go forward at the last minute? The Queen tried to calm herself with the signs before her: Gilbert had been in the secret since Wednesday, 28 August, and had said nothing to his superiors. The same was true of Sergeant Dufresne. The Queen had given him Rougeville's 50 louis d'or and there seemed to be nothing to worry about in that direction. There was one person unaccounted for: the woman Harel, who did not appear to be in the plot. If she had noticed anything would she keep silent? It was true that she had been brought into the Conciergerie by Michonis himself.

The night of 2-3 September closed over the prison. Through her two windows, which were open on account of the heat, the Queen could hear the yard bell ringing. It was the signal for the prisoners to return to their cells. But the prison did not go to sleep. Those who were due to "go up" to the Tribunal the next day had asked their cell companions to supper. There was much drinking and singing. The steps of the turnkeys on their rounds could be heard in the corridor.

Suddenly, just before eleven o'clock, the door opened. Michonis and Rougeville were there. On behalf of the Municipality the administrator had come to transfer Marie Antoinette to the Temple. At least, this was what he had said to the turnkeys and to Richard, who if he did not believe it pretended to do so. In reality the carriage waiting for the prisoner in the Cour de Mai was to take her to the Château de Livry, where Mme de Jarjayes lived, and thence to Germany.

Flanked by her two gendarmes the Queen walked quickly down the "black corridor."

At this point we must hear from Rougeville, for we have no other documents. "We had already passed through all the wicket-gates and only the street door remained to go through when one of the two guards to whom I had given 50 louis d'or came forward threateningly to prevent the Queen's leaving."

Which gendarme was it who took fright at the last moment and changed his mind? According to the turnkey Larivière and Rosalie Lamorlière it was the woman Harel who caused the escape to miscarry. But nothing is known for certain. However, on the next morning, in a report to Colonel Du Mesnil, Gilbert denounced Rougeville's visit of the week before, spoke of the carnation and of the "pricked note," but, obviously, concealed facts which would have established his and Dufresne's complicity.

While the colonel hurried to inform the Committee of General Safety, Michonis dined at Fontaine's house with Rougeville and Sophie Dutilleul. This was apparently in order to take the necessary decisions after the previous night's failure. Rougeville decided to disappear. On leaving Vaugirard he took with him "two shirts and several pairs of stockings." These precautions of the Chevalier confirm the truth of the night's events. If, like Lenotre and many other historians, one refuses to admit the complicity of Gilbert and Michonis and the conspirators' attempt to carry out their plan, then the attitude of all the actors in the drama becomes quite incomprehensible.

When dinner was over, and while Rougeville was escaping,

Michonis decided to go to the Conciergerie to see how the land lay. He still had the famous note in his pocket, but apparently, in order to make the matter of no importance, he had riddled the paper with pin-holes in order to make it illegible. On arriving at the prison, around half-past four in the afternoon, he learned that he was wanted by two deputies of the Convention, Amar from l'Isère and Sevestre from Ille-et-Vilaine, accompanied by citizen Aigron, aide-de-camp to the armed forces. They had been charged by the Convention's Committee of General Safety and Vigilance to inquire into Gilbert's denunciation. They had arrived at the office half-an-hour earlier and having "asked the officer on duty to give them six gendarmes," they had gone to the Queen's cell.

Both actors and supernumeraries were interrogated but they all concealed some part of the affair, either to exculpate themselves or to avoid compromising their accomplices. When Michonis arrived at the office the investigators were questioning the Queen in a "private room in the said house."

In spite of her anguish the Queen denied everything systematically. She could not remember anything.

"Did you not, a few days ago, see a former Chevalier de Saint-Louis?"

"It is possible that I may have seen a face I knew, as so many of them come."

"And the carnation?"

"No one gave me a carnation and no note fell to the ground that I could see. Something may have fallen, but I saw nothing."

The deputies pressed her hard.

"A few days ago a Chevalier de Saint-Louis entered your lodging and you started when you saw him. We ask you to say whether you knew him."

"It is quite possible that I saw faces I knew, as I said before and that, in the tense state of my nerves, I started, without knowing on what day, or on whose account, or why."

"We would mention to you, however, that it has been stated that you knew the former Chevalier de Saint-Louis and that you trembled lest he should be recognised. Those are the expressions you are reported to have used."

"One would think that if I trembled lest he should be recognised I would not have mentioned it, for I would have wanted to conceal it."

She skilfully denied having "written with a pin." One of the Commissaires then tried kindness.

"In your position it would be natural to take advantage of any means offered to you for your escape and for getting messages to those you thought you could trust. It would not be surprising, therefore, if this Chevalier de Saint-Louis were a person who might be an associate of yours and of whom you would consequently not wish to speak."

"It would be very sad if the people I were interested in made so little impression on me. If I were alone I should not hesitate to try every means to be reunited with my family, but as there are three people in my room, although I never knew them before I came here, I should never involve them in anything."

The investigators were hardly more successful with the woman Harel and with Michonis. If the first was to be believed, she was practically blind and deaf. As for the second, he presented the picture of a police administrator whose carelessness had outrun his understanding. He treated everything lightly and simply admitted to having been a "prisoner's showman." As regards the "Rougeville affair," he confessed to having shown him into the widow Capet's cell, but pretended that he had not known the Chevalier's name.

When it was Gilbert's turn there was a rush of details, but as we have already seen they were often in complete contradiction to the report the gendarme had sent that morning to his colonel. The woman Richard was then summoned. She too claimed to know nothing; she had handed the note to Michonis and that was all. Michonis was therefore recalled and he took from his pocket the note, which was completely unreadable. The Commissaires passed it from hand to hand, but with no result, and pinned it to the report, which made two holes more.

This time Michonis was interrogated at length. When one reads his clumsy and embarrassed answer it is impossible not to recognise in him an accomplice of Rougeville. He contradicted himself, and then confessed that he had advised the concierge's wife to keep quiet. He claimed not to know that the note handed to him by Mme Richard was intended for Rougeville, and then declared: "I considered the matter unlikely to have any consequences and so I did not give him the note."

The investigators were enabled to reply: "To the question first put to you, whether the note was intended for him, you replied in the negative and yet you have just said that among the reproaches you made him you had not forgotten to mention that the note might have been for him."

Michonis's position was quite indefensible and one of the Commissaires exclaimed: "You must have been either very blind or indifferent to your duties not to have had that man arrested the moment Mme Richard handed you that note!"

The deputies were not examining magistrates and were unaware of the first rule of the profession: not to leave witnesses and accused in the same room. Everyone appeared to be in Marie Antoinette's cell. Weeping, the Queen asked the two gendarmes "not to repeat what she had confided to them" and several times asked Gilbert if the Chevalier de Saint-Louis had been arrested. We learn this from Gilbert and Dufresne, who appear to have been indulging in an orgy of accusations. Admittedly, they had been holding their tongues for six days.

The Queen was now aware of the depositions of the two gendarmes. She also knew that Mme Richard and Michonis had admitted part of the truth. So when the investigators called her a second time she did not continue to deny. She recalled the part played by Rougeville on 20 June, admitted the visit on the preceding Wednesday, the handing over of the note in the carnation and confessed to having replied with the help of a pin. The most difficult part was to conceal Michonis's hand in the affair.

"Has the administrator Michonis ever made any proposals to you?"
"Never."

"Why do you show so much interest in seeing him again?"
"Because his honesty and humanity touched me."

"And yet this interest would seem to have another cause and to spring from the fact that he introduced into your room a man who offered to help you?"

"It would appear that Michonis did not know him himself."

Michonis had probably had time to inform her of his line of defence, otherwise how would she have thought of giving such an answer?

The interrogations continued far into the night. When she signed the report Maria Theresa's daughter had a movement of pride. She was ashamed of having previously lied to these boors and wished to explain that "if she did not tell the truth it was because she did not want to compromise that individual and preferred to harm herself."

"When I saw that all was discovered I did not hesitate to tell what I knew."

Before going to bed the investigators had Michonis arrested and imprisoned, at half-past seven, in the Conciergerie itself. Four days later they arrested Sophie Dutilleul, who declared she had "committed only one crime—that of having loved Rougeville."

On 4 September the Queen's cell was thoroughly searched. The investigators went so far as to "overturn the bed and the chairs." Bars and walls were carefully examined. The policemen themselves searched the prisoner, taking her two rings, confiscating her linen and leaving only her bonnets and fichus. Henceforth her chemises would be given to her one by one. There was a particular ban on giving her flowers. Even the food was reduced to a minimum.

From a distance, although without news, Fersen guessed the misery she was undergoing. On 4 September he wrote to his sister: "I often grudge myself the very air I breathe, when I think that she is shut up in a horrible prison. This thought pierces my heart and poisons my life and I am constantly torn between grief and rage."

Rosalie watched the unhappy woman, "anxious and abandoned," pacing for hours up and down her cell. She was quite broken. She was not even left in peace at night. The Commissaires forced her to rise so that they could search her bed. The accounts of Robert, the apothecary, reveal that on the 4th there was ordered for the widow Capet a soothing potion "composed of lime-flower water, orange-flower water, maidenhair syrup and Hofman's liquor." On the next day, and until the 16th, she was given a cooling and soothing soup "made in a bain-marie with lean veal, chicken and various plants."

The events of 11 September were not calculated to calm the sick woman. The investigators had doubtless discovered that the Richards were partly involved, for the concierge and his wife were arrested. On the same day six police officers arrived at the Conciergerie "to choose a place of detention for the widow Capet, other than the one where she is at present detained, which they consider to be too near the office," that is, too near the front door. After seeing "all the rooms," they chose "the one in which citizen Guillaume Lacour's pharmacy is situated." Between this room and the Cour de Mai there were six wicket-gates or grilles, three obstacles more than those passed by the Queen in the night of 2-3 September. But this room was not arranged as a cell. The police therefore ordered the window looking on to the women's courtyard "to be closed up to the fifth cross-bar." The rest of the window was to be grated with close-mesh wire. Another window looked on to the infirmary. This was to be entirely closed "by means of a sheet of iron." A third window looked on to the corridor; this was "to be entirely stopped with masonry." The administrators noticed that light came under the door, and they therefore ordered a piece of wood "three inches thick" to be placed there. A second door was installed.

The police worked quickly and summoned Lemoine, a mason from the Rue Vendôme, Leroy, a carpenter from the Rue des Capucines-Chaussée d'Antin, and the locksmith Gonvin from the Rue Antione. Citizen Gonvin's account includes iron bars, and the netting which had been ordered became a proper grille. The new door was two inches thick, "studded with big nails," and closed with "a strong lock." Two bolts and two "safety locks" were also placed on the first door. The cost to the State was 983 livres.

And so there was fulfilled the wish of the municipal officers of Chapelle-Gontier, who had demanded that "the Fury who had sworn their ruin should be imprisoned in the darkest dungeon."

On the 13th or 14th the cell was finished and the prisoner and her wretched belongings were transferred there. The woman Harel had disappeared; nothing more is heard of her. The two gendarmes had orders to remain, one of them in the corridor and the other in the women's courtyard. The latter was stationed just in front of the half-boarded window, where he could see everything that went on in the cell. The prisoner could not even go behind her screen without the gendarme hurrying forward.

The new concierge, citizen Bault, who had come from the prison of La Force with his wife, was answerable with his life for the Queen's person. Only he had keys to the cell and could enter only with an officer or under-officer of the gendarmerie. "When Bault came to the Queen for the first time," related Rosalie, who had been able to keep her post, "I was with him and I brought Madame her usual soup for breakfast. She looked at Bault, who in accordance with the fashion of those days was wearing an all-in-one jacket and trousers called a carmagnole. The collar of his shirt was open and turned down, but his head was bare. Holding his keys, he stood by the wall near the door. The Queen took off her nightcap, sat down and said to me pleasantly: 'Rosalie, you will do my hair today.'

"Hearing this, the concierge hurried forward, took the comb and said loudly, as he pushed me aside: 'Go away, I must do that.'

"Astonished, the Princess looked at Bault with an indescribable air of majesty.

" 'I thank you,' she replied, and rising immediately she rolled up her hair herself and put on her bonnet."

The Queen then took the white ribbon which Madame Richard had hitherto used for her hair.

"Rosalie, take this ribbon and keep it always in memory of me."

She wore a look "of sadness and dejection which went to my heart, and tears sprang to my eyes," Rosalie recounted.

Such was the end of the affair of the carnation.

Rougeville, whose head had a price on it, was hiding in the plaster quarry in Montmartre. He was writing a pamphlet: "The crimes of the Parisians towards their Queen, by the author of the carnations presented to the Queen in her prison." When he had finished he made a great many copies and before taking the road for Belgium went himself to place them in the bureau of the Convention and the Revolutionary Tribunal a few moments before the sessions opened.

When Alexandre Dumas wrote his famous *Chevalier de Maison-Rouge* he fell well short of the truth!

19

❧

The Anteroom to the Guillotine

IT IS DIFFICULT to pass by the Conciergerie without looking up at the first floor of Caesar's tower. There, at the beginning of year II, was the office of Antoine-Quentin Fouquier de Tinville, son of the "seigneur of Hérouël and other places," former prosecutor at the Châtelet and since March 1793 citizen Fouquier-Tinville, Public Prosecutor of the Revolutionary Tribunal.

From his window he could see the cartloads of condemned people crossing the Pont-au-Change. In this vaulted room, whose ogives and ribs date from Philippe le Bel and where formerly the gentlemen of Parliament came to take their refreshments, he carefully perfected his grinding machine during the months of July and August 1793. The Tribunal, which had been at work since 6 April, had already pronounced 63 death sentences in its first session, but at that time the judge still respected the formalities, and there were twice as many acquittals as condemnations. Moreover, for the past few weeks the magistrates and juries had been weary. They condemned "without zeal." On 17 July President Montané had tried to hold out "a safety plank" to Charlotte Corday, in the words of the scandalised Fouquier-Tinville. On 24 July the number of judges was raised to seven, and on the 30th to ten and on the same day Montané was sent to the prison of Sainte-Pélagie. On the next day Fouquier succeeded in having his tribunal divided into two sections, so as to provide more work.

The Convention's decree committing the widow Capet to his Tribunal had whetted his appetite. But he was greatly disappointed. Days passed and the Government seemed not to want to send him the prisoner. On 25 August he could bear it no longer and wrote to the Committee: "The Tribunal is attacked in the newspapers and in the public places because it has not yet dealt with the affair of the former Queen." On 2 September, therefore, just as Rougeville was leading the Queen to escape, the members of the Committee of Public Safety met in secret session at the house of Pache, the Mayor of Paris. There were present Cambon, Hérault, Barère, Jean Bon Saint-André, Hébert and a secretary. The secretary was a spy in the pay of England and on the next day he sent to the English Resident at Genoa a detailed report which was then sent to Lord Grenville in London.

Current business having been dealt with, Cambon opened the discussion of "the Queen's death" and informed his colleagues that one of the Committee's agents was at that moment trying to negotiate with Brussels, Vienna and Prussia.

"By postponing the judgement could we not turn this affair to great profit?"

There was a general uproar.

"The life of Louis XVII would answer exactly the same purpose."

"The Queen's blood is needed to bind the Revolutionary Tribunal to the Convention and to make the city of Paris a co-sharer in the destiny of the Convention!"

The editor of *Le Père Duchesne* could not be bothered with such subtleties; Hébert went straight to the point.

"I have promised Antoinette's head. I shall go and cut it off myself if there is any delay in giving it to me. I promised it on your behalf, to the *sans-culottes*, who have asked me for it and without whom you would cease to be. The instinct of the Republic leads them to wish to unite themselves with us by this expiatory sacrifice, and yet you are hesitating!"

Cambon pointed out that the Queen was a hostage whom it would be folly to get rid of, so Hébert promptly took on a prophetic tone.

"I know not if you still have any hopes for a Republic, a constitution and the safety of your persons, but I know that if you have you are greatly mistaken. You will all perish, anything else is impossible. I know not if it was well or ill done to bring matters to this point, but there they are. The Kings will harm themselves by wishing to annihilate us, who will annihilate them in twenty years. But we shall none the less perish. France will be in subjection. We shall all perish!"

But supposing the Queen's life could be used as a medium of exchange? Supposing that by using it an amnesty could be obtained?

"If we are promised an amnesty it will not be honoured, because it could not be. You will merely be knifed or poisoned instead of being torn in pieces. In these circumstances, therefore, we live only for vengeance, a vengeance which could be great. In perishing let us bequeath to our enemies the seeds of their own death and, in France, a destruction so great that its marks will never be effaced. To bring this about we must satisfy the *sans-culottes*. They will kill all our enemies, but their zeal must be nourished by the death of Antoinette. Remember that the way to make them dare everything is to persuade them of what I shout to them every day—that in this crisis, whatever the event, their obscurity is their safeguard and that we alone are answerable for everything. Thus they will give us every help, for the profits are for them and the danger for us. This is all I have to say to you to tell you of my opinion."

The secretary added: "So saying, he went out without staying a moment longer."

The debate went on all night, and finally Cambon was defeated. Dawn was breaking as Fouquier-Tinville was sent for, and asked what he intended to do and what was needed to be certain of the result.

"Renew the jurors."

They must have men on whom they could count. They must be permanently appointed and given a salary.

"A certain amount of rebellion is needed to overcome the fear of the Tribunal."

Some of the judges, indeed, were in favour of poisoning the Queen "so as to get rid of this thorn in our side."

Fouquier got his "certain amount of rebellion" two days later. The discovery of the conspiracy of the carnation having stirred up the half-hearted, the Convention decided on 5 September that the Tribunal would judge not only the nobles, priests and counter-revolutionaries, but all the "enemies of the people," that is, "the shopkeepers, rich merchants, former attorneys [Fouquier-Tinville was to be able to guillotine some of his old colleagues], ushers, insolent valets, intendants and men of business, men of private means, cheaters by nature, profession and education." It can be seen that no one was forgotten.

On 28 September the new judges and jurors demanded by Fouquier were permanently appointed by the Committee. The axe was ready to work.

After Rougeville's plot the number of petitions increased. The *Section de l'Unité* asked, nay begged, "that the widow Capet should be definitely judged." The Central Committee of the "Patriotic Society" demanded that "the modern Messalina, this woman who seems to be rejected by nature and society, should be delivered to the vengeance of the law." Letters flowed in to the Committees, the Convention and the Tribunal. Even children—the young citizens of the *Section des Piques*—took a hand, asking "if the crimes of Marie Antoinette, that impious woman ruled by a barbarous nature, need to become blacker still before her fate is pronounced?"

The provinces followed Paris's lead. Calais, Evreux, Riom, Pamiers, Laigle, Grignan, Louhans, Senlis, Sens, Charolles, Josselin, Orgelet, Mont-Terrible and even the fishermen of La Flotte-en-Ré asked for sentence on "the shameless and despotic woman," the "wretch Antoinette," guilty of the crime of *lèse-nation*. The town of Chantilly was even more impatient and begged simply "that the Austrian she-wolf should be delivered to it" without the formality of a trial. Crécy was of the same opinion. "Antoinette is a thousand times guiltier than Louis XVI and she must pay with her impure blood for the sea of generous blood she has spilled."

Finally, on 3 October, the Convention decreed that the Revolutionary Tribunal "shall deal immediately and uninterruptedly with the judgement": On 5 October Fouquier replied that the Tribunal wished to hold the trial, but that he still had no documents concerning Marie Antoinette.

Perhaps the Prosecutor informed Hébert and Chaumette of his lack, and was told that documents could be procured, for the two accomplices, together with Pache and some Commissaires, arrived at the Temple and went up to the apartment "occupied by Louis-Charles Capet to hear his declarations regarding conversations and events within his knowledge." This idea, admittedly, could spring only from the mind of a Chaumette or a Hébert—to make a child of eight give evidence against his mother.

The little boy was questioned about the Commissaires "who were in the habit of coming to his mother and his aunt and holding conversations with them." The child first accused Lepitre and Toulan and then those "who conversed with more familiarity than the others": Michonis, Jobert, Moëlle, Beugnot, Vincent and Lebœuf.

"During these conversations I was sent away."

With disarming seriousness Simon made his pupil say that "Pétion, Manuel, Bailly and Lafayette" had behaved "very mysteriously in the Tuileries, with his mother and aunt." In the Tuileries the child had been barely seven years old!

Hébert soon realised that gossip of this kind would not create a favourable "climate" for the trial. The two accomplices then began their revolting plot, "Louis-Charles Capet declares also that having several times been surprised on his bed by Simon and his wife, who were entrusted by the Commune with guarding him, while committing indecencies harmful to his health, he confessed to them . . ."

We need not publish any more; it is nauseating. The accusation may have appeared probable to these men, who for fifteen years had been hearing all sorts of calumnies against the Queen, but Fouquier was intelligent. It is surprising that he did not feel that he risked having everything "blow up in his hands," in his own words, by making use of such filth. But he noted his customary *hic* against the most odious passage of the report. "From the way in which the child expressed himself we gathered that on one occasion his mother called him to her and there resulted . . ."

Was it the Prosecutor who asked Hébert to have these declarations supported by the testimony of the sister and aunt? However that may be, the next day the little group, which had been joined by the painter David and the Commissaire Danjou, returned to the Temple and began by confronting the two children. "We immediately summoned Charles Capet and asked him to declare if what he had said yesterday relative to the attempts on his person was true. He persisted in his statement, repeated them and continued in them in the presence of his sister and persisted in saying that it was the truth. Asked a second time to declare if it was really true, he replied: 'Yes, that is true.' His sister said she had not seen it. It was pointed out to her that her brother appeared to us to have spoken the truth and that as they were nearly always together it was impossible that she had not noticed everything her brother had declared."

Madame Royale replied: "It might be that her brother had seen things she had not, in view of the fact she was occupied with her education."

Madame Elisabeth, summoned in her turn, was horrified and exclaimed: "Oh! the monster!"

Would Fouquier's prey escape him? Madame Royale's denials concerning her mother's conversations with Toulan and Lepitre admittedly lacked sincerity, but a wish to escape was merely a breach of the prison rules; it was not a crime against the Nation.

The Prosecutor again asked the Convention to send him the papers found in the Queen's apartments on the morning of the departure for Varennes, the documents of Louis XVI's trial and the interrogation of the accused after the failure of the conspiracy of the carnation.

On 11 October a letter from the Committee, signed by Robespierre, Hérault, Collot d'Herbois and Billaud-Varenne authorised the Keeper of the Archives to let the Prosecutor have the documents he required.

In the evening all that arrived in the office in Caesar's Tower were the two interrogations of the Queen on the night of 3-4 September. Fouquier opened the first one. The Queen's answers to Amar had been very skilful.

"Do you sympathise with the success of our enemies' forces?"

"I sympathise with the success of those of my son's country."

"What is your son's country?"

"Can you be in doubt? Is he not French?"

How cleverly she had avoided giving up her rights!

"As your son is only a private person do you declare that you have renounced all the privileges which formerly gave him the empty title of King?"

To reply "yes" or "no" was equally dangerous. She therefore replied: "There is none finer than the happiness of France."

The *hic* in the margin bit deeper. Another trap was set:

"You are glad, then, that there is no more King or monarchy?"

She exclaimed: "All we need is that France should be great and happy!"

There, again, she had not answered the question, and another *hic* marked the reply. She was now going to be asked to approve of regicide.

"You must therefore wish for the People to have no more oppressors and [that] all of your family who wield arbitrary power should undergo the fate undergone by the oppressor of France?"

"I can answer for my son and myself. I am not responsible for others!"

Hic, wrote Fouquier.

The Varennes episode enabled Sevestre and Amar to lay another trap.

"How was it that you showed such an eager desire to use every means to be united with your family at war with the French nation?"

Here was the only valid accusation. Marie Antoinette could have replied that in June 1791 France and Austria were not at war, but from her replies one can see that she had lost her footing.

"My family is my children. I can be happy only with them and without them in no place."

"You therefore consider as your enemies those who make war on France?"

She might have answered "yes," but she refused to lie. Fouquier was therefore able to write a victorious *hic* against these two lines:

"I regard as my enemies all who might do harm to my children."

"And what is the nature of the harm that might be done to your children?"

"Any harm . . . of whatever kind."

She was obviously confused, but was able to recover herself. When the two deputies spoke to her of the abolition of royalty "which she could not consider wrong," she cried: "If France is to be happy with a King I wish it to be my son. If she is to be happy without a King I shall share the happiness with him."

Corneille could not have found anything better, and this time there was no *hic* in the margin.

Fouquier took up the text of the second interrogation. Perhaps he would have more luck there. It must have been well on in the night of 3-4 September when the Queen came back for questioning, and so this time the Prosecutor might find what he wanted. Amar and Sevestre tried to make the accused assume her share in Louis XVI's "crimes."

"Did he inform you of his plans?"

"He told me what his trust in me prompted him to."

"Did you approve those plans?"

"Everything that might lead to the peace of all was his desire and mine . . . I felt his troubles keenly."

"How was it that if, as you say, the people's happiness was your one wish, the people were so unhappy and constantly harried and tyrannised over by the perfidy of the court and the treachery of the Ministry?"

"There was much treachery. I am not in a position to know it nor to speak of it. All I know is that his heart wished only for happiness."

Amar and Sevestre preferred to leave the matter there. Neither weariness, nor the anguish of that last week which had seen the birth and sudden death of the hope of freedom brought by Rougeville had managed to diminish the mental faculties of Maria Theresa's daughter.

Fouquier wrote no *hic*, but closed the dossier. An indictment should be supported by more solid documents. And so on that same evening, Saturday, the accused was to be questioned and the trial could begin two days later, Monday 14 October, or "23 Vendémiaire." The revolutionary calendar had just begun its poetic cycle, but unfortunately it was soon to evoke not rime, blossoms, prairies, mist and wind, but bloody days and murderous laws.

Had the Queen a presentiment of what was being plotted against her? Since 5 October she was no longer alone in her cell. An officer of the gendarmerie guarded her—Lieutenant Louis-François de Busne, who before the Revolution had worn the uniform of the *Royal-Dauphin* Regiment. Two sentries were stationed before the window, but by speaking very loudly the prisoners in the courtyard had managed to inform Marie Antoinette "that she was to go up."

On 12 October Marie Antoinette was suffering from the cold and from serious hæmorrhages. At dusk she put on her "night shirt," which Rosalie brought to her all warm from the kitchen, and went to bed. The pretty servant managed to drag out her "little evening tasks," in order, as she tells us, that the Queen should not yet be "in solitude and obscurity." Finally Rosalie went away and the cell was lit only by the lamp in the women's courtyard.

Marie Antoinette took a long time to get warm. She had indeed asked the concierge for an extra blanket, but without success. When he transmitted the accused's request Bault was sharply spoken to by Fouquier-Tinville.

"What's that you're daring to ask for? You deserve to be sent to the guillotine!"

The prisoner had been in bed for two hours when the two doors of her cell were noisily opened. An usher and four gendarmes had come to take her to be questioned. Behind the screen the Queen hastily put on her black dress and then, surrounded by her guards and preceded by a turnkey carrying a torch, she left the cell, turned to the left into a corridor where a lantern burned by day and by night, went through the two grilles of the parlour—a real animal's cage—and went down a short flight of steps into the men's courtyard, which at that late hour was empty. She crossed the court and mounted the "*Bonbec* staircase." The boots of her escort rang loudly on the narrow stone staircase. On reaching the first floor the group followed a winding corridor, interrupted by steps, and finally emerged in the former *Grand-Chambre* of Parliament, the "tabernacle" of the old régime where Louis XVI had held his *lits de justice,* that "basilica" of which a monarch had said: "It is in seeing such things that one is proud to be King of France!"

The vast room was now called the Hall of Liberty and had become the seat of the Revolutionary Tribunal. The tapestries with their fleurs-de-lis had disappeared and the Crucifixion by Albert Dürer or Van Eyck—it was not known which—had been replaced by a picture painted on paper and reproducing the Declaration of the Rights of Man. Coustou's bas-relief, "Louis XV between Truth and Justice," had given way to busts of Marat, Lepeletier and Lucius Junius Brutus, a man who at that time was generally held up as an example, since to show his love for the Republic he had condemned his own children to death for having conspired to restore the Tarquins.

The Queen was given a seat on a bench in front of Fouquier's desk. In the shadows behind the tall balustrade of the public gallery could be seen a few faces of privileged people invited by Fouquier. The Queen heard murmurs and looked towards the back of the hall, but her shortsighted eyes could distinguish nothing.

The enormous room was lit only by two candles on the desk of the clerk, Paris from Marseilles, who as a sacrifice to fashion called himself Fabricius. The *Grand-Chambre* appeared like a tomb and the Queen was already speaking of herself in the past tense.

"I was called Marie Antoinette de Lorraine d'Autriche."

The question had been put by the young President of the Revolutionary Tribunal, Hermann, who was to preside at the debates two days later and was this evening acting as examining magistrate and sat alone at his table. He affected an air of compassion, but he was a friend of

Robespierre, to whom he owed his promotion (four months earlier he had been only President of the Criminal Tribunal at Arras), and was entirely at the orders of his "chief," Fouquier-Tinville. The Prosecutor could count on him.

He went straight to the point. "Before the Revolution you carried on political relations with the King of Bohemia and Hungary and these relations were contrary to the interests of France, which was showering advantages on you."

Maria Theresa's daughter denied it, of course. But this was one of the points on which Marie Antoinette was terribly vulnerable. How Fouquier would have exulted if he could have taken from his dossier that letter of Mercy's of fifteen years before. There would have been a *hic* against every line: "The Queen has taken steps to bring the King round to her way of thinking and to set him in opposition, to some extent, to his Ministers. She deserves to be congratulated."

Without delay Hermann struck another blow. "Not content with squandering in an appalling way the finances of France, the fruit of the people's sweat, for your pleasures and intrigues . . ."

No proof was given. And yet it would have sufficed to open a few of the account books of the Queen's Household or to summon a few witnesses who in the old days at Fontainebleau had sat down at the faro table. This absence of proof enabled the accused to deny vehemently.

"Never! I know this argument has too often been used against me. I loved my husband too much to squander my country's money!"

Hermann continued: "Since the Revolution you have never for a moment ceased intriguing with foreign Powers and at home against liberty, when even now we have only the shadow of that liberty which the French people desires above everything."

"Since the Revolution I, personally, have forbidden myself all correspondence abroad and I have never meddled at home."

The accused denied what was a secret for no one in France. However, she did not feel in the least guilty. For her there was no State, there was only the King—it was the famous "*L'Etat, c'est moi!*" of Louis XIV. To call for help, to ask her brother to assist her in regaining the throne, to beg him "to put an end to the troubles of the Revolution," as she had asked him on 3 September 1791, was not in Marie Antoinette's eyes to behave like an Austrian. Far from committing a crime when she addressed herself to "the enemies of the Nation," she was saving the State!

Marie Antoinette was again to deny the evidence.

"Did you not employ secret agents to correspond with foreign Powers, in particular with your brother?"

"Never in my life!"

Hermann could exclaim quite honestly: "Your reply does not seem to us to be correct, for it is stated that at the former château of the Tuileries there were secret, nocturnal councils, over which you yourself presided, and where the replies to be sent to foreign Powers and to the Constituent and Legislative Assemblies were discussed, debated and drafted."

She denied it. But did she know that in the iron chest at the Tuileries the Republic had discovered letters from Barnave alluding to his correspondence, to her interviews with the Triumvirs and to the notes sent to Brussels? Fortunately there was so much lack of order that Fouquier-Tinville had not been able to get hold of the documents.

Hermann and the other members of the Tribunal—and they were perfectly sincere—approved of the Convention's vote of regicide. Louis XVI was guilty—guilty of having supported the non-juring priests, guilty of having opposed his veto to the decrees, guilty, as was proved by Barnave's reports, of having played "a double game." If they could prove that the Queen had been the prime instigator of this wavering policy she would be more "criminal" than her husband, who was decreed "irresponsible." This was one of the Prosecutor's aims.

"It was you who taught Louis Capet the art of profound dissimulation by which he so long deceived the good French people, who did not imagine that rascality and perfidy could be carried to such lengths!"

Need we recall that letter from the Queen to Mercy, dated 26 August, 1791: "All we have to do is to hoodwink them and make them trust us so as better to defeat them afterwards"?

When Hermann reproached the accused with the advice she had given "Louis Capet," advice which had gone so far as "persecution," so that the King should "put himself at the head of the malcontents," how can one not remember the Queen's admission to Fersen, the "hell" their home had become, the "serious obstacles" she met in trying to make her point of view prevail and which she mentioned to Mercy, the "great struggles" she was forced to have with her too hesitant and changeable husband?

To recall these documents is not to accuse the Queen, but to try to explain, otherwise than through fear of the guillotine, the behaviour of the judges and jurors who were to send this woman to her death, in the persuasion that they were acting justly.

In guise of proof Fouquier had only the documents relating to the flight of June 1791.

"You opened the doors and made everyone leave. There is no doubt that it was you who ruled the actions of Louis Capet and persuaded him to flight."

She replied, reasonably: "I do not think that an open door proves that one is constantly ruling a person's acts."

She seems to have made her reply somewhat ironical. The President exclaimed violently: "Never for one moment have you ceased wanting to destroy liberty. You wanted to reign at any price and to reascend the throne over the bodies of patriots."

Still ironically she replied: "We had no need to reascend the throne; we were there!" More seriously, she added: "We have never wished for anything but France's happiness. As long as she was happy, as long as she is so, we shall always be satisfied."

It was a fine phrase, but it allowed Hermann to remark that if the Queen had really wished for France's happiness she would have prevented her brother from breaking the treaty signed with the King. It was then easy for Marie Antoinette to reply "that it was France who declared war."

Hermann admitted it. "But the accused cannot be unaware that this declaration of war came only through the intrigues of a liberticide faction."

"The Legislative Assembly repeated its request for a declaration of war and my husband consented only after receiving the unanimous assent of his Council."

Hermann was not well placed and preferred to attack the unhappy woman on more shifting ground: the banquet of the bodyguards at which, it was alleged, they had "trampled under foot the tricolour cockade so as to wear the white cockade." Here again she was skilful in her replies.

"That can have been no more than the mistake of one or two people

. . . It is not credible that such devoted people should have trampled on and changed the sign worn by the King himself."

Without transition Hermann asked: "What interest do you take in the forces of the Republic?"

"The happiness of France is what I wish for above everything."

Now the questions came thick and fast.

"Do you think that Kings are necessary for the people's happiness?"

"An individual cannot decide such matters."

"No doubt you regret that your son has lost a throne to which he might have mounted if the people, finally conscious of their rights, had not destroyed that throne?"

"I shall never regret anything for my son when his country is happy."

The moment her son was in question Marie Antoinette found the right answer. Hermann therefore hastened to change the subject.

"What is your opinion on the day of 10 August when, by order of the master of the château, the Swiss Guards fired on the people?"

"I was out of the château when the firing began. I do not know how it all happened. I only know that no order was ever given to fire."

After several traps about the Temple and a long interrogation on the conspiracy of the carnation, Hermann put his last question.

"Have you any counsel?"

"No. I do not know anyone."

"Would you like the Tribunal to appoint one or two?"

"I am quite willing."

"Upon which we appointed, as official counsel and defenders, citizens Tronson du Coudray and Chauveau-Lagarde."

Fabricius handed the Queen the pen. She signed, and then Hermann, Fouquier and the clerk wrote their initials.

As the prisoner and her escort returned to the Conciergerie, Fouquier shut himself up in his office in Caesar's Tower to prepare the indictment. Right at the beginning he committed an historical error in comparing Marie Antoinette to Messalina, Fredegonde and Brunehaut, whom he described as "Queens of France." He began by writing "Bruneau," then feeling something was wrong corrected it to "Brunechaut" and, finally, "Brunehault."

Sprinkling his text with such phrases as "scourge and bloodsucker of the French . . . full of intrigues of all kinds . . . disordered pleasures . . . criminal intrigues . . . excessive squandering . . . perfidious views," the Prosecutor repeated and amplified all the questions put to the Queen by Hermann.

Needless to say, he paid no attention to the accused's replies, except for one point regarding the journey to Varennes. "That the widow Capet admits in her interrogation that it was she who arranged and prepared everything for the carrying out of this escape and that it was she who opened and closed the door of the apartment through which all the fugitives passed."

As regards 10 August, he alleged that on the evening before, Marie Antoinette had gone "to the hall where the Swiss Guards and others devoted to her were working at making cartridges; that while she encouraged them to hasten the manufacture of the cartridges, and in order to spur them on still more, she took some cartridges and bit on the bullets (there are not words to paint such an atrocious act); that on the next day, the 10th, it is well known that she urged and begged Louis Capet to go to the Tuileries, at about half-past five in the morning, to review the true Swiss Guards and the other rascals who were wearing the uniform, and that on his return she handed him a pistol, saying: 'Now is the moment to reveal yourself,' and that on his refusal she called him a coward; that although during her interrogation the widow Capet persisted in denying that any order was given to fire on the people, her conduct on the 9th, her actions in the Swiss Guards' room, the discussions held all night, at which she was present, the matter of the pistol and her remark to Louis Capet, their sudden retreat from the Tuileries and the shots fired just as they were entering the hall of the Legislative Assembly—all these circumstances together leave no doubt that it was agreed, during the council which was held during the night, that the people must be fired on, and that Louis Capet and Marie Antoinette, who was the prime mover in this conspiracy, herself gave the order to fire."

Fouquier-Tinville now came to a serious matter, so serious indeed that it would be unnecessary to seek further, if the Prosecutor were able to prove it.

"That it was by her manoeuvres and intrigues, always fatal to France, that the first retreat of the French from Belgian territory came about. That it was the widow Capet who conveyed to the foreign Powers the plans of campaign and attack which had been agreed on in the Council, so that by this double treachery the enemy was always aware in advance of the movements of the armies of the Republic, from which it follows that the widow Capet is the cause of the reverses suffered at different times by the French armies."

Before finishing the Prosecutor actually made use of Hébert's plot. "That, finally, the widow Capet, immoral in every way and a new Agrippina, is so perverted and so familiar with every crime that, forgetting her position as a mother and the line drawn by the laws of nature, she did not recoil from indulging with Louis-Charles Capet, her son, as is confessed by the latter, in indecencies the mere idea and mention of which arouse a shudder of horror."

By uncovering this garbage in court and providing details which would be eschewed by a writer of cheap melodrama—the Queen calling Louis XVI a coward, or biting bullets on the eve of 10 August— Fouquier imagined he would make a good impression on the jurors.

He had chosen them carefully. First there were the zealots: the Pyrenean surgeon Souberville, the printer Nicolas, both of whom were friends of Robespierre, the former *procureur* Thoumin, the valuer Besnard and the former Marquis Antoinette, who had been a deputy from Bouches-du-Rhône in the Legislative Assembly. Fouquier could be as sure of them as of himself. The others were rather simple-minded men, who liked ready-made formulas and believed in enormities: the wigmaker Ganney, the cobbler Desboisseaux, the café-keeper Chrétien, the hatter Baron, the musician Lumière, a certain Fiévé and two carpenters, Devèse and Trinchard, the latter being a former dragoon of the Bourbon Regiment. On the following morning the Prosecutor was to summon them.

That same evening Fersen wrote in his Journal: "The news of the Queen is a little more reassuring. The Public Prosecutor is complaining that he has no documents. It has been decreed that he should have them and this at least means a delay."

At his country house not far from Paris Chauveau-Lagarde, aged 28, was informed by the clerk of the court that on the previous day he had been appointed to defend "the widow Capet" and that the trial was to begin at eight the next morning.

The lawyer hastened back to Paris and at two in the afternoon arrived at the Conciergerie, where he showed the order signed by Fouquier. Preceded by a concierge he passed through the wickets and went down the corridor. "With trembling knees and moist eyes," as he related afterwards, he entered the cell. On the left were two armed gendarmes; on the right, behind the screen, the bed, table and two cane chairs. The Queen greeted him with "majesty and kindness." She had not yet received the indictment and spoke to her defender about the interrogation of the day before. To find out more about it Chauveau-Lagarde went up to the clerk's office, which led out of the waiting-room. According to custom Fabricius's clerks were making as many copies of the indictment as there were to be judges and jurors. The lawyer was given a copy and then asked to see the accused's dossier. The documents had finally arrived and the defending counsel was taken aback by the mountain of paper.

"I cannot possibly become acquainted with the documents in such a short time!"

Discouraged, the lawyer returned to the prison. Citizen Eustache Nappier, the court usher, had just given the accused her copy of the indictment, "speaking personally to her between the two wickets of that house, as in a place of freedom." Marie Antoinette was "accused of having conspired against France."

Together with his client Chauveau-Lagarde read the eight pages. In order to be able to reply to this farrago he would need the dossier.

"But I cannot get to know the documents in such a short time."

"To whom must you apply?" asked the Queen.

"To the National Convention," Chauveau-Lagarde murmured.

To those who had voted for her husband's death. "No, no, never!" she cried, "turning her head away."

The lawyer insisted. The Queen might, in the name of her defenders, make "a complaint against a haste which by the terms of the law amounted to a real denial of justice."

Marie Antoinette gave way. Without uttering a word she took the pen held out to her by Chauveau-Lagarde, "let fall a sigh," and wrote to ask the President of the Assembly for a delay of three days, as she owed it to her children "to omit nothing necessary for their mother's entire justification."

When the letter was finished Chauveau-Lagarde went again to the Tribunal and gave the request to Fouquier, who promised to send it to the Assembly. He took care not to do so, however. One day he was to give the letter to Robespierre and after 9 Thermidor it was found under the Incorruptible's mattress, together with the Queen's will.

At Brussels, on this same 13 October, Fersen was once more in despair. "Although there are no proofs against this unfortunate Princess, how can one hope for anything with wretches who manufacture proofs when they have none and who condemn simply on vague assertions and on suspicion! No, let us not hope for anything. We must be resigned to the divine will. Her fate is certain. We must be prepared for it and summon strength to bear this terrible blow. I have for long been trying to prepare myself for it and I feel that I shall receive the news of it without great emotion. Only God can save her; let us implore His mercy and submit ourselves to His decrees."

That evening Gluck's *Armide* was being performed at the Opera. How often, seated at her clavichord in the Trianon, had Marie Antoinette sung the famous aria: "Ah! if my freedom should be taken from me!"

20

❧

The Trial

A FEW MINUTES before eight the usher of the Tribunal, Lieutenant de Busne, and the gendarmes opened the cell door. The Queen was ready. She had put on her worn black dress and had managed to give herself a widow's headdress by adding "weepers" to her lawn bonnet and fixing a crêpe veil under it.

When the crowd saw her enter "free and without fetters," a murmur rang round the *Grand-Chambre*. The public crowding behind the rails had difficulty in recognising the 37-year-old Queen in this woman with white hair and pallid complexion. "She is prodigiously altered," wrote the *Moniteur*. During the last few months Marie Antoinette had grown so thin and her face had become so sunken that she looked about sixty. She was led to a little platform, where there was an armchair so placed "that the accused could be seen by all." Chauveau-Lagarde and Tronson du Coudray stood near the Queen. In front of her were the tables adorned with gryphons at which President Hermann was enthroned together with the judges Coffinhal, former clerk, former doctor, former lawyer, former errand-boy, former police officer and still only 31, Antoine Maire, who pleaded in that same hall in the time of the Parliament and who was alleged to be a son of Louis XV, born in the Parc au Cerf, the former deputy Deliège, who wore a wig, and the doyen Donzé-Verteuil, a man of nearly 60, whose tiny mouth was lost in the middle of a large, round face. According to some documents there were also present, as alternates, Etienne Foucault, once a farmer, whose large nose stood out in a face marked with smallpox, and Marie-Joseph Lane.

Marie Antoinette remained standing while the witnesses took the oath.

"The accused may be seated . . . Your name, surname, age, position, place of birth and residence?"

"My name is Marie Antoinette Lorraine d'Autriche [the scribe wrote *dautriche*], aged about 38 [she would not be 38 for another 18 days], widow of the King of France, born in Vienna. At the time of my arrest I was in the session hall of the National Assembly."

The clerk Fabricius then read the eight long pages of the indictment. Did she listen to the text she had read the day before with Chauveau-Lagarde? Somewhat irritated, "with seeming inattention," she moved her fingers on the arm of her chair "as though over the keyboard of her pianoforte."

The usher finished mumbling.

"This is what you are accused of," the President announced. "Pay careful attention. You will now hear the charges to be brought against you."

The first witness, who was to testify for two hours, was Laurent Lecointre, formerly a linen-draper and now a deputy to the Convention. It will be remembered that he was second in command of the National Guard at Versailles. "The witness," says the report, "entered into the details of the feasts and orgies which took place in the town of Versailles from the year 1779 to the beginning of 1789, the result of which was an appalling dilapidation of French finances."

We do not know these "details," but the text is much more precise concerning the "orgy" of the bodyguards.

"Have you anything to say about the witness's testimony?" Hermann asked the Queen.

"I have no knowledge of the greater part of the facts mentioned by the witness. It is true that we visited the table on the day of the bodyguards' feast, but that is all."

"It is notorious that throughout France at that time the rumour was that you yourself visited the three armed corps at Versailles to urge them to defend what you called the prerogatives of the throne."

"I have nothing to reply."

Hermann now came to the famous royal session of 23 June 1789, which he pretended to call a *lit de justice*.

"It was in your apartment that the articles [of the King's speech] were prepared?"

"This affair was decided in the Council."

"Did your husband not read the speech to you half-an-hour before entering the hall of the people's representatives and did you not urge him to utter it with decision?"

"My husband had great confidence in me and it was for that reason that he read it to me, but I did not allow myself any observations."

"What were the decisions taken to surround the representatives of the people with bayonets and to assassinate half of them, if it had been possible?"

There had been bayonets only in Mirabeau's famous phrase, and so the Queen exclaimed in astonishment: "I have never heard such a thing mentioned."

She lost ground when the President recalled the troop movements on 12 July 1789, troops which were placed under the orders of Maréchal de Broglie and Besenval.

"You are doubtless aware that there were troops in the Champ de Mars, and you must know why they were assembled?"

"Yes, I knew at the time that they were there, but I am entirely unaware of the reason."

"But as you had your husband's confidence you cannot have been unaware of the cause?"

"It was to re-establish public tranquillity."

"But at that time everyone was tranquil; there was but one cry, that of liberty."

Hermann's second attack also had its effect. These were, incidentally, almost the only attacks to reach their target throughout the long trial.

"How did you use the immense sums given you by the various Controllers of Finance?"

"I was never given immense sums. What was given to me I used to pay the people in my service."

"Why were the Polignac family and several others gorged with gold from you?"

"They had places at court which procured riches for them."

The vague testimony of a certain Lapierre, Adjutant-General on duty at the Tuileries on the evening of 20 June 1791, enabled Hermann to put some questions about Varennes. Roussillon, "surgeon and gunner," came next and alleged "that on 10 August 1792, having entered the château of the Tuileries and into the accused's apartment," he had "found under the bed bottles, some full and some empty, which led him to believe that she had given drink either to the officers of the Swiss Guard or to the Knights of the Poniard who filled the château."

It would soon be said at the Jacobins Club that "the testimony of Roussillon had been a fire burning like a fuse."

There was another "fuse" from the gunner-surgeon. "The witness affirms that the accused helped to bring France within an inch of her ruin by sending enormous sums to her brother [the former King of Bohemia and Hungary] to help in his war against the Turks and to enable him later to make war against France, that is, against a generous nation which was nourishing her, her husband and her family. The witness observed that he had this fact from a good citizeness, an excellent patriot, who had served at Versailles under the old régime, and in whom a favourite of the former court had confided."

Fouquier-Tinville pricked up his ears and immediately dispatched a summons in the name of "the good citizeness."

The *tricoteuses,* who were crowded behind the rails, constantly insisted by their shouts that the accused should reply standing, so that they should not miss anything. She murmured: "Will the people soon be weary of my hardships?"

With Hébert's deposition Marie Antoinette entered a new phase of her agony. In order to give substance to Toulan's conspiracy the deputy Prosecutor recalled the life of the prisoners in the Temple and put forward the declarations of "little Capet." He then stated coolly: "Finally, young Capet, whose health was worsening each day, was surprised by Simon in indecent defilements, baneful to his constitution. When the latter asked him who had taught him this criminal behaviour he replied that he owed his knowledge of this baneful habit to his mother and aunt. From the declaration that young Capet made in the presence of the Mayor of Paris and the Prosecutor of the Commune it was revealed that these two women often made him lie down between them; that there then took place acts of the most uncontrolled debauchery; that there was no doubt, from what Capet's son said, that there had been an act of incest between the mother and son."

One may imagine the Queen's horror and suffering at hearing the ignominy contrived by the abominable Hébert and the part her son had been forced to play. But Hébert had not finished.

"There is reason to believe that this criminal intercourse was not dictated by pleasure but by the calculated hope of enervating the child, whom they still liked to think of as destined to occupy a throne and whom they wished to be sure of dominating morally as a result of this scheme. As a result of the efforts he was forced to make he suffered from a hernia, for which a bandage was needed. Since the child has been away from his mother his constitution has become robust and strong."

Hermann questioned the accused. "What reply have you to the witness's deposition?"

In a trembling voice she replied: "I have no knowledge of the incidents Hébert speaks of." She eagerly refuted the details concerning Toulan which Hébert had given, but after a few sentences he interrupted her.

"I omitted one important fact, which should be brought to the attention of the citizen jurors. It shows the characters of the accused and her sister-in-law. After the death of Capet these two women treated little Capet with the same deference as if he had been King. At table he always took precedence over his mother and his aunt. He was always served first and sat at the head of the table."

Marie Antoinette turned towards the witness and asked him calmly: "Did you see that?"

"I did not see it, but the whole of the Municipality will confirm it."

Hermann cut this conversation short and asked the Queen about Rougeville and Michonis. Suddenly one of the jurors—his name is not known—rose.

"Citizen President, would you kindly observe to the accused that she has not replied concerning the incident mentioned by citizen Hébert, regarding what happened between herself and her son."

The President, perhaps unwillingly, repeated the question. The Queen rose, "much moved," according to the report.

"If I did not reply it was because nature recoils from such an accusation against a mother." Turning to the crowd she cried: "I appeal to all those who may be here!"

"At this sublime cry," wrote two eye-witnesses, the brothers Humbert, "an electric shock ran through those present. The *tricoteuses* were moved in spite of themselves and they nearly applauded ... Cries could be heard and the Tribunal had to threaten to call the disturbers to order."

For a few moments the session had to be suspended. The Queen called Chauveau-Lagarde and asked him in a low voice: "Was there too much dignity in my answer?"

"Madame," he replied, "be yourself and you will always do right, but why do you ask?"

"Because I heard a woman of the people remark to her neighbour: 'See how proud she is!'"

"This remark of the Queen's," wrote the lawyer, "shows that she still had hope. It also proves that with her pure conscience she was entirely mistress of herself, since amid the greatest agitation of mind she heard everything that was said around her and in order to prove her innocence she tried to regulate her silence and her words to suit the situation."

It was nearly two o'clock and the first session would soon be over. They were still hearing the trivial testimony of a certain Abraham Silly, "on duty in the château on the evening of 20 June 1791." However, this gave Hermann the opportunity to ask a series of questions about Varennes which were only remotely connected with the indictment.

"Who provided or caused to be provided the famous carriage in which you went away with your family?"

"It was a foreigner."

"Of what nation?"

"Swedish."

"Was it not Fersen, who was living in Paris in the Rue du Bacq?"

"Yes," murmured the accused.

At this name a tremor went through the public.

Followed by her lawyers and surrounded by gendarmes, the prisoner went down to her cell.

"The Queen asked me what I thought of the testimony we had just heard," wrote Chauveau-Lagarde, "summarising it quite correctly and complaining bitterly of the falsehood which filled most of it. I replied, as was true, that not only was there no proof of all the ridiculous calumnies of these witnesses, but there was not the slightest foundation for them and that they defeated themselves by their very grossness and by the vileness and meanness of their authors."

"In that case," replied the Queen, "I fear only Manuel!"

Marie Antoinette was wrong to fear him. When the session resumed, at about four or five, he opened fire. But as with the two succeeding witnesses, Bailly and Perceval, it was merely a matter of self-defence and personal questioning. They might have been in the office of an examining magistrate.

It was now Reine Millot's turn to appear in the *Grand-Chambre*. She was the "good citizeness" summoned by Fouquier, and had been fetched from the café of the Couronne-d'Or in the Rue du Bourdonnais. Formerly a servant in the château of Versailles, she alleged that she had "taken it on herself" to ask the former Comte de Coigny, whom she saw one day to be in "a good humour": "Will the Emperor go on making war against the Turks? Heavens, it will ruin France, on account of the great sums the Queen sends her brother, which must now amount to at least 200 millions."

"You are not mistaken," replied the "Comte" de Coigny (who in fact was a Duke). "Yes, it has already cost more than 200 millions and we have not finished yet."

"I would also mention," continued the witness, "that I was told by different people that as the accused had conceived the plan of assassinating the Duc d'Orléans, the King, having learned of it, ordered that she should be searched at once and that as a result two pistols were found on her. He then confined her to her apartments for a fortnight."

Marie Antoinette replied disdainfully: "It may be that my husband ordered me to remain in my apartments for a fortnight, but it was not for any such reason."[1]

The farce continued with J. - B. Lebenette, editor of the *Journal du Diable*, who declared with the utmost seriousness that "three individuals came to assassinate him on the orders of the accused." He did not explain how he had put them to flight.

With the gendarme Dufresne, the two Richards, the woman Harel and Gilbert they were back to the conspiracy of the carnation and, with that memory of the hope that had gleamed the month before, the first day's hearings ended at eleven o'clock.

Tuesday, 15 October, was the feast of Saint Teresa, her mother's feast-day and her daughter's. For the *sans-culottes*, who followed the new calendar, it was the feast of the Amaryllis.

[1] No mention of this punishment inflicted by the King is found either in Mercy's correspondence or in the memoirs of the time.

When Marie Antoinette crossed the courtyard at nine o'clock it was raining and the wind was blowing.

The session opened. The Queen listened, without interest, to the testimony, or rather the interrogation, of ex-Admiral d'Estaing, but her heart beat violently when she saw the approach of Simon, who must just have woken the little King. Louis XVII's "tutor" brought no serious accusations against the Queen. When the President asked him: "Is it within your knowledge that the little Capet was treated as a King, particularly at table?" he replied with restraint: "I know that at table his mother and aunt gave him precedence."

Fouquier was banking on vouchers signed "Marie Antoinette" which were said to have been discovered in the possession of Septeuil, the former Treasurer of the Civil List. Hermann began by asking the Queen: "Did you not sign vouchers to obtain money from the Treasurer of the Civil List?"

"No."

Fouquier rose and declared triumphantly: "I must tell you that your denial will soon be useless, seeing that among Septeuil's papers there were discovered two vouchers signed by you."

A little less boastfully he added: "As a matter of fact these two documents, which were deposited with the Comité des Vingt-Quatre, have temporarily gone astray, as the committee has been dissolved, but you will hear witnesses who have seen them."

There was only one witness—a common spy, who dignified himself with the title of "merchant." He was called François Tisset and recited the piece demanded by Fouquier.

"As an unsalaried employee, at the period of 10 August 1792, of the Vigilance Committee of the Municipality, I was sent on a mission to Septeuil, the Treasurer of the former Civil List. I was accompanied by armed forces of the Place Vendôme Section, now the *Piques*. I could not seize his person, as he was absent. Among Septeuil's papers were found two vouchers for the sum of 80,000 livres, signed 'Marie Antoinette,' which documents were all deposited with the Comité des Vingt-Quatre, which is now dissolved."

He was reciting a lesson, but he did not know it very well. The Queen, who was following attentively, asked very calmly: "I would like the witness to say what was the date of the vouchers he mentions."

"One was dated 10 August 1792; as for the other, I do not remember."

"I never signed any vouchers, and in any case how could I have done so on 10 August, the day on which we went to the National Assembly at about eight in the morning?"

The twentieth witness reminded the Queen of her "happy dream" of the preceding winter. It was Lepitre, who had been arrested the week before and brought from the prison of Sainte-Pélagie, and had been present at the trial since morning.

"Did you not procure means for the accused to learn the news by sending a pedlar every day to call out the evening paper near the Temple tower?"

"No."

Marie Antoinette explained: "I have never had any conversation with the witness. On the other hand, I had no need for pedlars to be hired to come to the tower. I could hear them well enough every day when they went through the Rue de la Corderie."

The Queen had then to submit to a painful experience: the opening by Hermann of the packet of possessions seized at the Temple on which the prisoner had put her seal when she was registered at the Conciergerie. In his Marseillais accent Fabricius read the inventory aloud.

"A packet of hair of various colours."

"They come from my dead and living children and from my husband."

"Another packet of hair."

"They belong to the same people."

"A paper with figures on it."

"It is a table for teaching my son to count."

"A hussif or little wallet fitted with scissors, needles, silk, thread, etc. A little mirror, a gold ring in which is some hair, a paper on which are two gold hearts with initials, another paper on which is written 'Prayer to the Sacred Heart of Jesus; prayer to the Immaculate Conception'; a portrait of a woman."

Hermann raised his head.

"Whose is that portrait?"

"Madame de Lamballe," replied the Queen.

"Two other portraits of women," cried the usher.

The President inquired: "Who are the people represented by these portraits?"

"They are two ladies with whom I was brought up in Vienna."

"What are their names?"

"Mesdames de Mecklembourg and de Hesse."

Fabricius continued: "A small piece of cloth on which is a heart in flames pierced by an arrow."

It was Fouquier's turn to intervene and to pretend not to know what a scapular was.

"I notice that among the accused who have been brought before the Tribunal as conspirators and whom the law has justly dealt with by striking them with its sword, it has been observed that most of them, or indeed the majority, wore this counter-revolutionary sign."

Under his judge's robes Fouquier himself wore a "counter-revolutionary sign." When the last surviving daughter of the Public Prosecutor died in 1856 at Saint Quentin there was found on her a paper enveloping a medal of the Virgin. On the paper was written: "He had it round his neck when he condemned the widow Capet."

The clerk rewrapped and carried away all those beloved and painful remembrances which recalled to the Queen so many well-loved ghosts.

The twenty-first witness was Philippe La Tour du Pin Gouvernet.

"Were you not present at the festivities at the château?"

"I practically never went to court."

"Were you not at the banquet of the former bodyguards?"

"I could not have been there, for at that time I was commanding in Burgundy."

"What! Were you not a Minister then?"

"I have never been a Minister and would not have wished for the post if those then in power had offered it to me."

The President, who thought the witness was lying, questioned Lecointre.

"Do you recognise the witness as having been, in 1789, Minister of War?"

Lecointre enlightened Hermann. Philippe La Tour du Pin had been summoned in error. The right one—Jean-Frédéric—was there and would appear. The former Minister came forward unmoved and made the Queen a respectful court bow. When he had finished his testimony he made another. Fouquier-Tinville would not forget these two greetings when on the following 28 April he sent La Tour du Pin to the scaffold.

There was another interrogation which stirred the audience. It concerned the King's departure for Rambouillet on 5 October and the disbanding of the army. Hermann finally came back to the trial.

"During your Ministry did the accused ask you to let her know the exact state of the French Army?"

"Yes."

"Did she say what use she wanted to make of it?"

"No."

"When you asked the witness for the state of the army," asked the President, turning to the Queen, "was it not to communicate it to the King of Bohemia and Hungary?"

"As it was publicly known there would have been no need for me to communicate it to him. The public papers would have told him all about it."

"What then was your motive in asking?"

"As there was a rumour that the Assembly wished for changes in the army, I wanted to know the state of the regiments to be suppressed."

Fouquier had scored a point.

It would be useless to look for the guiding thread in Hermann's conduct of the argument. He suddenly changed the subject and with three syllables reminded the Queen of her former happy life.

"Where did you get the money to have the little Trianon built and furnished, where you gave parties at which you were always the goddess?"

"There were funds especially for that purpose."

"These funds must have been large, for the little Trianon must have cost immense sums?"

"It is possible that the little Trianon cost immense sums, perhaps more than I would have wished. We were gradually involved in more and more expense. Besides I am more anxious than anyone that what happened there should be known."

"Was it not at the little Trianon that you knew the woman Lamotte?"

"I have never seen her."

"Was she not your victim in the famous affair of the necklace?"

"She cannot have been, since I did not know her."

"Do you persist in denying that you knew her?"

"I have no system of denial. It is the truth that I have told and will persist in telling."

The questions continued to rain down, and this time the accusations were just.

"Was it not you who appointed the Ministers and filled other civil and military posts?"

"No."

"Did you not have a list of persons you wanted places for?"

"No."

"Did you not compel various Ministers to accept the persons you indicated to them for vacant posts?"

"No."

"Did you not compel the Ministers of Finance to send you money and did you not threaten with your indignation those of them who refused?"

"Never."

"Did you not ask Vergennes to convey six millions to the King of Bohemia and Hungary?"

"No."

Fouquier, who had realised the bad effect made the day before by the testimony of the policy spy regarding the vouchers signed by the Queen, found at Septeuil's house and then mysteriously lost, summoned the former secretary of the Comité des Vingt-Quatre, a certain J. - B. Garnerin. There was no longer talk of two vouchers, but of one only "in favour of the former Polignac" which had come into the hands of citizen Valazé.

"Have you any remarks on the witness's testimony?" Hermann asked the Queen.

"I repeat that I never signed any vouchers."

On the same subject Valazé supported the Prosecutor. Among the papers that had been through his hands he had noticed two "which concerned the accused."

"The first was a voucher, or rather a receipt signed by her, for the sum of 15 or 20 thousand livres, as far as I can remember. The other document was a letter in which the Minister asked the King to be so good as to communicate to Marie Antoinette the plan of campaign which he had the honour to send him."

The latter document was obviously important and, if it had been produced at the trial, would have been a proof of great value for the prosecution.

"Do you know what has become of these two documents?" asked the President.

"The documents which were used in preparing the indictment of Louis Capet were claimed by the Paris Commune. I believe that now all these documents must have been returned to the Convention's Committee of General Safety."

Hermann avoided drawing attention to the confusion among the files of the young Republic and turned to the accused.

"What have you to say in reply to the witness's testimony?"

"I know nothing of the voucher or the letter he mentions."

Fouquier intervened. "It seems to be proved, in spite of your denials, that through your influence you made the former King, your husband, do whatever you wished."

"There is a great difference between advising that something should be done and having it carried out."

"You can see that it is shown by the witness's declaration that the Ministers were so well aware of your influence on Louis Capet that one of them asked him to inform you of the plan of campaign which had been presented to him a few days earlier, from which it follows that you made use of his weak character to make him carry out many evil deeds, for even supposing that he had followed only the best of your advice, you must admit that it was impossible to make use of worse means for leading France to the brink of the abyss which nearly swallowed her."

"I never knew him to have such a character as you describe," she said calmly.

But the blow had gone home. Admittedly Valazé did not produce the document, but he had seen it. He was, of course, a Girondin, and in prison, that is, a "counter-revolutionary," but to the jurors the former deputy to the Convention, the ex-member of the Committee of Vingt-Quatre, was the man who had drafted Louis XVI's indictment. He may have been suspect, but his testimony had the "official" ring of a man on oath, and it was with a certain feeling of anguish that the Queen left the court when the sitting was suspended.

When it was resumed a whole series of *commissaires* of the Commune and former municipal officers followed: Nicolas Lebœuf, August Jobert, Antoine Moëlle, J. - B. Vincent, Nicolas Beugnot. Their testimony concerning the life of prisoners in the Temple did not bring much for the prosecution. These "citizens" had "seen nothing," "noticed nothing," and had never had any conversation with the prisoners, or at least so they said. But some of their replies made the Queen's heart beat faster. On several occasions the names of "Thérèse Capet" and, in particular, "little Capet" were heard in the court.

"I would point out to you that as regards these facts your testimony is in opposition to your son's."

"It is easy to make a child of eight say whatever one wants."

"But there was not just one declaration. He was made to repeat it several times and on several occasions; he always said the same thing."

"Well, I deny the facts."

The testimony of Brunier, doctor to the little King and Madame Royale, once more reminded her of those from whom she was parted. Hébert, who had been silent for a long time, became excited and reproached the doctor "with having never approached the children of the accused without all the servility of the old régime."

"It was correct behaviour, not servility," exclaimed Brunier, whom Marie Antoinette had formerly blamed for his familiarity.

When Renée Sévin, Marie Antoinette's former "under waiting-woman," gave evidence there was laughter.

"In what part of the château did you sleep?"

"At the end of the Pavillion de Flore."

"In the night of the 9th-10th did you hear the tocsin ring and the alarum sound?"

"No, I slept in the attic."

"What! You slept in the attic and you did not hear the tocsin?"

"No, I was ill."

"And through what chance were you present at the royal review?"

"I was up at six o'clock."

"What! You were ill and you rose at six o'clock?"

"It was because I heard a noise."

"On the previous evening did you see the unusual mustering of the Swiss Guards and the rascals who had taken their uniform?"

"On that day I did not go down into the courtyard."

"But you must have gone down to take your meals?"

"I did not go out. A servant brought my meals."

"But this servant must have told you what was going on?"

"I never held any conversation with him."

"It would seem that you have passed all your life at court and have learned how to dissimulate."

Hermann then asked the Police Administrator Dangé some curious questions.

"What is your opinion of the accused?"

"If she is guilty she should be judged."

"Do you think she is a patriot?"

"No."

"Do you think she wants a republic?"

"No."

At half-past four the sitting was suspended. The Queen had eaten nothing since the morning.

"The accused is not coming down; they are asking for soup," Mme Bault informed her pretty servant.

"I immediately took some excellent soup which I was keeping ready on my stove," Rosalie recounted, "and I went up to the Princess. I was just about to enter the hall when one of the police officers called Labuzière, who was short and snub-nosed, snatched the soup-dish from my hands and, giving it to his mistress, who was young and covered with finery, he said to me: 'This young woman is very eager to see the widow Capet; it is a *charming* opportunity for her.' The woman went off at once, carrying the soup, which was half spilt. In vain I begged and prayed Labuzière. He was all-powerful and I had to obey. What must the Queen have thought when she received her soup from the hand of a person she did not know!"

It was nearly night when the sitting was resumed. Here and there in the large room a few candles were placed and behind the judges two wall-lamps with reflectors were lighted.

The interminable procession went on. The Queen followed the debates attentively. Michonis and Fontaine took her through the backstage events of the conspiracy of the carnation, about which she probably knew nothing. The trial dragged on with evidence of no interest: Tavernier, lieutenant on duty at the Tuileries on 20 June, who spoke of Lafayette; Jean Lebrasse, lieutenant of the gendarmerie, who again recalled "the carnation scene"; the painter Boze, who did a portrait "of the former King," but who had never spoken to the accused. For some unknown reason Fouquier had him arrested as he left the court. There was Michel Gointre, who accused the Queen of having had forged assignats made. Finally there was the usher Jourdeuil, who claimed to have found a letter from Marie Antoinette at the house of d'Affry, commander of the Swiss Guards. "Can one count on your Swiss?" the Queen was alleged to have asked the officer. "Will they make a good showing when the time comes?"

"I never wrote to d'Affry," Marie Antoinette exclaimed.

Faced with this new document, which was mentioned but not put in evidence, Fouquier felt obliged to bring himself into the matter.

"Last year, when I was leader of the prosecuting jury to the Tribunal of 10 August, I was entrusted with the preliminary examination of the trial of d'Affry and Cazotte. I well remember having seen the letter mentioned by the witness, but the Roland faction, having succeeded in abolishing the Tribunal, had the papers removed by means of a decree which they rushed through in spite of the protests of all good republicans."

With equal relevance Hermann asked: "At the time of your marriage to Louis Capet, did you not conceive the project of uniting Lorraine with Austria?"

"No."

"You bear its name?"

"Because one must bear the name of one's country."

Without any transition the President continued: "Did you not investigate feeling in the departments, districts and municipalities?"

"No."

Fouquier rose, triumphantly.

"There was found in your desk a document proving this fact conclusively, in which are written the names of the Vaublancs, Jaucourts, etc."

"The said document was read. The accused persisted in saying that she could not remember having written anything of the kind."

Hermann put his last question.

"Why, when you had promised to bring up your children in the principles of the Revolution, did you instil errors in them, for example by treating your son with a deference which made it appear that you still thought that one day you would see him succeed the former King, his father?"

"He was too young to be spoken to of that. I set him at the top of the table and myself gave him what he needed."

"Have you nothing more to add in your defence?"

Marie Antoinette rose.

"Yesterday," she declared with surprising cleverness, "I did not know the witnesses. I was ignorant of what they would testify. Well, no one has uttered anything positive against me. I end by remarking that I was only Louis XVI's wife and that I was bound to submit to his will."

The debates were over. The sitting was suspended. It was midnight.

When it was resumed Fouquier turned to the jurors. If the report is to be believed the Prosecutor attacked "the perverse conduct of the former court," rather than the Queen. Only at the end did he declare that he looked on the accused "as the declared enemy of the French nation, as one of the principal instigators of the disturbances in France during the past four years to which thousands of French had fallen victims."

Tronson du Coudray and Chauveau-Lagarde followed him. According to the report "they discharged this duty with as much zeal as eloquence." But Hébert has given us some details in his *Père Duchesne*.

"Is it possible that there should exist a rogue bold enough to defend her! And yet two babblers from the law-courts had that audacity. One of them carried his effrontery so far as to say that the Nation owed her too much to punish her and to assert that without her, without the crimes for which she is blamed, we should not be free! I cannot understand, damn it! how it can be endured that low-class pettifoggers, lured by the spoils of scoundrels, by a gold box, a watch, or diamonds, should betray their conscience and try to pull the wool over the jurors' eyes. I myself saw these two devil's advocates not only dance like cats on hot bricks to prove the slut's innocence, but actually dare to weep for the death of the traitor Capet and say to the judges that it was enough to have punished the fat pig and that at least his trollop of a wife should be pardoned!"

Chauveau-Lagarde pleaded for two hours regarding "the alleged conspiracy with foreign Powers." When he had finished the Queen murmured "in the most touching voice": "How tired you must be, Monsieur Chauveau-Lagarde! I am very sensible of all your trouble."

Fouquier suspended the sitting and called a gendarme. Chauveau-Lagarde was arrested in court. In spite of this warning, Tronson du Coudray pleaded with equal zeal "on the alleged conspiracy, on the enemies of the interior," and he underwent the same fate as his colleague. He was carefully searched, and on him were found two little gold rings and a lock of the Queen's hair, which she had asked her lawyer to give to a "citizen Mary or Maray," living at Ligny with citizen La Borde. This was Mme de Jarjayes.

Meanwhile the debates were resumed and Hermann pronounced an indictment.

"Today a great example is given to the universe and it will doubtless not be lost on the peoples inhabiting it. Nature and reason, so long outraged, are at last satisfied. Equality triumphs.

"A woman who was formerly surrounded with all the brilliant splendour that the pride of Kings and the servility of slaves could invent, now occupies in the Tribunal of the nation the place occupied two days ago by another woman, and this equality assures for her impartial justice. This affair, citizen jurors, is not one of those in which a single deed, a single crime is submitted to your conscience and your intelligence. You have to judge the accused's whole political life since she came to sit beside the last King of the French. But above all you must consider the manoeuvres which she has never for a moment ceased to employ to destroy the budding liberty, either at home, by her intimate connections with base Ministers, treacherous generals and faithless representatives of the people, or abroad, by negotiating that monstrous coalition of European despots which Europe will ridicule for its impotence and by her correspondence with the former émigré French Princes and their worthy agents."

Hermann had been a lawyer too long not to be obsessed by the absence of documents.

"The material proof," he explained, "is in the papers which were seized from Louis Capet and listed in a report made to the National Convention by Gohier, one of its members, in the collection of documents relevant to the indictment of Louis Capet by the Convention, and finally, and above all, citizen jurors, in the political events which you have all witnessed and judged."

In default of these absent documents, which should have proved "the accusation of high treason which lies heavily on Antoinette of Austria, widow of the former King," Hermann and Fouquier had only one resource—to assimilate the Queen's trial with the King's (a trial which in any case was only an elimination) and to affirm that she was "the instigator of most of the crimes of which the last tyrant of France was guilty."

"There is a general observation to be noted," Hermann went on, "which is that the accused agrees that she had the confidence of Louis Capet. It also emerges from the testimony of Valazé that Marie Antoinette was consulted on political matters, since the former King wished her to be consulted about a certain plan, whose object the witness either could not or would not declare."

He quickly tried to take from each witness's evidence one fact to illustrate his main accusation, but there was nothing to prove "intelligence with foreign Powers," or plots against the safety of the State. There was nothing but cockades distributed, empty bottles found under the Queen's bed on 10 August and "desires for vengeance" observed in the accused's expression. He shrank only from Hébert's plot, which he did not dare mention. He also slid prudently over the carnation affair.

"I shall not speak to you, citizen jurors, of the incident in the Conciergerie, the interview with the Chevalier de Saint-Louis, the carnation left in the accused's room and the paper pricked, or rather prepared for a reply. This incident is not more than a prison intrigue which can have no place in an indictment of such great importance."

In the final sentence of the indictment one can again feel the embarrassment of a lawyer confronted by an absence of documents.

"I end by a general reflection, which I have already made to you: it is the French people who accuse Antoinette. All the political events of the last five years testify against her."

The jurors were asked four questions:

(1) Is it established that there were intrigues and secret dealings with foreign Powers and other external enemies of the Republic, which intrigues and secret dealings aimed at giving them monetary assistance, enabling them to enter French territory and facilitating the progress of their armies there?

(2) Is Marie Antoinette d'Autriche, widow of Louis Capet, *convicted* of having co-operated in these intrigues and of having kept up these secret dealings?

(3) Is it established that there was a plot and conspiracy to start civil war within the Republic?

(4) Is Marie Antoinette d'Autriche, widow of Louis Capet, *con-*

victed of having taken part in this plot and conspiracy?

It was three o'clock in the morning.

When the jurors retired the judges remained in the *Grand-Chambre*. The public, who in spite of the cold had remained for the end of the pleadings, went into the waiting-room, which was almost in total darkness, to join the little groups of interested spectators, friends of the Queen, or Jacobins, striding up and down the room to get warm. Here and there in the darkness could be seen a few policemen, listening. Even Ducâtel, one of the murderers of the Princesse de Lamballe, was there, wandering from group to group. Outside there were not, as Hébert was to say, "two or three hundred thousand *sans-culottes* surrounding the Palace, and waiting in silence," but a few hundred sightseers.

Was she guilty? The trial had not proved it. Juridically she was innocent. Taking away the low gossip, the tittle-tattle of kitchens, backstairs, clubs and the Temple council room, what positive facts for the prosecution remained? The description of "orgies" at Versailles by witnesses who had not been there, the accusation—without any documents to support it—regarding the sums given to the Polignacs, the Queen's influence over her husband vouched for by people who had never been intimate with the royal family. Nothing, absolutely nothing, on what Fouquier called treason.

The trial had in no way shown that Marie Antoinette, more of an Austrian Princess than a Queen of France, obeyed orders from her mother and brother transmitted by Mercy. Nothing had been established, neither her culpable frivolity, her blind friendships, her fatal influence, her intrigues with foreign Powers, nor her vacillating policy, her over-tenacious rancour, her double game in 1791 and her "treachery" in 1792. But for everyone these were obvious facts. The way in which the second and fourth questions were worded, however, would have enabled the jurors to answer "no." Although guilty, the accused was not *convicted* of being so.

Such was the unanimous opinion. Mme Bault had just heard someone exclaim: "Marie Antoinette will get away with it. She gave her answers like an angel. They will only deport her."

This optimism was not blindness. It was still only the beginning of the Terror. The law on "suspects" was only a month old. The machine of death, prepared by Fouquier, started work with the Queen's trial.

In a room adjoining the *Grand-Chambre* Marie Antoinette waited in company with Lieutenant de Busne. The Queen, too, was full of hope. As she had said, no one had uttered anything positive against her. Her throat was dry from anxiety and she asked for something to drink. De Busne brought her a glass of water.

At four o'clock the Queen heard the President's bell in the distance. The minutes went slowly by. She could distinguish the voice of Hermann, who was exhorting the crowd "to the greatest possible calm" and reminding them "that the law forbade them any sign of approbation and that a person once overtaken by the law, with whatever crimes she might be covered, belonged only to unhappiness and humanity."

An usher came to fetch the accused. She was greeted by a menacing silence as she took her place on the platform. Chauveau-Lagarde and Tronson du Coudray, escorted by gendarmes, were also brought back into the hall. Hermann addressed the Queen with familiarity.

"Antoinette, here is the jury's declaration."

In dying Antonia was to return to her childhood's name.

As in a dream she heard: "Yes, to all the questions." Then Fouquier was heard, demanding "that the accused be condemned to death, in accordance with Article One of the first section of the first chapter of the second part of the penal code, which reads: 'All intrigue, all intelligence with the enemies of France tending either to facilitate their entry into the territories of the French Empire, or to deliver up to them towns, fortresses, ports, vessels, magazines or arsenals belonging to France, or to furnish them aid in soldiers, money, food or munitions, or to favour in any manner whatever the progress of their armies on French territory, or against our forces by land or sea, or to undermine the loyalty of officers, soldiers and other citizens towards the French Nation, shall be punished by death.'"

By death! Those must have been the only words she grasped from the text. These two syllables held the beginning and end of its pathos. But the dry, cutting voice continued: "And again, in Article Eleven of the first section of the first chapter of the second part of the same code it reads: 'All conspiracy and plots tending to disturb the State by civil war, by arming citizens one against the other or aimed against the exercise of the legitimate authority, shall be punished by death.'"

"Antoinette," resumed the President, "have you any objection to make to the application of the laws invoked by the Public Prosecutor?"

She had no strength to reply and merely shook her head.

Hermann then turned to the two defenders surrounded by their guards and put the same question.

"Citizen President," replied Tronson du Coudray, speaking as a lawyer attentive to formalities, "the jury's declaration being definite and the law in this respect clear, I announce that my services to the widow Capet are ended."

Hermann turned towards Douzé-Verteuil and Lane. The plumed heads bowed. For the last time Hermann spoke.

"The Tribunal, according to the unanimous declaration of the jury, which complied with the indictment of the Public Prosecutor, and according to the laws quoted by him, condemns the said Marie Antoinette, called Lorraine d'Autriche, widow of Louis Capet, to the pain of death; declares, in accordance with the law of 10 March last, that her possessions, if she has any within the territory of France, are acquired and confiscated for the benefit of the Republic and orders that, at the request of the Public Prosecutor, the present judgement shall be executed in the Place de la Révolution and printed and displayed throughout the Republic."

Overcome, she left the platform like an automaton. Without a gesture, her head down, "seeing and hearing nothing," according to Chauveau-Lagarde, she crossed the hall. When she arrived at the railings, where even the *tricoteuses* had fallen silent, she raised her head and left the hall. De Busne escorted her bareheaded. On arriving at the darkened Bonbec staircase which led to the courtyard, she murmured: "I can hardly see to walk."

The officer gave her his arm to the foot of the stairs. A few steps farther on she nearly slipped and de Busne helped her down the three steps leading to the courtyard. It was cold, barely 35 degrees, but the sky was clear. With their faces pressed against the bars of their cells the prisoners watched, in the feeble light of the yard lamp, the Queen of France go by with her hand on the arm of her last bodyguard.

Meanwhile the *Grand-Chambre* was slowly emptying.

It was an assembly of dying men who went their ways. Of the Prosecutor, the President and the six judges, only Douzé-Verteuil, Deliège and Maire would escape the guillotine, but the last-named was to slip one day on his hearth and perish with his head burned.

Chauveau-Lagarde survived, but Tronson du Coudray, a proscript of Fructidor, was deported and disappeared in Guiana.

Fourteen of the witnesses were to climb Sanson's ladder,[1] and three to perish by a violent death. Mme Richard was stabbed by a prisoner, the gendarme Gilbert blew his brains out for having embezzled his company's money, and the Girondin Valazé, hearing he was condemned to death, stabbed himself twelve days later in the same *Grand-Chambre*, and his body was carried to the foot of the scaffold.

Of the twelve jurors there were to escape only three, who when the trouble was over went to ground. Renaudin, Nicolas, Châtelet, Besnard and Deboisseaux mounted the scaffold. Trinchard, Antonelle, Jourdeuil and Chrétien were deported to Cayenne or "to the islands."

But during this night of 15-16 October they thought only of eating the lavish repast Fouquier had ordered to be prepared for them. They were convinced of having done their duty, as can be seen from the carpenter Trinchard, who proudly wrote the following note to his brother: "Je t'aprans, mon frerre, que jé été un des jurés qui ont jugé la bête féroche qui a dévoré un grande partie de la République, celle que lon califiait cideven de Raine." (I inform you, my brother, that I was one of the jurors who judged the mad beast who devoured a large part of the Republic, she who was formerly called Queen).

[1] Bailly, Manuel, Simon, Hébert, Jobert, Leb œuf, Michonis, Lecointre, Vincent, Dangé, Lebrasse, Estaing and the two La Tour du Pin.

21

✤

The Knife

"There is something worse than regicide there."

Napoleon.

SHE HAD BEEN able to obtain two candles, a sheet of paper, a pen and ink. While de Busne dozed in the corner of the cell, she sat down at her little white-wood table, and this woman who had lived through two days and one night of trial, this woman weakened by hæmorrhages, who had undergone a final session lasting more than twenty hours, was to write, while waiting for her executioner, the admirable letter which should be read yet once again.

"It is to you, my sister, that I write for the last time. I have just been condemned, not to a shameful death, for it is shameful only for criminals, but to rejoin your brother. Like him innocent, I hope to display the same firmness as he did in his last moments. I am calm, as one is when one's conscience holds no reproach. I regret deeply having to abandon my poor children. You know that I lived only for them and for you, my good and kind sister. In what a situation do I leave you, who from your affection sacrificed everything to be with us. I learned from the pleadings at the trial that my daughter was separated from you.[1] Alas! poor child, I dare not write to her, she would not receive it. I do not know even if this will reach you. Receive my blessing on them both. I hope that one day, when they are older, they will be able to join you again and profit to the full from your tender care

[1] Madame Elisabeth and Madame Royale were questioned *separately* in the apartment occupied by the Simons and the little King. Hence the Queen's misapprehension on hearing the report of the interrogations.

and that they both remember what I have always tried to instil in them: that the principles and the execution of their duty should be the chief foundation of their life, that their affection and mutual trust will make it happy. Let my daughter remember that in view of her age she should always help her brother with the advice that her greater experience and her affection may suggest, and let them both remember that in whatever situation they may find themselves they will never be truly happy unless united. Let them learn from our example how much consolation our affection brought us in the midst of our unhappiness and how happiness is doubled when one can share it with a friend—and where can one find a more loving and truer friend than in one's own family? Let my son never forget his father's last words, which I distinctly repeat to him, never to try to avenge our death. I have to mention something which pains my heart. I know how much distress this child must have given you. Forgive him, my dear sister, remember his age and how easy it is to make a child say anything you want, even something he does not understand. The day will come, I hope, when he will be all the more conscious of the worth of your goodness and tenderness towards them both. I now have only to confide in you my last thoughts. I would have liked to write them at the beginning of the trial, but apart from the fact that I was not allowed to write, everything went so quickly that I really would not have had the time.

"I die in the Catholic, Apostolic and Roman religion, in the religion of my father, in which I was brought up and which I have always professed, having no expectation of spiritual consolation, and not even knowing if there still exist any priests of that religion here, and in any case the place where I am would expose them to too much danger if they should enter. I sincerely beg pardon of God for all the faults I have committed during my life. I hope that in His goodness He will receive my last wishes, and those I have long since made, that He may receive my soul in His mercy and goodness. I ask pardon of all those I know, and of you my sister in particular, for all the distress I may, without wishing it, have caused them. I forgive all my enemies the harm they have done me. I say farewell here to my aunts and to all my brothers and sisters. I had friends. The idea of being separated for ever from them and their troubles forms one of my greatest regrets in dying. Let them know, at least, that up to my last moment I was thinking of them.

"Farewell, my good and loving sister. May this letter reach you! Think of me always. I embrace you with all my heart, together with those poor, dear children. My God! what agony it is to leave them for ever! Farewell! Farewell! I shall henceforth pay attention to nothing but my spiritual duties. As I am not free, they will perhaps bring me a [conformist] priest, but I protest here that I shall not say a word to him and that I shall treat him as a complete stranger."

At five o'clock the call to arms was sounded in Paris and cannons were placed "in strategic positions." At seven o'clock all the troops were mustered and patrols were scouring the streets. Day was just breaking when Rosalie entered the condemned woman's cell. The two candles had burned out.

A young officer of the gendarmes was standing in the left-hand corner of the room. It was no longer de Busne. He had just been arrested, on the denunciation of one of his men, who had seen him give the Queen a glass of water and walk back with her bareheaded.

Marie Antoinette had not undressed. Still wearing her black dress, she was stretched out on her bed. She wept quietly, facing the window, with her head resting on her hand.

"Madame," said Rosalie in a trembling voice, "you ate nothing yesterday evening and hardly anything all day. What would you like this morning?"

"My child, I need nothing. Everything is over for me."

Rosalie insisted. "Madame, I have been keeping some soup on my stove . . ."

Rosalie was weeping, too, and began to leave. The Queen called her back, fearing to have distressed her, and between two sobs whispered: "Well, Rosalie, bring me your soup."

She sat up, but could eat only a few spoonfuls.

"Come back at eight to help me dress."

She remained lying down for an hour, letting her mind wander among her memories. A pale light filtered through the barred windows. She watched her last day dawn. It was the feast of the Ox, which had replaced that of St. Gal, Priest.

Gradually the condemned woman pulled herself together, and when Rosalie returned trembling to the cell Marie Antoinette asked her to help in changing her chemise for the last time. She had lost much blood since the previous day. The unhappy woman laid her clean chemise out on the bed, slipped into the little passage between the camp bed and the wall and let fall her black dress. At a gesture from the Queen the young servant came and stood in front of her, but the officer of the gendarmerie came forward, leaned over the bolster and watched.

"In the name of decency, Monsieur, allow me to change my linen without witnesses."

"I could not permit it," the man replied shortly. "My orders are that I must keep an eye on all your movements."

The Queen sighed, and "with all the precautions and modesty possible" took off her stained chemise. Over the clean one she put on the white négligée she usually wore in the morning. She then took a large muslin fichu, which she folded high under her chin, and put on a white bonnet without a mourning veil. Rosalie then saw her "carefully roll up her pitiful bloodstained chemise, tuck it in one of its own sleeves, as in a sheath," and then "look anxiously around her as though seeking some object she feared not to find." Suddenly, with "an expression of ineffable satisfaction," she slipped the soiled linen into a hole she had just noticed in the wall behind a torn part of the hangings.

Without daring to say goodbye, Rosalie left her and the dreadful waiting began. In her thin white piqué négligée Marie Antoinette was trembling with cold. The Abbé Girard, a conforming priest sent by the Tribunal, advised her to put her pillow over her knees. He then offered her "the services of his ministry." She refused.

"But Madame, what will be said when it is known that you refused the help of religion in these final moments?"

"You will tell those who speak of it to you that God's mercy provided for it."[1]

The priest asked timidly: "May I accompany you, Madame?"

"If you wish."

A few moments later she asked the gendarme: "Do you think the people will let me go to the scaffold without tearing me in pieces?"

Larivière entered the cell and Marie Antoinette said to him in a small voice: "Larivière, you know they are going to put me to death?"

At the same hour conspirators were going towards the Rue Saint-Honoré, along which the condemned woman was to pass. As they went

[1] For the "Queen's communion," see the chapter "Sources," pp. 418-420.

to their posts they were full of hope. They would shortly number 500—1,500 even, some thought—and they would rush at the cart.

Who were these last defenders of Marie Antoinette, who were to lose their lives in trying to save that of the Queen? Former bodyguards? Former officers of the Queen's Household? Former friends from the Trianon, who would once have died to kiss their sovereign's rosy finger-tips?

No. At the head of the conspiracy was a former working-woman, who had lost her sight making lace—a hunchback from Auvergne, called Catherine Urgon, wife of Fournier. Her staff was composed of her son, a fourteen-year-old boot-black, and two barbers: Guillaume Lemille and Jean-Baptiste Basset. The latter, who was eighteen-and-a-half years old, had managed by himself to win over 460 men. Their headquarters were in a wine-shop in the Rue de la Vannerie, at the sign of *La Cave des Charbonniers.* The principal lieutenants were two locksmiths, three pastrycooks, two wine-sellers, two grocers, two butchers, two conveyors, two masons, a knife-grinder, a house painter, a gardener, a second-hand dealer, a lemonade-seller and four barbers. All lived in the *Section des Incorruptibles,* otherwise called the *Section des Arcis,* which lay to the north of the Place de Grève, a stone's throw from the Conciergerie. Their rallying-sign was a little round card bearing a heart in its centre, with all round the words "Long live Louis XVII, King of France."

Their main "forces" had been recruited from among the Volunteers barracked at Vanves and Courbevoie. There was talk of 1,500 men, and the blind, hunchbacked lace-maker knew how to speak to them.

"We do not want men who talk! We need brave men, people who can strike! They must all be Charlotte Cordays!"

At the beginning of the month they had wanted to storm the Conciergerie.

"We must act at once," cried one of the barbers. "Otherwise this unhappy woman will perish!"

Their arms consisted of 1,500 pistols. Their plan was ingenious, and came from young Basset. In the daytime they would light all the street lamps in the quarter so that, for lack of oil, they would go out during the night. Under cover of the darkness there would then have been a mass attack on the Conciergerie.

But six police spies got wind of the plan. Posing as ardent royalists, they managed to gain the barbers' confidence and have the attack on the prison postponed and held back for so long that the trial had already begun.

The hunchback then exhibited "a terrible despair." "There is not a moment to be lost in saving the poor Queen. It is absolutely essential that orders should be given to rally and kidnap the condemned woman on the way."

And the order was given to the conspirators to go to the Rue Saint-Honoré.

At the same time Hermann entered the cell with the judges Foucauld and Douzé-Verteuil. Fabricius followed them, holding a large sheet of paper. The condemned woman, who was kneeling by her bed, praying, rose.

"Pay attention," declared Hermann. "Your sentence will be read to you."

Contrary to custom the four men dressed in black took off their hats. They seemed "struck" by the majestic air of the condemned woman, who raised her voice to declare: "It is useless to read it; I know the sentence only too well."

"No matter," declared one of the judges. "It must be read to you a second time."

And the words as sharp as knives sounded in the low vaulted cell: ". . . . complied with . . . condemned . . . declares . . . orders . . . executed . . ."

The clerk had just uttered the word "Republic," which ended the decree, when, followed by Nappier, the usher to the Tribunal, a young man entered—the executioner.

He was Henri Sanson, son of the executioner who had guillotined Louis XVI and who since 21 January no longer exercised his duties. He came forward, seeming to fill the cell with his "enormous size."

"Hold out your hands."

The Queen recoiled two steps and asked in a frightened voice: "Are my hands to be bound?"

The executioner bowed his head. She exclaimed: "Louis XVI's hands were not bound!"

Sanson turned towards Hermann, who ordered: "Do your duty."

"Oh, my God!" cried the condemned woman, "all bewildered."

"At these words," Larivière recounted, "Henri brutally seized the poor Queen's hands and bound them too tightly behind her back. I saw that the Princess sighed, raising her eyes to heaven, but she held back her tears, which were ready to flow."

Then Sanson, who towered over Marie Antoinette, suddenly took off the bonnet she had arranged so carefully a short while before, and with a large pair of scissors cut off the wonderful hair which had gone white, but in which ash-blonde lights could still be seen.

The Queen thought she was to be executed there with an axe and she turned round, her eyes terrified. She saw the executioner putting in his pocket the hair, which was shortly to be burned. With his large hands he replaced the bonnet on the top of the Queen's head. Irregularly cut locks surrounded the freed nape.

It was nearly eleven o'clock.

The bystanders moved away from the door. In silence Marie Antoinette left the cell, followed by the executioner holding the ends of the rope, which pulled at her elbows. Walking between a double row of gendarmes, she reached the office and suddenly her eyes filled with horror. Beyond the rails of the little courtyard, beyond the two doors which had just been opened, she had caught sight of the ignominious cart. Louis XVI had gone to death in a coach. She would have to mount that garbage cart! A weakness seized her. She asked them to undo her hands and there, on the ground, in a corner of the office which was called the Mousetrap, she squatted down, then went and held out her hands again to Sanson.

The picture of the Archduchess, the features of that "charming and dangerous favourite of an old monarchy" become blurred and are effaced. Everything disappears—and should disappear—leaving to posterity only the picture of a woman in a white dress, walking to the guillotine like a true Queen of France.

The temperature was a little warmer—45 degrees at eleven o'clock. The weather was fine; a light mist, that indefinable Paris mist, blurred the horizon. In the Cour de Mai gendarmes on foot and on horseback, together with pikemen, surrounded the muddy cart. Here, in the happy years, the lawyers' clerks planted a beribboned may-tree each spring, a fine oak which the clerks went "in full battle array" to find in the forest of Bondy.

In the Rue de la Barillerie the crowd huddled in silence behind the beautiful gilt railings.

The white figure, which seemed to be held in leash by the executioner, appeared under the arcade, took a few steps and stopped by the cart. A small ladder of four or five steps had been placed there. The executioner showed the Queen where to put her foot and supported her with his hand while, holding her head high, she mounted the tail-board. It was noticed that she wore a black petticoat under her white dress. A narrow, uneven plank was fixed more or less securely to the sides, cutting the cart in two. She was about to step over it and sit down facing the two cart-horses, who were harnessed in tandem to the shafts. But the executioner and his assistant stopped her; she was to sit facing backwards.

The Abbé Girard climbed the ladder in his turn and sat down on the right of the condemned woman. Behind them, leaning on the rails, stood the executioner, holding the rope in one hand and his three-cornered hat in the other. His assistant, also bare-headed, was at the back.

It was a quarter-past eleven.

The cart set off noisily. The actor Grammont, on horseback and carrying a sword, preceded it; the gendarmes surrounded it; the pike-men followed.

The great gateway opened. The crowd was silent. Without a murmur or an insult they watched the passing of the woman whom they had acclaimed twenty years before. Marie Antoinette appeared unmoved and seemed to see nothing with her motionless, bloodshot eyes. As they crossed the bridge did she look at the towers of the Conciergerie, her last palace? Fouquier had no doubt left his files to watch the procession from his window.

Thirty thousand troops were lined along the route. At the entrance to the Rue Saint-Honoré the cries of hate could be heard. For a moment the cart stopped. Marie Antoinette looked round her. A smiling child, lifted up by its mother, blew her a kiss. The blood rushed into her cheeks and her eyes filled with tears.

At that moment the little King was laughing in the Temple with his municipal officers, while in the crypt of Saint-Denis the coffin of the first Dauphin, who had died at Meudon four years before, was being opened by order of the Convention and the body thrown into the common burying-ground.

The cart started with a jerk, amid cries. The Queen nearly lost her balance. A mocking voice shouted: "Ah! those aren't your cushions from Trianon!"

Cries of "Make way for the Austrian!" and "Long live the Republic!" broke out, but Marie Antoinette did not seem to hear. Her eyes rested unmoved on the narrow fronts of the houses, where tricolour flags and revolutionary signs waved gently.

The cart passed by the arcade over the passage leading to the Jacobins. A board carried the inscription–"Workshop of Republican arms to strike down the tyrants." She appeared not to have been able to read it, and for the first time turned to the priest and questioned him. The Abbé, who from the beginning had kept his eyes fixed on a small ivory crucifix, was about to reply, when suddenly Grammont "raised his sword, brandished it in all directions" and rising in his stirrups yelled: "Here she is, the wicked Antoinette! She is done for, my friends!"

He was answered by shouts. On the steps of the church of Saint Roch the *tricoteuses,* wearing red bonnets and carrying pikes, yelled.

The Rue Saint-Honoré seemed endless. And yet she knew it well. How many evenings had she gone down it in her carriage drawn by eight white horses! As she passed, the cannon in the Invalides fired a salvo and then, in the distance, that of the Bastille answered. Paris mobilised its guards and its cavalry of the watch to guard its sovereign. Paris placed twelve cannons in the Place Louis-XV which fired when twenty of the King's bodyguard galloped past surrounding the gold and silver carriage in which a young woman in evening dress and an extravagant headdress, almost lost in her glittering skirts, laughed so attractively.

The young Queen of twenty, the young Queen of the most beautiful kingdom in the world was going to the Opera.

On this October morning she was going to the scaffold.

The crowd became even thicker. Not far from Robespierre's house, and in front of the house numbered 404, a mother, hearing the procession approach, said to her daughter: "Above all, don't cry when you see her. You will have us guillotined."

The cart passed. "It bumped on the cobbles and could be heard to crack as though it would break." A woman's cry lashed the Queen.

"Death to the Austrian!"

She looked with an "expression of contempt," which faded at once. She had recognised a former waiting-woman from the château. Did she also perceive, at the corner of the street, a group of "honest folk," simply dressed? They were the defeated barbers. They numbered barely

eighty: about thirty small shop-keepers and workmen from the Arcis
quarter and 52 volunteers from Vanves. The spies had acted. The police
had done their work and "infiltrated" the movement. In vain did the
little boot-black cry out in despair: "We must go to the big merchants,
who want nothing better than to snatch her from the executioners!"

The wig-makers realised that everything was over.

The cart had gone by.

They remained there, deserted, haggard, waiting for the police to
pick them up.[1]

Noon struck.

Since eight in the morning the Place de la Révolution had been
filling up. It was now black with people.

When the cart was seen coming from the former Rue Royale, the
applause broke out and cries of "Long live the Republic!" were heard.
"The aristocrats are easily recognized," wrote a police-agent, "by their
closed lips and embarrassed faces."

It was a few minutes past noon.

The cart rattled over the uneven ground of the square. The Queen
was still impassive. "The slut was audacious and insolent to the end,"
Hébert was to remark. She turned her head, saw the Tuileries on her
right, changed colour and "became much paler." With a few more
turns of the wheels the cart arrived at the place of execution. The
cries and applause grew louder and hats flew in the air. The Queen
was still looking to her right. Through the great alley she could now
see the façade of the château. Twenty years ago, on the evening of
her joyful entry, the crowd packed in the Place Louis-XV applauded
just as today, and the men threw their hats in the air, when Marie
Antoinette and her husband appeared on the terrace. "Tears of affection
mingled with the cries of joy each time that M. le Dauphin and Mme
la Dauphine had the goodness to give the citizens signs of their
satisfaction."

"You have two thousand adorers there, Madame!"

The cart stopped.

Rapidly and without accepting any help, Marie Antoinette got
down, turned round and saw the two raised arms holding the heavy
triangle of steel. She hurried, climbed the steep ladder with such pre-

[1] The epilogue to the "Barbers' Conspiracy" was played out before the Tribunal.
See the chapter, "Sources," p. 422.

cipitation, "in bravado" one witness wrote, that she lost one of her little purple shoes *à la Saint Huberty*. On reaching the platform she trod on the executioner's foot.

"Monsieur, I ask your pardon. I did not do it on purpose."

These were her last words.

Marie Antoinette looked at the vast square around her. The assistants came forward. With a movement she let fall the bonnet from her head. She shut her eyes and felt that she was being dragged to the upright plank. She was tied on. It took long—horribly long. Finally the plank tipped over and she felt the heavy wooden collar fixed round her bared neck.

A click.

It was a quarter-past twelve.

Between the moment she appeared on the platform and the moment the crowd heard the dull noise four minutes had passed. One of the assistants picked up the head dripping with blood, held it up by the white hair and, to applause, carried it round the scaffold.

Suddenly the gendarmes in the front rank were seen to rush forward and arrest a man who had come out from beneath the scaffold. His shoes were covered with blood, he held a white handkerchief in his hand which was also bloodstained and between his teeth was a carnation.[1]

While he was being taken to the Tuileries section the crowd parted to make way for the cart streaming with blood. Its path could be traced to the Madeleine cemetery. There the executioners noticed that no coffin or grave had been prepared.

Anxious to get their dinners, they threw the body on the grass, the head between the legs.

The mist had quite cleared away, but the wind rose and from the north there came heavy clouds which gradually covered the whole sky.[2]

[1] For further details on this strange affair see "Sources," pp. 421-422.
[2] Archives of the Observatory (National Meteorological Office).

Sources

Would one, on the eve of the Revolution, have found a thousand French people bearing the same sentiments towards Marie Antoinette as we do today? The Queen was then frankly detested. Her martyrdom did not disarm the hate which some people continued to feel for her. To realise this one need only go through the vast files preserved in the National Archives and containing letters and petitions congratulating the Convention and the Revolutionary Tribunal for having rid the world of that "tigress thirsting for blood," that "poisonous viper," that "cannibal woman," "the implacable harridan who for too long profaned the holy land of liberty with her pestilential breath."

In order to make the reasons for this execration understood I wanted to avoid as much as possible following the example of most of my predecessors, who divided the first part of their character's life into a series of subjects (the favourites, the marital drama, Marie Antoinette and her mother, the feasts, the friends, the expenses, etc.). It seemed to me that this procedure did not lead to the presentation of an accurate picture of Marie Antoinette. I preferred to bring the Queen to life by following the chronological order. But in trying to carry out such a plan it was necessary to go back to the sources.

I do not know if I have succeeded with this scheme, but at least it enabled me—in dealing with the Queen's life as well as with that of the "widow Capet"—to lay my hands on numerous documents which have hitherto gone unnoticed and to use these forgotten texts of which one might say that "they were as good as unpublished."

I

VIENNA

I was able to reconstruct this part of Marie Antoinette's life with the help of documents which have never yet been used and which are preserved in the *Minoritenplatz* of Vienna (*Haus-Hof und Staatsarchiv*). Unlike those of the Rue des Francs-Bourgeois these series have not been given a serial number but a title.

Zeremonialakten, Sonderreihe. Bd. 52 (Feast given at the Belvedere Palace on 17 April 1770 and feast given by Durfort at the Liechtenstein

Palace on 28 April 1770; *Hausarchiv. Familienakten Kart.* 50 (Documents concerning the marriage by proxy and the various ceremonies). Little Antonia's history exercise is filed in Box 55 of the *Familienakten* series.

All the correspondence of Mercy, Durfort, Kaunitz, Choiseul is preserved in the archives of the Ministry of Foreign Affairs. I gleaned unpublished details in the collections *France 426, Vienne 285, 307, 308, 310, 311, 312*; and in the *Haus-Hof und Staatsarchiv,* dossier *St. K. Frankreich, Berichte (Fasz. 207, 208, 209, 210).*

Among printed sources the most important are the remarkable study by Maurice Boutry (*Le mariage de Marie-Antoinette*), the Comtesse d'Armaillé's book (*Marie-Thérèse et Marie-Antoinette*) and above all *La Correspondance secrète* between Mercy-Argenteau and Maria Theresa, Kaunitz and Joseph II, full collections published by Arneth, Flammermont and Geffroy, which form the basis of any study of Marie Antoinette. I mention these works here, but, as can be seen, I have obviously made use of them all through my work.

II

FROM VIENNA TO PARIS
and
THE MARRIAGE AT VERSAILLES

I have made use of numerous unpublished details from:

(1) Vienna Archives: *Familienakten Kart.* 50 (Formation of the procession, suite, journey to Günzburg and *Remise*). *St. K. Provinzen, Vorder Osterreich, Fasz.* 10 (The journey, the procession, the stages, etc.).

(2) National Archives: 01.3254 (*Remise,* Strasbourg, marriage feasts), K.1715 (Route and marriage feasts), 01.3791, 01.3793, 01.3797, 01.3252, 01.3253, 01.3254 (Household of Madame la Dauphine), K.506 (Etiquette, ceremonial), 01.1783 (Opera), K.1015 (Evening of 30 May 1770. Report on the accident).

(3) Foreign Affairs: *France 426, France 429, Vienne 285.*

(4) Manuscripts: *Nouvelles à la main* of the House of Penthièvre (Bibl. Mazarine), *Manuscrit de Hardy* (B.N.), *Registre de l'Intendant des Menus* (Mazarine), *Mémoire sinédits* by the Comte de Caraman (in the possession of Mme la Comtesse du Bouchage).

(5) Printed sources: *Mercure de France* (May, June, July and August 1770), *La Gazette* (same months), *Mémoires* by Weber, Goethe, Mme d'Oberkirch, Mme de Boigne, Mme Campan, Croy, etc. *Mémoires secrets, Correspondance* of Mme du Deffand, Mouffle d'Angerville (*Vie privée de Louis XV*) and: works by Pierre de Nolhac (*Marie-Antoinette, dauphine*),

Maurice Boutry (op. cit.), Funck-Brentano (*L'Affaire du collier*, 1st chapter), Lenotre (*Versailles*), L. Dussieux (*Le château de Versailles*), etc.

III

THE DAUPHINE

National Archives: Dossiers cited above and: K.1014, K.1016 (Ceremonial and etiquette), 01.3792, 01.3785, 01.3786, 01.3797 (The Dauphine's household), 01.1044, 01.903 (Death of Louis XV).

Private archives: *Mémoires* of the Comte de Caraman.

Printed sources: To the collections of Mercy's correspondence one must add, once for all, the *Correspondence* of Marie Antoinette edited by La Rocheterie and Beaucourt which is the only one which can be used without misgiving. The letters edited by Feuillet de Conches and by Hunolstein are, indeed, nearly all apocryphal.

Apart from the works already mentioned I used the *Mémoires* of Besenval, *La dernière maladie de Louis XV* by the Duc de Liancourt (published by Paul Cottin in the *Revue Rétrospective*), *Marie-Antoinette et l'art de son temps*, thesis by Jeanne-Armand Bouteloup, *Histoire de la Musique* by Jean Combarieu, *Gluck et Piccini* by Desnoiresterres, *Ch. von Gluck* by A Schmidt, *Histoire de Marie-Antoinette* by La Rocheterie, *Secret du Roi*, by the Duc de Broglie, *Madame du Barry* by Alfred Leroy, *Louis XV* by Pierre Lafue, etc.

IV

THE QUEEN

National Archives: 01.1044 and 01.903 (Accession of Louis XVI), K.1016 and K.1017 (Mourning ceremonial), K.1714, K.161, 01.3250 (Coronation of Louis XVI), K.505 (Accounts, expenses, voyage to Fontainebleau), 01.3791 (Mme de Lamballe, library, wardrobe, economies), 01.3194 (Candles), 01.3792 (Looting by Comte Jules de Polignac, the Queen's wardrobe), 01.3795, 01.3796, 01.3797 (Queen's Household), 01.3793 (Expenses), K.3796 (Saint Cloud), K.159 to K.164 (The King's papers), 01.1883, 01.1072, 01.1885 (Trianon), 01.3193 (*Menus Plaisirs* of Trianon), K.161 (Letter about Joseph II), K. 506 (Visit of Comte de Haga, Comte du Nord and Joseph II; etiquette, life at court), 01.1031, 01.1032 (Equipages), 01.903 (Carriages), 01.3798, 01.3799 (Household of the Children of France), 01.3469 and 01.3470 (Inventory of the château), etc. In the *Armoire de fer* of the Archives is the register containing the samples of Marie Antoinette's dresses. This folder bears the title: *Garde-robe des atours de la Reine. Gazette pour l'année* 1782.

In an important series of dossiers (K.1015 to K.1019) I discovered numerous unpublished details concerning the births of the Children of France, Marie Antoinette's lyings-in, the Dauphin's illness, the presents offered to him, his funeral, the mourning, the Queen's visits to Paris, her journey in a *hyac,* her evenings at the Opera, the feasts given in her honour, the gigantic fish brought to Versailles and, in general, the relations between the "Gentlemen" of the city and the royal family. These dossiers are supplemented by unpublished information coming from the King's Household or the Queen's: 01.3791 (entry into Paris), 01.3260 and K.161 (Births of the Children of France), K.903 (Illness and burial of the Dauphin).

Memoirs, Souvenirs, Diary: Works already mentioned, and: Tilly (edited by Christian Melchior-Bonnet), d'Hézèques, Ligne, Lauzun, Vigée-Lebrun, Saint-Priest (edited by Marcel Thiébaut), Levis, Augeard, Tourzel, La Marck, Papillon de La Ferté, Diane de Polignac, Luynes, Maurepas, Belleval, Richelieu, Liedekerque-Beaufort (published by the *Revue de Paris,* May 1952), Mme Eloff, Hanet-Cléry, Abbé de Veri (edited by Pierre de Nolhac), Talleyrand, Esterhazy, Stael-Holstein, Genlis, Volude, Lage, Frenilly, Aiguillon (Minister), *Mémoires* by Souslavie, Collé, Bachaumont, historical and anecdotal *Mémoires, Correspondance secrète,* correspondence of Métra, Grimm, Walpole, etc.

Several pages would be needed to give a complete bibliography of Marie Antoinette. We will merely mention the studies of P. de Nolhac (*La reine Marie-Antoinette, La Trianon de Marie-Antoinette, Autour de la Reine*), by M. Mauricheau-Beaupré (*Versailles*), Alméras (*Les Amoureux de la Reine*), by Stefan Zweig (*Marie-Antoinette*) and the works of Fleichmann, Maugras, Küntzler, Lescure, Serieys, Ségur, Viel-Castel, Otto Friedrich, Hilaire Belloc, Maurice de La Fuye, Jullien Kageneck, Paul Gruyer, Lenotre, Leroy, La Rocheterie, Baumann, Ed. Pilon, Robiquet, Renard, Geffroy, La Faye, etc., and the various books of the Goncourts.

V

FERSEN

The first place goes to Mme Alma Söderjhelm's book (*Fersen et Marie Antoinette*), written according to the private diary and correspondence of Axel preserved in the Archives of Stafsund, Sweden. Axel's letters to Sophie are at the castle of Lösta.

I have also consulted with profit *Le Comte de Fersen* by R. M. de Klinckowström, which is very incomplete, and the interesting books by Henry Valloton, *Marie Antoinette et Fersen,* Charles Kunstler, *Fersen et son secret,*

Paul Gaulot, *Un ami de la Reine*, P. de Witt, *Le comte de Fersen et la cour de France*, etc. The article by G. Laguerre on the *Mémoires* of Mme Campan appeared in the *Intermédiaire des Chercheurs et des Curieux* of 20 March 1906.

VI

THE AFFAIR OF THE NECKLACE

National Archives: K.162, K.163.

The accused and the lawyers published a mass of *Mémoires, Réponses, Précis* and *Exposés*. There is thus plenty to choose from when reconstructing the "affair." First place, however, must be given to the works of Campardon, remarkably well documented, and of Funck-Brentano. One may also mention the studies by Combes (very biased), G. Chaix d'Est-Ange and the *Mémoires* of Beugnot. Funck-Brentano has also published the *Rapport officiel* by the lieutenant of police at Crosne.

VII

THE REVOLUTION

National Archives: K.1719 (States General), K.506 (Plate sent to the Mint), K.164 (5 and 6 October), K.505 (Tuileries, Kitchens, wardrobe, installation), D. XXIX bis 31 to D. XXIX bis 38, F7.4385, F7.6762, M.664, AD.101, C.71, A.194, W.290 and W.33 (Varennes).

I also discovered in the Archives many unknown details concerning 20 June and 10 August.

In M.664 is the dossier No. 21, filed by error in a box containing documents concerning the King's flight. This unpublished and very important dossier provides us with many details on "the siege, invasion and sacking" of the château. I have also used documents from: ADI.101 (Eve of 20 June), ADI.102 (20 June), F7.4774,70 (Very important box containing the papers seized from Pétion), C.185 (Roederer's letters). To be noted also are: F7.3688, W.15, F7.4390, W.319.

In C.222 (Papers seized at the Tuileries) are many unpublished details, particularly the report Rougeville sent to the Queen and which was taken from the table of Mme Thiébault, the Queen's waiting-woman. It is quite certain that Rougeville would not have allowed himself to invent anything in a document intended to be read by Marie Antoinette. He therefore did play an important part on 20 June, whatever may have been said.

To reconstruct the period between these two dates, consult: C.222 (Papers found in Mme de Tourzel's possession), C.185 (Durathon's departure),

*ADI.*101 and *F7.*4387 (Defence measures, reports of eye witnesses, denunciations, "counter-revolution," etc.).

10 August. The short narrative by the Abbé Gallois, written during the night of 9 to 10 August, is also in *C.*222. Pétion's papers (*F7.*4774,70) give further important information. For lack of space I was not able to use the whole mass of unpublished documents in *W.*19, *C.*161, *F7.*4408, *C.*162, *F7.*4666, *M.*667, *C.*184, *F7.*4426, *C.*159, but I draw them to the attention of research workers.

Memoirs, Souvenirs and Correspondence: in addition to the works already cited: Roederer, Dumont, Mathieu, Dumas, Lafayette, Paroy, Gouverneur Morris, Mme de La Tour du Pin, Mercier, Mounier, Mme de Béarn, de Staël, La Rochefoucauld, Cubières, Rivarol, Mallet du Pan, Chastenay, Lindet, Mirabeau-Lamarck, *Journal d'un Garde Suisse,* published by A. Augustin-Thierry (*Revue des Deux-Mondes,* 1-VIII-1928), etc.

Printed works: For 5 and 6 October we possess a considerable number of depositions by eye witnesses published in the two volumes of *Procédure criminelle instruite au Châtelet de Paris.* Also on the same subject, the remarkable study by Dom. Leclercq, *Les journées d'octobre,* a work which is as full as one could wish. It is impossible to mention everything on the Revolution, but I should note: *La Révolution française,* by Pierre Gaxotte; *La Révolution française,* by Octave Aubry; *Crépuscule de la Monarchie* and *La Révolution* by Louis Madelin; *Les derniers mois de Versailles,* by Vte Fleury; *La Révolution française de 1789,* edited by P. Sagnac and J. Robiquet, etc. Also the *Moniteur* and the numerous newspapers and brochures of the time.

For the chapter "Lost Opportunities" I used Alma Söderjhelm's book, *Marie-Antoinette et Barnave,* based on their unpublished correspondence and, on the same subject, *Barnave,* by J. - J. Chevalier and *Marie-Antoinette et la politique,* by J. Arnaud Bouteloup. In *Varennes, le roi trahi* and in *Souverains en fuite* I was able to make use of many unpublished documents from the National Archives, from private archives and from inquiries made on the spot. This material helped me in writing the chapter "Varennes . . . or the Hand of Fate!"

Works to be consulted regarding the royal flight are *La Fuite de Louis XVI à Varennes, d'après les documents judiciaires,* by E. Bimbenet, and the many *Souvenirs, Relations* and *Récits* of the actors and witnesses.

VIII

THE FEUILLANTS AND THE TEMPLE

National Archives: *F4.*1310 (The Feuillants), *AA.*53.1486 and *F4.*1304 to *F4.*1314 (Supplies, accounts, corset-makers, mourning, etc.), *F4.*4390

(The furniture in the Temple), F4.1319 (Bath), W.400 (Toulan), F4.4391, F4.4392, F4.4393 (Life in the Temple).

Memoirs, Accounts, Souvenirs: Madame Royale, Pauline de Béarn, Mme de Tourzel, Cléry, Hüe, Turgy, Abbé Edgeworth de Firmont, Dufour (Feuillants), and the police officers, Danjon, Goret, Lepitre, Moëlle.

Newspapers: *Le Moniteur* (sessions of 10, 11 and 12 August), and the gazettes of the period.

Works by Paul Gaulot (*Un complot sous la Terreur*), La Morinerie (*Papiers du Temple*), Lenôtre (*La captivité de Marie Antoinette, Louis XVII*) and the works of Bord, Charles Kunstler, Louis Hastier, Viel-Castel, Reiset, Gautherot, Funck-Brentano, Maurice Garçon, etc.

IX

THE CONCIERGERIE

We possess a vast number of documents on the last nine weeks of the Queen's life. First of all there are accounts of eye witnesses. The most important is undoubtedly the *Déclaration de Rosalie Lamorlière, native de Breteuil en Picardie, servante à la Conciergerie durant la captivité de Marie-Antoinette,* and Mme Simon-Vouet's research, which supplements it. Next come the *Relation de Louis Larivière, porte-clef à la Conciergerie* and the *Souvenirs de Mlle Fouché.* The *Relation de la femme Bault, veuve du concierge de la prison de la Conciergerie,* I used with reserve, for it seems to me to be full of errors. Note also: *Clubs contre Révolutionnaires* by Challamel and *Marie-Antoinette* by Saint-Hugues, published in 1815.

Several boxes in the National Archives provide important details, some of which are unpublished or little known: W.15.534 (Prison register), F7.4392, W.296, F7.4393, Wia.112 (Accounts), F7.1319, and W.151 (Prisoner's state of health). The prison register and Wia.121 also give the list of objects possessed by Marie-Antoinette.

On the Conciergerie itself, on the topography of the district and on the Palais de Justice I consulted with profit: C.226, F13.1528, F13.1279, AF.11, 22.170,55, F16.580, F13.1279 and the following works: *Souvenirs* by Berryer, *Etude sur les Tribunaux de Paris,* by A. M. Cazenave, *Guide du voyageur et de l'étranger* (1787), by Thierry, *La Sainte-Chapelle et la Conciergerie,* by F. Gebelin and, in particular, *Mémoires d'un détenu,* by Riouffe.

X

THE CARNATION

Our information on the affair of the carnation comes from the interrogations, the originals of which are preserved in the Musée des Archives

(*W.296 [No. 261], Armoire de fer*). We possess two interrogations of the "widow Capet," two of Michonis, one of the woman Harel, two of the gendarme Gilbert (plus his report of the morning of the 3rd, which set matters off), two of citizen Fontaine, one of Sergeant Dufresne, two of citizeness Richard, one of Lieutenant Brasse and finally, two days later, that of the woman Dutilleul. Moreover, at her interrogation of 12 October and during her trial Marie Antoinette was again questioned on Rougeville's conspiracy and during the debates the principal actors—in particular Michonis—were in the box. Other important information is in the Archives, in the Rougeville's dossier (*F7.6413*), in particular his petition and the draft of his letter to Metternich. Also worthy of mention is Michonis' dossier (*W.296,261*). In the Archives de la Guerre there is information on the military side, principally regarding Rougeville's Cross of St. Louis (Série E, Saint-Louis, 13 *A,V° 197, No. 93*). *Autour du Temple,* by Gustave Bord, and *Le vrai Chevalier de Maison-Rouge,* by Lenôtre (although our theory is quite different from that of the latter work) were of great use. Also the two little volumes by Pierre-Etienne Regnaud published at the beginning of 1795, which recount the events of 10 August and the role played by Rougeville during July and August 1792.

With regard to the changing of the Queen's cell, which ended the affair of the carnation, besides Rosalie's *Relation* and the report of the police officers published in the issue of 14 January 1883 of *La Révolution Française,* and besides the report preserved in *W.296,* I discovered in the dossier *F7.4392* the bills for "the work carried out in the former dispensary," which appear to have remained unnoticed until now.

XI

THE QUEEN'S COMMUNION

For the Queen's confession and communion I consulted *Souvenirs* by Mlle Fouché, the *Déclaration* of the Abbé Magnin (*Le Monde,* 23 July 1864), *La Communion de la Reine à la Conciergerie* (*Le Monde,* 31 May 1863), *L'Eglise de Paris sous la Révolution,* by the Abbé Delare, *Vie de l'Abbé Emery,* by the Abbé Gosselin, *Un Episode de la Terreur* (1864), by A. de Ségur, *Revue des questions historiques* (1870), *Marie-Antoinette, la Captivité et la Mort,* by G. Lenôtre, and *Autour du Temple,* by Gustave Bord.

In her will Marie Antoinette wrote: "Having no expectation of spiritual consolation, and not even knowing if there still exist any priests of that religion here, and in any case the place where I am would expose them to too much danger if they should enter."

How can this sentence be reconciled with the confidence made by the

Abbé Emery, according to which he was able, shortly before the trial, to get a note passed to the prisoner: "Prepare yourself to receive absolution. Today, at midnight, I shall be before your door and I shall pronounce the sacramental words over you"? Still according to this account, the almoner of the Conciergerie went to the Queen's door at the hour fixed, heard "the sighs of that unfortunate Princess" and "spoke with her for several moments before giving her absolution." This scene can have taken place only before 14 September, when the Queen did not have two heavy doors separating her from the corridor.

The will can be reconciled with Abbé Magnin's account and that of Mlle Fouché. When Marie Antoinette wrote "if there still exist any priests here," she might have been implying "as there did formerly." Again, "the place where I am detained would expose them to too much danger" could imply "whereas where I was formerly imprisoned it was possible."

Yet Mlle Fouché and the Abbé Magnin asserted that Bault let them into the cell *after* 14 September. But the priest's own words must be heard:

"The memory of what happened when Louis XVI was in the Temple, in the same situation, and the sentiments which inspired the Queen caused me to suggest that I should say mass in the obscure cell she occupied and give her holy communion. I assured Her Majesty that it would be easy for us to bring all the objects for these august ceremonies. We had, indeed, for our use in those terrible days very small chalices which took to pieces, small 18mo missals, portable altar-stones a little longer than the base of a small chalice. All these articles fitted into a small work-bag and we could easily hide them in our pockets.

"The Queen accepted gratefully and thanked us. Among the gendarmes employed in guarding the cell we had noticed two who, by their respect for their Sovereign and the open display of their religious feelings, inspired us with complete confidence. As they were well known to the concierge I did not hesitate to tell them of the happiness that the Queen was about to enjoy, and these Frenchmen, good Christians and faithful subjects, revealed their desire to share in this glorious opportunity.

"The day for the holy work being fixed, the concierge came to fetch us during the night, at an appointed spot, and led us through the night. I heard the Queen's confession. Mlle Fouché had prepared herself to receive her God, and the two gendarmes told me that they also were prepared and that they ardently desired to communicate on this occasion, as fortunate as it was unexpected. Without losing a moment, we prepared everything needed on a little table.

"I celebrated the august sacrifice of our altars and I gave communion to the Queen, who by the nourishment of the eucharistic bread received from her God the courage to bear, without complaint, all the torments awaiting her. Mlle Fouché and the two gendarmes were also admitted at the time to the divine feast.

"The promise I have made to be brief in my narration does not allow me to depict the emotion caused by such a touching scene, which took place at the beginning of October 1793. I fell ill shortly afterwards and it was the last time that I had the honour of seeing Her Majesty. Mlle Fouché, more fortunate than myself, presented M. Cholet, a priest from the Vendée, to her. This priest gave the Queen communion during the night of 12-13 of the same month."

The Abbé Magnin explains the sentence in the Queen's "will" as follows: "Prudence and a desire to shield the priests who had helped her, as well as the persons who had helped to introduce them, were enough to give rise to the phrase in question, or to any similar phrase. However that may be, the facts speak."

What must one conclude? The presence of the two gendarmes seems all the more unusual since the Queen was alone in her cell from 4 September to 5 October. At the time of the Restoration did the fact that the Queen might have died without being in a state of grace determine the priest to utter a "pious untruth"? For myself I cannot believe it, particularly since the Abbé Magnin, on being violently attacked, entered the pulpit and, turning to the altar, "raised his hands and affirmed before God that everything he had said was the pure truth."

XII

THE TRIAL

First of all one must mention *Histoire du Tribunal Révolutionnaire,* by H. Wallon, *Le Tribunal Révolutionnaire de Paris,* by Campardon, and in particular *Le Tribunal Révolutionnaire,* by G. Lenôtre.

On the important question of the route taken by the Queen to or from the Revolutionary Tribunal I am in disagreement with G. Lenôtre and I owe the reader an explanation. This master of "little history" makes Marie Antoinette go by the chapel staircase, the foot of which was undoubtedly nearer her cell but which came out rather a long way from the *Grand-Chambre,* right at the end of the *Galerie des Peintres,* now the *Galerie Saint-Louis.* My opinion is supported by two texts written by eye-witnesses. The Lieutenant of gendarmes, de Busne, who was arrested the day after the trial for having brought the prisoner a glass of water and offered her his arm, wrote in his petition: "I offered her my right fore-arm and she descended the staircase in this way; she took it again in order to descend the *three slippery steps of the perron.*" And a prisoner wrote: "The Queen's trial began on Monday morning. *We saw her pass through the courtyard four or five times,* modestly dressed in black." (*Un épisode de la Terreur,* written by Barthélemy B. de La Roche and published by the Comte de Ségur.) On the evenings of the 14th and 15th, it was not from the court-yard that the prisoners saw the Queen pass but from the windows of their cells looking out on to the courtyard. On the mornings of the 14th and 15th and at four o'clock in the afternoon of the 14th she must have twice crossed the yard where the prisoners were free to walk between sunrise and sunset.

The text of the Queen's trial, the interrogations of 5 and 6 October (Louis XVII, Madame Royale and Madame Elisabeth), the interrogation of the Queen on 12 October and the indictment were published, from the originals, in *La Révolution Française* directed by August Dide (1883 and 1884). But the dossier W.290 gives us the report, the times of suspension of sessions, which are not in the document published by Dide, and the names of the judges and jurors, which differ from those given by *La Révolution Française*.

I also consulted with profit the *Souvenirs* of Chauveau-Lagarde, the dossier for Chauveau-Lagarde and Tronson du Coudray, *La Souveraine devant la Justice*, by Marcel Rousselet (F7.4774,94), the dossiers W.295, 296 and 297, AE.15, 18, F4.1319, Wia.121, F13.1279, etc., the *Déclara-tion* of the brothers Humbert discovered by Mme Simon-Vouet, *Marie-Antoinette et la Révolution*, by Viel-Castel, etc. The dossiers C.166, C.271, 272, 276, 279 to 286 contain the petitions for the Queen's trial and the many congratulations from municipalities after her execution. Trinchard's famous note is in the Bibliothèque National *Mss. fr.* 12759, and the account of the secret session of the Committee of Public Safety was pub-lished by Francis Drake in *Historical Manuscripts Commission; The Manu-scripts of J. B. Fortescue, Esq. preserved at Dropmore* (Vol. II).

XIII

THE EXECUTION

The details of the Queen's last hours are taken from the *Relation* of Rosalie and from accounts by eye-witnesses: Louis Larivière, the gendarme Léger, Desessarts, Charles Desfossés, Rouy, Hébert, Lapierre, Notelet (letters published by Jules Mazé), from the unpublished report of the police officer Roubaud (F7.3688,3) and of an unknown police officer (*Fic. III*, 13). The archives of the Observatoire (preserved at the O.N.M.) show the weather hour by hour on 14, 15 and 16 October. In the dossier W.291 (183) are the details of the curious affair of Maingot, the man who came out from under the scaffold all covered with blood after the execution. He was arrested by those standing in the front row. His name was Maingot and he was a second-hand dealer. The presence of a carnation aroused interest. "Do you know Rougeville, the former Chevalier de Saint-Louis?" He denied this, he was searched and on him were found two holy pictures, "a rallying sign for the enemies of the Republic." Moreover, he was curiously tattooed with a blue cord in a saltire, on top of which was a cross, on the chest the letters G.B., on the right arm J.H.S. and on the left arm a crucifix. There was enough there to have him sent to the guillotine the same day! Maingot appeared twice before the Tribunal—once for the blood and the carnation and once for the tattooing and the holy pictures —and was acquitted! He was even given back his bloodstained possessions. He had succeeded in proving that "the stigmata on his skin" dated from 1787, when he was a soldier "in the regiment of Neustrie" and that he had found the pictures on the ground. As for the blood, he claimed "to have been pushed by the crowd" and to have "walked in the blood with the intention of effacing it."

What was the end of the pitiful barbers' conspiracy, details of which are in the dossier *W.311* of the National Archives?

The day after the execution the heads of the conspiracy, numbering 29— the Volunteers were left alone—were arrested and sent to the Conciergerie.

On 17 January 1794 Fouquier-Tinville brought the 29 to trial as "guilty of having hatched a plot to kidnap the widow Capet in order to preserve her from the vengeance of the Nation." There were 54 witnesses: hatters, dyers, launderers, weavers, charcoal-burners—and barbers. Urged by fear, they brought overwhelming evidence against the lace-maker, the Lemille family, Basset and the little boot-black.

After three days' trial Basset and Lemille, together with his wife, and the woman Fournier, the head of the conspiracy, were condemned to death. Thirteen other conspirators were imprisoned "until the peace." The little boot-black, "in view of his age," got off with 20 years' imprisonment. While the verdict was being announced the poor blind lace-maker embraced her child. "She was suffocated by sobs," a witness said. All during her journey in the cart she was heard to repeat, weeping, *"Pobré pitit! . . . Pobré pitit!"*

The barbers died bravely. The lace-maker struggled so violently that the knife took off only part of her head.

Two days later, on the same spot where his mother had died, the little boot-black was placed on the scaffold and tied to a post on which were written his name, his age, his profession and the text of the verdict.

Such, in Nivôse of the Year II, was the end of the last defenders of the Queen of France.

In the registry of the Conciergerie (*W15.534* [11]) is the inventory of the widow Capet's effects made after her death (chemises of fine linen, mantle of *raz de St.-Marc*, two pairs of black stockings, a lawn headdress, a crêpe sash, etc.). All these clothes were given, according to custom, to the Salpêtrière, to be distributed among the prisoners. The legacies of the two people the Queen most detested are also inscribed in the registry not far from hers. After reading of "the swansdown puff and the little tin pomade box" which end the inventory of the widow Capet, one has only to turn two pages. There, after Bailly, who left only a gold watch and a key, is the legacy of Philippe-Egalité. It is a real dandy's wardrobe, the most luxurious of all the prisoners. There is a long list of breeches, waistcoats, cravats and dressing-gowns. There are even sets of silver plate, a picnic basket and a travelling suitcase. Turning another two pages, one can see, under the date of 19 Frimaire, the inventory of the du Barry's effects. After she left for the scaffold there was found in her cell only a white wood box containing two teapots and two cups—nothing else.

When did the grave-digger Joly bury Marie Antoinette's body? How long did the corpse remain lying on the grass? We do not know exactly. It was not until 1 November that the grave-digger sent in his bill.

The widow Capet, for the coffin	..	6 livres
For the grave and grave-diggers ..	..	15 livres, 35s.

The authorities waited nearly four years to be reimbursed. Only in the Year V did the Commissaire Dardoize put up for auction the objects seized in the Temple and unpacked during the trial. There remained only the little green morocco hussif, which reached 5 fr. 75, and the three little portraits in shagreen cases, which reached 4 fr. 40. The rest had disappeared, stolen, nobody knew by whom.

"This being done, and seeing that there remains nothing to say, do or sell, we have closed the account of the said objects at the sum of 10 fr. 15 centimes." (Archives de la Seine.)

This was the sum produced by "the goods acquired and confiscated for the profit of the Republic."

To end with, we reproduce the Queen's death certificate.

"Death certificate of *Marie-Antoinette Lorraine d'Autriche*, on 25 of *last* month, *aged* 38 *years, widow of Louis Capet*. On a declaration made to the Commune by ...., aged .... years, profession ...., living at .... The said declarant said .... Dated ...."

No one had dared to go to the Hôtel de Ville to declare the death of the daughter of the Empress Maria Theresa of Austria, widow of the King of France.

Index

Abrieu, Chevalier d', 78
Achet, Louis François, 194
Adelaide, Mme, 25, 26, 41, 45, 49, 53, 54, 78, 164, 260
Adhémar, Comte d' (Montfalcon), 88, 143, 144, 171
Affry, d' (Commander of the Swiss Guards), 391
Aigre, President d', 214
Aigron, Citizen, 353
Aiguillon, Duc d', 52, 71, 72, 77-79, 92-93, 101, 192; dismissal from office, 79, 80; exile, 91-92
Aiguillon, Duchesse d', 75, 77
Albert, Prince of Saxe-Teschen, 13
Alembert, Jean le Rond d', 68
Alliance, Franco-Austrian, 3-4, 54, 128-129, 132, 185
Amar, Deputy, 353, 364-366
Amédée, King of Sardinia, 6
Anckarström, Captain, 295
Andlau, Comtesse d', 141
Angoulême, Duc d', 189
Angoulême, Duchesse de. See Mme Royale
Antonia, Archduchess. See Marie Antoinette
Artois, Comte d'. See Charles X
Artois, Comtesse d', 202
Assembly, Legislative. See Legislative Assembly
Assembly, National. See National Assembly
Athalie, 40
Aubier, M. d', 314
Aubrey, Octave, 258
Audiat, Pierre, 184
Augié, Mme, 250, 314
Austria, war with, 295-298, 318, 321, 335, 336, 372
Austrian lip, 153
Autigny, M. d', 20
Ayen, Duc d', 164

Bagatelle, Château, 125
Bailly, Jean Sylvain, 233, 253, 260, 287, 363, 382, 398 n.
Balsamo, Joseph. See Cagliostro
Balue, Cardinal de la, 211
Barère de Vieuzac, Bertrand, 336, 360
Barnave, Antoine, 182, 257, 258, 280-282, 285-288, 290-293, 328, 369
Barrière, Jean-François, 183-184
Barry, Mme du, 3, 25, 26, 29, 40, 49-52, 68, 70, 71, 75, 77, 79; relations with Queen, 49-56, 92, 193
Barthélemy de la Roche, Jean Jacques, 316, 338, 343
Bassenge, Paul, 189, 195-197, 215
Bastille, the, 215; capture of, 234-235
Batz, Baron de, and plan for rescue of Queen, 331-332, 347, 348
Bault, Citizen, 357, 366
Bault, Mme, 395
Bavaria, 128-130, 186
Bavaria, Elector of. See Maximilian-Joseph
Bayon, M., 270-274, 276
Beaudeau, Abbé, 77-78
Beaumont, Archbishop, 71, 72, 74
Beausire, Sieur de, 214
Beauvau, Prince de, 77
Beauvilliers, Mme Adelaide, 155
Benedict XIV, Pope, 51
Béranger, Farmer General, 197
Bernardin de Saint-Pierre, Jacques Henri, 219
Bernis, Cardinal de, 154
Bertin, Rose, 84-86, 136, 173, 220
Besenval, Baron de, 15, 89-92, 100-103, 106, 108, 113, 126, 137, 140, 146, 170, 182, 222, 234, 378
Beugnot, Nicolas, 201, 208, 304, 363, 388
Bevi, Comte de, 134
Bignon, Mayor, 42
Billaud-Varenne, Jean Nicolas, 364